The Collected Sermons of

Fred B. Craddock

The Collected Sermons of

Fred B. Craddock

Fred B. Craddock

WESTMINSTER
JOHN KNOX PRESS
LOUISVILLE • KENTUCKY

© 2011 Fred B. Craddock
Foreword © 2011 Westminster John Knox Press

Originally published in hardback in the United States
by Westminster John Knox Press in 2011.
2011 paperback edition
Published by Westminster John Knox Press
Louisville, Kentucky

11 12 13 14 15 16 17 18 19 20—10 9 8 7 6 5 4 3 2 1

Unless otherwise indicated, Scripture quotations are from the New Revised Standard Version of the Bible, copyright © 1989 by the Division of Christian Education of the National Council of the Churches of Christ in the U.S.A., and are used by permission. Scripture quotations marked RSV are from the Revised Standard Version of the Bible, copyright © 1946, 1952, 1971, and 1973 by the Division of Christian Education of the National Council of the Churches of Christ in the U.S.A., and are used by permission.

Excerpts from *The Cherry Log Sermons*, by Fred B. Craddock, and *Speaking of Stewardship*, by William Carter, are reprinted by permission of Westminster John Knox Press. Used by permission. All rights reserved. Excerpts from "Doxology," "Asleep in the Storm," "Nothing Is Impossible with God," and "And They Said Nothing to Anyone" are used by permission from *As One without Authority*, copyright 2001 by Fred B. Craddock, published by Chalice Press, www.chalicepress.com. Excerpts from "Being a Friend of Jesus" used by permission, from *Preaching the Gospel of John*, copyright 2008 by Chalice Press, www.chalicepress.com.

Book design by *Sharon Adams*
Cover design by *Lisa Buckley*
Cover photo: © *Bryan Meltz/Emory University Photo/Video*

Library of Congress Cataloging-in-Publication Data

Craddock, Fred B.
   The collected sermons of Fred B. Craddock / Fred B. Craddock. — 1st ed.
      p. cm.
   ISBN 978-0-664-23457-7 (alk. paper)
   1. Sermons, American.   2. Bible—Sermons.   3. Christian Churches (Disciples of Christ)—Sermons.   I. Title.
   BX7327.C65C65 2011
   252'.0663—dc22

                                                                    2010034959

ISBN: 978-0-664-23858-2 (paper edition)

Contents

Sermons

In Memorium

Foreword

The book you hold in your hands is like no other book you have ever read. This is fitting, since Fred Craddock is like no other preacher you have ever heard. If you have worshiped with him, then I need say no more. You know all about the voice, the timing, the stature, the gaze. If you have not worshiped with him, then prepare to be a little disoriented, for you are about to overhear sermons that happened without you.

"It's good to see you again this morning," the first one begins, but who is "you" and when was the last time, so that this time is "again"?

"This is a very refreshing place and we all need it," begins another, but where is this place and who are "we"? Who, for that matter, are Steve, Bill, Robin, Richard, Wesley, or Birdie, who show up in these sermons as naturally as Peter, James, or John?

"As you know we are now one week away," begins a third sermon, but by now you are getting the hang of it. You have walked into the middle of a conversation between this preacher and the particular people sitting right in front of him. Even if *you* do not know what will happen a week from now, *they* do—just as they know who they are, where they are, and who is standing in the pulpit before them speaking directly to their condition.

This comes as something of a relief since it means the reader of this volume is not in charge. You are a guest here, not a host. You do not have to know everything about the people sitting around you. You do not have to understand the relationship between this preacher and these people. You do not even have to know what day it is. All you have to do is settle down so you can overhear the gospel, which may be how you discover that these sermons speak directly to your own condition too.

How can this be, since the preacher has never laid eyes on you? I could not begin to say. All I can say, with complete confidence, is that reading these sermons one after another will take you places you have never been between the covers of a book.

As Fred says in his introduction, there is a big difference between reading speaking and reading writing. The sermon is "an event in the world of sound," he says, a "self-consuming artifact" that lives for the ear, not the page. Things can happen in a sanctuary between a preacher and a congregation that are not reducible to print. What caused one person to doze while another wept? Why did people laugh at the first story but not the second one? What made all the babies stop crying at once?

Worship is like that. However tight the script, the Holy Spirit moves between the lines. However sure the preacher is about where she is going, everyone in the room can end up somewhere else. There is a "surplus of meaning lurking in every good sermon as in every biblical text," Fred says, keenly aware of how much this surplus depends on the physical presence of a trusted speaker with a familiar audience. For this reason among many, a book of sermons is a very odd duck.

If you are reading this one for your own soul's health, then my advice is not to think about it too much. Just let the words do their deeply intuitive work, leading you to notice things you have never noticed before, feel things further down than you are used to feeling them, and think things you want to think about some more. You need never fear that this preacher will use these things to bend you to his will, because he is not like that. He gives you his words, trusting you to know what to do with them.

If, on the other hand, you are reading this book because you want to preach more like Fred Craddock does, then proceed with caution. I once witnessed a seminarian the size of an NFL linebacker try to impersonate him in a sermon and it was not a pretty sight. The voice was all wrong for the body. The posture did not go with the words. The bad news, I am afraid, is that to preach like Fred Craddock you have to *be* Fred Craddock. Flip this truth over, however, and you find the good news on the other side: if you want to preach like he does, then be who *you* are—inhabiting your own body, using your own voice, finding your own language, noticing your own life.

This may take some practice, since it is often hard for preachers to trust that the standard equipment package for human beings is adequate for the proclamation of the gospel. Surely a deeper voice would help, a taller frame, a more sophisticated vocabulary, a less routine life . . . ? While there are certainly things preachers can do to enrich both the interior and exterior worlds they inhabit, the first and best thing they can do is to come home to themselves. How does a preacher discover her voice? She learns to use the voice she has. How does a preacher establish his authority? He abandons all guile.

The first time I heard Fred Craddock was 1978, when he delivered the Beecher Lectures on Preaching at Yale Divinity School. I had been out of seminary for two years by then, working as a secretary during the week and helping out at a local church on weekends. While I was just beginning to imagine myself an ordained minister, imagining myself a preacher was not part of the deal. The Episcopal Church had only been ordaining women priests for a couple of years. I had never seen a woman in a clerical collar, much less heard one preach. With a little effort I could imagine myself a pastor, a teacher, a counselor to youth. When I tried to imagine myself a preacher, my mind went blank.

The lights came on for me the day Fred Craddock stepped into the pulpit of Marquand Chapel. His head and shoulders were just visible above the top of the podium. He made a joke about this as he cranked the microphone down to his height. "They always set these things for adults," he said, or "I *am* standing up." I have heard him begin like this so many times through the years that I no longer remember what he said the first time I heard him. Whatever it was, it let the rest of us know that we could laugh with him— because the truth is often funny, and things so seldom turn out the way any of us expects.

For the next hour he continued to foil our expectations in memorable ways. His voice went with his body. He could do things with it that stayed in the ear long after he finished speaking. There was no separating *what* he said from *how* he said it. He spoke of Kierkegaard as easily as he spoke of the Indianapolis 500. He quoted Kafka as helpfully as Corinthians. Clearly, this was a man with great skills in the disciplines of theology and philosophy as well as biblical studies and homiletics, but he was also someone who noticed a lot about ordinary human life on earth.

Time and again, he said things I wanted to say but did not know how. He put words to my music, gave voice to my better angels. *Yes,* I thought, *that's exactly what it's like. Yes, that's just how it feels. Yes, I've always wondered about that but I never heard anyone say it out loud before.* Every now and then he would reach high over my head to bring something down where I could handle it for myself, but he did this so unassumingly that I never felt stupid.

"You know as well as I," he said, when I did not know.

"As you probably have already anticipated," he said, when I did not have a clue.

"All of you will be aware," he said, when I was not aware—yet the cumulative effect of such phrases was to lift me up and draw me in to the conversation he was having with his listeners. I wanted to know what he thought I already knew. I wanted to join the community of the aware.

By the time Fred finished his last lecture, he had not only described another way to preach; he had also shown me how it was done, so that for the first time it was possible for me to imagine myself a preacher too.

In the years since then I have heard him preach a hundred times without ever figuring out how he does it. How does he use such simple language to convey such luminous and sometimes difficult truths? How does he see the sorts of things we all see—people eating in restaurants, children pushing each other around—and see more than we see? How does he say what he sees so that it goes straight to the heart?

Part of the problem, of course, is that there is no analyzing Fred while he is talking. The minute he starts I am a goner. All I want to do is listen to the stories, join the laughter, make the connections. After about twenty minutes I always start getting anxious because I know he is going to sit down soon—always too soon!—and I know the whole sermon is going to snap back on itself depending on where he decides to end it. I am not sure even he knows when he is going to end it, but nine times out of ten it takes my breath away.

For this reason among many others, being able to read a whole volume of Fred's sermons provides a different kind of pleasure than hearing them in person one at a time. There is still plenty in these pages to grab the heart, spark the will, and work the mind—indeed, it is hard to recall a single page that does not do one or more of those things—yet there is also the opportunity to note how this preacher does what he does even when he is not standing right there in front of you.

Here are some things I notice about how Fred does what he does.

He trusts emotion and intuition to light the way into a text as much as he trusts education and intelligence. Just try to reduce one of these sermons to outline form and you will see what I mean. There you are sailing along, thinking you know what this sermon is about, when all of a sudden Fred starts telling a story that has no apparent connection to the theme you had picked out for him. Stick with him and the connection will become apparent—or not—but either way this preacher does not map his sermons with a ruler but with a heart. He speaks to his listeners the same way the text speaks to him, which almost never involves the shortest distance between point A and point B.

He uses lovely and concrete language to evoke visceral response. Both descriptors are necessary, I think, since lovely language is more likely to woo the ear than language that is merely correct. Fred chooses his words with such care that they arrive like specially selected gifts—never too pricey, never too precious—just exactly the right words to describe what he wants to convey. Their concreteness has everything to do with their familiarity. When he describes a potato as small as a marble, it is so real you can hold it in your hand. When he repeats a conversation between two people in a church parking lot, it is so recognizable that you can almost name the people.

He tells the truth about things, even when the truth is that he does not like a particular parable much or that he once avoided eating lunch with a man who drooled. Whether he is telling you something about himself or about someone he knows, the frankness of his observations can strike so close that you want to cover your head. *How did he know that about you?* Since he is believable at this level, he becomes believable at every level, even when he moves on to things as high as the meaning of the cross, the purpose of the church, or the love of God. I do not know what it costs him to be so candid, but it constitutes one of his greatest teachings.

While it helpful to notice how Fred does what he does, it is also helpful to notice what he does not do.

He does not talk down to his listeners. He assumes from the start that we are capable of attending to the text, handling some scholarship, dealing with open-ended stories, and drawing our own conclusions. He does not tell us what he is going to tell us, tell us, and then tell us what he told us. He sits down before we are ready. He lets us chew our own food.

He does not make use of caricatures or stereotypes. When he has an argument to make, he does not set up a cardboard opponent. Whether the adversary of a story is a Pharisee or a church member who thinks the parable of the Prodigal Son needs fixing, Fred goes to some trouble to present the other person's point of view. In this way he both honors and engages the complexity of most arguments worth having.

He does not turn to popular culture for material. His stories come from real life, not the movies. He may cite Shakespeare or the evening news but there is not a single reference in this volume to a sports event or television show. Of course this may simply reflect Fred's tastes, but I think it is more than that. The sources a preacher consults suggest to listeners where God may be found. Fred's sources point to the full range of human experience that is available even to those without cable connections.

But do not let me hold you up another minute. It is time for you to begin, so that you can engage this master preacher—this consummate human being—in his own words. Somewhere in these pages he says that gratitude is the central virtue of Christian life. If that is true, then he has made virtuous people of us all.

Barbara Brown Taylor

Acknowledgments

I wish to express my gratitude to Dr. Donald McKim, editor at Westminster John Knox, who invited me into this project and was my conversation partner throughout. A special thanks also goes to those who helped me harvest recordings of sermons preached hither, thither, and yon. Among those essential helpers are Ann Knox at the William Smith Morton Library at Union Presbyterian Seminary in Richmond, Marilyn Schertz of the Media Center at Candler School of Theology, Atlanta, and John Craddock of Bell Tower Productions, Marietta, Georgia. And a most special thanks to Kay Zimbrick, Ellijay, Georgia, who listened to all the recordings, transcribed them, and put them in an order fit for a publisher, and who never lost her sense of humor.

Of these fifty-five sermons, ten had previously appeared in print elsewhere. My thanks to the following publishers for granting the right to include them here:

> Westminster John Knox Press, *The Cherry Log Sermons* (2001)
> "God Is with Us"
> "Why the Cross?"
> "Throwing Away the Good Stuff"
> "How Long Does Easter Last?"
> Geneva Press, *Speaking of Stewardship* (ed. W. G. Carter, 1998)
> "A Note of Thanks"
> Chalice Press, *Preaching the Gospel of John* (eds. D. Bland and D. Fleer, 2008)
> "Being a Friend of Jesus"
> and *As One without Authority* (Fred Craddock, 2001)
> "Doxology"
> "Asleep in the Storm"
> "Nothing Is Impossible with God"
> "And They Said Nothing to Anyone"

And finally, more than gratitude to Barbara Brown Taylor, whose Foreword makes me want to rewrite the book to make it more deserving.

Fred B. Craddock

Introduction

The editors of this volume offered me the opportunity to write an introduction to this collection and I jumped at the chance. I need to talk to the reader about these sermons whether or not the reader needs it. Every preacher, whether published or not, needs now and then to back away and bring to the conscious level what she is doing. Because repetition is a major component of the preparation and delivery of sermons, habits develop, and that is not a bad thing. Habit is a best friend of the preacher, but habit can contribute to a degree of deafness and blindness, which can dull the edge of communication.

The first thing I want to say is that these sermons were prepared to be heard not read. They were from the time of conception aimed for the ear not the eye. For there to be a collection the first task was to locate recordings of sermons delivered, transcribe them, edit as needed, and then to present them to you to be read. Your task would be far easier if you were reading writing but, in fact, you are reading speaking. Of these fifty-five messages, only one existed as a manuscript to be read before it was delivered from a pulpit. (I expect the readers will have little difficulty identifying which one it is.)

For most of my years in the pulpits of chapels and churches, my preaching has been attempts to implement the definition of a sermon as an event in the world of sound. Hearing is a world away from reading. A sermon is heard while seated among other listeners; one most often reads alone. A sermon is heard in a context of worship; one may read a sermon at home, on a plane, or in a library. Listeners to sermons often have a relationship of mutual respect and trust with the preacher; readers of sermons often do not know, have never met, the writer. A preacher may trust a familiar audience with a half-sentence, knowing they will complete it; may pause in silence; may gesture with a hand, a shrug of the shoulders, a look of disgust or doubt or bewilderment. A preacher may make wordless noises—grunts, groans, sighs, chuckles. A writer, even a good one, can barely approach conveying such nuances. A preacher and a writer can both use repetition, but for the preacher the range of communicating meanings and emotion is far greater. Repeating words or phrases, when speaking, may slow down a message so the listener can catch up, or may underscore, or transition, or question, or even contradict. Such is a voice in the room; only partially so is the word on a page.

Enough of this: my intent is not to create a competition but rather to point to a difference. I am aware that, unlike the manuscript, orality can tempt the preacher into a casualness that approaches sloppiness. "I enjoy just conversing with the congregation," said the preacher as an excuse for poor preparation, lack of focus, sparse content. Preaching *is* conversation but it is serious conversation; two persons (or a preacher and congregation) with enough in common to be able to communicate, with enough difference to need to communicate, and each with an open willingness to be influenced by the other.

Obviously, the differences between the spoken and the written word are sufficient to call for editing when moving from one to the other, in this case from the voice to the page. The ideal is to produce a script which reads well but which prompts the reader to say, "As I read I could hear the sermon being preached." Such editing is difficult and only partially approaches the ideal. The temptation is to provide the reader with explanations, descriptions, and footnotes to ease the transition. One could argue for the benefit of such aids, but losses are greater. It is better to turn the sermon loose, to let the reader deal with it without the preacher, to make discoveries even beyond the intention of the preacher, and to find that surplus of meaning lurking in every good sermon as in every biblical text. In other words, trust the reader as the preacher trusts the listener.

Having said this, perhaps it would not be too intrusive on the reader for me to comment in general on my sense of what constitutes effective preaching. I will attempt to organize my thoughts by pointing out the major influences on my preaching life.

I must speak first of the Scriptures, and I will do so in two ways: the study of biblical texts and the texts themselves. Exegesis of texts begins in a sense of distance between oneself and the text. This distance is to be respected, and even enjoyed as one enjoys listening in on a conversation. The exegete does not become impatient and collapse the distance too soon. Rushing from *then* to *now* interferes with honest listening. The sermon that is in a hurry to speak to us today can be heard as lacking confidence in the Scripture's capacity to gain and hold attention and robs the sermon of anticipation by a lack of restraint or an unwillingness to delay in arriving at the point. As in much of life, anticipation is a major source of pleasure as well as a precondition of learning.

And as we all know, exegesis is by its nature inductive. That is to say, one works with the details of the text under consideration and out of those details comes the message. This is the opposite of the deductive sermon, which moves from a general theme to the particulars of application and exhortation. This difference between induction and deduction was in my early pulpit years a source of constant agony. I knew that honest exegesis dealt with the details interior to the text, out of which I arrived at a conclusion as to the meaning to be preached. This induction I did in my study, in private, but then I went into the pulpit with my theme or conclusion and started with that, breaking it down into particular points as I went along. No wonder I was uncomfortable in the pulpit; my listeners had to accept my point without participating in the process of arriving at it. Relief from that pain came when I began doing my exegesis in the pulpit in the company of those who had as large a stake in the message of the text as I did.

But the biblical text gives me much more than a method or movement of thought, a way of unrolling the sermon. The text gives my sermons rich vocabulary and phrasing, words concrete and particular, words that appeal to the five senses, giving the listener something to touch, to see, to taste, to hear, to smell. Very seldom does the Bible deal in abstracts such as morality or mortality or spirituality. In addition, the text gives my sermons a popula-tion. A sermon consisting only of ideas, regardless of their truth or merit, is unreal. No one lives in such a world, and as long as our sermons are related to Scripture we will be reminded to include the names of actual persons. The Scriptures, by naming the sister of Moses, the husband of Naomi, the parents of John the Baptist, the Roman soldier who guarded Paul, and the brother of Jesus, instruct us not only to tell its stories as stories of real people but also to bear witness to the lives of those about us. I often review my sermons listen-ing for names and places and specific events. The more specific, the more applicable to more listeners.

Finally, the Scriptures remind me that lively and engaging preaching con-tains conversation. Relating a message in the form of conversation is not a homiletical gimmick; it is the way the biblical texts tell their stories. Adam said, Eve said, Noah said, Sarah said, Moses said, Elijah said, Amos said, Mary said, the angel said, the demon said, Jesus said, Paul said, Peter said, James said: so the stories are told. The Scriptures are so bold as to say, "God said." How much more engaging is a conversation than a report or an expla-nation. Conversations hold the camera on what is being said. Conversations make the absent present. The preacher who studies the sacred text and then converts it into summaries, explanations, and syllogisms has robbed the text of much of its power.

All this is to say that biblical preaching means much more than using Scrip-ture to give authority to the sermon. And it means more than informing the listeners. There is informing, to be sure, but the informing is most effective when it comes as reminders. "You remember when Jesus, on his way to Gali-lee, stopped at a well to get a drink of water?" Then the preacher tells the story completely because many listeners do not remember. Since some do and some do not remember, the formula for narrating biblical material is this: tell it as a reminder as though all know it; tell it completely as though none know it. In the course of time there will be enough Scripture in the congregation's memory bank that the preacher can make allusions to texts and receive from the listeners a nod of recognition. What a delightful moment that is!

I am talking to you about major influences on my preaching and I began with the major influence, the Scriptures. I have, for purposes of discussion, separated out as a second influence that which is in fact a portion of Scripture: the parables of Jesus. I have done so because the parables have functioned for me as a way of communicating apart from their status as biblical and therefore normative texts. Parables are metaphorical and therefore expect an interpretive contribution from the listener. The parable gives freedom of interpretation, and therefore responsibility of interpretation to the hearer. Congregations long accustomed to being told what everything means will likely have lazy ears and will resist this offer of responsible listening. But in the course of time they will come to accept it as their delightful duty. After all, the Scriptures belong to the whole church, not to the clergy alone, to be dispensed in such doses as the clergy deem appropriate.

Let me be clear: parabolic preaching is not a game one plays with the congregation. "I bet you can't get this one." The subject is serious: the reign of God, and the sermon is an invitation to participate in mind, heart, and action. Underscore "invitation." No one wants to listen to pulpit bullies, behaving as though they had walked all around God and taken pictures. Not only listeners, but preachers, too, stand before a double mystery: the mystery of God and the mystery of the human longing for God. Preaching that is aware of this does not seek to coerce but, as C. H. Dodd said of the parable, to "tease the mind into active thought."

I must mention but not discuss too lengthily the influence of Søren Kierkegaard on my preaching. A chance encounter with Hermann Diem on a street in Tübingen, Germany, in the summer of 1969 began my relationship with Søren Kierkegaard. I expressed to Professor Diem my frustrated search for a way of preaching in a time when the authority of the pulpit could no longer be assumed. Professor Diem turned to leave, paused, and said over his shoulder, "Read Kierkegaard." I did, and the immediate result was the Beecher Lectures at Yale published under the title *Overhearing the Gospel*. I need not repeat what is said there, but if anyone wishes to engage Søren Kierkegaard's method of indirect discourse, I suggest his *The Point of View of My Work as an Author*. His indirect method of communicating led me to narrative in general and in particular to the parables of Jesus, which took on new significance in my search for a way to preach.

I turn now to a final resource influential in the development of my preaching style. I say "final" fully aware of many influences along the way, which may actually be more important because they lie beneath the surface of conscious recovery. But, the "final" influence is Thomas de Quincey, a mid-nineteenth-century English essayist. His brief essay *Literature of Knowledge and Literature of Power* is worthy of every preacher's careful reading. De Quincey distinguishes between literature with the purpose of imparting knowledge and literature with the purpose of creating an experience in the reader; the one *informs*, the other *forms*. As an example of the former he offers the cookbook; as an example of the latter he offers John Milton's *Paradise Lost*. It is no difficult matter to bring to bear on preaching the insights of de Quincey. Some sermons have as a primary purpose the instruction of the listener, and so are framed to be remembered. Other sermons are intended to create in the listener a new experience and so are framed not so much to be remembered as to be life altering, to be what Stanley Fish calls "self-consuming artifact." To be sure, many sermons in some measure pursue both purposes, but it is helpful for the preacher to ask in each case, "What am I really trying to do?" De Quincey has served me well in my continuing quest to find a more effective way to preach. I say "continuing" because it is, and it will be until the pulpit is vacated and the book closed.

Fred B. Craddock
Cherry Log, Georgia

Sermons

1

Only One God but Just in Case

Genesis 31:17–32

It's good to see you again this morning. When I looked out and saw the darkened sky this morning I thought, "Who would show up in this dreadful weather?" So I sat there in my room and made a list of the good and faithful people who are abounding in steadfast love. I looked over the crowd and you are exactly the ones I listed. It's amazing. I appreciate also the many solicitations concerning my health and whether the chores here are a bit much for me. They are not. This is Thursday; I have begun to accumulate a little weariness but it's all right. I'm back to my usual routine as a six-mile runner. I don't run it every day and I don't run it all at once. The six miles are the total I have accumulated over eleven years.

I hope the discussion of these biblical characters has been in some way helpful to you at the point of some identification or clarification. I have wanted to be clear in speaking to you, but I have not wanted to simplify their lives in terms of unusual good or unusual flaws in their faith. But to maintain the complexity and tension of it, I have tried to talk to you as adults, I suppose. I have been offended in recent years by the use of the word *adult* and what constitutes adult entertainment. It's really insulting to adults; violence and bloodshed and crashing and bombing, nudity, profanity, and that's adult. There is nothing they offer really that I haven't heard or seen or read on the walls of public toilets since I was six years old.

I'm talking about adult in the sense that it was used early in the movie industry. I remember the first adult western. It was called *High Noon* with Grace Kelly and Gary Cooper. It was advertised as an adult western. There was no nudity, no profanity, and a minimum of shooting guns. What made it adult? A Quaker woman marries a police officer, a marshal. He is sworn to protect the town; she is sworn to pacifism and nonviolence. In their marriage, he commits himself to her and will take off his gun. In the marriage, she commits herself to him and will support and care for him. The rogues, the thugs, the villains that he has sent to prison return to town on the wedding day. They both have conflicting commitments, to peace, to each other, to protect the town. It was called adult. That is adult. Everything is not neat and simple and clear. Decisions have to be made and pains borne and sorrows expressed.

We come today to the beautiful Rachel; beautiful of name, Rachel, beautiful of face, Rachel. She has captured the heart of Judaism from the beginning. She has captured the heart of the church and Christianity. She was like Sarah, barren most of her married life. She was like Hannah, barren most of her married life. But it is Rachel that has captured the hearts of so many people. When Jeremiah is expressing in great lamentation the desolate condition of Israel, he says, "I heard a voice in Ramah, the voice of Rachel, crying for her children and she would not be consoled because they were gone" (Jer. 31:15, au. trans.).

When Matthew told the story of the infancy of Jesus and the wicked king trying to destroy Jesus by killing the boy babies in the Bethlehem area, Matthew says, "I heard a voice in Ramah, the voice of Rachel weeping, weeping for her children, and she would not be consoled because they were gone" (Matt. 2:18, au. trans.). Rachel. Of the many sons of Jacob, the twelve tribes of Israel, really Rachel bore only two sons. First there was Joseph, who later was to save the whole family from famine because of his position in Egypt, and then the beloved Benjamin. She died in childbirth when Benjamin came and she named him Ben-Oni, Son of My Sorrow. But when she died, Jacob renamed him Benjamin, Son of My Right Hand. She's buried near Bethlehem and some of you have visited the historic marker said to be the place of her tomb near Bethlehem. She is like Mozart, Amadeus, beloved of God.

I was just reviewing before coming here some of the literary figures who have loved her and spoken of her in symbolic ways as well as theological ways. Charles Lamb, Herman Melville, William Makepeace Thackeray, T. S. Eliot, Charles Dickens, they have loved her and she has appeared in their poems and their stories. But in the text that was read a few moments ago, Rachel is in a point of transition, a radical dislocation. When Isaac knew that there wasn't room in the land for his warring sons, Jacob and Esau, he said to Jacob, "I don't want you to marry one of the Palestinian women. I want you to leave. I want you to go to the East Country. Your mother has relatives there; I want you to marry among those people." So he went far to the east and he met Rachel, daughter of Laban.

Jacob said, "Laban, I will work for you seven years for her," and he did. The day of the wedding, here came Leah. Jacob said, "I said Rachel."

"Well, Leah is older and in our country, the older girl marries first."

Jacob worked seven more years, fourteen years for this woman. Now that is extraordinary. I mean, Jacob was shrewd, but right now it looks like he doesn't have the brightest porch light on the block. Fourteen years! But he did, he loved her. They were married and they stayed on six more years with Laban before the time came to leave. Jacob said, "It is time for us to go, to go back to the land of my people, land of my father, land of my inheritance. It is time to go back to the land of my God."

She agreed. "Your God is my God. Your land is my land. Your family is my family." And so begins for her a time of radical dislocation. She had, even after her marriage, not only her years growing up in the home, but even after her marriage, lived in her father's house for six years. It was home and she had such a strong, protecting father who loved his daughters and cared for them in every possible way. Everything was so secure. And now, move. Moving is, on the stress list, number two, right after funerals. It's painful; it's difficult because furniture and houses that we get used to mother us. Just to come in and take off your jacket or your coat or toss your purse in a chair, kick off the shoes, this is home.

Once, somewhere in North Carolina, I was housed by the Ministerial Association in a local retirement center. I didn't get the point of it but that's where I was quartered. I was told when I went there and took my room, "Now in the morning when you come down for breakfast, you wait until everybody is seated before you take a seat. Everybody always sits in the same place. Don't upset it." Don't move the furniture in the home of an elderly person. Don't create any upsetting circumstance. Because, you see, routine has a composing quality to it. You know routine has been underrated. Routine is extremely important.

The father/husband dies, the mother/widow there, children there, the grandchildren there, the funeral is over. You see the mother/widow at the sink washing. "Mother, don't do the dishes, we'll take care of the dishes." You see mother slip down to the corner grocery to get a quart of milk. "Mother, send one of the boys down there to get the milk." You see mother scraping out table scraps for the dog. "Mother, the boys will feed the dog. Sit down, Mother." You see mother a little later fixing supper for the folks who are there. "Mother, we'll take care of it." Leave her alone; she's trying to stay alive.

And Rachel moves. She has to go a journey of weeks and weeks and weeks in the tent, going with the animals and the children and the servants and all, back westward to the land and the God and the faith of her husband. You can call it a pilgrimage if you want to and on good religious days that's a nice way to say it. "She was on a pilgrimage." But you know what pilgrimage is, don't you? It means transient; it means temporary; it means paper plates and Dixie cups. It means a bunch of children asking, "Are we there yet?" It means asking your husband, "Is this it?" Pilgrimage sounds nice but what that means is very temporary.

I remember hearing Joachim Jeremias of Germany telling of the time when he was in Israel and invited by some friends to help them or join them at least in observing the Feast of Tents. They had erected a little brush arbor in the backyard to help them remember the days in the tents in the wilderness. He said, "When I went into this little hovel they had built, on one side of the doorway was a slip of paper attached that said, 'From God.' On the other side of the doorway was another little slip of paper that said, 'To God.'" And in between, tent.

Now we know, all of us know in our heads that it is true, that all of us are just moving along. Everything is temporary but we don't like all these extra reminders. We have enough already—the seasons. In the spring, when the world is a poem of light and color and the meadows are turning somersaults of joy, it doesn't last long. It gets hot, heat waves come up off the highway and the railroad tracks and somebody's fumbling with the thermostat and everybody's trying to stay cool, but it doesn't last long. Comes a little chill in the air, the autumn weather turns the leaves to flame, somebody kicks a football and a whistle blows and a school bell rings, but not for long. Pretty soon the bony fingers of the trees will pray to heaven for some cover and down comes the snow to blanket them. The flying cloud and the frosty light and the year's dying in the night and somebody says, "Happy New Year." Just like that. We have enough reminders. Even our own bodies: look at yourself in the mirror.

A small boy can hop up on a rail fence and balance himself for half a mile. But in a few years he'll walk around in his front yard as though it were a foreign country. A child can hear a cricket in the grass. In a few years she'll walk in front of a honking automobile and swear she never heard a sound. A boy can see the quail in the brush but in a few years look upon the face of his closest friend and say, "I didn't catch the name." That's just the way it is. We don't need more reminders.

Every day with Rachel, temporary, moving, moving, moving, moving, the loss of place. What a tragic thing. You know place is important to everybody. Whatever you may think about it, it is extremely important. If you've been involved with Habitat for Humanity and had the additional pleasure of being there when the family comes, you know. The house is complete, here's this young mother, three children, and they're holding to her skirt. One will dart off in this room and dart back, "Mama, Mama, there's a bathroom, there's a nice bathroom." One will dart off this way, "Mama, there's a bedroom and there's another one. Can I have my own? Is this our home? Is this our place?" "Yes, this is our place." That's it.

"Now, Mother, now that Dad has died and you're alone, you're going to have to come and live with me. I can't stand being there in Albuquerque thinking of you here by yourself. I don't know what might happen so you're going to come. I'm going to stay over a few extra days for you to pack your things. Maybe we'll get rid of a few things you don't need and you're going to come with me."

"I'm not coming to live with you."

"Mother, you'll have your own little place to the side. You'll have your own kitchen, your bathroom. You can have your own television. We won't interfere."

"I'm not coming."

"Mother, I can't stand . . . now you're coming."

"I am *not* coming. I have my friends; I have my neighbors; I have my place; I have my church. Leave me alone."

It's true even of young people. If you have a son or a daughter away at university, and after a few weeks there, the home phone rings, "What are you guys doing?"

"Oh, nothing much, just sitting here watching a little T.V. What are you doing?"

"Oh, I thought I'd come home this weekend and see how you all are doing."

"Well, okay, if you want to, but it's a long way."

"It's not bad, I'll get in late Friday night."

"You think that old car will make it?"

"Oh, it will make it fine. I'll be in there Friday night."

"Don't you need to study?"

"I'll bring some books with me. I just want to check up and see how you all are doing."

Come in late Friday night and go up to bed. Come down next morning. "Same old bedspread, same old curtains, I thought maybe you'd change things." Been gone a month, you know. Come down to the kitchen, eat breakfast. Same old refrigerator. "Dad, why don't you get Mom a new refrigerator? This one is getting all worn around the handle and everything." Same old refrigerator. Goes out, looks around, same old town.

Sunday morning, "Get up, we're going to church."

"Aw, can't I sleep?"

"No, you knew we go to church when you came home. Now get up."

Go to church, come back. "Same old sermon; I knew in three minutes everything he was going to say. Same old songs, same old prayers." Sit down to the pot roast; same old pot roast. Dad has the blessing. "Bless this food to our body's use and us to thy service."

"Same old blessing, eh, Dad?" Sunday afternoon, "Well it's time to go back." Now, why did he come home? Because it's the same ol', it's the same ol'. It's tough at school; it's competitive. I don't mean just in the classroom but in every way. People have values or no values, ideas and notions and classroom teachers that are strange and all that. It's just tough. So when they call on some Friday and say, "I just thought I'd check up on you and see how you're doing," say, "Okay, we'd be glad to see you." Just have to have a place.

But Rachel has no place now. Oh, she has a place way down the road and she says as surely and as firmly as anyone, "There is no God but my husband's God, the God of Israel." But before she leaves, she steals the family gods, puts them in the saddlebags of her camel, just in case. These have been the little gods on the altar, little candle on either side, and these little gods, they brought the rain, they caused the cows and the lambs to come. They caused the children to be healthy; they caused happy marriages. These were her household gods all of her life.

Oh, there's only one true God, the God of . . . but just in case, a little backup, you see, just a little backup. Do you find that is really the way it is? Just a little backup. Most of us need some backup. How many people have come to this country from other countries, put their children in schools, pretty soon they're going to a church, and pretty soon they become Christian. They didn't grow up Christian; they were in another religion in another country. Now they're in America; now they're citizens, they're belonging to a church. You go into their home; they show you the home, "Isn't this nice?" And upstairs in the hall is a little table with two little candles and something in between. "I know, I know this doesn't fit in. We're Christian and all, but all my life. . . ." A little backup.

Paul ran into it in his churches. In the church in Colossae, they believed in Jesus Christ, they'd been baptized, they were worshiping together, but they got into this angel business. Oh, they loved those angels. They said, "Oh yes, we believe in Christ and Christ died for our sins and Christ was raised and we can say the creed with the best of them, but these angels, you know they never die. They can come in and help you. Christ is fine but when you're in a crisis, you know, a little angel won't hurt." They had a little backup and Paul said, "If Christ is not sufficient, forget it. Forget this angel stuff on the side as backup."

In the church at Corinth, they believed in Christ, they recited the creed; they believed what Paul preached. They had become members of the church but they still wanted a little backup. And when Paul wasn't there, all these high-powered preachers came, standing tall. They thumped their suspenders and did wondrous things and people said they could heal and they could work miracles. There was a big crowd and pretty soon they were saying, "You know

Paul was all right. He wasn't too attractive; he wasn't really a good speaker and he was all beat up from the stuff he's been through. We like these new ones; they've got the power. Oh, the Gospel is fine and the Bible is fine but we want some miracles just, you know, as backup."

And Paul said, "You want backup? I'll give you backup. I have been whipped five times for my faith. I have been beaten with rods three times for my faith. I have been shipwrecked; I have spent twenty-four hours in the water. I have been wet and cold and hungry, chased in the city, chased in the country, alone and stoned and left for dead. Are you getting the picture, folks? Is that not enough? Do you still need some backup?"

One of the brightest seminarians I had left school. He said, "I believe the Gospel and I believe in God and I believe in Christ and I believe what the church teaches. I want to be a minister but I want something more." He went to California; it was in the days of psychedelic music and psychedelic lights and psychedelic drugs. He became brain damaged, ending what could have been a fruitful life.

I said to him once, "What was that experience like?"

He said, "Well, well, well, it was, it was . . . everything was just, everything was kind of orange."

What did he want? He wanted a little more than what the Gospel provided.

I had a Bible class, in a way it was a Bible class, for a group of women who were forming on a Tuesday, I think it was, Bible study in Atlanta. They told me one day, "We'll have to leave early today because this is the day we go out to Lake Lanier."

And I said, "Lake Lanier? You go to Lake Lanier?"

They said, "Yes, this is the day we go to Lake Lanier."

I said, "Why?"

"Well, we go out there and we get on this nice boat that one of the husbands owns. We reach over and get some water from the lake and we all put our hands in the water and get in touch with the primal source and try to remember when we were here before."

Well, I mean these are all committed churchwomen. They're in the choir and all that. Plus, plus, a little backup.

In Jerusalem, there is by the sheep gate, a pool called in Hebrew, *Bethzatha*; it has five porches. At that pool there's a legend that every once in a while an angel will come down and stir the water and the first one that gets in is healed. All the believing, God-believing people bring their sick folk and lay them by the pool just in case today an angel will stir the water. Oh, they're still in the synagogue, they're saying the Eighteen Benedictions and they're having the prayers and giving the alms for the poor, but still, there's a little more. Now some people quit the synagogue and some people quit the church. I've known in every town, people who quit their church and say, "Well, we go to the pool now."

"We've been missing you in Sunday school."

"Well, you see, we're going to the pool now."

"Well, what's going on down at the pool?"

"The first one who gets in when the water is stirred is healed."

Hey, back up! Now who gets in first? Severely crippled, twisted, arthritic, in pain people? Oh no, no, no. The people who are able to get in first, somebody with chapped lips or a hangnail. What a commentary on the kind of stuff people pursue. And it's my experience that most of the people who are pursuing that backup are doing quite well in the world, thank you.

One day, one day, the disciples could understand it no more. Jesus was talking about leaving and he said to them, "Farewell; in a little while you won't see me."

They couldn't stand it so finally Philip, speaking for the group, said, "Show us God and we'll be satisfied. Just show us God."

And Jesus said, "Oh, you want to see God." And a child, epileptic, falling in the fire, falling in the water, worrying his parents to death, is brought to Jesus and Jesus hugs him and touches him and heals him.

The disciples said, "Well, yes, that's nice and all, but we want to see God." And a leper comes and Jesus reaches out and touches the leper and heals him. The disciples said, "But we want to see God. We want to see God."

And Jesus said, "Oh, you want to see God."

So some young mothers come with their little babies. They're crying and the mothers are sticking the pacifiers in their mouths. They have to change a diaper and it's a little disturbing and noisy and the twelve apostles come in and say, "Get the kids out of here; we're trying to have the kingdom."

Jesus said, "Let the children come to me. Don't you stop the children, for of such is the kingdom of God."

"But we want to see God."

He said, "Oh, you want to see God."

They said, "Yes."

So he took a towel and a basin of water and he washed their feet. They cried, "Oh no, don't, don't, no, we want to see God."

He said, "Oh, you want to see God." And so he picked up a cross, started up the hill, turned around and looked at every one of us and said, "Have I been with you all this time and you don't know that whoever has seen me has seen God?"

Is this enough? Or do you need a little backup?

2

Back to Basics

Exodus 20:1–17

You've heard it now twice, once from Richard in the Call to Worship and once from John in the Scripture reading that there are ten, and not eleven, Commandments. I hope those in this church who have been insisting that there are eleven will knock it off; there are ten. The eleventh one is spurious, does not exist, is not in the Bible. "Thou shall barely get by" is not one of the commandments.

We hear a lot about the Ten Commandments now, and have for several years, whether or not it is possible, or right, or legal to post them in courthouses and legislatures, in the classrooms of public schools. Some who advocate this are simply, I think, testing the principle of separation of church and state, but some are sincere people concerned about the sagging morals of the country and feel that the posting of the Ten Commandments might bolster morality a bit. Commit no act of violence, don't lie, don't steal, don't commit adultery, don't covet in a greedy way what belongs to other people. Perhaps it would help. There are those who wish to use the Ten Commandments as perhaps a way of scotching the decline and the decay of the American family. Honor your father and mother who brought you into the world and loved you and made you safe. It might help.

There are some who simply, plainly put, wish to bring the country back to God. "I am the LORD your God . . . you shall have no other gods before me" (Exod. 20:2–3). You're not to turn me into a trinket or an idol or something you can put on a bumper sticker or put around your neck, or post on a board, or make into a cute saying. I'm more than that. I am the Lord your God. It might help. Do not take the name of God lightly. Don't be heard saying "My God" and "Good God" and all like that and then excuse it by saying, "I didn't mean anything by it." When you use the name of God, mean something by it. It might help.

I thought a lot about the Ten Commandments recently. In a restaurant in Blue Ridge I ran into an old classmate of mine and I thought of the Ten Commandments. I'll tell you why. I hardly recognized him. He's not only gotten old, I don't know what's the matter with him, but he still had egg on his face. We were in a class together, taught by a Jewish rabbi, on Jesus and Judaism. It was a good class, about twenty of us, and he was, I guess you would say, the class clown. It's nice to have a clown in class, it breaks it up. But once in a while the clown gets into trouble and it's hard for a clown to get out of trouble because everything that's said digs it a little deeper. The rabbi, our teacher, was talking about the Ten Commandments and our class clown, with whom I visited in the restaurant in Blue Ridge, said, "Well, Prof., if God had written on both sides of the tablet, he could have gotten it all on one tablet, making it easier for Moses to carry down the mountain."

We all waited; how's the rabbi going to take that? I mean, the rabbi even looked like God. And the rabbi said, "If you would read your text that we had for today, Exodus 32, you would know that God wrote on the front and on the back." I was ready to drop it. I was ten or twelve feet away, but you know, those things can ricochet. But the clown wouldn't leave it alone. He said, "Well, if God had written in smaller print, he could have gotten all ten on one tablet and wouldn't have had to use two; would have been easier for Moses." And he looked around at us to see if he had any support. He had none.

And the rabbi said, "God did get all ten of them on one tablet. Both tablets had all Ten Commandments." Jaws dropped. I didn't know that. The clown didn't know that, but he hated to lose. So he said, "Then if they were both the same, why two copies? Oh, one for the file; I see." Didn't work.

The rabbi said, "They were both for the file. They were both kept in a beautiful wooden box, overlaid with gold, with gold cherubim above the box facing each other, and everywhere that Israel went they carried these tablets because these were the Tablets of the Covenant, ten on one, ten on the other. One was for the people and one was for God and they carried them with them to remind them to remember, remember God." Tough assignment. Oh, on a clear day, on a real clear day like today, I can remember God, but usually you have to work at it.

"I am the LORD your God who brought you out of Egypt, out of the house of slavery. I want you to remember that. Your life was nothing, you were nobody, you weren't citizens, you had no name, you had no address, you were strangers and aliens in a foreign land. You were slaves; you worked and broke your back to fill the pockets of other people. You were living, but only partly living and I gave you freedom. I want you to remember that."

I've thought about that a lot of times. Wouldn't it have been better if they'd just forgotten it? Just forget it; I've said that to folk who still carry the burden of the Depression with them. They were born during the Depression, the gnawing poverty, the homelessness, the same old plain food or no food at all. I've said "forget it" to people who grew up in families where alcohol had broken every dish in the house. Grown up peeking from behind the couch. Violence, anger, cursing, swearing, finally dissolution. "Forget it, move on." I've said that to people who've had nice homes, three cars, in fact everything they wanted, except the one thing they wanted most: love. "Forget it, move on."

And God said, "Don't forget it. That has shaped you to be what you are. You can't forget it. The tides of a thousand oceans could sweep ashore and roll over the sand of your mind, but when the tide went out, you would still remember. That's who you are."

A halfway house near Plainview, Texas, I think it is. A place where prisoners, hardened prisoners, have served most of their time in the state system of Texas, and are now moving toward rejoining society. These are still tough customers with all the dissipation of crime and misuse on their bodies, getting ready to go out. They had a Sunday school class in First Christian Church in Plainview. I taught the class twice. It was a tough bunch. They said it straight, no tiptoeing around and filling the air with righteousness and stewardship and going forth unto victories. No, they just called it like it was. Kind of scared me but I never in the two Sundays I was with them, I never heard any of them blame anybody else. "I am a convicted felon. That's who I am."

Nettie and I and the kids lived in Enid, Oklahoma. I worked with Alcoholics Anonymous. I wasn't an alcoholic but they were nice to me. In fact, the week before we left to move to Georgia, I was the honored guest at AA. They had a sheet cake there wishing me farewell, and underneath it, "For Fred, our honorary drunk." I liked that title but I never, never heard any of them say, "I used to be alcoholic but I've forgotten all that." They say, "I am an alcoholic."

God said, "Remember you are liberated slaves. And I want you to remember it because when you're in a land of your own, there will be strangers come, people that you can take advantage of because they don't know the language, they don't have a home, they don't have an education. Oh, you can work them for nothing practically, you can really take . . . No! When a stranger comes among you, remember you were a stranger in Egypt."

But wouldn't remembering, wouldn't remembering keep alive a kind of hatred among us for the Egyptians? They enslaved us, they hurt us, they took away our lives. Won't that just keep alive a kind of prejudice against the Egyptians? And God said, "No."

You see, when God delivered Israel from Egypt, God was busy at the time and gave the assignment to a group of angels to take care of it. And when the fleeing Israelites got to the Red Sea, these angels empowered of God parted the water. The Israelites went through on dry land and then when the pursuing Egyptians got there with horses and chariots, and fire in their faces, when they got in the middle of the Red Sea, the angels released the water. And horses and chariots and men went tumbling, drowning, tumbling, drowning. The angels said, "We got 'em, we got 'em, we got 'em."

And God came along and God said, "What are you cheering about?" They said, "Look, we got 'em." And God said, "You're dismissed from my service. I can use you no more." "Why? We got 'em."

"You don't understand. The Egyptians are also my children. And I want you to remember that I am the one who gave you food, bread from heaven, and water for the journey. All the way through the wilderness to the promised land, I fed you. I gave you birth, I nurtured you, I nursed you, I gave you love, I gave you safety. Don't forget. I gave you water from a rock, I gave you manna from heaven. I fed you every day. Don't forget. The time will come," God said, "you'll be in the land, you'll have a nice home."

"Sure thing; we put up a nice place there; our summer place. Half-million dollars; real nice."

"Oh, there'll be a time when you don't need to drink from the streams anymore because you'll say we have our own well now, we have our own well. We provide for ourselves; we don't have to raise any food, we go to the market. And you will have the illusion that you're sufficient to yourself. So I want you to do this. One week every year, I don't care how nice your home, how deep your well, you will spread a tent in the backyard and live in the tent for a week. To remember, to remember. Secondly, one day out of every seven, you will give to me. You're not to work. One out of every seven belongs to me. It is a God day. It's a remember God day. Get rid of the frantic, always on the cell phone, always on the e-mail, always on the wheel, always on the go."

"If we drive all night, we'll get to the beach by sunrise and we'll have two full hours before we have to go back. Wasn't that a great vacation?" Frantic leisure, frantic work. "But if I don't work on Sunday, if I don't work on the Sabbath, somebody may get ahead of me. Somebody else may get the deal. Somebody else may make the sale."

"True, true, but if you don't, if you forget, what difference does it make? What difference does it make? And I want you to do this. When you put the bread and drink on the table, I want you to say grace. 'Blessed art thou, O Lord, Creator of the Universe, you care for all your creatures and fill our hearts with good things. Amen.' 'For health and strength and daily food, we give you thanks, O Lord.' 'Bless this food to our body's use and us to thy service. Amen.' 'God is great, God is good, let us thank him for our food.' Every day, every day."

The class clown couldn't leave it alone, had one more question. "Yes?" "I still don't understand why God had a tablet. I understand we need a tablet but why would God need a tablet?" And still with complete patience, the rabbi said, "To remind God to remember us. The oldest prayer in the world is, 'Please God, don't forget us.' Think about it. 'Remember me, the one who inhabits eternity, who dances among the stars.'"

Think about it. Knows where Cherry Log is, knows where you live, knows the names of your family members, knows where you hurt, why you ache, what makes you happy. God knows when the sparrow falls and God remembers you. So God has a tablet, too. To remember.

Years ago when we were in Germany, I was holding a retreat for chaplains, army chaplains, at Berchesgarten, Germany. I went over to the General Walker Hotel to get my supper and there was a young woman there singing that evening while we had our meal. She was from London; her name was Julie Rayne. She sang while we ate, songs of the '40s and '50s, nice songs from musicals; very nice. And then without a break or without an introduction, right in the middle of the concert, she sang Psalm 121. "I lift mine eyes to the hills from whence comes my help." It was strange and the people were awkwardly quiet. I saw her the next day. I thanked her for the concert. I said, "But would you tell me, why that Psalm 121? It didn't seem really appropriate for your concert."

And she said, "If you knew what my life was like on the streets of London, you'd realize that was the most appropriate song I sang." She spoke briefly about that life; horrible. And I said, "Wouldn't it be best just to forget it?" And she said, "No, no."

3

Grace and Disgrace

1 Samuel 28:3–25

Watching the choir leave clarified a passage of Scripture for me. I hadn't thought about it before. "They all forsook him and fled." It's good to see you this morning. I hope you had a pleasant day and evening. Some of you were out a little late because I saw you at the opera myself. It's good to see you this morning.

I've been given permission by a number of you to dress less formally and as I look at you, I think, "Is that less formal?" Maybe I should do that. In fact, one person asked me if I ever wore Bermuda shorts. I *am* wearing Bermuda shorts. I didn't come here to be made sport of.

I hope the holding up of these biblical characters is of some value to you. I hold them up, not as windows into the past and history, but as mirrors in which we may more helpfully look at ourselves, in a better light, a clearer light, and in that light, maturity. We all are in the process of maturing but we do it so unevenly. We go forward and become even sophisticated in some areas and in other areas, we're still in high school or junior high. It comes out in ways that are very irritating, even to ourselves, but behind most decisions that people make, behind most actions and behavior, even that of which we do not approve, there lies a severe struggle of faith and values.

I was asked some years ago by the president of the university where I was teaching at that time to go with him to receive the first installment of a major, major, major gift to the theological school of that university. Since I taught preaching and the donor was interested in giving money for the improvement of programs of preaching in the seminary, I was asked to go along.

We arrived; the donor was all ready, papers before him to be signed. This was going to be, as I say, a major gift. On the way over we were celebrating the growth of this person's life who had made so much money. At first, he was quite selfish, but now was concerned about his church and the education of ministers, so he was making this gift. When we arrived and sat before his desk in his office, he then said, "Before I sign this, let's have a word of prayer," and he led us in prayer. Then he took his pen and paused just before signing and said, "Now you understand all of this is to go for the education of ministers."

"Oh, yes sir, yes sir."

He started to write and then said, "Now none of this is to go to women and blacks."

And without hesitation, the president of the university stood and said, "We cannot accept your money."

He had grown in the quality of generosity but he was still far behind in something else. We're all that way in some fashion so we do not make excuses, but neither do we judge. Even the Apostle Paul: "I don't understand my own actions," he said, "in my mind I serve God but there is another law at work in my members that interferes with and wars against the law of God in my mind. And the things that I say I will do, I don't do. The things I say I will never do, I do. I'm crucified between the sky of what I intend to be and the earth of my performance. Who is going to deliver me from this?" (Rom. 7:15–24, paraphr.) And so it is in the life of faith.

We come today to Saul, the first king of Israel, Saul of the small tribe of Benjamin. If you have tears, prepare to shed them now. I did not ask that the closing scene for Samuel 31 be read, because it is prophesied in the passage we heard. The battle is joined between Israel and the Philistines and the Philistines have overcome the army of Israel. Saul is dead; his three sons are dead and their bodies, now beheaded, are hanged on the wall of the Philistine city of Beth-shan so that the passersby could look at them in triumphant scorn. But the penultimate scene, the scene before the last scene, was read for you.

Saul is in his tent, this giant of a man, tall and handsome, the Scripture says. Now middle-aged, pacing in his tent, he calls an aide. He is absolutely anxious and terrified about what's going to happen. And he says, "Go find someone who communes with the dead; find me a medium." Remember he had just issued an edict. "Anyone practicing fortune-telling, reading tea leaves and crystal balls, anybody communing with the dead and all of that other tripe will be executed because it's contrary to Israel's faith in the one God. None of that stuff!" And now in his crisis he says, "Find me someone who is a medium."

They said, "There's one in Endor."

He puts on a disguise, a fake beard and a wig and old clothes, hoping no one will know who he is, the king of Israel. He makes his way to the tent of the medium at Endor. "Woman, I want you to call up someone."

She says, "You know the edict of the king. What is this, some kind of sting operation? Are you trying to trap me here?"

And he says, "No harm will come to you. Call up someone."

"Who is it?"

"Samuel."

She said, "You're Saul."

"Woman, nothing will harm you. Call up Samuel."

And she goes into her ritual and in her ritual she says, "I see some kind of ghostly being coming up out of the ground."

"What does it look like?"

"It's an old man in a robe."

He says, "It's Samuel."

Samuel said, "Why have you disturbed my sleep? Why?"

"Help me, tell me what to do."

And Samuel said, "It's too late; you'll be with me tomorrow."

You will not find in all of literature a scene more tragic than that. I think what adds to the pathos of this extraordinary man is the fact of his former glory. There's a pathos about people who once were high and lofty, who had something to give to the world, who attracted attention. When they walk into the room, everyone senses, "Somebody came in." And then it's gone, like the hall-of-famer, standing on the street of our nation's capital with an old, faded football jacket, begging for money to feed his habit. In a way it's no more pitiful than any beggar on the street, but Hall of Fame? And then the plummet.

Like the old man who comes into the barbershop where I go—once a year in case you're interested. He comes every day and sits in the corner. There's still a little fading glory about him. If I mentioned his name, some of you would recognize it if you keep up with the Upper 400. He was the CEO of this extraordinary company. Everything was going his way and then the bottle and then the bottle and then the bottle. Lost the wife, lost the children, lost the job, lost the boat, lost the house, lost the vacation home. Then a stroke and he sits in this little neighborhood barbershop with a drool, mumbling things we don't understand. But you still see a little bit of CEO and it hurts.

Like going to worship and across the aisle and two rows down near the front, she stands with her husband. There was a time she wouldn't be standing beside him. She would have been up front. The announcement that this marvelous soprano was going to sing would have brought the crowds. Now she's standing beside her husband. Alzheimer's has taken everything away. But in the course of just an ordinary hymn, "How Great Thou Art," here she goes, and for a few bars, everybody stops. It's a solo and she lifts the room. You stand there with goose bumps and tears, and then she stops. She doesn't know where she is or what she's doing and the congregation tries to continue. There is a pathos about those who once had it but don't anymore.

Now, what Saul did was cheap. Going to a fortune-teller was unbecoming a king. It was unethical; he violated his own principles and it was illegal. It broke the law. I can make no excuse but something in me wants to defend him in this hour. Remember, he didn't ask to be king. His father, Kish, of the tribe of Benjamin, one morning at breakfast said, "Saul, some of our donkeys have broken out of the corral. I want you to pack a lunch, take a servant and see if you can get them." They were farm people. So this big, tall, handsome young man, with a servant and a packed lunch, went out looking for these jackasses.

In the course of the search, he met the prophet of God, Samuel, and that evening Samuel said, "Tell your servant to go on down the road." And Saul did. And Samuel said, "Kneel." Saul knelt before the man of God and the man of God took out the oil of anointing and poured it over the head of this young man, Saul, and said, "God has chosen you to be the first king of Israel. I anoint you king of Israel." The oil went down his face and into his beard and he rose from the dirt of that road, king of Israel. Now he had to go home with that awful, burdensome secret. What does he do with it? Samuel says, "Oh, the time will come. It will be announced. It will be public. Go home."

And he has to go about his chores, chasing donkeys, emptying wastebaskets, working in the fields, carrying the burden of future greatness. How can anybody do it? And now, at this point in his life, his successor has been chosen and he has to live with that. Who can live with that? Who can go about his or her work in a normal fashion, every day having to look out and see a handsome young man about whom God has said, "I've already picked him as king"?

When the associate rises above the senior minister, there's trouble in the church. He doesn't have any support, even his family's support. That alone, to me, creates a most tragic scene. How can anybody get up and go to work in the morning without the support of a family that loves and cares? But I know people who do, who go to work in important jobs, men and women, the spouse no longer cares, no longer supports. I know ministers who step out of domestic wreckage into the pulpit to preach the word of God. How they do it, I don't know.

They have abandoned Saul. He has tried; he has tried to communicate with God. Samuel is dead, he calls in some other prophets and they said that there was no word from God. He lies down on his couch to go to sleep, thinking, "God will speak to me in a dream." There's nothing. He gets out the ancient Urim and Thummim, these dice-like things, to toss them and see what is the word of God; there is nothing. He has tried, and he has tried, and he has tried. Now in his desperation, he goes to a fortune-teller. Don't be too hard on him.

I know families who in desperation go to quacks. She teaches English; he is head of a prosperous company. They have a daughter, twisted in an iron chair. The doctors have shaken their heads; they've been everywhere, to the specialists all over the country. Then they read an article that there's an old man in Brazil who makes a little pottage out of bark and root, and it heals. They beg, borrow, and steal to get to Brazil. There is an old woman in the Alps who is said to have the power of healing. There's an evangelist on the West Coast who has the power. Here they go, here they go, here they go. Why? They're educated; they're sophisticated, intelligent people. They are desperate. Please, please, please, don't sit on your patio in the high noon of your tranquility and make light of the huts that people build in the midnight of their desperation.

Now what's happened to him? Why is he here? A man who should be riding down the street to a ticker-tape parade, a man who should be standing Gibralter-like before his troops is lying in the dirt of a fortune-teller's tent crying and saying, "Tell me what to do." What happened? Specialists in this story have written, disagreeing with each other. Some have used the word *fate*; some have said *God-forsaken*; some have said *star-crossed*. Others have said that Saul had a fatal flaw, like Herman Melville's Billy Budd, the perfect young man with but one little flaw. He stuttered, and it cost him his life. Others have said that Saul was simply a pawn of God. God said, "You want a king, you want a king, all right, here's a king. Is this what you want?" I don't know. I do know this: There is in the story of Saul the repetition of a phrase that begins to haunt him and finally to destroy him and that is, "I did what the people wanted. The people wanted it." Do you remember? There was to be a great worship service; all the people of God were gathered and the prophet was late. Samuel was late; he was getting old so he was late. The people said, "I'm not going to wait much longer." They're looking at their sundials. Some of the people said, "Saul, you're the king; why don't you just preside at the altar as the priest?" And he did.

He's in the middle of the liturgy and Samuel comes. "Saul, what are you doing?"

"Well, the people said, 'Go ahead, Saul.'"

"But you are not ordained of God."

"But the people wanted me to . . ."

Before an important battle Saul said, "We must have the favor of God if we are to win. I declare among all my troops that there will be fasting. No soldier, no soldier shall eat. Until the battle we must be in prayer and repentance before God." And then the word came that one of the soldiers has been eating.

"Bring him here." It's his own son, Jonathan.

Jonathan said, "Yes, I have broken the law; I have broken the fast. I know the punishment."

And the people said, "Aw, cut him some slack. My goodness, a little bread and honey? What's the deal?" And the people said, and the people said, and the people said.

After the defeat of the great army of the Amalekites, the word of God was clear: "We do not go into war in order to collect spoils and take the property and possessions of our enemies and, therefore, to prevent that selfishness, everything you take is to be destroyed." Samuel comes upon the victorious army with Saul out there celebrating and he hears the bleating of lambs and the mooing of the cows and he says to Saul, "What is this, the lowing of the herd and the bleating of the sheep?"

Saul said, "Well, the people . . ."

"Look, you know the law, everything was to be destroyed."

"Well, the people said, 'Why don't we save some of it and have a big celebration and thank God for the victory.'"

To obey, to obey is better than sacrifice. But the people said. . . .

Saul had this insatiable appetite for public approval. He was intoxicated by applause. He had to have it and in my judgment, that's what brings him down. Do you remember in George Eliot's novel *Adam Bede*, how she, the writer, predicts the tragic fall of one of the characters with one sentence? "The opinion of others formed the very air he breathed."

"The people wanted me to."

Why could not he, why could not he have been satisfied by just touching his beard, touching his head and feeling still the oil of God's anointing and just say, "It doesn't matter what the people think, God knows I'm king, God made me a king. As long as God knows, that's all that matters." Isn't that a wonderful thing to say? I hear people say that once in a while. "Well, I just don't care. God knows the truth of the matter and I just don't care." After they have said that to everybody they know about ten million times, it's not persuasive really.

Can you, can you, can you be satisfied by simply saying, "But God knows"? You have been charged with something you did not do. Can you say, "Well, it doesn't matter, God knows"? No, you can't do that. You have family, you have friends, you have church members; you can't do that. They must know that your name is clear. You've been criticized, unduly, improperly, unjustly, criticized and you say, "Well, I don't care; God knows." Oh, no, I must let the people know it's wrong. I didn't do it. I didn't say it; I was not there. Why? Because we have to have some support, some community, some respect. We can't live without that. But the question is, when does that desire for approval cross over into being diseased, erosive, finally destructive? When can I know? When can I know that I'm beginning to silence my own conscience and convictions so that I can better hear the approving voice of others and hear their applause? When can I know? That's a decision, a determination you will have to make.

I have been most of my life a teacher, a teacher of future ministers in seminaries. I try to find in my students some early indication that they are moving across the line because, in my judgment, the most unbecoming quality in a minister of God and a servant of Jesus Christ is arrogance and intoxication by applause.

I gave a student a C on his sermon. He was upset; he thought it was a grand sermon. I didn't think so. There were some things to be improved. There were basically two things wrong with it: What he said and how he said it. So I gave him a C. I thought it was sort of a sign of encouragement. Just keep working; it'll be a B and then an A. He came in a few weeks later and flopped that C sermon down on my desk and said, "Prof., I preached that sermon in my home church and I got a standing ovation." He picked it up and stomped out. Has he passed the point? The last time I saw him, he was hanging onto the furniture to keep from ascending. Is he still teachable? It won't be long until he will be standing at the door of his church somewhere, people filing by, "Good sermon, Pastor."

"Good sermon, Pastor."

"Good sermon, Pastor."

"Good morning, Pastor."

"Uh, oh, I wonder what's the matter with her? I'll have to call on her in a pastoral way."

It can happen. There is a very outstanding minister in this country who calls me once in a while and says, "Fred, the sermon I preached yesterday, the people say it's the best I've ever preached."

"Wonderful."

And then he says, "But what will I do next Sunday?"

That's fatal, fatal for a minister to begin to compete with himself or herself. "What do I do to top that? Will they stand when they applaud next time? Will the house be even more filled?" Whew.

"The people said; the people said."

"But what about your integrity? What about the word of God? What about your conscience?"

"But the people said."

His house is coming down around his ears. The roof leaks, the rent is due, and he hears the rats gnawing in the wall. It's over for him and in the hour of his desperation, he goes to a fortune-teller.

There was, you know, another Saul of the tribe of Benjamin. A Jewish couple in Tarsus in southern Turkey had a son and because they were of the tribe of Benjamin, they named him after the first king. Saul of Tarsus; some of you know him as Paul. Saul of Tarsus of Benjamin; he, too, was in great conflict with himself. When he was fighting with himself, he made casualties of Christians. In a great crisis, a moment of truth in his life, he, too, fell to the earth with his face in the sand. But in that moment of truth, he did not go to a fortune-teller. He went to God and it made all the difference, all the difference in the world.

4

Does Money Carry Germs?

2 Kings 5:1, 14–27

This is a very refreshing place and we all need it. Regardless of whether or not you love your job, love your neighbors, love your colleagues, love your church; it's good to get away. This is a marvelous place to be refreshed and to be renewed. I recall reading about Pablo Casals. The cello was his life; it was his love. He went hiking with his hosts when he was in the States, in some of the mountains in the West. He fell and hurt, rather severely, one of his hands. Everybody was concerned, rushed him to emergency, but he said, "My first thought was, when I looked down at my hand, 'Oh boy, now I don't have to play the cello.'" I understood exactly that feeling. I think all of you do. From the very thing you love the most, it's nice to have a break.

But we are here to talk about Gehazi. You heard his story read a moment ago. We begin with Naaman, Commander in Chief of the Syrian army, a great man in favor with his king, but he has leprosy. In the course of one of the Syrian raids on Israel, they had captured a Jewish girl. The Jewish girl was kept in the house of Naaman as a housekeeper. She felt rather bad about her boss's leprosy and she said to her mistress one day, "If my lord would go over into Israel, there's a man over there who can heal him by the power of God." Naaman went to his king, who said, "I'll prepare the papers immediately." So he sent papers to the king of Israel, from his Excellency to his Excellency.

When the king of Israel got the letter, he began to tear his clothes and scream and say, "What are you doing? You're making fun of me? I'm not a healer; I have no power. This is not a matter of government. What are you doing?" When Elisha the prophet heard about it, he said, "Tell Naaman to come to my house." And so this marvelous entourage of horses and chariots with fine gifts comes up before the little cottage of Elisha. Elisha sends a servant out and says, "Tell Naaman to go wash seven times in the Jordan."

Naaman was indignant. "Do you mean he's not coming out himself? He's not going to come and wave his hand over the ailment and heal me with great ritual and demonstration? Where is the liturgy here?" He was upset and started to go home and one of his servants said, "My Lord, if he had asked you to do a difficult thing, would you have done it?"

He said, "Yes."

"Then why not do the easy thing and go to the Jordan and wash?"

He did and he was cleansed. He goes back to the cottage of Elisha and says, "You must accept a gift."

Elisha said, "No."

"You must accept some gift."

Elisha said, "No. This is not a financial transaction," and so he returns to his cottage. But the servant of Elisha, Gehazi, can't stand it. He goes running after the chariots, and says, "Sir, we've just had company come in unexpectedly, some prophets from the hill country. Could you give us a couple of suits of clothes and maybe a talent of silver?"

"Oh sure, take two talents" (that's about $2,000). To his servants, Naaman said, "Bundle up some fine clothes and send servants back with Gehazi." And when they arrive at Elisha's cottage, Gehazi says, "Just leave it there." Gehazi hides the clothes and silver. He goes in to Elisha and Elisha said, "Gehazi, where have you been?"

"I haven't been anywhere."

"My spirit was with you. I know where you've been; I know what you've been doing. Don't you understand? This kind of thing is not a financial matter. Look at your hands. You now have the leprosy."

Now this is a complicated story. The complication consists of two elements. You have a good man, Gehazi. I have no question; he's a good man. It is too bad when we run across a character in life or in Scripture who makes a mistake and we paint them in ugly colors. Practically all the cheap art in the world paints Judas hunched over, eyebrows knit together, dark hair, dark beard, piercing eyes, deceptive face. No, no, no, that's too obvious. A good artist would paint Judas just as handsome as John.

Gehazi's a good man; I have no doubt about that. He's committed and loyal to his master; he's committed to the ministry. He's not ordained. In the military he would be called a chaplain's assistant. He is administrative assistant to the minister. He is the servant of the servant of God, a humble position, and almost no pay, I am sure. But he did it; he wanted to serve. I'm sure his parents weren't pleased. "Why are you going to do that? You'll never have anything and what will you say when you go back for your class reunions?

You're a servant of a servant of God? Oh, come on!" And I'm sure his family, wife and children suffered. Barefoot children, wife with seldom a new dress. There's no reason to question that he is a good man.

And then there's the money. Now when you bring up in church the subject of money, it is not appropriate suddenly to go into a tirade against the rich and become soft and sentimental and poetic about the poor. It's a very complicated subject. It's beautiful and it's ugly. One of the most beautiful things we do in the house of God involves money. The ushers come with the baskets and receive the gifts, which are elevated in the presence of God. We stand and sing the doxology; there's a prayer of dedication and people we don't even know around the world are blessed. There's nothing more beautiful than this. And yet, this: "He married her for her money. Thirty pieces of silver. Oh, it was the money. Money talks." It's a mix. The Bible argues with itself about it. Psalm 1: "Whoever meditates on the law of the Lord day and night and loves the teaching of God is like a tree planted by a stream of water. Everything he does will prosper" (paraphr.). In other words, godliness is in league with riches. You do what is right, you'll prosper. You do what is wrong, you will not prosper. And then Psalm 73: "When I saw the prosperity of the wicked, I was confused and envious" (paraphr.). Something is out of joint; it's not so simple.

Phillips Brooks, the great American clergyman, believed that prosperity went along with godliness. He said one day in one of his sermons, "Show me a poor man and I'll show you a sinner." But it's not that simple, Mr. Brooks. "Blessed are the poor." You cannot look at a prosperous person and say that God is blessing that person. Remember Solomon? Solomon sinned greater than his father, David, so God punished Solomon with a greater punishment. What was it? God gave him everything he wanted. Yuck! But to the observer: "Oh, that person must really be favored of God." Money is a complex matter, so we have a complicated story. A good man faces a financial opportunity and by defrauding, he gets the money.

Now the Bible, as is its custom, does not give us the workings of Gehazi's mind. The Bible usually gives us just the person's speech and action. Not much psychological insight in Scripture, so I don't know what thinking went into this man's life at this point when he saw the opportunity. It might have been no thinking at all. He might have just been overwhelmed by it. You know there are certain moments in life when you can be caught up in some pretty heady stuff. Here's this poor man and he sees all these beautiful horses and chariots and gold and silver and everything glistening in the sun. He didn't know how poor he was until he saw all that. Then it gets to him. It can happen.

A few years ago, I spent about ten months working with the speeches of a candidate for president. He was not successful. I did what I could. I remember the first time I went to Washington and was shaking hands with all these important people. My land, that would get to you. When I went back home to Atlanta, my kids wanted to talk to me. I said, "Make an appointment." Listen, that will get to you. In fact, it might still be with me except Nettie said, "Would you take out the garbage," and then it all went south.

It could be that Gehazi just said to himself, and quite reasonably so, "The service of God deserves more than I'm getting. If it's all this important, if it really is the salt of the earth, the light of the world, the glue that holds civilization together, then surely it's worth more than the pittance I get." It is surely.

Here's a young minister, wife, small baby, in a shoebox called a parsonage in western Kansas. It's hot; there's no air conditioning. There's one little window fan. They're smothering in there. Knock at the door Saturday morning, here comes one of the parishioners, a wealthy man, owns half the county, oil, cattle, wheat. He has something in his hand. "Won't you come in." It's a television. It's kind of a small television; it's kind of an old television. The parishioner says, "My wife's in Europe shopping with the girls but I thought I'd surprise her and have one of those big screen televisions here when she comes back. I tried to trade this one in but they wouldn't give me anything for it so I said, 'Well phooey, I'll just give it to the minister.' Now it still works even though the knob is off there. If you take a screwdriver and slip it right in there, you know . . ."

"Thank you, sir, thank you very much." Watch the muscles in the jaw; look at the stare and the clenching of the soul of the young minister. Gehazi is worth more than he's getting. He probably said, in fact, he did say, "Naaman's a Syrian. What's wrong with socking it to the Syrians?" You see, I want you to follow this now; your ethics or your morals can be determined by the other person. There are some people you would never lie to. There are some people you might lie to. There are some people you would never cheat; there are some people you might cheat. That is, it is possible to let your ethics be determined by the nature of the other person. Now Gehazi knows that's wrong; his own Bible tells him it's wrong. "You shall love the stranger as yourself. Whenever the stranger comes within your gates, you treat that person with protection and care as though that person were a member of your family." He knows better. But it's a Syrian, for goodness' sake.

We know better too. Jesus said, "You're not nice only to people who are nice to you. What is that? You're not generous only to people who are generous to you. Pagans do that. You're to be children of God who never react according to the other person, but according to God's own nature." So you are to be children of God and live out of your own character, not wait and see what the other person is like.

When I was working my way through school in a box factory making crates for tomatoes, I worked beside a black man who drove the same number of nails I did; it took twenty nails for each box. We were side by side. Friday afternoon we got our checks. He said, "How much did I make?" He had never been to school. I looked at his check; I looked at mine and said, "Oh, there's some kind of mistake. Yours is $15 less than mine." I went with him to the office. "There's been a clerical error here. Our checks are not the same." There was muttering, there was going into the back room, there was coming out, and he had another check. It was the same as mine. Then the boss said to me, "We didn't know he could read." Do you know what I'm talking about?

There is an inner circle of real honesty, another circle of "usually" and then, "Well, he's a Syrian." He might have thought that. He might have just thought, "Well, I'll never see him again. We'll never see him again; he'll go up to Syria, I'll be here, that's it." Out of sight, out of mind. Now let me explain this to you. Seeing is a powerful force in the way we behave. You've heard the expression, "I don't see how I'll be able to face her." Why? It will be seeing her that will make all the difference. You remember that Chinese story of a king who saw two men leading an ox to be sacrificed at the temple. The king was moved with pity and he said, "Release the ox and go get a sheep." And they did. Later, one of the men of the court said, "King, do you favor ox over sheep?" And he said, "No, it's just that I saw the ox." Seeing it makes the difference.

There are people who would never snatch a purse from an elderly woman. There are people who would never, never, never steal from a neighbor that they see every day, but would steal from an insurance company or the government. What do you see? What do you see? "I'll never see him again." So the moral standards are different.

It's possible he thought, "Why, this amount I'm getting is just peanuts. He has so much it's just spilling over everywhere. This is nothing."

Now, let me tell you how that works. You calculate the seriousness of a breach of ethics by how much was involved. Ten dollars? If you steal ten dollars, that's not as bad as a hundred. And a hundred is not as serious as a thousand and a thousand is not as serious as ten thousand, ten thousand is not as serious as a hundred thousand. How much was involved? Only a couple of bags of silver. No sweat. It's easy to think that way. I would like to suggest exactly the reverse. The smaller the amount involved, the greater revelation of the soul.

I saw in an airport some years ago, when there still were small boys hawking the newspapers, a well-dressed man in tweed jacket with leather at the elbows. He was gray at the temples, wore a nice hat. He saw the boy hawking the papers turn his back to go the other way and picked up a newspaper from the stand. He put it under his arm and walked on out without paying. In those days, what was the price of a newspaper, ten cents? What's the big deal?

A couple of businessmen in front of me going through the line at the cafeteria talking big deals, big deals. One of them, when we came to those little pats of butter, you know, what are they, a nickel, dime? He took a pat of butter, lifted his cup, slid it under the saucer, came to the cashier, didn't pay for it. Oh, what's the big deal? Ten cents? Here, take a quarter; what's the problem? Let me suggest: Stealing a pat of butter was a greater revelation of the character of that man than embezzling a quarter of a million. Plutarch said, "Do you want to know the real character of a person? Then listen to the slight, the small remark, the insignificant act." "Trifles light as air are proofs as strong as holy writ," said Shakespeare. It's true.

I don't know what Gehazi is thinking. Scripture doesn't say. He could just say that it's a cruel world. It's an uneven world; it's an unfair world. You have to take when you can take. Everything is uneven, what are you talking about? You get a chance to take, you take. It's easy to think that way. I'm tempted to think that way. I get sometimes so upset at the unevenness and inequality before the courts and before the cashiers and in the grocery stores of the world.

As a boy preacher, I was in West Virginia in a little mountain town. There was a woman there who had gotten one of the tickets for a drawing of groceries at the store. They were going to have a drawing for a $25 basket of groceries. In those days, a $25 basket of groceries was something. She said, "I don't have any way to get to town but I want to go in there and see if I won." She had her three grandchildren with her. Where was the mother? Nobody knew. Where was the father? Nobody knew. She had these three little girls. I borrowed a car and took her in. We stood out on the hot pavement until the announced hour and the loudspeaker came on. "Look at your tickets now." She held that ticket in front of her as though she were in prayer. I know she was. She held the ticket. The numbers came out over the speaker and a young woman in a late-model convertible already dressed for the tennis court started jumping up and down. "I won, I won, I won, I won, I won!" This old woman looked down and said, "Them that has, gets."

Gehazi, go ahead, take the silver. You know how he must have felt. Well, the tragedy in his act, whatever his thinking, was that he had damaged his life. He had damaged his soul, not beyond repair, but he had damaged it. Already the destruction of his act sets in. He has the leprosy. What was it Flaubert said in that marvelous book *Madame Bovary?* "A demand for money being of all the winds that blow on love, the coldest and most destructive." Leprosy already. Spiritual dissipation has set in. Is $2,000 enough? How much will be enough? How much more will he need? Does his new lifestyle demand another level of income? How much is enough? When will he have enough? Oh, a terrible thing has happened. He's already into it. The magnificence of the promise will be lost in the poverty of its achievement and then what? And then what?

And the illusion, oh, he started down that street, the street of illusion of what the money will get. Now what will the money get? "I'd like to buy a home."

"Well, you can't buy a home; you can buy a house."

"I'd like to have a friend."

"Well, you can't buy a friend; you can buy a companion for the evening, but you can't . . ."

"I'd like some love."

"You can't buy love; sell you a romance novel."

"Like to have some peace of mind."

"Well, we don't have any. Got some nice Bibles here."

"Like to buy a little time."

"Oh, you can't buy any time. Got some nice watches. Would you like to buy a watch?"

Where is the market that will give him what he wants and what he needs? The saddest thing in the world is to see a man with a fistful of $50 bills running up and down the hall of a hospital, stopping every orderly, every nurse, every doctor, every intern. "In Room 320, that's my wife under the oxygen tent, if you'd just look in, if you'd just, there's something here for you." "Mister, your money has absolutely nothing to do with you and your wife."

But worst of all, he has damaged all of his relationships. They're all tainted now. He lied to Naaman to get the money. He's lied to his beloved friend and boss, Elisha. "I haven't been anywhere." Now, let me ask you something. What is he going to tell his wife? "Well, honey, where did you get all this money?" "Uh." And when the kids come home from school, "Daddy, where did we get all this? And that suit you're wearing? Daddy?" What is he going to say?

Now, may I make two suggestions? One, in life the issue is not do you have money or do you not have money? Rather, the money you have, can you speak of it with celebration and love with your own family? Will you still have the respect of your children when they learn about you? The most awful, awful thing is for a child to lose respect for a mother or a father. Children will lie to defend their parents. Children will believe the best of us when we're at our worst; they just want us to be . . .

In a little mining town in Kentucky after the services one night, a little girl lingered. I think she was about nine years old, barefooted; but it was summertime so that was okay. She wore a little faded dress that belonged, I'm sure, to her sister who had gotten it from an older sister. She always sat on the front row. She came up to me and she said, "Can I talk to you?"

I said, "Sure."

She waited until everybody was gone and then she said, "Do you know what?"

I said, "No, what?"

She said, "Guess what."

And I said, "What?"

She said, "My daddy's coming with me tomorrow night."

You should have seen her eyes. I've seen children's eyes reflecting the candles on a birthday cake. I've seen children's eyes reflecting the bulbs on a Christmas tree, but no eyes like her eyes. "My daddy's coming with me tomorrow night." He didn't come; he wasn't coming. He was a drunken bum and a wife beater, but it was her daddy. Please, never an act, never a word that causes a little girl or a little boy to lie just to hold on to respect for you.

Suggestion number two: Can you say grace over your possessions? Can you bow your head and say a word of thanks. "Thank God for this." This is the final test, because gratitude is the central virtue of the Christian life. There is no other virtue like gratitude—none. I've never known a person who was grateful who was, at the same time, mean or small or bitter or hurtful. Not when you're grateful.

When our kids were small, if an angel had come into the room and said, "Now you may receive one virtue, one quality for each child; what will it be?" I am sure my wife and I would discuss it, but I already know what my request would be. Make them always grateful.

5

A Little Less Than God

Psalm 8

The worst place in the world to locate a pulpit is between hungry people and the dinner table, so I will not be long. I just want to make sure you don't forget what Bill read to you a moment ago, Psalm 8:

"O Lord, our Lord, how excellent, how majestic is your name in all the earth."

Such a huge statement made by the psalmist, probably living in the desert of Israel. How could he say, "in all the earth"? Probably had never seen huge chunks of icebergs break off and plunge into the sea. Probably never saw a flight of flamingos startled by the appearance of a person. Never saw alligators dozing in the sun along the Amazon. Never saw the fjords rushing with melting snow down the Scandinavian mountains. Never saw the ugly ostrich stride across the savannas of South Africa. Probably never heard the trumpet of the elephant. Never heard the chattering of a tree full of frightened monkeys, probably never. How could he say, "in all the earth"?

Because he is in a worshipful mode. He may have talked to some travelers who had seen some things and heard some things that he didn't know, but not necessarily. He had his faith in God as the one God of all creation and he had Genesis 1: "In the beginning God created the heavens and the earth." Everything that is, is from God. So he didn't need to travel to say that. There are many people who travel all over the world, buy a lot of trinkets, complain about the service, and come home exactly the way they were. You can stand in the doorway of your cabin in the Appalachians and say in worshipful tones, "in all the earth." Or read again the beautiful cadences of Genesis 1 and let your mind go free as you imagine what fun it was for those beginners when God said, "Now it's your job to name all the animals." Wouldn't that be a pleasure?

"Well, Adam, what are you going to call that one?"

"I was thinking maybe giraffe."

"Eve, what did you have in mind?"

"I like the word 'mouse.'"

"But it doesn't look like a mouse."

Isn't that a delight? It's all about creation. The majesty and power of God reflected in what was made. "How majestic, how excellent is your name. Everywhere." And then in the desert of Israel it grew dark, camp was made, temporary corrals for the animals. The camels now kneeling and blinking in the swirling sand, calves released to their mothers, and it is dark. That's the wonderful thing about remote rural areas; it gets dark at night. With all the increase of population up here, the one thing that is most disturbing to me, and I'm a latecomer, is the increase of light. In Atlanta we had to get in the car and drive out in the country to see a shooting star. The lights competed with the lights. But up here it gets so dark; it's supposed to be dark when it's dark. And then you see the stars.

And the singer of Israel looked up and said, "When I consider the heavens . . ." Note the plural, heavens; heaven was not a single word then. There were many heavens. How many? Three? Seven? Some said 365. And at the top of the highest of the heavens is the throne of God. I look at the moon and stars. How long has it been since you did that? One of the most wonderful experiences for a parent or a grandparent is finally to get a small child to see the Big Dipper. Have you shown the Big Dipper to a child? Children's eyes just go everywhere and you say, "There it is, see. The four stars make the little cup and then that's the handle, you see it?" "I hear a bird." "No, now do you see that? Look at it. Watch my finger—out that way." Then that final time when he/she says, "I see it, I see it!" That's important because we don't want our children to be like some of the rest of us, so small of mind and thought.

When I consider the moon and stars, who are we that you think so much about us? We're so little. That's such a grand expanse and here we are, so small, some of us really small. Did you know there are people whose world is so very small, same few people every day, same few people every day, family, friends, family, friends? You could develop a prejudice if you are not careful. Same few people. I know some people do it deliberately because, "If I keep the pond small, I seem like a big frog. If I am in a small world, then it looks like I have increased in size. And in my own opinion, I get to be rather huge."

The man's name was Robert Williams; he died and he went to heaven. He was checking in at the Pearly Gates and the angel at the desk said, "And the name?"

He said, "Williams."

"First name, please."

"Robert. Everybody knows me."

"Well, Robert, we have here 413 billion Robert Williams. Could you be more specific?"

"But, you know, here in Gilmer County, they always just call me Bob."

"That helps, Bob. We're down to 193 billion."

"My close friends call me Buddy."

"OK, Buddy, now we're doing well, 97 billion. Could you help me a little more?"

"Well, I lived out on the road going out . . ."

"No, what planet?"

"Well, it was the earth, it was the earth."

"That's good. What country?"

"The US of A."

"Would you give me the state."

"Georgia."

"Would you give me the county."

"Gilmer."

"Now, would you give me the address. Ah, I see, you are Robert Williams."

It's easy to think so small. But to look at the moon and stars and to know that there are people every hour of every day, it's dark somewhere all the time, every hour of every day there are other boys and girls and adults looking at the same stars, wishing on the same stars, looking at the same moon. Teach your children that; show them the moon and stars and say, "Just think, in Japan and in Korea and Yugoslavia and Uganda, they're seeing the same thing. And they are wishing the same thing."

When I started out in the ministry, I thought in terms of right and wrong and true and false and biblical or unbiblical. But now that I've gotten wise, there is a bigger category, more important to me; small and big. When I consider the moon and stars, O God, why do you even think about us? We're so confused. The moon and the stars go in their courses every day. We can count on it; we can chart it. Whatever the century, whatever the country, we know exactly where every star and all the moons will be. We know exactly because they are ordained of God. But we are so confused. You said, "I'll give you dominion over land and sea and all that is in the sea and all the beasts of the field, the fish that go in the sea. Over everything, I give you dominion." And we don't know what it means. Some people think it means rape the land, you own it. Soil the streams, you own them. Darken the air, it's yours. Toss your McDonald's trash all along the highway, "This is my land." Some people think that's what it means. "You shall have dominion."

There are other folk who think it means that you shall accumulate. It's yours, so accumulate. And some never think about the fact that the more they get, the less somebody else has. If you get a huge meal, somebody else is hungry. That's the way it works. What does it mean, "You shall have dominion"? It seems that we can just grab, hold, collect, hoard. After all, we have dominion.

A hundred years ago there was published in the *San Francisco Chronicle* a poem, "The Man with the Hoe," by a public school teacher there in California. His name was Edwin Markham; he taught high school. His poem became the call for revolution around the world:

> Bowed by the weight of the centuries he leans
> Upon his hoe and gazes at the ground,
> The emptiness of ages in his face,
> And on his back the burden of the world.
> Who made him dead to rapture and despair,
> A thing that grieves not and that never hopes,
> Stolid and stunned, a brother to the ox?
> (*San Francisco Chronicle*, Jan. 15, 1899)

Who made him this way? "I have so many people working under me and I give them almost minimum wage, but I am the owner." And the voice says at night, "You fool; you're history." Now who gets it? The relatives? Is it going to be piled up in the front yard, strangers picking over it while an auctioneer gavels off your precious goods? What does it mean, "have dominion"?

When I consider the moon and stars that God has ordained, why does God pay so much attention to us? We're so mixed up and we're so temporary. The moon and stars, the moon and the stars forever. As for me, I'm just a blip on the screen. There was a time I did not exist. There will be another time I will not exist, but in the narrow time between whence and whither, what am I going to do? Why does God pay attention to us? We're so brief. We see it in the seasons: spring of the year, all the world is a poem of light and color, then it gets hot and the grasshopper drags itself along and the thermostat's broken and everybody's mad. Then it cools off; you grab a sweater, kick a football in the air; it's beautiful, but not for long. The cold weather blows the leaves off the trees and bony fingers on those trees beg for cover and down comes the snow, the flying cloud, the frosty light, the year's dying in the night. "Happy New Year." What happened?

Do you live as though you're going to live forever? At our little place over a creek, a couple of years ago I was out working in the yard, and I found a beautiful arrowhead, beautiful, beautiful and perfectly shaped. I picked it up and said to myself, "Fred, you're not the first one to live here." And the plow goes along and hits something hard. The farmer stops and goes around to pull out what might be just a little boulder. It's a cornerstone, actually a hearthstone. There was once a family here; made popcorn balls, pulled molasses taffy, sat around the fireplace and sang from the old paperback book, "Bring Them

In," "Oh, How I Love Jesus," "O What Wondrous Love Is This." They put
poultices on the sick, put camphor salve on the breasts of the children, put
salve in their noses, cooked collards, and laughed and cried; gave birth and
died, right here. We're not the first ones; we're not the last ones. Life is just
so brief. It's true of everything we do. Consider the buildings we build; we put
up a beautiful building, bring in a speaker from California, great orator, for
the dedication. "When we build, we build for a thousand years." He pauses
in his oratory and you hear a not very religious repairman addressing a leaky
faucet or a broken brick and you say, "We haven't even paid for it yet." Why
does God pay attention to us? So small, so wrong, so brief.

And the psalmist says, "I know. God made us in God's own image. When
God made the duck, God said, 'That's good.' When God made the elephant,
God chuckled and said, 'Well, that's good.' When God made the dogwood
tree, God said, 'That's good,' and so with the squirrel and the quail and the
grouse and the turkey. 'That's good.' But it wasn't enough and finally God
said, 'I'm going to make something just like myself, my very image. I'm going
to make something that, when people look at it, they're going to say, "God."'
And that's when God made you."

Now we don't want any of that stuff like, "We're only human." I'm sick
of that. A shortstop catches the ball without mistake 300 times and finally
he drops it and somebody says, "Only human." What was he when he made
the play? She bakes a cake eight inches tall, beautiful. Then the church has
a fellowship dinner so she wants to outdo herself. She makes one, looks like
the sole of your shoe. "Well, I'm only human," she says. What was she when
the cakes were eight inches tall? When the singer climbs the silver stairs and
leaves every note as clear as the morning dew, what do people say? "Oh, that
was wonderful." If her voice cracks, "Well, she's only human." Why, why,
why do we say we're human when we make a mistake? Weren't you made in
God's image? Don't ever say, don't ever say, "I'm only human." When somebody says, "That was beautiful," you say, "Well, after all, I'm human." When
somebody says, "Best I've ever eaten," you say, "After all, I'm human." When
somebody says, "That was a beautiful prayer today," you say, "Well, after all,
I'm human." Would you do that?

I know sometimes we don't act like it. You take the expression "You have
made us but little less than God," and then hold it up beside the daily newspaper and it doesn't seem to fit. Left a baby in a trash bin? Hit a pedestrian and
didn't even stop? Took people's money that was supposed to go for Medicare,
Medicaid? It doesn't seem to fit, I know, I know, I know. But once in a while,
once in a while . . .

When I was minister in the mountains of east Tennessee, the church had
vacation Bible school in the summer. I had these kids, I don't know, third or

fourth grade. The thing lasted two weeks. I was ready at the end of one day to call it quits. Took about twelve kids, all day, two weeks. The lesson that year was on, you know, nature. Well, I use up that stuff all in one day; then what am I going to do the rest of the time? I thought of something. I'll send them out into the woods and let them get something that reminds them of God and bring it back. I rang a bell and I said, "Now when I ring this bell, you go out into the woods, find something that reminds you of God, and when I ring it again, bring it back and tell us what it tells you about God."

So I rang the bell and they scattered. My plan was not to ring it again, but I did. I rang it again and here they came. And I said to her, "What do you have?"

She said, "A flower."

"And what does that tell you about God?"

"God is beautiful." Now that's good.

"And what do you have?"

"A rock."

"What does that tell you?"

"God is stout." Hey, that's good, that's good.

"And what do you have?"

"Huckleberries."

"Well what does that tell you?"

"God is good; God feeds us and feeds the birds." Another good answer.

Well, here's Jim East, meanest kid I ever saw, but he was always there. You didn't want him to be there all the time, but . . . So I said, "Well, Jimmy, what do you have?" He was holding the hand of his sister from the kindergarten group. I said, "What did you bring, Jim?"

He said, "My sister."

I said, "What does that tell you about God?"

And Jimmy said, "Uh, uh, uh, I don't know." And that's it, that's it. This mean little kid recognized there wasn't a thing in the forest that told him as much about God as his sister. That's it.

In *The Education of Little Tree*, that marvelous story about a Cherokee Indian boy in western North Carolina, raised by his grandparents, poor as Job's turkey, didn't have a thing. He knew the grandparents had nothing to get him for Christmas; they had no money. But he wanted to give his grandmother something so he got some leather hide and sewed a little pouch, a coin purse I guess you would say. He didn't want to give it to her and hurt her feelings because she would have to say, "Well, Little Tree, I don't have anything for you."

So you know what he did? You remember the story? He pushed that little coin purse that he made down into the bin of dried beans. They ate dried beans all winter. He pushed it, he said, down into the beans about Christmas deep. She would start reaching into that bin every day, October, November, and December. Then about the middle or toward the last of December, she'd say, "Little Tree, Little Tree, look what I found, look what I found." And he would run over and look at it, "What is it?" She said, "It's a Christmas present. I don't know who. . . ." And Little Tree said, "That's beautiful."

A little less than God. I know, I know, some of us act like garbage sometimes. But I looked out one day and saw our garbage can with stuff spilling out the top and I thought, "That's awful, that is really awful." But during the night it snowed and the garbage can was a mound to the glory of God. How does Paul put it? "You are created in God's image. You are recreated in Christ Jesus. You are God's masterpiece."

A little less than God. Amen.

6

Whatever Became of Sin?

Psalm 51:1–12

As you know we are now one week away. According to my calculations, if we continue at our present pace, next Sunday morning about this time we will arrive in Jerusalem. After the long Lenten journey we'll be there, join the crowds, shouting, waving palm branches, celebrating the presence of Christ among us. Joyful to enter the Holy City; it's an exciting time, the air will be electric. In the language of Shakespeare, "Let the drum speak to the trumpet, let the trumpet speak to the cannon, let the cannon speak to the sky." It is an extraordinary day.

Now I remind you we are not going to Jerusalem as tourists. Leave your camera at home; don't get excited saying, "But we may see some camels." We're not going to take side trips to Rachel's tomb. We're not going down to David's boyhood home in Bethlehem. We're not going to take the kids on a picnic in Gethsemane. We're not tourists. We're pilgrims, pilgrims in whose hearts are the highways to Zion.

We've been in prayer and penitence and preparation forty days. There is a strong likelihood, a very, very good chance that we will see Him, on the street, in the temple, on the cross. And I've been trying to think what I would say. Maybe you already know what you will say. What will we say?

The receptionist buzzes the secretary and says, "The nine o'clock appointment is here." The secretary buzzes the boss and says, "Your nine o'clock appointment is here."

"Who is it?"

"It's Reverend Nathan."

"Well, send him in."

"Good morning, Reverend. To what do I owe the honor of this visit? I know, I know, I know I've missed worship a few times lately but the war, the economy, a lot of family things going on. A few trips to take, I've been busy. But I sent my pledge in; it should arrive early next week. I don't know why you came but I've taken care of those things. How are you doing?"

"I just came here to tell you a little story."

"Oh, I love your stories. That's one reason I come to worship, to hear your stories, I like your stories. I was just telling a friend of mine one of your stories the other day. What is it, Reverend?"

"Well there were two men in this certain village, one was very rich, one was very poor. The rich man had sheep all over the hillside; you could hardly count them. The poor man had one. It was rejected by its mother; he raised it from a little lamb, fed it with a bottle. It was in the house most of the time, sometimes slept with its head on his lap, drank from his cup. His children loved it; one ewe.

"The rich man had company arrive and he wanted to feed them well so he went out to get a sheep to slaughter for the feast. He did not take one from among his hundreds. He went to the neighbor's and took the only sheep the neighbor had. Slaughtered it for the feast."

"Slaughtered it, stole it?"

"Yeah, the only one he had, took it, he had plenty . . ."

"Why, goodness, I've never heard of anything so insensitive, so cruel, so greedy, so selfish, so . . . I tell you he ought to pay back fourfold. Ah, no, that man should die for what he did."

And Nathan said, "David, you are that man." David knew, he didn't have to be told. It was on his mind night and day. He remembered all the details. It was in the spring of the year when kings go forth to war and he had returned to Jerusalem for a little R & R. He saw this beautiful woman and brought her to the palace. After all, he is the king. And who is she? Her husband is a soldier in the army and he's gone. These are difficult times, yakkety, yakkety yak. She becomes pregnant. He sends for her soldier husband to come home and the soldier husband, Uriah, is a good soldier. "I can't take my wife out to dinner and sleep in my own bed and have good meals in the comfort of home when my buddies are out on the cold ground eating K-rations." And he would not go home. Plan A didn't work.

Plan B: He sends word to the commander to have Uriah's troop pressed to the front to take the city. And when he is out front, withdraw and leave him there vulnerable. And soon the word comes back; "Uriah was killed." The king comforts the poor widow and marries her.

"You are that man."

Samuel tells us that he fell prostrate, would not be consoled, and according to tradition, he prayed Psalm 51: "Have mercy, have mercy."

"It's always in front of me. I wake up with it; I go to bed with it. It's against you, God, that I sinned; it's against you. The one relationship that means more to me than anything else and I stained it. Don't leave me alone. I've lost all my joy. I feel like my bones are all broken. I can't do anything right. If you withdraw from me, I'll become an animal, I'll be grazing with the jackasses, I'll be nothing. Don't turn your back on me. Clean me up. Give me a clean spirit. Forgive me."

I've been wondering what I would say when I very likely will see Him in Jerusalem, on the street, or in the temple, or on the cross. Very likely you will see Him. What are you going to say?

The receptionist buzzes the secretary, "The nine o'clock appointment is here."

The secretary buzzes the boss, "The nine o'clock appointment is here."

"Who is it?"

"It's Reverend Nathan."

"OK. Morning, Reverend. I know why you're here. You've heard about it, the whole town's heard about it, it's been in the papers. And I admit it; I made a mistake, so what? Cut me a little slack here. It's not like I'm the only one in the world who ever made a mistake. I mean these are war times and in war times you have an emergency situation, you relax all these moral restraints. We suspend the ethical; it's just a difficult time for everybody. I know I've upset my kids, my wife, but they'll get over it. I'm not a bad person.

"You know I was anointed by the prophet to be the king when I was still just a boy in my father's home. I've had a favored place in God's sight; I'm not a bad person. When Israel was paralyzed in fear of the Philistines, I'm the one who killed their champion Goliath. You remember that? I'm the one that gave a home to the ark of the covenant and set up a place to worship. I'm the one that's been wanting to build a temple to God. You remember the grandson of old King Saul, Mephibosheth, crippled boy? I brought him into my house and treat him like a son. I'm not a bad person. Hey look, we're all human, we make mistakes. Nobody's perfect. It's not the end of the world. The way I look at it is this. There's enough bad in the best of us, enough good in the worst of us, that it behooves none of us to say anything critical about the rest of us. You know the way I look at it, Reverend? Life just kind of ends in a draw, right? That's the way I look at it. How's your family?"

I've been trying to think what I would say 'cause we're going to see him. Back in the '70s, Dr. Karl Menninger, Topeka, Kansas, great pioneer psychiatrist, wrote a book, which he entitled *Whatever Became of Sin?* I was embarrassed when he asked me one day, "What did you think of my book?"

I hadn't read it. I said, "It's on my list, Doctor."

He said, "I'll send you a copy."

And he sent me a copy. We were at Chautauqua at the time and the next morning at breakfast, he said, "What did you think of the book?"

Well, I was on page 32; give me a break here. I read the book. We had a chance to talk about it a little bit. And he asked me, "Whatever became of sin? I don't hear much about it anymore. And I don't know why. We still have violence and greed and infidelity, and lying and stealing and oppression of the poor. We still have inequity in so many things. We still have violation of family life. So what's happened? Is it just that we don't call it sin anymore or are we just used to it?"

I had no answer for him, nor for you. I don't know whatever became of sin. I do know what can become of sin.

May I suggest something? If you will this next week slow down, quit breezing along doing as you please, calling it freedom, treating every relationship as though it were casual and every value as though it were relative. Slow down. Not just to pass by the altar and leave a little gift and pay your regards to God, but stop in front of it. Just stop. You know the light at the altar is different from every other light in the world. You see things you don't otherwise see. If you are at the altar offering your gift and there you remember somebody has something against you—it causes that to happen, you know—just slow down. All locomotion has to stop. Then the feeble excuses stop and the explanations stop and the comparing and being compared as though we expected God to grade on the curve, all that stops. And if you stand there, you will kneel there and you might even say, "Have mercy on me. In the multitude of your tender mercies, clean me up. Don't back away from me, don't take away your Holy Spirit; forgive me."

If you'll do that I have every, every reason to believe that you will hear God say, "Yes, yes, yes."

7

God Opens the Ear

Isaiah 50:4–6

You heard the text read, and read very well, but the lines of haunting poetry are so full of pain and mystery that it seems unfair not to let our ears feast on them once more. Listen:

> The Lord GOD has given me
>   the tongue of a teacher,
> that I may know how to sustain
>   the weary with a word.
> Morning by morning he wakens—
>   wakens my ear
>   to listen as those who are taught.
> The Lord GOD has opened my ear,
>   and I was not rebellious,
>   I did not turn backward.
> I gave my back to those who struck me,
>   and my cheeks to those who pulled out the
>   beard;
> I did not hide my face
>   from insult and spitting.

That this is poetry is clear enough, at least a fragment of a poem. It is written in first person, but by whom? It is the kind of poetry left on the wall of a prison cell following liberation. We know the place is the exile, that forced removal of Israel from altar, hearth, and home, to live among strangers with strange language, strange dress, strange food, strange worship. Such a circumstance could account for the mystery in these lives and the pain in their voice. The writer obviously has a mission: "That I may know how to sustain the weary with a word." Equally clear is the painful preparation for that mission: a bleeding back, torn cheeks, a face covered with the spittle of the tormentor. But central to the preparation is God's awakening of the ear every morning. The awakening is painful: "The Lord GOD has opened (literally, dug out) my ear." Apparently listening is difficult, so difficult, in fact, as to require an act of God.

Jesus has told us as much. When the sower goes out to sow the Word, some of the seeds do not even sprout. They fall on the path hardened by frequent travel. Sparrows from the rooftop, chickens from the barn come peck, peck, pecking, and in the blink of an eye there is no evidence there ever was a sower or seed. So much goes unheard, with no chance of making a difference. A prominent Texas preacher often complained that he was not heard. Not even, he said, during the announcements. According to him, announcements of church functions were published in the weekly parish paper, reprinted in the weekly worship bulletin, and again repeated orally by the pastor during the informal moments of Sunday worship. And, he said, "During the benediction I pray, 'And please help the people to remember the fellowship supper on Wednesday at 6:30.' But invariably, at the door following worship someone will ask, 'Are we going to have the fellowship dinner?' Do I delude myself with the idea that anyone hears my sermons? Not at all."

A bit more promising, says Jesus, is the fact that some seeds sprout and spring up. But the soil is shallow and so are the roots, the sun is hot, the air is dry, and soon promise of a harvest wilts. This pitiful drama is sadder than the first because the promise unkept is more painful than no promise at all. You are, I'm sure, familiar with this type of non-listener. He attends twice a year, but already dressed for the lake outing to follow worship. In fact, his Suburban with boat attached sits out back astride five parking places. "Well, Reverend, are you going to make another one of your good talks?" What do you say? Or, she is the first one out the door following the benediction. She rushes up to the preacher: "What were you saying at the end of your sermon? Everyone seemed to be listening." "Oh, I'm sorry you were late for the service." "I wasn't late, but I brought my daughter today, there were not two seats together, so she sat on one side and I on the other. The only way we could communicate during the service was by text messaging." Shall the preacher repeat the sermon?

More promising yet, says Jesus, is a harvest from seeds falling among the weeds. There is almost a harvest; the potatoes are small, like marbles, the green beans are blisters, and the corn is but nubbins. The weeds take a lot of nature's attention; in fact, they choke the crop. I was a guest in an Atlanta pulpit. The pastor and I were to lunch together after he picked up trash and discarded bulletins. I helped. One bulletin lay open and caught my eye because it bore handwritten notes. In one hand, "Shall we close the deal today?" In another hand, "But it's Sunday." In the first hand, "But if we don't close it today we may lose it." What, could you not pray with me one hour? Weeds.

Thank God, Jesus assures us that some seeds fall in good soil. But even so, listening is not easy. And for many reasons. For example, we eventually get used to a noisy clock, or to loud music in the next room, or to huge trucks groaning down the highway near the house, and eventually we no longer hear these intrusive sounds. Else we would be driven crazy. Or, it may be that we think we are listening when in fact we are remembering. In art there is a phenomenon called "pentimento." When an artist applies a base color to the canvas, changes her mind and puts on another, in time the original color may bleed through to the surface. This is pentimento. It happens all the time when listening to sermons. An image, a line of poetry, a text of Scripture, a phrase of ancient origin; these or countless other sounds prompt the memory of another preacher, another sermon, a wedding, a funeral, and one is no longer listening but remembering. And then there is preoccupation, the tangle of ideas, plans, duties, promises, and regrets already running around in the brain, refusing to sit down and listen. They are with us when we sit down, when we rise up, and throughout the sermon. Bill Muehl, when professor of preaching at Yale, often reminded his students, "Remember, about half of your congregation almost didn't come this morning." In other words, a line has already formed and is begging for attention before Moses or Nahum or even Jesus arrives.

But perhaps chief among reasons for the difficulty we have with listening is that the subject matter is vitally important; that is, possibly life changing. It is a very real possibility that the one who listens can, as a result, be radically affected in relationships, in ethical standards, in moral decisions, in how money is made and spent. In other words, in every way. Who wants that? No wonder some people prefer a poor preacher to a strong one. The weak pulpit provides two benefits: a Sunday morning nap and the grounds for complaining about the poor preaching. But when the pulpit is strong, laying on the listeners the full claims of the Gospel, the one who sits before such a pulpit may look for an escape. Perhaps rather frequent absences. Or perhaps, be present but distracted. Count the light bulbs in the ceiling; guess the ages of the worshipers; make lists of things to do; catch the preacher in a grammatical error; read from the pew Bible passages totally unrelated to the message and its text—Bible against Bible. One woman, attending a service at which I was guest preacher, told me that if she anticipated that a message might lay a claim on her life, she brought her three small children into the sanctuary with her. The distraction, she said, usually worked. It probably worked as well for those around her, but their angry stares were a small price to pay for going home scot-free.

"And you do not recall ever being in church before today?" I asked a young (25–30) visitor.

"I'm sure this is my very first time."

"Well, how was it?"

"A bit scary."

"Scary?"

"Yes, I found it a bit frightening."

"How so?"

"The whole service seemed so important. I try to avoid events that are important; they get inside your head and stay with you. I don't like that. To be honest I prefer parties."

"Then will you come back?"

A long pause. "Yes."

Of course, there is resistance. Who wants to be disturbed by the truth: three thousand children killed by gunfire every year; twelve million children go to school every day in charity clothes; thirteen million children go to bed hungry every night? Who wants to have a nice day ruined by Jesus: If you have two coats; go the second mile; turn the other cheek; if you love only those who love you; forgive seventy times seven; love your enemies; your will be done on earth as it is in heaven; I was hungry, naked, a stranger, in prison; you fool, where is all your stuff now; God is kind even to the ungrateful and wicked; do not be anxious about tomorrow?

George Eliot said it well: most of us are "well wadded with stupidity"; that is, with deafness. How comfortable! And then it happens: God opens my ear. Life is never again the same.

8

Two Faiths in One Heart

Jonah

It is an honor to be invited to Chautauqua. It may be true that you cannot go home again but you can return to Chautauqua and I am pleased about that. I regret very much having to cancel in 1993; I was paralyzed with Guillain-Barré Syndrome, a rather rare disease. I received many calls and letters and cards from persons I had met at Chautauqua and prayers were said here for me; I appreciate that very, very much. I hope you will not, now that I'm on my feet, cease your prayers; as you can tell I am in much need of them.

Some years ago I was invited to speak at Ebenezer Baptist Church in Atlanta. Joe Roberts is the pastor but it is known as the church of Martin Luther King Sr. and Jr. At the time of the sermon one of the associates introduced me simply by name and said that Mr. Craddock will read his own text. And I got up to do just that. It was Mark 1, and I had begun to read when the pastor, Joe Roberts, seated nearby, began to hum. But that's all right, I can use a little humming. And then he began to sing and it interfered with the flow of my words. And then the associates on the platform began to sing. The instrumentalists went to their instruments, a guitar and drums and organ and piano, and they began and people were singing. I'm standing there in the middle of my text. The people began to sing from all over that auditorium and I thought, well, I'm the one up front, I must be the leader, so I began to clap my hands and they began to stand and sway and sing. It was a great time; the song was "I Feel Much Better Now That I've Laid My Burdens Down." It was a grand moment and then Joe said, "Yes" and everybody sat down.

I continued the reading, I had my sermon and afterwards I said to Dr. Roberts, "You got me off doing that. I didn't know you were going to do that."

And he said, "I didn't know I was going to do that."

47

And so I asked him then why he did it. He said, "When you stood up to preach, one of the associates leaned over to me and said, 'That boy's going to need some help.'" And I did. And I do.

It is my desire this morning and each morning through Friday to talk to you about biblical characters, Old Testament and New, male and female, who trusted in God, but whose faith was troubled, sometimes divided, full of impurities and difficulties, source of a great deal of pain as faith can be, as hope can be, as love can be, a faith much like our own. I want to talk about them but I want you to understand that I'm not doing this to topple them from some pedestal in your mind. I don't like toppling heroes and heroines. I hate those books like *Mommy Dearest* and things like that. If Abraham Lincoln told dirty jokes, don't tell me about it. If George Washington did not kneel for three months in the snow at Valley Forge, don't tell me about it.

I remember how disappointed I was when I read the essay of Thomas de Quincey about William Wordsworth, the poet. I love William Wordsworth; "My heart leaps up when I behold." I just love it. And here was the essay. Wordsworth belonged to a literary circle whose members took turns going to each other's homes for dinner, once or twice a month. And it was the custom of Mr. Wordsworth when he went to the home of his host to ask, "Have you received any new books?" "Well, they're on my desk."

Mr. Wordsworth would go into the desk of his host, get the books and in those days, the pages had not been cut apart; that had to be done by the reader. He would take a stack of these books to the dinner table and sit there and cut the pages apart with the knife that had butter and jam on it. I hated that essay.

Nor do I have in mind comparing ourselves favorably with them. Comparisons are not good. Comparing ourselves with each other and being compared by others is a sick business. It's a sorry unfruitful thing. In the dim lamps of this world you can play that game and we'll all come off looking pretty good; everybody passes. If you believe that God grades on the curve, everybody wins. But it's a fruitless thing and useless among us.

I don't have that in mind. What I have in mind is simply helping us to understand what it is to live in trust, to live before God, and to understand the tensions and the troubles and the pains that are in that experience. And sometimes it helps us to understand our own life and our own faith. If we look at someone else, we receive truth, as Emily Dickinson said, "On the slant."

And so I begin, as Sister Christine read, with a man you know, a man in whose heart were two faiths, Jonah, the prophet. The story you know; I briefly remind you. Jonah, son of Amittai, prophet in Israel, received the word of God to go and preach in Nineveh, a great and wicked city about 175 miles northwest of the present city of Baghdad on the River Tigris, the enemy of Israel. And God said, "The wickedness of that city just smells and it has reached me. I want you to go and preach against it."

But Jonah would not go; he caught a ship to Spain, to Tarshish. God sent a great storm and troubled the ship and the sailors, afraid they were going to die, called on their gods and cast lots. "Who on board is the cause of this?" Eventually they tossed Jonah overboard. God appointed a great fish to swallow him and three days later he was belched out upon the land and he went, reluctant still, to preach to Nineveh.

He preached and started the countdown for the destruction of the city, but it was not destroyed. When Jonah had finished, God sent a gourd vine to cover him and shade him from the sun and he was pleased about the gourd. Then God sent a worm to cut the gourd down and it withered and Jonah was angry. Then God sent an east wind to burn his face and head and he said, "I wish I were dead." That's the story.

Here is a man of profound faith and commitment to his vocation. His faith is very deep. It's Abraham-and-Sarah deep. His faith is Exodus deep. His faith is Israel deep. He has the faith of his parents and his grandparents and their parents, all the way back to the beginning. Here is a man who loves his country and is faithful to its institutions and to the God who called them to be God's people. "You alone of all the nations of the earth have I called." That's his faith. A faith that is deepened and confirmed with every slur he gets at the market. A faith that is deepened by every ugly insult he got on the playground as a child. A faith that is deepened more by the ugly things painted on the garage door. A man whose faith is deepened by every spitting upon his gabardine, every slurring of the word "Jew"; deeper and deeper it goes. His faith is full of "My Country 'Tis of Thee." The most favored nation; that's his faith.

I don't think that Jonah was aware of all the components of his faith, just as I am not of mine, you are not of yours. They're in there deep, elements that are added from culture and from nation and from poetry and from conversation and reading and from pains and war and loves and hates and prejudices all mixed in together. We don't really know.

There is a phenomenon in art (and here I don't know what I'm talking about), there is a phenomenon in art: if an artist puts the base color on the easel and then changes her mind and puts on another color and goes on with the painting, and the original color bleeds through, it's called pentimento, pentimento. And everybody here's faith is pentimento. Stuff bleeds through. Stuff we don't even like to think about, we don't even know about. It's a part of the way we worship God and think about God and read the Scripture. It bleeds through. So it was with Jonah, but it was a strong and popular faith.

He would get ovations, I'm sure, when he spoke because he knew how to draw a line in the sand, he knew who they were, and he knew who he was, and he knew the difference.

What's the point of taking a stand if you don't take a stand over against somebody else? He knew who the enemy was and he was not soft on Assyrians. No siree. During the Gulf War, we had a prayer meeting, an ecumenical prayer meeting in Atlanta. Quite a few came. We sang hymns, we prayed, we read Scripture, and a young fellow there, I suppose about 18, prayed an unusual prayer, different from all the others. "God, please care for the women and children in Iraq who will be killed during this war."

A man in his middle 50s, I suppose, came over to him afterwards. "Are you on Saddam's side?"

And he said, "No sir."

"Well, you're praying for the wrong people."

Never Jonah; he knew where the line was. My country, my nation. "You alone of all the nations." And there's a lot of pleasure in that. Part of the pleasure of having a faith is knowing how different it is from everybody else's and how superior it is to everybody else's. When you get in a room full of people whose faith is like your own, it is rather bland. But get some opposition, some over against, now that's when it really comes through.

Thomas Hardy once said that just as the color of the skin is not determined by the rays of the sun that the skin receives, but by the rays of the sun that the skin rejects, so we come better to be known by those things which we reject than those things which we accept. It's true, and there's pleasure in it.

Imagine a small boy standing before the ticket taker at the circus. He wants to go to the circus. The ticket taker says, "Son, aren't you going in?"

"I don't have any money." He stands outside consoling himself with the sounds of what's going on inside.

The ticket taker, in a moment of generosity, said, "Son, come tomorrow after school, we're having a matinee, I'll let you in free."

Whew! He couldn't pay attention in school the next day. School lasted a hundred years. "When are we ever going to get out of here?" Finally the bell rang and down to the circus grounds, standing right before the ticket taker, waiting, waiting, waiting, waiting, and finally the ticket taker said, "All right boys and girls, you can go in." And he looked around and there must have been forty or fifty. He turned and walked away.

The ticket taker said, "Son, aren't you going in? It's free."

And he said, "I don't think I want to."

Why? There's something about feeling that you're the only one that is dulled a bit when you discover that someone has said "everyone."

And so Jonah, as Herman Melville says at the beginning of *Moby Dick*, "With slouched hat and guilty eye goes aboard ship." Why is he running away? My impression is this would have been the ideal assignment for him because God has said, "Go and preach against the wickedness of that great city." My, wouldn't that be a grand assignment? Just to go and start the countdown for the destruction of Nineveh. Ten, nine, eight, seven, and then lean over the banister and say, "Gotcha! Burn, baby, burn." Just watch it all and be pleased and let it confirm the superiority of your own life and faith. Why does he run? Why does he run?

Because in that same heart is another faith. When pressed by the sailors on board, Jonah said, "I am a Hebrew and I reverence the Lord God of Heaven who made the sea and the land" (Jonah 1:9, au. trans.). What?

He also believes that God is the God of all creation, that God is the God of every living being, that God is the God of everything everywhere. As the Apostle Paul said, "Lord of the Totality," which incidentally would include the Assyrians. He knows that, he believes that. So God begins to work on him, not by reminding him of the exodus, not by reminding him of Abraham and Sarah, not by reminding him of the Ten Commandments. God begins to work on him how? Through creation. "You do believe that I am the Lord of sea and land."

So what does God do? God stirs up a storm; God creates a great fish. God appoints a gourd; God sends the worm. God sends the east wind, all acts of creation. "What's the matter, Jonah? You said you believed in the God of all creation." And he does. Deep down in there, that's his problem. He believes it. And he's not alone among his people in believing that.

The Rabbis used to tell a story of the exodus. At the time of the exodus God was very busy and so appointed a committee of angels to take care of the Red Sea. And so the angels, looking over the banister of heaven, when the Israelites arrived at the sea, used the power of God, parted the waters. The Israelites went through. Here came the Egyptians, horses and chariots. So the angels waited and when they got out in the middle of the sea, they released the water and the Egyptians went tumbling and drowning. The angels were clapping and singing and clapping and singing and God came by and said, "What's all the celebration?"

They said, "We got 'em, we got 'em, we got 'em."

And God looked over the banister of heaven and said, "You're no longer in my service."

"But, we got them."

And God said, "Don't you know? The Egyptians are also my children."

Who tells that story? Jewish Rabbis. Jonah knows. That's the pain of it; he knows the impartiality of God's love and grace. When he got to the city and preached and everybody repented, the Scripture says that God repented of the calamity that was going to be sent upon Nineveh and the city was saved. And Jonah said, "Didn't I tell you? This is the very reason I didn't want to come. I knew you would love them and forgive them and accept them because you're always so full of mercy and grace."

I tell you, take a moment, take a moment. There is sometimes nothing harder to take than the grace of God when it is shown to someone else.

Luke says, "God is kind to the ungrateful and to the wicked." That bothers me. How are the ungrateful and wicked ever going to learn about gratitude and generosity if God is kind to them? It looks like they're just being blessed in what they're doing. The difficulty with forgiveness, you see, is it looks a lot like condoning.

And the mother said to the daughter, "Martha, what are you doing?"

"I'm packing my suitcase."

"Packing your suitcase?"

"Yes, Mother, I'm packing my suitcase."

"Where are you going?"

"I'm going back to Jim."

"You're going back to Jim?"

"Yes, Mother, I'm going back to Jim."

"How could you go back to Jim?"

"Mother, he's my husband and I love him."

"But you know what he did to you."

"Yes, Mother, I know what he did."

"But you're still going back?"

"Yes, Mother, I'm going back. I forgive him, I love him, I'm going back to him."

"Well I never thought a daughter of mine would condone a thing like that."

"Mother, I didn't say I condoned it, I said I forgive him."

"Well, it looks the same to me."

About a block away, it looks the same and when Jesus said, "God sends the rain and the sun on the just and the unjust, the good and the bad alike," don't tell me that doesn't bother you. No line in the sand? The good and the bad alike? The sun and the rain on the evil and the good alike? That's no way to run the world. If I were running the world, the rain would come on the righteous right up to the fence, but the unrighteous, not a drop. And I'll guarantee you this, that old boy over there who never darkens the door of a sanctuary, after about nine years without rain, he might suggest to the wife and kids, "Why don't we go to church this Sunday?"

The sun would come shining in all its glory upon the good, but on the evil, gloom and darkness. That's the way to run the world. If I were running the world on Sunday morning when the wife and children go to church and he goes with the clubs out to play eighteen holes, about eleven o'clock when everybody was starting the Call to Worship, he'd hit the ball, it would go straight up and come right back down and fall between his legs. A few shots at that ball and right back down, and he'd begin to say, "Well, I might as well be with the family in church." Now that's the way to run the world.

But look at this, look at this. Absolute impartiality of God and Jonah knows it, he knows it in his heart and he's mad as a boiled owl about it because he said to God, "I knew you would forgive them. That's why I didn't want to come."

In his heart and in his faith, "You alone of all the nations have I chosen." In his heart is the faith, "I worship the Lord God, Creator of everybody, everywhere, everything, the God who daily runs along after me and blows across the sand and erases all the lines that I have drawn." Who can live with both? I do, maybe you, maybe you.

In the summer of 1992, Václav Havel gave an address at Lehigh University. In the course of that address, Mr. Havel said, "No member of a single race, no member of a single nation, of a single sex, of a single religion, may be endowed with any basic rights different from anyone else's." Do I agree with that? Yes, yes, I agree with that. The Lord God who made heaven and earth, and all . . . Totality. I agree with that. But there is something else in me that once in a while wants my faith to support me in the desire for, the appetite for, the feeling that I'm a little different from, maybe a little superior to, maybe a little better than . . .

When I was paralyzed in the hospital and totally dependent on the ministrations of strangers, I got down a time or two and I tried to think of things that would lift me up and give me a sense of worth and value. And so I tried to imagine into what kind of room could I walk and I would be superior to someone there. And do you know what I pictured? I pictured myself walking into a room of people caught, trapped in gnawing poverty, and I imagined myself walking into that pocket of poverty and I didn't feel any better.

So I changed the scene. I pictured myself walking into a room of illiterates. I have a good education, so I walked into a room of people who could not read or write and in my mind I thought, this will do it: Dr. Craddock. I didn't feel any better. I tried again.

I imagined I walked into a room of people in prison and I walked up and down the corridor and looked at them behind the bars, caged like animals. I felt totally free, able to leave at anytime and I thought, ah, this is it. But I felt no better, because I had to face the fact, no human being, by that I mean no human being; to put it another way, no human being is better than any other.

And my friends, if there is still in your heart the residue of such phrases as "better than," "greater than," "superior to," take a moment to ask Christ to pluck that from your heart, cast it into hell, let it burn to a crisp. And then the day will come when you will look back and laugh at yourself and say, "Who was I? Who was I to think that I could resist God?"

9

Who Am I to Hinder God?

Jonah 3:1–5

I hope you noticed that was Steve's arrangement of "Shall We Gather." Marvelous. And choraliers, A+. I'll remember you when I come to my grade book. That hymn sings of Revelation 22: "The new creation, the new heaven and the new earth and the river of the water of life that flows from the throne and down the middle of the street of the city. And on either side of the river is the tree of life and the leaves of the tree are for the healing of the nations" (au. trans.).

Revelation 22 echoes Genesis 2: "And there was a river that flowed through Eden to water the garden and it divided into four rivers, the Pishon, the Gihon, the Tigris and the Euphrates" (paraphr.). But between Genesis 2 and Revelation 22, between when "morning has broken" and "shall we gather at the river" is a long painful story; and there are rivers and there are rivers. For instance, if you go to Baghdad, which is on either side of the Tigris River, and go up the river for about 200 miles, on the eastern bank of the river you will find the excavated site of the ancient city of Nineveh, the grand and glorious and idolatrous and violent capital of Assyria, the apple of the eye of Sennacherib.

And God cared for Nineveh. God was concerned about Nineveh and so God looked around for a prophet to go and speak to Nineveh and found the son of Amittai, Jonah, an Israelite. And God said to Jonah, "Shall we gather at the river?" And Jonah said, "No way." And so from the Tigris he went down to the great sea and he went just north of Tel Aviv to the port of Joppa, paid his fare and as Herman Melville says, "with slouched hat and guilty eye he skulked on board."

He went to the hull of the ship, to the bottom of the ship, and went to sleep. God wasn't through. God hurled a tempest, a strong wind against the

55

ship and they were afraid, these sailors, and they threw things overboard. Finally, in their own scattered and nervous way, they said, "There must be someone on board guilty for all this to happen. The gods are angry." They cast lots; the lot fell upon Jonah. "Who are you? Where are you from? What are you doing? What's your country?" He said, "I'm a Hebrew and I fear the Lord God of heaven, the creator of the sea and of the land" (au. trans.).

They threw him overboard and God appointed a great fish to swallow him. After three days and three nights, God said, "Shall we gather at the river?" Jonah said, "As you wish" and he went. He preached there on the bank of the Tigris, 200 miles north of Baghdad. He preached, not expecting anybody to listen, but they did and there was a national repenting. The city was in sack cloth and ashes and praying to God and even the beasts of the field and the cattle, the cattle repented. And there was a great reformation and God repented and said, "I will not destroy the city."

Jonah was mad as a boiled owl. He did not plan it that way and he said to God, "Now do you see why I didn't want to come here in the first place? I knew you were a God of tremendous mercy, abounding love, steadfast grace, and willing to repent from punishment. I knew you would do this."

What's the matter with Jonah? Jonah has whistling through his soul now two theologies. Some of us don't have one; he had two. Most of us have more than one; that's our problem. He had two. He had the theology that we can surmise from the story and that was that he was a Hebrew. And he had the theology that said, "Of all the nations of the world, Israel alone have I chosen. We are Abraham's children." Here was a prophet who knew who was in and who was out, who was for God and against God, who was under grace and who was under judgment. There was a God of we and a God of they, and we know the difference. And Jonah could preach those sermons; sometimes I'm sure to standing ovations. Preach a sermon in favor of Israel and a sermon that includes a curse of Assyria; standing ovation. There is nothing more powerful if you love applause than to play upon the hatreds and the prejudices of people. Draw them out, say their hatreds for them and then receive the accolades. In fact, in some quarters it is called conviction. And it generates enthusiasm to be clear about who's wrong, who's under judgment, who is outside.

Thomas Hardy said once that just as the color of our skin is determined not by the rays of the sun that our bodies receive, but by the rays of the sun that the body rejects, so it is among us that we are most often known by those things we oppose than the things we embrace. Easy to preach that sermon.

But there is in Jonah another theology. "I am a Hebrew and I fear the Lord God of heaven who created the sea and the land." His is a God not only of the selection historically of Israel, but his is a God of creation, all creation. What's he going to do with that? Is he going to preach that? That God loves and cares for all creation. What he runs up against in this beautiful story is the God of creation. Notice the language. "And God prepared a strong tempest and God appointed a whale, a great fish." Later on it will say, "And God appointed a plant to grow up over Jonah and give him shelter." And then it will say, "And God appointed a worm to cut it down" (paraphr.). The King James has instead of "appointed," "ordained." "God ordained a worm." I like that.

And then it says that God appointed an east wind to blister him. And Jonah wanted to die and God said, "You're concerned about the wind? Did you know that I have in the city of Nineveh 120,000 babies that don't even know right hand from left and many cattle? Jonah, I am the God of creation." But he knew that; he knew that. But he didn't want to preach that. He wanted to preach the other. You preach inclusivity and people say, "Oh, all right." You preach the other and they say, "Sic 'em; good stuff." He knew it but he didn't want to preach it. It was such a painful clash within him that he wished he were dead. A theology of creation and a theology of historical selection and particularism, it was painful. Shall we gather at the river?

Lest you think this story is just a quaint story from ancient Israel, let me remind you how Luke in the New Testament loves the character Jonah. For in Jonah is captured so much that is going on in the early Christian movement. And so it is that Luke tells us a story about a man named Simon, Simon Bar-Jonah. Remember? He was selected by God and God said, "Simon Bar-Jonah, shall we gather at the river?" In other words, "Shall we go and preach to the nations?" And Simon Bar-Jonah, who was at the time in Joppa, had the vision. All these unclean, nonkosher things on a sheet and a voice that said, "Get up, Peter, kill and eat it." He said, "No, I don't eat that stuff." "Get up and eat it." "I don't eat that, it's unclean." "Get up and eat it." "I don't . . ." "If I say it's clean, it's clean."

Reluctantly, with the reluctance of the first Jonah, Simon Bar-Jonah left his Joppa and went to Caesarea and in the house of an Italian military man, as foreign as you can get, with the army of occupation in Israel, the Holy Spirit fell. Simon Bar-Jonah looked around and said, "Well, looks like God accepts these people." And then he said, "Can anybody here hinder these people being baptized?" And there was silence and they were baptized. Can anybody here hinder it? Luke loves that word, "hinder." You remember the Greek word for that, *koluo*. "Can anyone here *koluo*?" and nobody spoke up. And they baptized these Italian military people at Caesarea.

He was called on the carpet. He went back to Jerusalem and they said, "We understand you went in and ate with some Gentiles." And Simon Bar-Jonah said, "I did, but who am I to *koluo* God?" It's painful to think about. But can you identify with Jonah, with Simon Bar-Jonah? When there is in all of us the particularism, the cultural, historical, national, economic, educational shaping of our lives a certain way and then God taps us on the shoulder and says, "Shall we gather at the river?" And we look; where is the river?

And it means moving outside Tennessee or Alabama or Akron, Ohio or San Francisco, Opelika. But this is who I am. This is the way I live. These are the values I have. This is the way my family talked. This is the way we thought and this and that. And God said, "But I am the God of the sea and the great fish and the wind, the plants, the worms and the cattle and I have a lot of little children there."

It is so difficult to go into the ministry unless you want to get ordained and just go repeating the same. You can do that you know and you will be applauded. I'm sorry, but you will. It is so difficult.

Paul told about Simon Bar-Jonah coming to Antioch when they had the church dinner there and there were Jews there and Gentiles there but now they'd all become Christians so it was an integrated fine congregation at Antioch of Syria. They had the fellowship meal and Simon Peter was eating with all the others. This fellow was eating with all the others until some came in from Jerusalem from James. And he took up his plate and his glass of iced tea and they formed a separate table, a separate table. This is the same man who stood up on the day of Pentecost and said, "The promise is to you and to all your children and their children and to as many afar off as God will call" (paraphr.). He said it. But when it came right down to it, my grandparents and my parents said this is what I eat and this is with whom I eat and this is the way I eat and this is the way I talk and this is the way I pronounce words. It's painful.

The gentle snow reminded me this morning of being caught in a blizzard in Erie, Pennsylvania, once some years ago. No planes flying, no buses, no trains, nothing there. Checked all the motels, they were full. Finally, last effort, came to one of those little bitsy ones at the edge of town, had a blinking light and said innerspring mattress, phone in office, one of those little things.

I went in, said, "Do you have room?" "No, we're full up, about to close, but you can sleep here in the office if you want to." Well there were two of us; there was another fellow there. I learned that he was Navajo, he was a Navajo Indian, a big man, from Arizona. He had no place either; I had no place. And so the motel man just said, "Here you can sleep in the office. I'm closing up."

There was a chair and there was a couch. This large Navajo said, "I'll take the couch." And I said, "Well, I'm sort of attracted to that straight hard chair over there." So we settled in for the night. He removed his shirt and there were huge scars on both shoulders and down the arms. I said, "Are those ceremonial? Are those ritual?" He said, "Yeah, yeah." I said, "Why?" Because he had earlier in the conversation told me he was a Christian and how long he'd been a Christian and we talked of Christian things. Then he takes off his shirt and I said, "Oh, then you were into all of that before you were a Christian."

And he said, "No." He said, "Two years ago my father died. I grieved, I was paralyzed, I was immobilized, I was lost, I just stumbled around. I couldn't get any relief from my grief and finally one night I went to our old Medicine Man and he bled me of my grief." I said, "You . . ." He said, "I know. I should be able to say I did that before I became a Christian. The fact is I did it after I was a Christian."

It is so hard. You don't just come to Candler; you come to Candler from somewhere. You come every morning and it's still hard.

Can anyone hinder? Oh, Luke loved that word. He used it a lot. Do you remember once in chapter 9 when there was an exorcist who was not of the band of Jesus' followers? And the disciples came to Jesus and said, "We saw a man casting out demons but he was not in our group. And so we *koluoed* him." And Jesus said, "You don't *koluo* them. If they're not against us, they're for us. Don't do that."

In chapter 18, some mothers were bringing their babies, the other Gospels say children, Luke says babies, infants. The mothers were bringing their infants and they were listening to Jesus but apparently the infants, the babies, were a disturbance so the Twelve Apostles came in and said, "Get the kids out of here. We're trying to have the kingdom, so get these out of here." And Jesus said, "Permit the children to come and don't *koluo* the children, for of such is the kingdom." They said, "What? They can't even take care of themselves, they can't sing in the choir, they can't teach, they can't take up the offering, they can't participate in the liturgy. They even have to have other people take care of them. They're a burden; they're an expense. You mean to say that people like that belong in the kingdom?" And Jesus said, "Yes." No *koluo*.

Can anyone hinder? Luke loves that word. He used it once in chapter 8 of Acts in the story of a man who was an Ethiopian eunuch. Get it now? Ethiopian eunuch, riding along in the chariot and the evangelist, Philip, comes along and Philip gets in the chariot and begins to talk to him about Jesus and about Isaiah. Finally the eunuch stops the chariot beside some water and says, "Here is water. Can anybody *koluo*?" And I know something in Philip was saying, "Yeah, I can. I mean you're an Ethiopian. I mean let's face it, you're an Ethiopian and you're a eunuch. My land of living, Ethiopian, eunuch, can anybody *koluo*? Yeah, in fact everybody in my home church would *koluo* just like that."

"Can anybody *koluo* my being baptized?" And nobody raised a word. He was baptized.

Shall we gather at the river? It's so hard to do. And it's not solved by some of the little schemes we have. Some of us think we solve it but we don't solve it. I notice some of the piddling efforts of some of us to be inclusive and you know the way we do it, we become generic, not inclusive, but generic. Just start using a lot of words that don't mean anything and, therefore, nobody will be offended. We get into "personhood" and "humanity" and all like that as though there was ever any such person. There was never any such person. There is no human being at large. There is no humankind humanity anywhere. There's a difference between being inclusive and being generic. Generic is nothing. People live in particular places with names and loves and hates and pains and joys and expectations.

I remember when I was in seminary school and my family was way below the poverty line. There was a man in the church, the little church where I served, and he worked for Stokely Van Camp. He was a chemist and his job was to sample the cans. Every so many cans he had to open one to see what was supposed to be inside. So he had a lot of cans; he would pull them off the track, you know, and open one and look at it. But he would just collect a bunch of cans. It was before the cans had labels. He would bring them over to the parsonage. He'd bring a box of cans with no labels and give them to us. Well, we were extremely grateful but when I would say to Nettie, "What are we having for supper?" She'd say, "I don't know, I haven't opened the can yet." Just generic.

Now I know we're against labels, but the fact of the matter is there is no unlabeled human being. When God chose to say, "I am the God of all creation, of land and sea, and I love you," when God decided to do that, God didn't roll up all the thunder into one big ball and say, "I love you." God didn't dip the finger in the cloud and write across the sky, "I love you." God sent a Jew of Nazareth in Israel.

When I was over at ITC to preach a few years ago, I worked so hard on that sermon to be totally generic because I was so afraid that I would offend somebody and reveal the deep, deep problem I have had with seeing whole. I worked on it and I had all the bland vanilla language you can get. I mean nobody would be offended because in essence I wasn't saying anything to anybody.

And when it was over, a very attractive young woman came over to me and thanked me for the sermon. She said, "Do you have a piece of paper?" I said, "Well, yeah, why?" She said, "I want you to write this down." I said, "OK." Then I couldn't find a piece of paper so I said, "I'll remember it. What is it?" She said, "My name is Marlene. I'm from Birmingham, Alabama. I am here because I've been called to the ministry. I am a woman, I am black, and I'm going to make it." And I said, "Thank you." I didn't honor her. In all my piddling effort to be inclusive, all I had done was become generic and there wasn't a generic person in the house.

Shall we gather at the river? We cannot do it; we cannot do it as long as we are unwilling to move out past our own culture and background and proverbs that were heard around the supper table and listen to the God of sea and land, of fish and storm, and plant and worm, and cattle and 120,000 children in Nineveh.

See, the burden on us when we enter the ministry is to preach out past, bigger than, beyond than, greater than all of our own feelings. If we just get up and preach our own feelings and pull everything we say through the knothole of our own small backgrounds, the kingdom can never come. Just because I'm a wren doesn't mean I can't preach an eagle message. Of course I can. Is that a lack of integrity if I preach something bigger than I can even feel, if I preach a message that I haven't even grown to? That's not a lack of integrity. That's accepting the call. That's what it is because there's too much at stake to do otherwise.

And so God says, "Shall we gather at the river?" And it scares me to death, but who am I that I can *koluo* God?

10

God Is with Us

Matthew 1:18–25

This is the fourth and final Sunday of Advent, and so we have now arrived in Bethlehem. The baby is due anytime, and all we have now to do is wait, which is the hardest part.

It is hard to wait. In a hospital sometimes the most miserable room is the waiting room. You don't have any information; you stop every nurse. "No, sorry, that's not my patient. The doctor will be out later. Maybe tomorrow." That sort of thing. You're helpless; you can't do anything. The time creeps by. No one waits very well.

So I suggest this morning, in order to occupy ourselves until the birth, that we do what Matthew did. Matthew went outside and took a stroll through Jesus' family graveyard. He starts his Gospel with a genealogy. Some people say, "What a horrible way to start a book. It's just a list of names you can't pronounce." Dwight Eisenhower said that in his family they had to read the Bible through completely every so often but that he was given permission to skip the genealogies. Well, we're not going to skip the genealogy; we're going to join Matthew for a walk through the family graveyard of Jesus.

Some people think going to a cemetery is morbid, but it doesn't seem that way to me. One summer not long ago our family visited Arlington National Cemetery. Far from being morbid, it was very inspiring to be there. Once when I was in New Haven, Connecticut, and my host was showing me around town, we toured the town's historic cemetery, and suddenly I found myself standing in front of the grave of Nathan Hale, the man who said, "I regret I have but one life to give for my country." It was an awesome moment, an inspiring moment. Some of you have been to these places. You just cannot believe all the feelings that churn.

Sometimes, though, it can be embarrassing to visit a cemetery, because you come across the graves of folk you wish you were not kin to. I remember that my sister was once in pursuit of information about an ancestor by the name of Ruby Craddock. The other Craddocks had come to this country from Wales, but not Ruby, so my sister, who was heavily into genealogies, was pursuing Ruby.

Eventually she reported, "I found Ruby."

"Good," I said. "What did you find out about Ruby?"

She said, "You don't want to know." It seems that Ruby, instead of coming to America with the rest of the Craddocks, went to London instead and opened a brothel. I assured my sister that this was another branch of the family and not to worry about it.

Going to cemeteries can be a strange, mysterious thing. South of Atlanta— it still haunts me to think about it—there is a cemetery in a small town where the members of a very large family are buried together in this one plot, all, that is, except for one. By the inscription on the marker, this one family member was a son. He is buried fifty yards away, I would say, all by himself. I just hate all the thoughts that come to my mind.

Other graveyards are mysterious in other ways. Last week, Fred Dickey from California wanted to take me up to Hogback Mountain to see the Dickey family graveyard. The Dickey graveyard is an unusual one and very, very old. The Dickeys have become particularly famous through one of their members, James Dickey, who wrote *Deliverance* and many other works. Mrs. Dickey was a member of President Zachary Taylor's family. All of this seemed very important, and I told Fred that I'd like to see that graveyard.

So we went out early on a Saturday morning to Hogback Mountain and found the cemetery. It was about forty feet square with a concrete wall, now broken in places. At one end of the cemetery stood two stones marked "George Dickey" and "Hanna Dickey." Twenty-seven other markers were there, but with no names on them—just fieldstones stuck in the ground at different angles. There were twenty-nine graves in all; two with names, twenty-seven with no names. The twenty-seven were for slaves. The slave owners buried with their slaves? I wish I knew about how that came to be. Cemeteries can be strange places.

So off we go with Matthew to the cemetery that holds the remains of the family of Jesus, and there at the entrance is the patriarch of them all, Abraham. A simple marker stands for Abraham; he was a simple man. He was a man of faith, and on his tombstone it said in small print, "He was a pilgrim on the earth seeking a city with foundations whose builder and maker is God." He was buried with his son Isaac and his grandson Jacob.

There is no marker there for Sarah, his wife; no marker for Rebekah, his daughter-in-law; no marker for Rachel, his granddaughter-in-law. I regret that very much, but you know how they felt about women back in those days. They were just sort of "also" people. You know what the Bible says about the crowd that Jesus fed, that there were five thousand men present, not counting the women and children.

But there are women in this cemetery of Jesus' family. There is Tamar. You remember Tamar. She is not really a savory character, but she was clever; she chased Judah, but he did not run as fast as she did. Then there is Rahab. Rahab in Jesus' family was like Ruby in mine. Also, there is Ruth, the Moabite woman who loved her mother-in-law with a love that has been sung about at weddings for hundreds of years: "Entreat me not to leave you." There is Bathsheba. She is not even mentioned by name; she is simply called "Uriah's wife," and she was. Uriah was a soldier in the army, and while he was away she had an affair with the king.

I am surprised there are women's names in Jesus' family cemetery. Maybe this is prophetic, pointing toward the coming day of the one we remember, pointing toward the one who is the climax of the whole genealogy, Jesus of Nazareth. Maybe including these women is prophetic, promising that someday, someday, under the good gracious eye of Jesus Christ, those distinctions will not be made—certainly not in churches. Maybe someday.

What strikes me about these women is that none of them were Jews. Did you think about that? Tamar was an Arab. Bathsheba a Palestinian. Ruth— today we would say she was Jordanian. None of them were Jews. Maybe this is prophetic too, announcing that the one who comes at the end of that genealogy, Jesus of Nazareth, will bring it to pass that the blessing of God will be showered on all people, Jew and Gentile alike, making no distinction.

Maybe those markers out there in that cemetery are really important. Over there is Judah—there is a big marker for Judah—a very important man. He gave his name to the people, Judeans—the Jews. He gave his name to the land, the land of Judah. He gave his name to the religion, Judaism. He is very important.

And over there, of course, is David. The central marker in the graveyard, the tallest of all the markers, is David's. The first part of the genealogy leads up to David, and the rest of the genealogy flows away from David. David is the centerpiece of the graveyard, just as he is the centerpiece of Jewish history. David was a remarkable man—a shepherd, a musician, a poet, a soldier, a king—a man of remarkable ambivalence, a man of powerful contradictions. He had an immense capacity to weep over his own sin: "O Lord . . . my sin is always before me . . . create in me a clean heart, O God. Renew a right spirit within me. Restore the bones you have broken; do not take your Holy Spirit away" (Ps. 51, paraphr.). But then, David could be hard and cold. He is back at the palace, his soldiers are in the field; across the way he sees a woman bathing. He sends for her, has the affair.

"Who are you, woman?"

"I'm the wife of Uriah. He is out fighting in the army."

Uh-oh. So David has Uriah killed, and then he takes in the poor widow, bless his heart. He could be cold as the edge of steel. The way he replaced his predecessor, Saul, was cold and calculating too, and yet, and yet . . . every night when David sat down to supper, there was a crippled, sickly, club-footed man named Mephibosheth, the grandson of the man he had destroyed. My sin is always in front of me.

Following David comes that line of kings, some of them not even worth mentioning. Uzziah became king when he was sixteen, a teenager. He died a leper. Then there was Manasseh, who ruled longer than anybody else. He ruled for fifty-five years, but I daresay he paid for his own monument. He was no good, and he stayed in power all that time by compromise and total lack of conviction. To him, every kind of religion was the same. Sure, come on in. Read the tea leaves, gaze at the crystal balls, practice the superstition, do the witch dance, trust in God, bring it all in. He did not have a spine, this Manasseh. And there was Josiah, who should have been a preacher, not a king. He was so in love with Scripture. He wanted to make the Scripture the center of the life of the people. Then comes the last name—Joseph. The last one in the graveyard is Joseph.

Does this mean that Joseph is the father of Jesus? If Jesus is the son of David, then Joseph must have been his father. Was Joseph his father? Well, no . . . yes . . . no. This is the way it worked: Joseph was engaged to a woman named Mary. Remember, engagement back then was a legal thing. You did not get engaged at the drive-in some Friday night. Engagement was a serious business, and it could be broken only by going to the courts. In effect, it was the same as marriage and binding in nature. So Joseph was engaged, may have been engaged for years. Engagements lasted a long time. The two families came together, signed the papers, and when the young people became of age, they married.

Joseph is engaged to Mary, but he discovers that she is pregnant. Now what is he going to do? Joseph's fiancée is pregnant. Joseph is a good man, a righteous man, a man who wants to do the right thing. That's great, but how do you know the right thing? What is the right thing to do? Here is a carpenter in the community engaged to a woman named Mary, and it is evident she is pregnant. What is Joseph to do?

There are two options available to Joseph. First, he could get the opinion of people in town. Somerset Maugham said one time that the most fundamental

and strongest disposition of the human spirit in civilized society is to get the
approval of the people around you. Go to the coffee shop, "What do you
think I ought to do?" Get on the phone, attend the sewing circles, take your
problem to work, talk about it over coffee, talk about it everywhere, tell everybody. "Did you hear about Mary? What do you think I ought to do?" Spread
it everywhere, spread it everywhere. But Joseph will not go that way. He will
not disgrace Mary, will not expose her, will not humiliate her. Then what is
he going to do?

He has some friends just fresh from the synagogue who say, "Just do what
the Bible says. You can't go wrong if you do what the Bible says." What about
that for an answer? I have heard that all my life. "Just do what the Bible says."
Well, I will tell you what it says. From Deuteronomy 22: "She is to be taken
out and stoned to death in front of the people." That is what the Bible says.

I get sick and tired of people always thumping the Bible as though you can
just open it up and turn to a passage that clears everything up. You can quote
the Bible before killing a person to justify the killing. "An eye for an eye and a
tooth for a tooth," the Bible says. Do you know what the Bible says? "If a man
finds something displeasing in his wife, let him give her a divorce and send her
out of the house." It's in the Book. Do you know what the Bible says? "Let
the women keep their heads covered and their mouths shut." Do you want me
to find it for you? It's in there. I run into so many people who carry around a
forty-three-pound Bible and say, "Just do what the Book says."

Joseph is a good man, and he rises to a point that is absolutely remarkable
for his day and time. He loves his Bible and he knows his Bible and bless his
heart for it. But he reads his Bible through a certain kind of lens, the lens
of the character and nature of a God who is loving and kind. Therefore, he
says, "I will not harm her, abuse her, expose her, shame her, ridicule her, or
demean her value, her dignity, or her worth. I will protect her." Where does
it say that, Joseph? In your Bible? I'll tell you where it says that. It says that in
the very nature and character of God.

I am absolutely amazed that Joseph is the first person in the New Testament who learned how to read the Bible. Like Joseph, we are to read it
through the spectacles of the grace and the goodness and the love of God. If
in reading the Bible you find justification for abusing, humiliating, disgracing,
harming, or hurting, especially when it makes you feel better about yourself,
you are absolutely wrong. The Bible is to be read in the light of the character
of God. As my old friend down on the other side of the mountain in east Tennessee used to say over and over again, "Well, Craddock, I know one thing,
God is just as good a Christian as we are." That's not bad; that's not bad at all.

You know, I am feeling good about Christmas. The baby is not born yet;
Mary is not even in labor, but it is Christmas already because of Joseph.

Through an angel, God said to Joseph in a dream, "I want you to marry Mary. I want you to go ahead and marry her. I want you to take care of her. I have chosen you to raise her boy." So please do not forget Joseph. God said, "Joseph, I want you to raise the baby. You feed the baby. You care for the mother. You care for the baby."

Christmas for me has already started because I know that when Jesus is born, the man who will teach him, raise him, care for him, show him how to be a carpenter, take him to the synagogue, teach him his Bible, and teach him his lessons is a good man and he will do right. When you have somebody like that, it is already Christmas, and Christmas will last as long as God can find in every community one person who says, "I will do what is right."

What is right is to read the Scripture and to read the human condition in the light of the love and grace and kindness of God. As long as there is one in every community, it will be Christmas. The question, of course, is whether or not you will be that person.

11

If at the Altar You Remember

Matthew 5:21–26

About two months ago Steve Kraftchick called me and said he thought it would be safe for me to return. It's been eight years and most of those who knew me are gone, physically gone or have gotten so old they don't remember. So I am grateful to be back. I'm grateful to Barbara and to the Dean as well as to Steve.

It's especially a good time for me to be with you on the eve of your beginning forty days of preparation so that you may be able, I may be able, to approach the mystery of the passion of Christ. It is especially a good time for me because I get the *Emory Report* and know that the service today is set in the context of a yearlong observance of reconciliation by the university and by the visitors who come to make presentations. So I am pleased. Actually I would have been back sooner but someone is sitting in my chair and he has used it all up.

"If you are offering your gift at the altar, and there remember that a brother or sister has something against you, leave the gift, go be reconciled to the brother or sister and then come back and complete your act of worship" (au. trans.). Strange statement. We all know that Jesus spoke in parables. Sometimes we forget that he also spoke in hyperbole, exaggerated speech, what Stephen Webb calls "blessed excess." Overstating in order to underscore, to accent. We do it all the time, especially in worship. "O for a thousand tongues to sing." Well not really, but it's the way to say it.

"Were the whole realm of nature mine, that were a present far too small." That's the appropriate way to speak. Jesus talked that way a great deal. "If your eye causes you to stumble, pluck it out, throw it away." "Take the log out of your own eye and then you'll be better able to see the splinter in your neighbor's eye." That's the way he talked. "You strain at gnats and swallow

68

camels." He talked that way a lot, hyperbolic speech, overstatement, exaggeration, excessive.

The text that I chose has in it the portion I paraphrased and it bears all the marks of overstatement, hyperbole, exaggeration. You're at the altar worshiping, the sacred moment, then you remember someone has something against you and you leave. Really? It seems exaggeration but may I say to all of you who are in the business of interpreting Scripture, it's very important that you decide whether or not it is hyperbole, because it makes a difference. If you take it literally it seems to me you could change the church into a circus. We'd all be running around, "Do you have anything against me? Do you have anything against me? Have I offended you in any way?" You know that could really be terrible. We'd never have class, never have any worship service, just up and down and running around. Surely not.

You come to me about eight or ten times with that, "Do you have anything against me?" and I would say, "I'm beginning to. You're getting on my nerves really." Surely you don't take this literally. It's exaggerated, exaggerated speech. I have to be confident that Jesus believed, understood and knew and assumed that we knew, that when the body of Christ is healthy, it can receive, can swallow, can digest, can assimilate a thousand bruises and blunders, and not make a big deal out of it.

Calling people like us together and calling us church. Just think about it. It's impossible unless there is an atmosphere of not taking too seriously what otherwise might be regarded as a slight. It just happens. Nobody intended to hurt your feelings. The person just happens to be under socialized, socially awkward, didn't mean anything by it. Went down the hall, didn't speak to you, preoccupied. Did you know that some faculty and students come to school some days at war with themselves? And when you're at war with yourself, it's very likely you'll make casualties even of your friends.

Did you know that there are faculty and students who come to class, try to do the work, stepping out of domestic wreckage? But still so preoccupied they didn't notice you. Didn't hear you say, "Hello." Surely you can handle that.

We're socialized or not socialized in so many different ways. One student sits through a whole semester, never says a word, never asks a question. Another student's hand is in the air all the time. "I don't mean to be disrespectful but could it be that you're wrong, Professor?" There are some people that are just energized by confrontation. Others would never be confrontational. No, no, no.

A teacher in an elementary school raises her voice at two pupils, Mary and Billy. "Mary, if you don't sit down in your own seat, I'm sending you to the principal's office." And Mary nudges her friend and says, "Miss Crabtree's really going to miss me when I move to the next grade."

"Billy, did you write these words on the board?" And he slinks into his seat, sullen, silent, but never forgetting until it breaks out in incendiary form and he's a violent person.

We all come together and make up the church. Jesus surely knew that there would be abrasions and bruises and slights all the time, but we can handle a thousand a day without changing our nature as church and community of faith. Surely he knew that. So you don't take things like this literally, do you? And especially when you think about the little slights and social awkwardness that infect us in the light of the larger picture, the cosmic picture. There are national and racial and gender and ethnic conflicts all over the world. Now where does my little whimpering fit?

"She didn't speak to me in the hall." Listen, Jew, Gentile, slave, free, male, female, now there is an agenda worthy of a seminarian. If you want to go to work on reconciliation, take on that agenda. The world is out of joint and what's your problem? "Well, I thought the professor answered my question with a little condescension."

"That's the second time I've passed him in the hall and he has not spoken. Some of the students over in Turner Village got together and had a little cookout and I was not invited." And the world is in the shape it's in and you have a problem. Get over it. Christian faith should be made of sterner stuff.

But then I remembered something that Elias Kennedy said. You may not know that name, but Elias Kennedy said once, "When I was in an academic community, as I look back on it, everything distant laid a claim on my life. Everything within a half hour was as strange as the other side of the moon." There is no more sophisticated nor justifiable escape from our problems with each other than to enlarge the screen until we're made to feel silly for complaining about that slight or that bruise or that bump or that hurt or that condescension.

I remember reading years ago a statement by a woman who served as a receptionist/secretary in an office in Geneva, Switzerland, where there was headquartered an international organization for peace and reconciliation. She quit her job; it was a good job and a well-paying job, but she quit it. She'd been there six years but she said, "In the six years, all those marvelous people coming and going, trying to bring about the healing of the nations, never spoke to me. The people for whom I worked never called me by name." Does she have a legitimate hurt?

There is no more painful, there is no more painful dismissal of my hurts than trivializing them in the light of the cosmic situation. If I hurt, I hurt, where I hurt. So, I go back to the text. If you are offering your gift at the altar and there you remember that a brother or sister has something against you, you leave the gift. You go first and be reconciled to the brother or sister and then come back and finish your worship. In other words, Jesus wants you and me to image ourselves in the most serious, most significant, most seriously sacred place and moment in our lives at worship. The hour, the central hour of the week; every door in the place has on it "Do Not Disturb." Shhhh.

Worship here, people are at the altar here. Be quiet; be respectful. Don't you know what's going on? The altar is the oldest piece of furniture in the world. That's the first thing God made. "And God set the whole universe on an altar." And if the prayers and praise of the saints ever stops, down it goes. That's the end of it. The world cannot survive.

And people are there. That altar will be there when everything is gone. Read the book of Revelation. The closing scene of all that God intended is a sanctuary scene, the altar and the worshipers. Shhh. Do not disturb.

Now if you're offering your gift at the altar and there you remember, and you will, you will remember. That's the thing about the altar. It's a dangerous place, the altar. I want to warn the students that are students here now. Be careful about going to chapel. It's a very serious thing and it can affect you in ways that will touch every moment of your life after this. There's something about being at the altar. I would avoid it if I were you. I would be truant in worship. I would absent myself from every chapel service if I did not wish to be influenced by my own memories, if nothing else, because it will happen to you. It really will happen.

And if at the altar you remember, I don't know why at the altar. Yes, I do. I think it may be because when we are at the altar, we are not defensive and self-protecting. We're vulnerable; we're open. We're not impressing and being impressed. We're not convincing and being convinced. We're not comparing and being compared. We're just there before God and being that open and free, you remember.

It is my judgment, and this happens to correspond with absolute truth, it is my judgment that the greatest moral and ethical force in the world is worship. Nothing else comes close, for two reasons. At the altar, being open and not protecting oneself, there a moment of truth likely will happen. Oh you can stay away and say, "Who's preaching?" "I don't know; I think it's another student." "I don't know, I think they're having an old man come back." "You going to go?" "I don't know, are you going?" "I don't know, I think I need to rest. You know we've got a lifetime of this church business. Why do it now?"

Fill up Brooks Commons, play the cards, eat the sandwiches, but don't come in here because truth, a moment of truth, floats around; you're dreaming of palaces and patios, and come in here and discover that your roof leaks and the rent is due. Turn the volume up, make the noise factor the controlling thing in your life. Put on the plugs; listen to nothing else. And there's still the sound of the gnawing of the rat in the wall. And how shall I escape that? I'll not go to chapel today. I cannot stand the truth.

The other reason is memory. Memory is such an extraordinary thing. You think you have something pushed down in Augustine's cave, to the deepest level, and it will never emerge again. And then I'm at the altar, in posture at the altar, in the presence of God, and that which I thought was totally and completely and finally buried comes to the surface. Now what am I going to do with it? Memory is a strong moral force, the ground for moral and ethical duty.

Do you remember God speaking to Israel in Leviticus 19, a most neglected book, and a most powerful book? "You are to love the stranger, the outsider, as you love yourself" (au. trans.). Why? "Remember, you were strangers in Egypt." If anyone knows what it is like to be a stranger, it's you. The memory of your own experience compels you to love the stranger.

Remember it from the New Testament. Paul has gone to Jerusalem. He anticipates a big quarrel with those who are the pillars of the church, James and John and Cephas. They have a confrontation. They agree to disagree. Cephas will go to the Jews; Paul will go to the non-Jews. They all shake hands, right hand of Christian fellowship. Paul turns to walk away. He's still not clear in his mind. He still has to throw a few darts. "The pillars of the church or whatever they were, I don't really care." You know he does that sometimes. He said, "When I started to walk away, they turned around, James and John and Peter, and said to me, 'Remember the poor.'"

He couldn't get it out of his mind. He said, "I have, I have, I have never forgotten the poor." In fact, it was concern for the poor and an offering for the poor that took him to Jerusalem for the last time, that put him in position to be arrested, that sent him to Rome a prisoner, and brought about his death. Doing what? "Remember the poor."

Memory is a powerful stab of awakening to face our duty. If you're at the altar and you're offering your gift and then you remember, then leave it and go. And it's urgent; it's urgent, do it immediately. Don't wait; delay is deadly. It will fester. Trifles light as air will become proofs as strong as Holy Writ and you will find yourself in a daily ritual of going into the backyard and lifting the stone to make sure the snake is still there. That is now defining your life. Oh no, go first. That is something that takes precedence over prayer and that's my relationship to you.

A friend of ours, now deceased, I think she was past sixty when she told me this. She said that when she was a little girl, there were six children in the family. She said that the happiest time in their home was at supper. She called it supper. "We laughed and talked about school and what we'd done and this and that. Mom and Dad would talk and it was just such a wonderful time."

But she said, "I remember, I was about six or seven years old, just before supper, Mom and Dad got into some sort of quarrel. We'd never heard them quarrel. It reddened their faces, increased their voices. They were actually screaming and when we children came in, they fell silent. My mother turned her back, stirred in a few pots, put it on the table and said, 'Let's eat.' That's all that was said that night. That's all that was said the next night. That's all that was said the next night." She said, "It seemed weeks that we did not say anything at the table. By and by Mom and Dad started speaking. They became civil to each other. We talked a little bit, but our family was never the same. Never the same. They never dealt with it."

So if you're at the altar, deep in worship and it comes to the surface, take care of it, take care of it. You can come back later and worship.

12

It's What You Say that Counts

Matthew 12:33–37

Either make the tree good, and its fruit good; or make the tree bad, and its fruit bad; for the tree is known by its fruit. You brood of vipers! How can you speak good, when you are evil? For out of the abundance of the heart the mouth speaks. The good man out of his good treasure brings forth good, and the evil man out of his evil treasure brings forth evil. I tell you, on the day of judgment men will render account for every careless word they utter; for by your words you will be justified, and by your words you will be condemned. (RSV)

It is the common experience of Christian people that reading Scripture encourages, refreshes, nourishes, stirs, challenges, and judges. And when caught up in such meaningful moments, some wonder why they read the Bible so seldom. Some on those occasions even repeat the ancient resolution so often said and so often broken, "I will read my Bible every day." But such are not the only experiences of the readers of Scripture. Some passages put on the reader a burden, a burden that is not easily unloaded. It may be a burden on the mind or on the reason. For example, Mark's story of Jesus cursing a fig tree because it had no figs because it was not fig season. How can we understand that? Or, for instance, Jesus casting demons into a herd of swine and they rush headlong over a cliff, drowning in the sea. How are we to understand that? Or for instance, Jesus telling Simon Peter to go and catch a fish, open its mouth and there he would find two coins, one to pay tax for Jesus and one to pay tax for Peter. How are we to understand that?

Reading Scripture can be a puzzling, mentally demanding experience. Then again there are some passages that put a burden on one's moral capacity. "Whoever looks upon a woman with lust has already committed adultery with her in his heart. If anyone asks of you your coat, give your shirt as well.

74

Rejoice when people persecute you for the sake of Christ. If anyone slaps you on one cheek, turn the other cheek as well. Do good to those who violate you. Forgive those who offend you seventy times seven."

These will send you searching for a friendly pastor or a comfortable book that will relieve you with words like hyperbole and exaggeration. But there are also passages that put a burden on one's observation and experience of the way life really is. Such is the passage before us today. "By your words you will be justified and by your words you will be condemned" (Matt. 12:37). That sentence contradicts our common experience of the low esteem in which we hold words. The reader of this passage immediately looks to the footnotes to see if perhaps there has been a scribal error, to see if there is another rendering of the text. Did not Jesus say earlier in the very same paragraph that a tree is known by its fruit? Surely all of us know that when the Bible speaks of being known by your fruits, it is not talking about what you say but what you do. In fact, how many of us have quoted a passage like this to minimize speech and to elevate the importance of action and deed. "It is not what you say that counts, it is what you do." Right?

In this same book, the Gospel of Matthew, did not Jesus say earlier in the Sermon on the Mount, "By their fruits you will know them" (Matt. 7:20, au. trans.)? Surely we are to assume that the accent he is placing is upon the life, the act, the deed, aren't we? When we look more closely it is evident that this is really not the case. Oh, I'm not saying that it is unimportant how one lives or acts or does, of course not. What I am saying is this is not what the passage means. In the Sermon on the Mount, Jesus says you will know a tree by its fruit. If you examine the passage carefully, you notice he is talking about false preachers or false prophets. "These who come among you dressed as sheep are really within themselves wolves. When they begin to preach or prophesy, in other words, to speak, you will know how false they really are" (Matt. 7:15–20, paraphr.). The stress is not upon their deeds at all. In fact in their actions they are like sheep. It is when they speak that their wolfishness appears. "By their fruits you shall know them," means by their speech you shall know them. And so it is here. In the passage before us a tree is known by its fruit. "How can you, if you are evil, speak good. Out of the abundance of the heart, the mouth speaks. In the judgment you will give account of every careless word you speak. By your words you will be justified, by your words you will be condemned."

In fact in the paragraph just preceding is that strange and difficult discussion about a subject much debated and much defined, the unpardonable sin. With all the clouds of uncertainty hanging about that passage, one thing is quite clear. The sin referred to as "unpardonable" is a sin of speech. "Whoever speaks against the Holy Spirit will not be forgiven." Needless to say it is difficult for us to evaluate our words in the way this text does. Part of the difficulty lies in our culture. We simply do not take speech that seriously. We say it is deeds not words. Talk is cheap; anyone can talk. Words, words, words, sticks and stones may break my bones, but words will never harm me. What can words do? The general impression is they can't do anything. Trying to change the conditions of our world by speaking is like trying to break up a concrete floor by dropping a light bulb on it. But whatever our culture's estimate of words, the very fact of Jesus stressing the serious nature of human speech forces us to think about it anew, to reflect upon its significance in our relationships to each other.

The moment we begin to roll the thought around in the mind, it becomes clear that it is erroneous to be contrasting words over against deeds because words are deeds. A word is an event in the world of sound. Instinctively we know how significant words are. We know it by the very fact of the difficulty of speaking. There is nothing we do more demanding than speaking. I'm not referring to chatter; that's easy. I'm referring to significant speech; talking to one another about something very important. Every one of us has experienced how hard that is. The more significant the conversation the more difficult it is. How do you get it started? How do you bring up the subject? Have you talked to your daughter about this? Oh no, no, no. Have you talked to your son about this? Oh no, no, no. Have you and your wife, have you and your husband discussed this? Oh no. It just seems we can't get around to getting the subject started. Maybe sometime it will come up casually and we will be able to speak about it.

Have you spoken to your minister about this problem? Oh no, I could never do that. Why is it that some husbands find it so difficult to say to the wife, "I love you"? Why is it that some men will spend a great deal of money on candy and flowers for that appropriate occasion rather than saying the words? The husband knows with all her expressions of gratitude, she would prefer the words, but still he growls awkwardly, "Be quiet, smell your flowers and eat your candy." He knows she wants to hear it. Why is it so difficult to say?

I'm sure you've noticed that when you're deeply moved, the first thing to go is your voice. It is true, isn't it, that the fundamental human sacrament is speech. Sure there's cheap talk; there's easy talk, but that is not the point. We do not allow an account of rape to provide for us our definition of love. Neither shall we allow idle chatter to define for us the significance of speaking with each other.

What is it really to speak? It is to break the silence. The proper context of all words is silence. If the opposite for you is true, if silence is an interruption in the flow of words, then you are probably caught in a massive, vulgarization of the sacrament of speech because words come out of silence. To speak, therefore, is to hurl a word against the clear glass of silence and break it. That's an awesome thing to do for someone. You have broken the silence.

What is it to speak? To speak is to create a new situation. Walk down a hospital corridor and if you find a door ajar, put in your head just far enough for the patient to see you and say, "Hello." That word turns on the light, straightens the bedcover, opens the blinds, fluffs the pillow and changes the face of the patient; just the word.

A young couple nervous, frightened, tense, stands before a minister. The young man says, "I will." The young woman says, "I will." And the minister says, "By the authority invested in me." By those words a new institution, a home, is created.

A man sat a table with his friends. When supper was over he asked for the cup in which there remained some wine. He asked for the bread that was left over from the meal and he said, "This is my body, this is my blood." By those words a supper became a sacrament.

What is it to speak? To speak is to commit yourself; to commit yourself in the way that I'm told folks once did when they entered a business agreement. "I give you my word."

A small boy was finally eight years old, finally eight years old. He is now able to play Little League ball. He has a cap much too large for his head; if it weren't for his ears he would smother. He has a glove. He stands in front of the mirror popping his fist into the glove and he waits and he waits and he waits that eternity before ball practice begins. He worries his mother to death, "When are we going to practice?"

"I think you're to practice on Tuesday, Jimmy, Tuesday afternoon."

"I'd better call the coach. Coach, this is Jimmy, when are we going to practice?"

"We're going to practice on Tuesday afternoon at 5:00, Jimmy."

"Thank you, Coach."

The next morning, "I think I'd better check with the coach to be sure about the time of practice." He calls the coach.

"We will practice Tuesday at 5:00, Jimmy."

"Thank you, Coach."

That afternoon, "I'd better check with the coach about the time for practice." He calls again.

"Tuesday afternoon at 5:00, Jimmy."

He's worrying everyone into the ground. A little after noon on Tuesday, it begins to sprinkle. The mother is ironing. She says to Jimmy, "I sure hope it doesn't rain much. You've been so anxious to begin practicing ball." About 3:30 it really begins to rain. About 4:30 it's raining a downpour. She looks over at Jimmy. "Jimmy, I really am sorry it's raining so hard. Jimmy, Jimmy, Jimmy!"

He's already out the door, his cap on his head, his glove on the handle-bars of his bicycle; off in the rain he goes. The practice field is on the school ground. The coach, who lives across the street, looks out the window; it's raining too hard to practice. But as he watches the rain he sees a small boy standing where home plate once was. The small boy is up to his knees in water. The coach says to his wife, "Some stupid kid is over there on the ball field. I guess I'd better go over there and rescue him." He puts on his rubbers and raincoat, grabs his umbrella and swims over there. "Jimmy, what are you doing here? Can't you see it's too wet? We can't practice in this weather."

Jimmy looks up at his coach and says, "I told you I'd be here, Coach." Poor Jimmy, he hasn't learned what you and I know but we will, of course, instruct him. Don't ever say with certainty that you're going to do something. You say, "If it doesn't rain, if I have the time, if things work out, if I get through my tough schedule, then I will try to be there." He'll learn, won't he? We've all learned and so will he. But in the meantime may I suggest that in that small boy's response to his coach, "I told you I would be here," there is the basic raw material for changing every life, every home. In fact, there is the raw material for changing the world. It is there in that simple line, "I give you my word."

"By your words you will be justified and by your words you will be condemned."

13

Seek and You Shall Be Found

Matthew 14:22–33

It is not uncommon in the church for us to urge each other to witness to our faith and sometimes we do so as though it were easy to do. It is not. Our faith is so profoundly intimate and important that we draw our breath in pain to tell the story of our faith in God. And to find the appropriate word to speak even to a receptive mind is difficult. Especially if the opportunity that presents itself comes as a total surprise. Such was the occasion that I'm about to relate to you.

A conference of church leaders from across the country had come to an end after four days. Lot of sermons, lot of lectures, lot of seminars, lot of discussion, but it had come to an end, thankfully so. I don't know if it will disappoint you but sometimes even as ministers we OD on religion. We don't need another sermon or another lecture; we need a break. So they provided a break.

After the last session there was a large reception to which all were invited and all were there. I had missed lunch so I pushed my way quickly to one of the serving tables. And it was there that I met him. We exchanged names but I was not able to shake hands as I had a cup of punch in one hand and a little plate of goodies in the other. But he couldn't shake hands with me either as he was occupied with a large camera. I said, "Well, you're going to do some serious picture taking."

"Well, it better be serious. I'm here to cover this event for a local newspaper."

I said, "You're the religion editor?"

"No, no, no, she's sick and I was asked to fill in at the last minute. I've never been to an event like this before."

I said, "Well, what did you think of the message tonight?"

"Oh, I didn't hear it."

"I'm sorry you weren't there, it was exceptional."

"I was there. I just didn't hear it."

I tried to act shocked that anybody could be present and not hear it. I said, "Why?"

He said, "Guess I was preoccupied. I'll have to have some help reporting on that message."

And I said, "You're in luck; the one who gave it is still here at this reception. I'm sure she'd be glad to give you an interview."

"Maybe later but right now I want to talk to you."

I said, "About what? If it's about that speech, I think you ought to talk to the one . . ."

"It's not about the speech."

"Well, what's it about?"

"It's about me. I was told that you might give me a few minutes."

And I saw in his face not the curiosity of a reporter but the distress of a troubled spirit. We moved aside to a corner to get as much privacy as an occasion like that will provide you. And he said, "I don't know where to start. I'm discontent. I think in the church you would say I don't have peace of mind."

I said, "You're discontent with what, your work?"

"No, I love my work. I've always wanted to be in the newspaper business."

"So you love your work but you want more, is that it?"

"No, well, everybody wants more, but it's not more, it's different, I want different."

"Are you discontent at home?"

"No, no, I'm well-married. We have three great kids. Many weekends when I'm off we go to the zoo, go to the lake, go to the movies, get a babysitter, my wife and I go out to dinner. Everything's fine."

I said, "Then you're bored."

"No, no, I'm not bored. I wish I were bored. If I were bored then something inside me would be asleep or dead and that would be better than this."

And I said, "What do you mean, than this?"

He said, "I feel like I've been running the bases but didn't hit a home run." He said, "Did you ever notice kids in a small town, cruising Main Street back and forth, round and round, back and forth, round and round. They burn a tank of gas and go home. That's kind of the way it is."

I said, "Do you have any friends who feel this way?"

"Well, no, I don't know; we don't talk about it. They seem to be satisfied but I really don't think they are. They talk too loud, they laugh too soon, they compliment too quickly, they meet folk too easily, they join all the clubs too readily. I don't think so."

Does anybody here know what in the world he's talking about? Here's a person whose life seems to be carried not by purpose but by calendar. January becomes July, July becomes January. Parents have children, children become parents, parents become children, round and round, there it goes. While he was talking I remembered an image that Wallace Hamilton used in one of his sermons of a small boy with his books open in front of him, his chin in his hands, and he was saying, "I wish my arithmetic was done and I was married and was dead."

But for some reason while I listened to him, I remembered listening to a large pink seashell that was used as a doorstop in the house where I grew up. Sometimes my sister and brothers and I would pass it around and listen to the shell and ask our mother, "What's that noise in the shell?"

And she said, "Oh, that's the sound of the ocean and it will make that sound until someone takes it back to the ocean."

I don't know why I thought of that as I listened to him talk. I do know that there are some things I decided not to say to him. I didn't want to share some old useless threadbare philosophy about how to find happiness or peace of mind like the old stoics did. The way to have peace of mind is not to have what you desire, but to have no desire at all. Kill all desire. Desire nothing and then you will have peace of mind. Make your heart a desert and that will be your peace. I didn't want to say that.

I didn't want to go back to that old philosophy, I think originated with Plato, that the reason you're restless is that you're young, we come from eternity into this world, we come from another world into this world. "The soul that rises with us, our life's star, hath had elsewhere its setting and cometh from afar," said Wordsworth. The soul originates in eternity and then it comes into this body and while you're young, you still have memories of the way it was in eternity and it makes you restless. "Whence did I come, whither do I go?"

But as you get older you gradually forget. Make a few mortgage payments, buy a bad car, have a few sick kids, work a little extra hard to keep your marriage together, lose a job or two, go too heavily in debt, and by the time you're 48 or so you just forget where you came from or where you're going and then you're "at peace."

I didn't want to say that. So I decided to say this: "If you're wanting me to give a name to the way you feel I would say that you are searching for God. I know you're not surprised by that word because the whole human race is searching for God. It is the one common quest we all have. With some people it comes and goes, it rises and falls, it haunts the edges of their minds all the time. With some it's as quiet a quest as a monastery, but with others, like a clap of thunder, dramatic and loud and cataclysmic. But for all of us it's the same; sometimes clear, sometimes very vague and ill defined, but even so, it's there.

"But also there on every corner of town are people giving you advice on how to find peace of mind and happiness and fulfill your quest. Now please, let me warn you, don't become a professional seeker after God. Don't make a career out of looking for God. There are people who do that. There's always one more set of tapes to listen to from someone in Dallas. There's always another guru out in the Nevada desert you need to go hear. There's always another circle you want to sit in on and hold hands and get in touch with the way life was before you were born.

"Then there's hypnosis, then there's astrology; study the charts. Maybe the sun and moon will tell you who you are and where you're supposed to be going. And you need to check out the psychedelic lights and the psychedelic music and maybe the psychedelic drugs. It may help you get there. And then brush up on the angels; you know they're popular now. Brush up on that. You can make a career out of all this seeking, but don't do that.

"Let me warn you; too intense a search pushes away the very thing you search for. Like trying too hard to have a good time. You just work at it so hard you're tired and have no fun. Like trying to go to sleep: I must go to sleep, I work so hard at going to sleep, I can't go to sleep. Like trying to make a friend, just pressing so hard to have a good friend, you drive everybody away. Like wanting to have a deep and meaningful conversation and you approach everybody to say you want to have a deep and meaningful conversation and you drive everybody away and reduce them to silence. Don't do that.

"If you were asking me how to find peace of mind, I would say to you: Let God find you. After all you're not the only one searching. You're searching for God, that's true, but God is searching for you. That also is true.

"When our parents, Adam and Eve, left the garden of Eden, God whispered in their ear. And God said, 'I will come for you.' They didn't understand that as a promise; they thought it was a threat and so they ran. And they've been running ever since, hiding in the mist of tears, hiding under running laughter, hiding in shopping sprees, hiding in travel, hiding in the upward spiral of strength and power, hiding in bad relationships. Sometimes even hiding in churches. You can hide from God in a church. Hiding in groups that are searching for God. Let God find you.

"I think the story I'm telling you, Thomas, is really the Christmas Story. God has come to us, not in power of government or sword or military might, not down some winding staircase of pomp and circumstance like a debutante. Not as though rolling up a ball of thunder and rolling it across the sky, 'I'm coming for you.' Not having an angel dip a finger in a cloud and writing across the sky, 'I'm coming for you.' No, no, that would scare us to death. God has come to us in a baby, fragile, vulnerable little baby, beginning life with the same birth cry as the rest of us, quieted at his mother's breast, growing up with the comfort and yet the restraints of a home and family and community and government and nation. Learning what it is to work hard and get tired, learning what it is to love and be loved and then have people betray you. Learning what it is to have a wonderful dream for the world, a vision for the world, be consumed with the vision to make it better, to make it different.

"And to have that vision rejected, to have even close friends turn against you, to suffer for that vision and to die for it. That's how God has come searching for you, as a person like yourself. This is why the ancient word was clear, 'And you shall call this child Emmanuel which means, God is with us.'"

I know I had tears in my voice as I told the story. He had tears in his eyes as he listened to the story. And I said, "Thomas, T. S. Eliot was right: 'We shall not cease from exploration and the end of all our exploring will be to arrive where we started . . . and know the place for the first time.' Because the life you seek is not in knowing but in being known, not in seeking but in being sought, not in finding but in being found.

"Tom, the one you're looking for, the one you're looking for is here . . . right here."

14

Hoping or Postponing?

Matthew 16:13–17

The imitation of hope is postponement. We sometimes prefer to hope than to have, and so we talk of hoping while delaying and postponing. This is quite understandable. It's a whale of a lot easier to believe a Messiah *will* come than to believe one *has* come.

For all of its alleluia and hosanna, Palm Sunday marks the beginning of what writers on the life of Jesus once called the Jerusalem Winter. These were the barren days marked by the disaffection of friends, the collapse of hope, the cold and bitter taste of death. But it was not always so. Those same writers spoke also of the Galilean Spring of Jesus, that early period in his ministry in which he enjoyed immense popularity. And I must say the Gospels yield some evidence for the truth of this.

Jesus was a teacher, a healer, an exorcist. To his ministry of healing and teaching and casting out demons, great crowds of people came. He was in a house and they came in such large numbers that desperate friends lowered a mattress through the roof to bring a cripple to the attention of Jesus. Sometimes the crowd was so large he had to get into a boat and push away from the land in order to have room to speak. When the crowds in the villages so swelled that Jesus could not minister, he moved into the open country. The multitudes on the hillsides sometimes numbered above five thousand. Jesus needed help; he chose a few, a few more, and finally, twelve. According to the records of his Galilean ministry, Jesus was extremely popular and the text for today explains what lay at the base of that popularity.

> Now when Jesus came into the district of Caesarea Philippi, he asked his disciples, "Who do men say that the Son of man is?"
> And they said, "Some say John the Baptist; others say Elijah; and others Jeremiah or one of the prophets."

He said to them, "But who do you say that I am?"

Simon Peter replied, "You are the Christ, the Son of the living God."

And Jesus answered him, "Blessed are you, Simon Bar-Jona! For flesh and blood has not revealed this to you, but my Father who is in heaven." (RSV)

"What is the public opinion of me?" he asked. And the answer was "Some say you're John the Baptist come back from the dead. Others say you are Elijah; some say Jeremiah or one of the prophets." These terms from the public opinion were not simply complimentary comparisons. These terms were titles, titles for the one who would be the forerunner of the Messiah. Before the Messiah comes, there will be one like Elijah or Jeremiah or one of the prophets. When the crowds said Jesus was John or Elijah or Jeremiah or one of the prophets, what they meant was, "We believe that Jesus is the forerunner of the Messiah." In other words, their opinion of him was the same as our understanding of John the Baptist.

If Jesus was regarded by the Galileans as the one announcing the coming of a Messiah, then it is no wonder he was popular. He drew crowds for the same reason that John the Baptist did. "The Messiah is coming," said John. "The kingdom is at the door," said Jesus. That message would certainly bring a crowd. School was dismissed early, bread left in the oven, shops unattended, plows dropped in half-drawn furrows. Everyone came running, totally unaware of anything except the thrill of one message. "The Messiah is coming. He will be here soon. The Messiah is coming." And why not? Every beautiful story that they knew began, not with *once upon a time*, but with the words, "When the Messiah comes."

To every blind beggar seated on the street, hollow eyes gazing over an empty cup, "I'm sorry, friend, but when the Messiah comes . . ." To every cripple with twisted body folded beneath him, "I'm sorry, friend, but when the Messiah comes . . ." To every beggar, clutching his rags with one hand and with the other reaching up for alms, "I have no money, friend, but when the Messiah comes . . ." To every prisoner, straining after that one little ray of light through the narrow window, "I'm sorry, friend, but when the Messiah comes . . ." To every couple, married now over fourteen years and still rocking an empty cradle, "I'm sorry but when the Messiah comes . . ." To every father seeking to calm a sobbing daughter assaulted by a Roman soldier, "Now, now, my child, when the Messiah comes . . ."

When I imagine these crowds drawn by messengers regarded as forerunners of the Messiah, it seems natural to envision even larger crowds when the Christians came announcing, "The Messiah is here. The Messiah has come. The Messiah has come." You would think so. After all, if the promise brought thousands, would not fulfillment bring tens of thousands? But they did not come in larger numbers and they do not come in larger numbers. The crowds, in fact, were smaller. Why?

If anticipation is a way of life, you do not want fulfillment. Looking forward to something can be the way you spend your whole life and you really are disappointed if it comes to pass. Why is it that Christmas Day is the saddest day of Christmas? Because Christmas is looking forward to Christmas. In much of life the pleasure is more in the chase than in the catch. The magnificence of life's promise is often lost in the poverty of its achievement. And as long as life remains an image in the mind, then life can be shaped to the contours of desire. While I am looking for a Messiah, I can make him what I want him to be. If I'm hungry, I can make him one who feeds. If I am tired, he is one who gives rest. If I am at war, he gives peace. If I am poor, he gives prosperity. If I am alone, he brings fellowship because I have created him out of the emptiness of my life. When I think about the Messiah coming, I know what he's going to be and I know what he's going to do for me. And I really do not want that dream exploded by anyone, not even a Messiah. I prefer the dream.

My wife and I have a cabin at a lake near our home. When I leave the office in the afternoon, we can throw a few things in the car and in less than an hour, be at our cabin. It's on a small lake, clear, deep and blue. It's peaceful there. Willows line the shore, very nice neighbors, very quiet, good fishing, a very relaxing place. We have never seen a mosquito, not a bug or a fly. We have never had any vandalism. The plumbing always works perfectly. Do you know where this cabin is? It's in our minds. And you're crazy if you think we're going to trade it in on a place like yours.

Beyond this, looking forward can be a way of handling by postponement all the problems of life. Every time I see injustice, inequity and misery in the world, I can say to myself, "But when the Messiah comes, all this will be changed. When he comes we'll hear 'The Battle Hymn of the Republic.' When the Messiah comes, we'll hear the hammers of justice, the bell of freedom, the song of love. Upon his arrival, there will be the redress of grievances, the taking up of the cause of the oppressed, but in the meantime, we must continue to look forward to his coming."

It is easier, really, to believe that a Messiah *will* come than to believe that one has *already* come. You see there is always enough misery in the world to make the announcement that a Messiah *will* come, believable. There is always enough misery in the world to make the announcement that a Messiah *has* come, unbelievable. How, then, are we to account for Simon Peter's confession? If the public opinion of Jesus was, "You are the forerunner of the Messiah?" how are we to account for Peter's answer to the question, "And who do you say that I am?" "You are the Messiah."

Has Simon Peter seen something that others have not seen? Has he detected in the Galilean something of the strength of Samson? Has he seen something of the shrewdness of Gideon, the leadership of Moses, the kingly qualities of Saul or David, the heroics of Jephthah? Has Simon Peter gotten something that the rest had missed? If he did, he certainly had a keen eye because it was not obvious. This Jesus went about his ministry without anyone ever hearing his voice aloud in the street. He incited no riots; he shouted no propaganda. This is the Messiah? A bruised reed, he would not break; a smoking wick, he would not quench. He had such a tender care for the weak, for the violated, for the crushed, and even for those as obnoxious as a smoking wick. This is the Messiah?

Has Simon Peter detected that this Jesus has begun to make a move, a move that could be called messianic? If he has seen it, he certainly saw more than others saw. In fact, most of Jesus' followers grew a bit restless with his wasting so much time on the cripples. Stop to pick up every cripple along the way and this army will never march. And the children; we stop to have a session along the road and in come some women with small children. The children fret and begin to whimper and cry. "Get these children out of here. We're trying to get the kingdom started."

And Jesus said, "Leave them alone. Bring the little children to me for of such is the kingdom of heaven." This is the Messiah?

One day Jesus attracted a large crowd and a poor widow suffering from a hemorrhage came pushing through the group to touch the hem of his garment. She claimed that she was healed. "Who touched me?" said Jesus.

"Who touched you? What do you mean who touched you? Everybody here is pushing and shoving. We have our biggest crowd."

A blind beggar heard him coming and cried out, "Jesus, thou Son of David, have mercy on me."

"Get away from here; we're busy."

"Call the man here."

And they bring the beggar to Jesus. More delay. This is the Messiah? And now contradiction of all contradictions, Jesus is saying something about going to a cross, going to be killed.

Has Simon Peter picked up something that everybody else has missed? If he did, it certainly was not obvious. In fact, it was incomprehensible. And yet Simon Peter said, "You are the Messiah." How could he say it? The answer was and is simple. Flesh and blood did not reveal this to Simon. He did not get this by observation; he did not come to this understanding by listening and watching. On the contrary, listening and watching could lead to one conclusion. Jesus is no Messiah. It is absolutely impossible to say Jesus is the Messiah except by the revelation of God. As Paul expressed it, "No one can say Jesus is Lord except by the Holy Spirit."

The central miracle of the Christian faith is just this; that anyone would say, "The Messiah has come and it is Jesus." Why? Because this confession calls for a grasp of the fundamental secret of the kingdom, a reversal of one's whole perspective on life. A view that once dreamed that wherever the Messiah is, there is no misery, has been forged into the present conviction, wherever there is misery, there is the Messiah. That reversal of judgment can come about only as Jesus expressed it. "Flesh and blood has not revealed this to you but my Father who is in heaven."

The Messiah has come and it is Jesus of Nazareth, and the first great task of the Messiah is to get us to quit looking for one.

15

It Is Necessary

Matthew 16:21

From that time Jesus began to show his disciples that he must go to Jerusalem and suffer many things from the elders and chief priests and scribes, and be killed, and on the third day be raised. (RSV)

With these words Matthew introduces the subject, which is at the center of Christian reflection, the death of Jesus. For some, such as Paul, it was the subject not simply for meditation during Holy Week, but it was the consuming subject of his life. Christ crucified. To the Greeks, foolishness. To the Jews, a stumbling block. This Paul understood to be the offense that lies at the heart of the Gospel. In fact, in the western world and in western Christianity, the central symbol is the cross. For the Gospel writers this was the area of greatest demand upon their faith and upon their theology, and upon their understanding of Scripture. They had to face the death of Jesus, make some sense of it, and set it in the context of God's searching grace. After all, the early church had to embrace the execution of its leader and shape its understanding into a proclamation.

In the four Gospels, more than 35 percent of the narrative is devoted to the death and suffering of Jesus. All of the Gospel writers introduce it into their stories quite early. Mark has hardly begun the story of Jesus when he says as early as chapter 2, "The days will come when the bridegroom will be taken away."

Here in Matthew, eleven chapters before the event itself, the long shadow of the cross falls across the page. Near Mount Hermon in the north, Jesus turned his disciples toward the south and showed them Golgotha. Matthew is certainly not seeking to create emotional effect, not squeezing pathos from the reader. A novelist might introduce into the story of the hero or the heroine some dreaded childhood disease as a fatal flaw, a shadow that appears and reappears to haunt every page of a brief but beautiful life, but Matthew is no novelist. And more is at stake than sustaining the interest of an easily bored reader. The way the subject of the death of Jesus is introduced here by Matthew is most attractive and yet most disturbing. He says that Jesus must go to Jerusalem and suffer and be killed. There is here no whining, no whimpering, no sighing and beating the breast. There is here the clear-eyed embrace of that horrible future. Sentimental biographers wrote of him as brave, bold, heroic. Psychiatric studies of Jesus upset us with phrases like "death wish" and "martyr complex." But even more disturbing is Matthew's way of putting it. "Jesus must go. He must go to Jerusalem and suffer and be killed." How are we to handle that word "must"? He "must" go. What is the source of that "must," that sense of necessity? Is it excerpted from the eternal will and purpose of God, unavoidable and inevitable? Harsh as that may sound, there is a way of reflecting on the death of Christ that properly describes it in precisely those terms.

After the resurrection, the disciples of Jesus were quickened and enlightened to see the meaning of the events surrounding and including Jesus' death. And they saw them as the gracious hand of God. They reread the Old Testament and rethought the tragedy until light dawned and the cross was no more a tragedy.

In biblical thought, strange as this may seem to you or to me, once an event is over, the result of that event is viewed as having been the purpose of it from the beginning. Even after a tragedy, biblical writers are able to say that from the beginning it was to be so. Recall a few painful passages. Jesus chose as one of his friends and helpers a man named Judas Iscariot. He shared with Jesus the joys and pains known only to the inner circle. He was trusted as treasurer of the group. In the critical and intense days in Jerusalem Judas betrayed Jesus and delivered him to the enemy for thirty silver coins. When it was all over, the tellers of the story said briefly, "He was a devil from the beginning." The end was seen as the beginning.

Isaiah of Jerusalem was called to prophesy, the net result of which were deaf ears, hard hearts, turned backs. Later Isaiah reflected on that result and understood it as the purpose of his calling. Paul was converted and called to be a missionary in his mature years. He wrote of it later as a necessity laid upon him, having been set apart from his mother's womb. Result was interpreted as purpose. Strange you say? Yes, to us. The result of Jesus' ministry was crucifixion. And so they were able to write, "The purpose was crucifixion." It could have been no other way, they said. This is how they understood it. This was for us and our salvation. He was delivered up according to the plan of God. With Joseph in Egypt in that beautiful moment of reconciliation with his brothers who had sold him into slavery years before, one could say here,

"You intended it for evil, but God intended it for good." He is able to make even the wrath of man to praise him.

But is it really this unusual perspective on events that bothers us about the "must" of Jesus going to Jerusalem? Is the statement that he must go to Jerusalem and suffer and be killed really a theological problem? Sure we join battle on the issue because it poses a threat to that most prized possession, our freedom to choose our paths and our destinies. But does not our real problem lie in our having no place in our lives for the word "must"? You must do this; I must do that. We hardly know how to pronounce it. It's too heavy, it's too burdensome, it's too confining.

Many of us and our children have been reared on the principles of self-expression, self-assertion, self-fulfillment. Some of us as young parents were so afraid we would damage the fragile psyches of our children that we dared not intrude into their lives a crippling "must," even if they were setting fire to the living room or sawing the family dog in half. There simply is no room for "must," especially in religion, certainly not in religion. All right, so we admit sometimes that we must go to work or we must go to school, but who is going to say that I must go to worship? Surely no one. In religion the guiding principle is wanting to do it, enjoying it. Have you not said or heard it said, "If you don't enjoy it, you won't get any good out of it. If you don't really want to, it has no value. All religion is to flow from a free and willing heart, otherwise it is just sheer hypocrisy, right?"

And so, when we meet those who speak of their religion and faith with "must" or "have to," we say they need therapy. Do they? Maybe. But it also may be that this common resistance to must and have to is really a massive copout, a rejection of responsibility on our part. When this country was faced with the ugly truth about the treatment of blacks, many church people said, "Well, you can't compel morals, you can't legislate morals. When all of us feel right in our hearts, then we'll not have this problem." How many hundreds of years can one say that? How long will this subjective captivity of the church last? Just how does one get to feeling right in order to act as a Christian? Is it not true that feeling right most often comes after and not before doing right?

Suppose getting out of bed, facing freeway traffic, cleaning carpet, preparing for exams, shoveling snow, or grading papers, waited upon our having hearts aflutter and leaping up with love of the task. The world would grind to a halt. Our organist is not playing today because his heart was not in the prelude, and he certainly did not want to be a hypocrite. The pulpit is empty today because the minister's heart is down and we all know one cannot preach up when one is down. Ridiculous. And yet the church sits in our world before a green light, with traffic backed up to Alaska, while she tinkers with her soul to bring it to a fine tune.

Maybe our resistance to must and have to really accounts for the poor record that some of us individually and some of our churches have in terms of effectiveness in making a difference in the life of the world. For so many of us everything has to remain optional. No assignments, please. We don't want to box ourselves in with obligations or burdens. But look for a moment at the major contributors of our lives. For instance, consider Madame Curie, pioneer in the field of science, who isolated radium and with that breakthrough, opened many new avenues in the field of medicine. You remember how it was with her, with frostbitten toes out there in the shed, with inadequate food, no financial support, working night and day, through tons of rock, to isolate this one element. Step out there in the shed and ask her about it. "Are you having a good time, Madame Curie? Isn't science wonderful?"

Stop the Apostle Paul, if you can, for a brief interview. Converted as an adult, sick much of his life, imprisoned often, stoned, beaten, rejected, shipwrecked, exiled, chased in the country and trapped in the city, and yet one who was able to say in his later years, "I have labored more abundantly than all of them." Stop him and ask him. "Isn't missionary work really just a piece of cake? I wager you're having a ball, and all that travel; I love to visit exotic places, don't you?" And hear him say, "If I preach the Gospel I have nothing to boast about for necessity is laid upon me."

Or Jesus. "Jesus, some of us have been thinking about having a picnic in the Garden of Gethsemane. We understand it's nice there. Do you recommend it?"

And he says, "I have not come to do as I please; I have come to do the will of him who sent me."

They did what they had to do and that is the key to achievement. You never know what you can do until you have to. Ask the man who lies in a hospital bed, his body wrapped like a mummy, cooked and rotting away with severe burns, "How do you stand the pain?" "You never know what you can do until you have to."

Ask the widow on pitifully meager pension, "How are you able to feed, clothe, and school those three children?" "You never know what you can do until you have to."

And until we have to, as long as everything is optional, as long as we spend our energies protecting all our alternatives, keeping them alive and well, we will achieve very little. Do you recall meeting now and then a really significant person? Someone who impressed you as really making a difference? Then I'm sure you noticed one thing about her. She possessed a sense of having something she had to do. To others she may look burdened, perhaps obsessed. But to herself, her joy is in knowing her work is more important than how she happens to feel about it on any given day. The really burdened person is the one who gets up in the morning, goes to bed in the evening, struggles with great issues such as what should we eat, what should we drink, what should we wear? Gets up in the morning, goes to bed in the evening, grows old, and dies, without a burden.

Here's the way the story of our redemption begins: "From that time Jesus began to show his disciples that he must go to Jerusalem and suffer . . . and be killed."

16

When He Shall Come

Matthew 25:31–46

I hope you're not one of those people who gets discouraged if you read or hear a passage of Scripture and it is not immediately clear or understandable. If that is true then you will be disheartened, not only by this, but by many other passages. It is not simply a problem of the Bible being in another language, in another culture and long ago. That distance is there and has to be negotiated. But part of the problem is that we have believed the Protestant fiction that anyone can read the Bible and immediately understand it. That simply is not true.

Jesus was a teacher and the church arose out of the synagogue which was as much a school as a place of worship. Wherever the church has gone, the first task was to begin a school. It is not a mere accident of history that the church launched education in America, with teaching the Bible at the heart of the curriculum. Then, too, difficult passages remind us we are impatient seekers after truth. We want things simple and immediately clear. We like summary sentences, one brief statement on the problem with the government, a one-liner capturing the very essence of religion, a catchy motto on the meaning of life. If you can't put it on a bumper sticker then I don't want to hear it. I don't have time for vague discussions. Religion is now being plagued by this huge appetite for super simplification.

But don't you think much of the distance between a modern reader and the Bible is due to the drying up of the life of the imagination? In a culture that pursues facts and information, the rich imagery of the Bible sounds unbelievably alien. For Bible writers the imagination is the home of faith. For a modern mind the imagination is the home of the fanciful, the untrue, the naively and childishly false. As long as this difference prevails, just believing the Bible, much less appreciating it, will be a critical issue for many people.

The image before us in this text is central to the Bible's understanding of life in history. The scene is the final one. The Bible conveys the unwavering conviction that history and human life have direction and purpose. Life and history are not according to chance or caprice or accident. Neither is life a cycle of repetition or an endless return of the same old thing. Life does not turn upon a great wheel. While one can find in the Old Testament a residue of nature religion which structured its faith and ritual upon the routine of returning seasons, the principal story shatters that cycle. History has an Alpha and an Omega, a beginning and an end. There was a genesis of all life; there will be an end to all life.

In the scene before us, it is God who finishes history. The creator of all things is the completer of all things. God did not begin the world and then abandon it, leaving us all victims of some cosmic accident or meaningless coincidence or cruel surprise. The central drama in the final scene is judgment. Here judgment does not mean a final put-down, a scathing criticism or vindictive anger without principle or norm. Judgment here means clarification, a bringing to light what really is the truth, revealing what actually has transpired in human behavior and in all our relationships. The very thought of judgment in this scene is immediately awesome. Imagine the truth being known. The possibility of such a moment of truth seems incredible. Each of us is such a tangle of ambiguities, mixed motives, subterranean drives, confused goals and contradictions. Enlarge the scene to include family, community, and national interests and the complexities are overwhelming. The apparent and the real are indistinguishable. Disguises are so carefully constructed the genuine look suspicious in comparison.

I recall reading that Charlie Chaplin once came in fourth in a Charlie Chaplin look-alike contest. In such a world, who is innocent and who is guilty? Who is right and who is wrong? Certainly no one is innocent and sainthood is attained by a slim 51 percent. Very soon all gives way to fear. Who wishes to be fully known? By the dim lamps of appearance and deception, we compare ourselves with one another and come away with passing marks. After all, when we grade ourselves on the curve, everyone gets through the course. But it's a weary business and we tire of it. There's no future in dreaming of palaces and patios when the real truth is the roof leaks and the rent is due.

The passage before us then as a scene of final judgment is not altogether a frightening one. It is in a way a welcome one. Let there be adjustment in the inequities that all have experienced. Let there be redress of grievances even when the fault is found to be with us. Let the clouds be removed from haunting uncertainties. Let justice be established as the governing principle of God's world. It is no wonder that early Christians prayed the prayer that seems so strange to some of us, the prayer that said simply, "Come, Lord Jesus."

The Gospel of Matthew places this grand image at the close of the public ministry of Jesus. It is the last message of Jesus before his death. This very location persuades me Matthew wants to underscore it, as though he were saying, "If you forget the other things he did and said, please remember his final message." And what is his final message? This is how it shall be when life ceases. This is how it will be when history ends and every person is openly and clearly seen under that light which makes no shadow. When the Son of Man comes in the clouds of glory attended by myriads of angels, every person who ever lived will stand before Him and He shall be the judge. He shall be the judge in that final court beyond which there is no appeal. Then will be the ultimate, the unambiguous, the complete moment of truth. And what is the truth? The truth, which will come to light, according to this text, is that there is an eternity of difference in people. And according to what standard is that difference measured and now made apparent? In response to what question is the distinction made?

That final question, the one essential question by which all are measured is really a surprising one. You may not think of it as a surprise, but I do. I am surprised by it because listening to people who are fairly deep into religion nowadays, one gets the clear impression that some other question would be the main question. Churches and Christian groups quizzing ministers and each other very often do not ask the question that is here considered the ultimate one. The religious air is filled with questions about the end of the world, visitors from other planets, heaven, hell and unusual gifts of the Spirit.

When I listen to people talk, sincere and dedicated members of various churches, it is very seldom that I hear a discussion that centers upon this question, which is, in the mind of God, the ultimate question. I have known ministers who have been dismissed from their parishes because they failed the question. But it was not this question. I do not wish to make light of the concerns people have. I do wish, however, to underscore this one thing, which lies in the arena of common sense. Let me put it this way. If we know we are going to face a final exam of one question and we are told by the examiner what that question is to be, is it not reasonable to suppose that one question would gather to itself the interest and the energies and the concerns of all of us?

Now here is the question. How did you respond to human need? That's it. That is the question.

"I was alone. I had no one in the world. My husband had died. My children lived in another state but I stayed in that big empty house. Did you or did you not come?"

"I was in prison, cut off from society for my misdeeds. A criminal, yes, but still a human being. Did you or did you not visit?"

"I was hungry, peering into a world of banquets and diets. I saw more food flushed down disposals than my entire family had eaten. Did you offer me anything to eat?"

"I was without clothing, looking into the shop windows, gazing at the wardrobes of the world. I waited for styles to change hoping for an old coat or dress. Did you offer me anything to wear?"

"I was a stranger, new at the job, new in the city, new on the street, new in the neighborhood, new in the apartment building. I did not know a soul. Did you introduce yourself to me?"

Moved by this final scene and feeling the burden of that one question, Christian leaders centuries ago made a list of sins. At the top of the list they placed what they called the Seven Deadly Sins, sins so scaly and serpentine as to destroy a person completely. In the list of seven, they included *akedia*, a word which means, "I don't care."

When everything is over and the streets have been rolled up, when all the switches have been thrown, when everything we have been doing has been done for the last time, the Creator and Judge will call the world to account with one question. "How did you respond to human need?"

17

He Could Have but He Didn't

Matthew 26:47–56

This is our text: Matthew 26:47–56.

> While (Jesus) was still speaking, Judas, one of the twelve, arrived; with him was a large crowd with swords and clubs, from the chief priests and the elders of the people. Now the betrayer had given them a sign, saying, "The one I will kiss is the man; arrest him." At once he came up to Jesus and said, "Greetings, Rabbi!" and kissed him. Jesus said to him, "Friend, do what you are here to do." Then they came and laid hands on Jesus and arrested him. Suddenly, one of those with Jesus put his hand on his sword, drew it, and struck the slave of the high priest, cutting off his ear. Jesus said to him, "Put your sword back into its place; for all who take the sword will perish by the sword. Do you think that I cannot appeal to my Father, and he will at once send me more than twelve legions of angels? But how then would the scriptures be fulfilled, which say it must happen in this way?" At that hour Jesus said to the crowds, "Have you come out with swords and clubs to arrest me as though I were a bandit? Day after day I sat in the temple teaching, and you did not arrest me. But all this has taken place, so that the scriptures of the prophets may be fulfilled." Then all his disciples deserted him and fled.

The Word of God.

Well it's almost over, as you know. He's in Gethsemane and it's becoming increasingly obvious that he's not going to fight. There was a skirmish there when he was arrested but he was not involved in it and he did not approve of it. In fact, he disapproved of it and, according to Luke, healed the one who was wounded and reprimanded his friend. "Put your sword away. That's not how we do it."

He's not going to fight apparently. He could have, oh, he could have. Matthew has absolutely no doubt he could have. In fact he said, "Don't you know I could ask God right now for twelve legions of angels and they would be here to fight for me?" He could have, says Matthew, but he doesn't. Not much time to decide to do that either.

When he's on the cross, there was a good time for him to do it. With all the taunting, just reading the taunting makes me want him to do something. "If you're the Messiah, why don't you jump down? Everybody will believe in you. If you're the king, come down. If you're the Son of God, God would surely love you and get you down."

That would have been my cue to act. Pull a little whammy. Motivate and energize the crowds and they would take care of it with garden tools and everything else and we'd be on our way. But it's obvious that he's not going to fight, although he could. How does the Appalachian singer talk about Jesus? You know that song "I Wonder as I Wander."

> If Jesus had wanted for any wee thing,
> A star in the sky or a bird on the wing,
> Or all of God's angels in heaven to sing,
> He surely could have it 'cause he was the King.

Matthew, more than anyone else, likes to call Jesus the King. He could have done it, but he didn't. And I don't know why I'm always surprised when I read this because I know better. Matthew has told us all along that he's not going to. Is he the King? He's the King. Is he going to fight? No. The title for every chapter in Matthew is this: "He Could Have but He Didn't."

Even when he was an infant and the magi came to Jerusalem and said, "Where is he that is born King of the Jews?" there's going to be trouble you know. You don't ask the king, "Where's the real King?" It's upsetting to the king. And the soldiers come in large numbers to the little town of Bethlehem and mothers huddle with their children behind cellar doors, but where is the King? The King is on his way to Egypt.

Joseph takes Mary and the boy to Egypt to get away from Herod. When he learns that Herod is dead, he takes mother and the boy and goes back to his home, Bethlehem. But he heard that Archelaus was ruling in Herod's stead and he knew that Archelaus was more violent than his father so the King is again on the run. Retreating up north into Galilee, out of the clutches of Archelaus, to a little hill town, remote, private, Nazareth. There he grows up.

When he begins his ministry, he's stirring around in all of Galilee and he's down by the valley of the Jordan. He hears that John, John the Baptist, has been arrested. And so he goes back into Galilee, goes to Nazareth, collects his belongings and, Matthew says, moves his residence over to Capernaum. The King is still on the run.

He hears about a plot, Herodians and Pharisees plotting against him. They plan to assassinate him. He hears about it and he quickly retreats. He's the King but he's on the run. He heard later that John the Baptist had been killed and Matthew says that Jesus got a boat and went out in the boat by himself to a remote place.

A delegation of official investigators from the capital came up into the hill country of Galilee to investigate this teacher, Jesus, and Jesus hears about the delegation and he quickly retreats into Lebanon. The King is still on the run. When is the King going to turn and draw a line in the sand and say, "Enough is enough"? Personally I don't like for him to retreat so much.

When he goes to Jerusalem he's safe in the daytime because the people come in great crowds and listen to him. This serves as a kind of buffer zone about him, safety. But at night when they go home, Jesus goes to spend the night out at Bethany and in particular in a place called Gethsemane. He's safe there; it's remote there. It's private there. Only he and a few others know, but one of those others went to the authorities and said, "I know where he spends the night." And so here we are. Not alone in prayer in Gethsemane, but being grabbed and pushed and shoved.

It's time to fight. He could have. "I could ask for twelve legions of angels and they'd be here." And Matthew has no doubt. If he wanted to fight, he could fight, and successfully, too. But he doesn't. I have written it across the Gospel of Matthew from first to last. "He could have but he didn't."

I think that is something that Jesus picked up from God. You know he was the Son of God and I get to thinking about God and the Scriptures. In Genesis, God said to Adam and Eve, "But if you eat of that tree, you're dead." They ate of the tree and God said, "Well you're going to have to leave the garden." And before they got out of the garden, God said, "Wait a minute. You're naked as jaybirds." And God made them some clothes.

But things got worse and worse and worse and by the time you get to Genesis 6, God said, "I repent that I ever made anybody. The thought of the human heart is wicked all the time, day and night, nothing but wickedness. I am sorry that I made anybody. I'm going to wash it all away." And the heavens opened and the floods in the deep opened up. It rained and it swelled from the ground. "I'm going to destroy all of it. Except those in the boat." And there's Noah and his wife and three boys and their wives. I don't know why God just can't do it.

God said to Jonah, "I want you to go up there and preach and tell them in forty days this place is coming down around their ears. I am sick of the wickedness of Nineveh. It stinks in my nostrils. This is the end of it. In forty days, it's gone." Then in forty days, God said, "You know I'm sorry I said that." And not a stroke, not a stroke.

Like Jesus going through Samaria. The doors were closed; the windows were closed. Nobody spoke to him; their backs were turned. No hospitality. "Would you like to spend the night here?" No, no, no. "Would you share a meal with us?" No, no, no. Nothing! And the Twelve came to Jesus and said, "Do you want us to call down a bolt of lightening from heaven and burn this whole town?" And Jesus said, "Let's go to another town."

When is he going to turn and draw a line and say, "Enough is enough already"? He could have, but he didn't because he has in him the character of God. And the character of God is not just power but the restraint of power. The most marvelous picture of God in the Bible as far as I'm concerned is in the book of Revelation, chapters 4 and 5. When the seer, the prophet, the sage John on the Isle of Patmos, is given this vision, he is told to come up and enter into this house of terrible splendor and he can hardly stand it. And holding his hand over his eyes, he goes into this place brilliant with the light of God and angels wing tip to wing tip singing, "Nothing is impossible with God. God Almighty, Holy, Holy, Holy, Almighty God." Everything is possible with God. That's the creed behind all creeds. God can do it.

And John says, "I went inside and I saw this throne, this terrible, beautiful throne, the very symbol of power upon power and I looked more closely and I saw in the midst of the throne a lamb, bleeding." This, too, is God. Not just power but the restraint of power. That's why I think those two fellows are wrong who have written those Left Behind books, LaHaye and Jenkins. Their last one is called *Glorious Appearing*. And you know what they say? They say that so far it's been the power and the restraint. It's been the throne and the lamb, but the lamb part is going away and it's going to be only the unleashed power of God. I'd like to say to them if you see them, they're wrong. It's like saying there will be a time when God ceases to be God, because God isn't just power; God is restraint of power.

Twenty-five years ago or something like that, what's a year, I think it's twenty-five years ago that I was asked to speak at a president's prayer breakfast. At that time, these prayer breakfasts were held in this country and around the world where we had troops and consulates. I got a letter from Washington asking me if I would hold one of these. I said I would and they said the place we want you to go is Seoul, South Korea. "Well, sure, I'll just stop by on my way to Candler." But I was glad to go and I went.

The general in charge, and my host, was General Stilwell, four stars. He gathered officers and enlisted people in this large room and we had the president's prayer breakfast. We had a nice breakfast and then we had prayers. It was not just prayers in name only. The general's assistant, a colonel, had the soldiers there enter into a period of sentence prayers. I really was surprised. I associate sentence prayers with an old Wednesday night service somewhere in the country. They had sentence prayers for mothers and fathers and sisters and babies and for my wife back home and for peace in the world, moving prayers.

There was a young man brought in from Formosa, a private who played the bagpipe. He played "Amazing Grace" on the bagpipe just before I spoke. The general sat there with tears and he said, "I love that song."

I spoke; he and I talked awhile. There was a benediction; the room began to empty. I shook hands with the general and thanked him for his gracious hospitality. He said, "I want you to remember us in prayer."

And I said, "I will, you know I will."

He said, "Not for more power, we have the power. We could just one afternoon destroy this whole place. Pray that we have the restraint appropriate." It was such an unusual request. "Pray that we have the restraint." He knew his history. He knew he was American and restraint is built into our history. Why do we have executive, judicial, legislative branches except to build in restraint? Why is it said that we shall allow a person only two terms as president? Restraint. Why do we say that the commander in chief of all armed forces of this country will always be a civilian? Restraint.

The general knew. It's not the power; it's the restraint of power. The mark of a civilized society is the restraint of power. The mark of a civilized human being is restraint of power. Every time I read or hear of a man or a woman shaking a baby to death, "You're bigger than the baby. What are you doing?" You know you can. Of course you can.

When I left the room everybody was gone except the general and his aide, a colonel who said, "General, shall I bring the car around?"

He said, "Not now, I want to sit here awhile." And he asked the private from Formosa to stay and the young man did, of course. When I looked back before I went outside, there was the general seated alone in this big room. There was a private out in front of him playing on the bagpipe "Amazing Grace." Now isn't that a picture? Four stars shining, listening to a voice of restraint.

God didn't send his Son into the world to destroy the world. "*If Jesus had wanted for any wee thing,*" but he didn't, only that the world through him might be saved. "For God so loved the world."

18

The Announcement

Matthew 28:1–10

I am grateful and honored to be back here. I can't recall how long it's been, two, three years. I should have written, but you were always on my mind. And I'm grateful for the gracious gesture of Wesley for relinquishing the pulpit this hour for me.

I have come to make an announcement, a brief announcement. Perhaps Wesley has told you. If he didn't, you know it's coming after the music we just had, which declares that an announcement is forthcoming. What marvelous words Steve has rendered from Psalm 68. God marching up in victory to the holy mountain where there is to be a banquet for all of God's people, and ahead of God goes the strong voice of God to make the announcement. Frankly I'm a little bit embarrassed about it. Hear the tympani, the solo voice, and the trumpet and the grand choir, and then I get up here like a piccolo. It doesn't come off too well.

I recall years ago when our kids were small. In a fit of patriotism I spent about $6.00 on a firework, I guess you can use that in the singular, can't you? It would go "boom" up into the air and explode and send sparkles everywhere. I wanted the children to understand about the Fourth of July so we went out into the country to a farm, cleared off a place. I gave a couple of lines from Washington's Farewell Address to the troops, dipped into the Declaration of Independence, closed with the Gettysburg Address and lit the fuse. When it began to sparkle, we all looked upward not wanting to miss anything and waited and waited and finally looked down and that pitiful thing just sort of threw up on itself and went "poof" and that was it. I don't know why that came to mind this morning. But I will make the announcement.

This morning, a little while before daybreak, God raised from the dead Jesus of Nazareth. That's really my whole assignment, to make the

103

announcement. I know it's difficult to hear. Announcements are always difficult to hear. Nobody pays attention to announcements. The announcements about the church's life put in the bulletin midweek, printed on the back of the worship bulletin on Sunday, read to you as though you couldn't read by the worship leader or minister. And then included in the benediction, "Lord help the people to remember the fellowship dinner Wednesday night." And then somebody at the door asked the minister, "Are we going to have the fellowship dinner?" I know it's hard to listen to announcements. One reason is we hear them over and over and over again. If I wanted to make someone deaf, I would do it by repetition.

Jesus warned his disciples that when you go out to sow the seed, which is the word of God, be ready for it. Some of the seed will fall on the path where the repeated passage of people, back and forth and back and forth, will harden the path like concrete. The seed falls on the path and the sparrow from the rooftop and the chicken from the barn peck, peck, peck and they're gone. Nobody received it.

It's never been easy to hear this announcement. You heard the Gospel lesson. The women running from the tomb when they got the announcement. They ran, afraid, traumatized, in total silence because they were absolutely terrified and said nothing to anyone. Who can hear this announcement? That's Mark. Matthew says, "And they gathered with Jesus on a mountain where he had wanted them to meet and there they worshiped him," but, but, but, some doubted the resurrection. Luke says, "They were terrified, paralyzed by fear." Tried to put it aside like a wives' tale, something the women are repeating at the well, but, of course, we men don't believe what they're saying. And then Luke puts in that extraordinary phrase, "They disbelieved with joy" (Luke 24:41, au. trans.).

It's not easy. And John, John says that one of the people closest to Jesus said, "I won't believe it, not until I touch his side, not until I touch his hands, not until I touch his feet. I will not believe it." It's never been easy to hear this announcement. But I want you to know that I'm not going to make it easy for you. I'm not going to trivialize it by just speaking of eggs and flowers and daffodils and things. No, no. There's a cross in this resurrection here. I'm not just going to fill the air with good cheer and let Easter evaporate into a vague cloud of good feelings. I can't do that. My job is simply to make the announcement. And the announcement is this: Sometime this morning before first light, God raised Jesus of Nazareth from the dead. I can't, I can't shrink it by giving you a few minutes of explanation as to what resurrection means. I'm not going to shrink it by trying to give you some scientific parallels so that it will help your believing. No, no, no, no. I will tell you that for a lot of people it is very, very important.

There was an early Christian leader by the name of John who was in exile on the Island of Patmos and he said on Sunday morning, "I was in the spirit." He was trembling, trembling not because of fear for himself, but fear for the church, because the whole earth was shaking with the marching of soldiers. They'd been sent out from Rome, column after column after column, against the church. Already Antipas killed and here they come. And in that trembling moment, John got the announcement and when he got the announcement, he said, "Choose your fastest runner and have that runner go to Rome and tell the Emperor, 'Wait, wait, wait, you can't win, you can't win.' God has pulled the sheet off the coffin and made it the cloth for the banquet table for the disciples. And there's going to be a lot of good, rich food, a lot of aged wine, and there will be dancing and singing, and God will move among us and wipe away every tear from the eye." That's what it meant to him.

It meant a lot to Paul in strange ways. I never cease to try to understand how the announcement affected this man. I don't know if this man was sick most of his life or had gotten some kind of sickness in his ministry, but he had an abused body, a painful body. He said, "I groaned in the body. Just when my spirit is getting richer and fuller and finer and more alive, my body is going down and down and down and my spirit going up and my body going down and all I can do when I lie down at night is groan. When am I going to have the redemption in my body?" Why is it so that the more we live and become qualified to live, the more we live and become qualified to witness for our faith, the body won't go? Some of the finest volunteers I've ever known in the church were on walkers, in wheelchairs, and groaning.

Paul said, "I die every day." What a shape his body must have been in. He said, "Three times I have been shipwrecked; I've spent twenty-four hours in the water. Three times I have been beaten by the Roman mallet, which is designed to break the bones. Five times I have been beaten by the whip in the synagogue, five times, thirty-nine stripes each time. I have been stoned and left for dead, those stones hitting the face, knocking out teeth, crushing the eyes, breaking the ribs, leaving me limp on the ground. I carry around in myself," he said, "the dying Jesus. I die every day. I groan, longing for the redemption of my body so that I will have an instrument adequate for my work." And then he heard the announcement and he said, "Death is swallowed up in victory. Death is dead and all her daughters are dead. Cynicism, criticism, fear, despair, discouragement, they're all dead." For Paul, too, dipped into the text you heard earlier from Isaiah 25. "Death is dead."

But, you will have to make of the announcement what you will. I can't tell you. I was just given the assignment to make the announcement. I can personally witness to you that the supreme importance of the announcement to me is not just for the resurrection from the dead but the resurrection of Jesus of

Nazareth from the dead. Who was raised from the dead? Jesus of Nazareth. Not King Herod who tried to stab that baby while it was still in the cradle, not Pontius Pilate who as the governor screamed in the face of Jesus and said, "Don't you know I have the power to kill you in this minute? I can do it, I can do it!" Not Tiberius Caesar who sat like a marble statue in Rome and said, "I have nothing really to do with peasants, especially Jewish peasants. What was his name again? Jesus? Never heard of him." Who was raised from the dead? Jesus of Nazareth. Do you know what that means? It means that God lifted up this person and said, "This is the one I've vindicated. This is the one I affirm. This is the one I confirm. This is the one I exonerate. This is the one that tells you this is what I had in mind when I created you in my own image. Look at him, totally without violence. You could walk among the people of his land and say, 'Can anybody here raise a hand if Jesus ever spoke ill of you? Criticized you? Put you down? Laid hands against you? Betrayed you? Lied to you? Can anyone?' No, no, no."

Do you see how it's important that it was Jesus of Nazareth God raised from the dead and said, "Now this is what I have in mind for the world"? You know that. In fact in every church I've visited there are a few sitting there who started out in the ministry. A few who went a year or two, I think, maybe four or five. "I never thought it would be like this. I don't like to row upstream. I don't like to be the only one who shows up. I don't like to live in a shoebox on half salary. I entered the ministry and found myself at Golgotha and I said to myself, 'Who needs this?'" I want to say to you that God raised Jesus of Nazareth from the dead.

Practically everywhere I go I meet somebody who started out on the path of generosity like Jesus. Do you see that woman over there putting in two coins? Yeah, yeah, yeah. She's given more than everybody else in the house and she's still rich. Really? Oh that'd make good preaching. I can preach that. Hey, that's a good sermon. But after awhile I can't do that; I can't do that. Everybody around me going for profit and for preference and I'm preaching about two pennies and a widow? No, no, no, no.

I talked to a man recently who just built, I think, the biggest house in North Georgia. He's got to have room, you see; there's his wife, there are two of them. Oh it's a beauty and dazzling and he said to me, "Did you know that I started out in the ministry?" I said, "I didn't know that." And he said, "Now look at me." And I said, "Why would you do this?" And he said, "Simply because I can." And I said, "You can't afford this house."

I want everybody who's traded it off to know that God has vindicated this life, Jesus of Nazareth. Look at him. Nonviolent, never violent, turn the other cheek, love your enemies. "How often must I forgive, Jesus? Seven times?" "No, no, no, seventy times seven." "But when I get kicked in the groin time and time and time again . . . I don't need this!" I want you to understand this is the life that God has raised from the dead and said, "Look, this is what I had in mind."

I know the experience; you know the experience, volunteering to be a chair of a committee. You'll be sponsor for the youth group, a few other jobs like that and you get in the boat all excited and start pulling at your oars. You look around and everybody else's oars are in the boat; they're not pulling. You're the only one tugging at the oars. Who needs this? Why this is the kind of stuff Jesus had to put up with. Exactly. But I want you to understand God has raised him from the dead. Do you see what that means?

I was up at Virginia Wesleyan. Is that where it was, Virginia Wesleyan, a few weeks ago. In a workshop for ministers I saw again Karen Banning. Some of you may remember Karen Banning. She went to Candler; she's a minister in Virginia. But I remembered her because when she was here she told me things about Carl Sandburg. She had worked as a "whatever," cleaning woman or something, at Flat Rock, North Carolina, at the home of Carl Sandburg, a National Historic Site. She had an interesting story. She told me that in the family, Carl Sandburg was called Charlie and some of his poems were signed "Charles Sandburg." She said one day she was cleaning out a cubbyhole in that old house trying to straighten up and she came across a piece of paper that had at the bottom of it, "Charles Sandburg." She read it; she'd never seen that before. She copied it off and gave it to me. This is what it said: "So take up your cross and walk the thorn way. And if a sponge of vinegar be handed to you on a spear, take that too. The soul is woven of endurance. God knows. Charles Sandburg." I think Mr. Sandburg wrote that after hearing the announcement.

You don't have to be in a hurry to make this something important in your life. Easter lasts fifty days, you remember? We think of today as Easter Sunday. Whoopee, here we go. But Easter, according to the church, lasts fifty days. Easter ends June 4 so don't be in a hurry. Take the afternoon, take the evening, take next week. You have fifty days. For some people it takes longer.

During one of my recent confinements due to various ailments, I read again a book I enjoyed twenty-five years ago. Adela Rogers St. Johns—probably the most important newspaperwoman ever in this country—sixty years at it, worked for William Randolph Hearst newspapers. She covered everything: the Lindbergh baby kidnapping trial, heavy weight boxing matches, presidential elections, visits of kings and lords and ladies, she covered it all. What a heady life! The important people in Hollywood were screened and said, "She was there; she wrote the story." A powerful woman. In Hollywood she met a cowboy actor named Tom Mix. Some of you are old enough to remember Tom Mix; he was one of the good ones. Weren't any women in his movies; he just kissed his horse and rode away. Tom Mix from Dewey, Oklahoma, a real cowboy, went to Hollywood, was making westerns. She didn't know who he really was. She loved to hear him recite Shakespeare. He was a Shakespearean scholar and memorized lengthy passages. She said, "I have never heard from the public stage anyone who moved me like Tom Mix." One day she was talking to him; she was about seventy-five when she told this. She said, "I was talking to Tom Mix and we got to discussing religion. And I didn't really have anything to do with religion. 'Do you believe in God?' 'Well I don't know, probably not.'" Shrugged her shoulders. And Tom Mix looked at Adela Rogers St. Johns and recited two lines from an Ezra Pound poem. "I have seen him eat from the honeycomb since they hanged him on the tree." When she wrote her memoirs she gave this title to the book: *The Honeycomb*. She heard the announcement; took her a long time. Take your time.

My assignment is simply to announce to you that this morning sometime before sunrise, God raised from among the dead, Jesus of Nazareth. You have fifty days. In fact, I'm sure if you applied, you could get an extension.

19

Have You Heard John Preach?

Mark 1:1–8

I recently spoke to a woman who was attending a church not her own and I asked her why. She said, "I go there for the music." And I considered that in a way a good reason because music is so vital to the life of the church. No nation can survive without parades and I don't think a church can survive without music. The hymnbook has always been the companion to the Bible even from the first century. The pioneer preachers moving westward across this country had in the saddlebags a Bible on one side, the hymnbook on the other.

I recall hearing a man from London, England, say that when he had to be rushed for emergency to a hospital, he asked that there be brought to the hospital his Bible and his hymnbook. In my particular denomination we have recently made an effort to get the hymnbook not only in every pew but also in every home so that the singing of the hymns of the church would be part of the family life of the members.

One of my early recollections from childhood days was the presence in our home of about a dozen old hymnbooks. The backs had been torn off and they were very simple, kind of "Gospel song" hymnbooks. But on Saturday nights neighbors would gather at our house and my mother would sometimes play the harmonica and the group would sing. I remember those songs: "Blessed Assurance," "Amazing Grace," "Bringing in the Sheaves," "Just As I Am." You remember those songs. And of course at Christmas we sang the carols.

But recently I've come to love a hymn that was not in that book. It's an old hymn; Charles Wesley wrote the hymn in 1744. It is not a Christmas carol; it is an Advent song. It's a song that we sing during the four weeks preceding Christmas that we call Advent, the time of preparation, the time of anticipation of the coming of Christ. The hymn is entitled "Come, Thou Long-Expected Jesus." It continues, "Born to set thy people free. From our fears and sins release us. Let us find our rest in thee." It's a beautiful song. I'm sure you know it. It's being sung a great deal in the churches.

This is Advent. This is the season of preparation and all over the world today in churches that observe Advent, all those churches will be reading texts about the one whom God sent to prepare the minds and the hearts of people for Jesus Christ. Jesus did not just suddenly appear; people were prepared for his coming. I want to read one of those texts, the briefest of them, from the first chapter of Mark, verses 1–8.

> The beginning of the good news of Jesus Christ, the Son of God. As it is written in the prophet Isaiah,
>
> "See, I am sending my messenger ahead of you,
>   who will prepare your way;
> the voice of one crying out in the wilderness:
>   'Prepare the way of the Lord,
>   make his paths straight,'"
>
> John the baptizer appeared in the wilderness, proclaiming a baptism of repentance for the forgiveness of sins. And people from the whole Judean countryside and all the people of Jerusalem were going out to him, and were baptized by him in the river Jordan, confessing their sins. Now John was clothed with camel's hair, with a leather belt around his waist, and he ate locusts and wild honey. He proclaimed, "The one who is more powerful than I is coming after me; I am not worthy to stoop down and untie the thong of his sandals. I have baptized you with water; but he will baptize you with the Holy Spirit."

So let's catch ourselves up on what we already know about John the Baptist. When Jesus was about thirty, Luke says that he shook the shavings from his carpenter's apron and folded it on the bench and went to the house and said goodbye to his mother and his brothers and his sisters. He made his way southward into the desert, which is another way to translate the word "wilderness." Wilderness in the Bible is usually not a jungle like a Tarzan jungle; it's a desert, a barren place, a neglected place, a wild place.

John was preaching in the desert. Jesus came under the influence of this desert preacher named John. According to Luke, John and Jesus were cousins; at least their mothers were cousins. They were near the same age. John was about six months older than Jesus. John's parents were Zechariah and Elizabeth; they were old when he was born. He was apparently their only child and they were well along in years and had given up having a family when he was born. Zechariah was a priest in the temple at Jerusalem.

From his birth, John was set aside as a Nazirite. A Nazirite in those days was a person who was devoted to God and therefore lived away from society, like in a desert place. They would go into the cities and into the towns but they were not social creatures. A Nazirite was totally devoted to God; did not trim the beard, did not cut the hair, lived in an unusual way. John was a Nazirite. He lived and worked in the desert and the word of God came to him in the desert and Jesus came to hear him preach and was baptized by John in the Jordan River.

When John was put in prison, as you recall in his vigorous preaching, he said to the ruler of Galilee that it was sinful for him to take his brother's wife. The ruler and his new wife, who had recently been his sister-in-law, were angry with John and shut him up in prison. When the word came to Jesus that John was in prison, Jesus took up the ministry himself, preaching very much at the beginning as John had preached. And then when the ruler of Galilee had John executed, Jesus moved his residence. I don't know, he may have thought that his life was in danger, but he moved from Nazareth over to the town on the north shore of the Sea of Galilee, a town called Capernaum. It was out of Capernaum that he conducted his ministry.

When the word came to Jesus that John was dead, Jesus mourned his death and preached his funeral, a beautiful oration. "What did you go out to see? A reed shaken in the wind? What did you go out to see? A man dressed in fine clothes? Oh no, no, they belong in kings' houses. He was the Prophet of God; he was God's preacher." And what an extraordinary preacher John was.

Have you ever heard John preach? If you haven't, you will, because on your way to Bethlehem for Christmas, you have to go through the desert and that's where he is. His preaching is extraordinary; it's just riveting. Crowds came from everywhere. Mark says they came from all over Judea and they came from the towns and from Jerusalem. Plows were left in the furrows, bread was left in the oven, shops were left unattended, school was let out early because the crowds were moving out into the desert to hear this extraordinary preacher.

I'm sure that many of the people who went were just curious, curious about the way he looked and the way he talked. This shaggy fellow eating locusts and wild honey, wearing camel's hair with a leather band around his waist. I'm sure some of the young people went out there just out of curiosity, nothing to do, sat out on the hoods of their camels and just watched the crowd and listened to John with no special interest, bored perhaps. But most of the people who went were very sincere.

Here was the scene: With a stump for his pulpit, with the stars for the chandelier of his cathedral, with the Jordan River for his baptistry, John preached. It was not smooth and beautiful. He never claimed to be a chef offering up fancy dishes. He just broke the bread of God with his bare hands and said, "Eat it and live."

He was no beautiful candle burning softly in a sanctuary. He was a prairie fire, the very fire of God scorching the earth. He was no diplomat trying to make yes sound like no and no sound like yes to please everybody. He just said, "The Judge is coming and I'm here to serve subpoenas." And still the people came.

There was something persuasive about him. Persuasive I think in his character; the rough grain of his character shown through clearly. And being in his presence made a radical difference. Luke says that huge crowds came and asked John, "Well, what are we to do in view of the coming of God's Christ?" And he said, "If you have two of anything, share one of them with someone who is poorer than you are. If you have two coats, you don't need two coats. Give one of them away to a person who is cold and poor."

Soldiers came, Roman soldiers came to hear him preach and at the end of his sermons, the soldiers gathered around and said, "Well, what are we to do?" And John said, "Don't be violent. Don't intimidate the citizens. Don't throw your weight around to subsidize your salary; be content with your wages."

Tax collectors came, surprising a lot of people. They lingered when the crowd began to move away and they asked John, "What are we to do?" And he said, "Do not collect any more tax than is your due. Don't add on anything; keep yourself free of graft and corruption." John talked to them real straight and apparently they wanted to hear it because they kept coming.

Did you ever hear John preach? It's frightening really. You know when John preached you felt like you were at the altar of God, in the presence of God, and the light at the altar is different from any other light in the world. It just makes things clear and true. There's no dark corner for deception or being deceived. It is what is called in literature "a moment of truth." No one there but you, in the presence of God, no deception. You may have spent the week before dreaming of palaces and patios but now, through the preaching of John, you know the roof is leaking and the rent is due and your life needs some attention.

Whenever you listen to John and grow quiet for a little bit, it's quite different from those days when you kept the radio or the noise of music blaring so that you didn't have to listen to anything really. Just keep busyness going and keep noise going and life doesn't have to really face anything. But when John preaches, you can hear the rat gnawing in the wall and the ugly dog growling in the cellar and you know that your life needs a little bit of attention. All busyness stops, no more locomotion, no more running.

I'm sure you have, as a youngster at least, taken flat rocks and skipped them on the water, seeing how many times you could make them skip, one, two, three, four, five. It's a lot of fun. But in every case, no matter how many skips, when the rock slows down, it sinks. Busyness stops, running stops, noise stops. And John preaches and you're in the presence of God.

I remember years ago a novel called *The High and the Mighty*. It was made into a movie. I'm talking ancient history here now. Most of you won't remember it, may not even go to the movies. I remember it was the story of passengers on an airplane that was trying to come in over the ocean into California but was running out of fuel and had engine trouble. The news got worse and worse and worse for all the passengers. There was a woman on the plane on whom the camera was fixed a great deal. She was an attractive woman, well made up, a lot of diamonds, a lot of jewels, a lot of rings, a lot of earrings shining. Just really dressed to the nines. Beautiful clothing, well made up with all the best of cosmetics. She was listening to the captain saying, "It looks less and less likely that we will arrive at the destination of our choice. It looks like we will not make it. In other words, it looks like we're going to be meeting our Maker before this is over."

She listened to that. She began to remove some of the jewelry. She took off the rings, she took off the necklace, she took off the diamond earrings. She removed the false eyelashes, she removed a lot of the mascara, she removed the cosmetics all over her skin. She came clean. She had a bad scar on one cheek; she was not really all that attractive but she was what she was, who she was, and it was her choice to meet her end, real and true, without deception, without makeup.

Well, as you may remember the story, they did arrive safely but she had learned something about herself. And I think of that story, *The High and the Mighty*, when I read about John and the response of the people when he preached.

Did you ever hear John preach? It's very refreshing really because he permitted the people to come and make open confession. Confession in the Bible is used in two ways. It's used to speak of one's expression of faith, to confess one's faith in God. It's also used to speak of one's coming clean about life and that's what John offered, the opportunity for people to just come clean. He had some marvelous analogies or images or figures of speech that caused people to see clearly what he was after.

He said, "This moment in history is like an axe being laid at the root of a tree. If the tree has not borne good fruit, it comes down." He said, "This moment in history and in your life is like the moment when a person has harvested the grain but it's still full of chaff. And so he takes a large fan and while the grain is being poured from one container to another, the fan is used to blow away the chaff. This is repeated several times until all the chaff is blown away. The grain is saved but the chaff is burned. And I'm here to talk to you about someone whose winnowing fork, that is, whose fan is in his hand, he's blowing away the chaff and the grain he will save. But the chaff, that which is useless, will be burned with fire. In other words, there is one coming after me, I'm not even worthy to stoop down and untie the thong of his sandal. He is so much stronger than I; he is so much greater than I. He is coming. And one thing that he will do is cause truth to come clean and clear. No more deception, no more pretending, off come the necklace, off come the earrings, off come the rings, off come the false eyelashes. This is who I am."

People came to hear John preach and I'm sure that many of them never, never intended it, but after hearing him, they confessed. They confessed to their life of deception, distorted values, loss of priorities, irresponsibility. They came, they said it, and they were baptized. They were baptized for the forgiveness of sin, for the beginning of a new life.

About four years ago I was in Atlanta visiting, over a light lunch, with a fellow that I had met not long before. He was not in church; he had been as a youngster, same story you hear a great deal. "Oh, I used to go when I was a kid." He had been in a church when he was growing up but hadn't been inside of a church in years. The conversation came around to my work, which has always been the church and ministry, his in the business world. He said, "Well I guess I came to doubt." I said, "What doubt? Doubt in the existence of God?" He said, "Oh no, no. I think I came to doubt what the church was saying." I said, "What did the church say that you doubted?" And he said, "I think I came to doubt that it was possible for a person really to be forgiven and begin a new life." I said, "It's true, it's true, you can." He said, "Really? Do you believe it?"

And he began to talk to me about his life and his need to turn a corner and begin anew. He had lost so much, including wife and children and business. "Is it really true?" I said, "Yes, it's true." He acted as though the message of the Christian faith had just come from Mars and I got to wondering later. Are there a lot of people in the world who really do not think that it is true? What is true? The message that the Bible presents, that John the Baptist presented. It comes in a lot of figures of speech. Sometimes it's called a New Creation, just imagine that, first day of the history of the world. "Morning has broken like the first morning; Blackbird has spoken like the first bird." Everything new, New Creation.

Sometimes it's spoken of as a New Birth, like a new baby, guilty of nothing, brand new, fresh. Father, mother, uncles, aunts, looking through the glass in the nursery at the new baby. The room is full of new babies. Can't tell which one really is Elizabeth, the newborn in this family. "I think that's Elizabeth over there." They all have those little bands around that little wrist where the deep wrinkle is, where the wrist joins the hand, but you can't read it through the glass, too far away, the print's too small. "Yeah, that's Elizabeth over there. Just look at her, no hair, no worry, no stain, no mark, no mistake, brand new."

This fellow said, "Is that true?" I said, "It's true, it really is true." Just imagine a garbage can in your backyard one winter night, ugly, it's full, stuff has poured out over the top and you can't get the lid on. There are one or two sacks of junk sitting around the garbage can. "When are they going to pick this up?" But during the night it snows and you look out the kitchen window the next morning and where that garbage can sits, is now just a mound of pure white. "It shall become as white as snow," says the Scripture. Really? Is that really true? John says it's true. It is true. Countless millions of people will tell you it is true.

Sometimes it is presented as a New Leaf or a New Page of a tablet. Imagine a child in school doing arithmetic, it's the third grade, doing math I suppose. Makes a mistake, tries to erase it, tears the page. Teacher says, "Turn in your papers." She starts crying, "I've torn the page; I was trying to erase it. I wanted to get it right and I've torn my paper." The teacher says, "Why don't you just take a new page and do it again?"

Sometimes the Bible uses that image, a New Beginning. That's what John preached. It was very, very refreshing to all who heard him.

Have you ever heard John preach? If you haven't, you will, because on the way to Bethlehem you will have to go through the desert. Well actually you can get to Bethlehem without going through the desert, but if you do, it won't be Christmas. If you've heard John preach, I'm sure you remember.

20

Asleep in the Storm

Mark 4:34–41

I know that I read it, and it's in there, but it's hard for me to image Jesus asleep. In the gallery of images I have in my mind, his being asleep is not one of them. I can image him, I can picture him staying up all night in prayer; I picture him in Gethsemane praying until the early hours on the morning he was arrested—but not asleep. Now I know he had to sleep; everybody has to sleep. I don't have a spooky view of Jesus, that he never had to sleep. He had to sleep, just like I have to sleep, like you do, even on Sunday morning. But I think I don't want to picture him asleep. Sleeping is a very private thing. I don't think anybody should intrude on anyone else's sleep. The psychologists who study privacy and shame and embarrassment list among the intimate things that people do that are totally private—sleep. And I can understand it. We are vulnerable when we are asleep. We can come apart when we're asleep. Some people, when they're awake, hold themselves together quite well; when they go to sleep they kind of sprawl out all over the bed. They're awkward looking, unattractive. Some people drool, and I now and then hear reports of snoring. It's a very private thing, but it's a very complex thing. Sleeping is not just resting; sleeping is also a way of avoiding. It's a way of avoiding boredom. People who are bored, people who live in dull communities, people who have very dull jobs, according to the report, sleep many more hours than other people.

Sleep is a complex thing. It is for some people a way of avoiding responsibility. "Well, I was asleep. I was hoping it would be over when I woke up." Jonah was also a prophet in Israel, and he was also on a boat. He was also asleep, but he was running from responsibility. He got on a boat, bought a ticket to Tarshish, went down into the bottom of the boat, and went to sleep, hoping he could get away from God in his sleep. That's not what we have here. If there is a need to interpret the sleep of Jesus, I guess we could call it an act of total, complete trust. With a storm raging, dark at night on the Sea of Galilee, Jesus is in the back of the boat asleep. Usually if there is one in a group who is asleep, the others are given some calm by that, are put at ease by that. "It must not be as bad as we think if he's asleep. Why are we anxious?" As a mother during a thunderstorm will say to a child, "It's just clouds bumping together—don't worry about it, don't be afraid." Of course, if she says that while she's crawling under the bed, it doesn't really work. But one calm person in a group usually calms the group, and it may have here for a time. But when the waters start coming over into the boat, and they begin to bail the water, they rebuke Jesus: "Don't you care? We're dying here. Get a bucket, do something! It doesn't seem right that the leader should be asleep when we're feverishly fighting the storm and it looks like we're sinking."

I don't know what they expected, but he got up and rebuked the storm. "Hush!" The sea became glass, the winds stopped, and then he rebukes the disciples. "What's the matter with you fellows, have you no trust?" And they were even more scared, because if the storm is fierce, here is one stronger than the storm. And Mark says they were even more afraid.

I really, however, don't think it's necessary to interpret the sleep of Jesus. I think it makes more sense simply to say that he's totally exhausted. Mark uses an expression in this passage that is quite unusual. He said to his disciples, "Let's go over to the other side. And they took him . . ."—listen to this— "in the boat, just as he was." What does it mean, "just as he was"? Whipped down, bedraggled, hungry, bent over already half asleep, in pain? What does it mean, "just as he was"? No time to clean up, freshen up, dress up, change clothes? Just as he was they took him. He's worn out. But that is unusual, isn't it? What's he been doing? He's been teaching. He's been preaching, he's been healing, he's been helping—aren't all these things exhilarating? "I could just do this all the time, helping, healing, teaching, preaching, giving, going, doing for people." Isn't that the most uplifting thing in the world? Why is he so whipped? He isn't coming off a twelve-hour shift in a factory. He hasn't been digging potatoes all day. He's been helping. What is so exhausting about Christian work? What's so exhausting about ministry?

Well, this is a church of volunteers, you know as well as I do. My feeling is that part of the reason is that all Christian ministry, lay ministry, minister ministry, whatever kind—all of it grows out of idealism. There are people that God has placed in the world who feel keenly—*keenly*—the distance between what is and what ought to be. And they have this dream of making a major difference in the world, to cure all, fix all, help all, change all—everyone is going to be helped. It doesn't work that way. And the person falls into collapse and discouragement, and many times quits.

When I first was clear that God wanted me to be a minister, I had all these dreams when I said, "I give my life to Christian ministry." What does that mean, "I give my life"? I pictured myself swimming out there and rescuing someone drowning, jumping in front of a car and pulling a child back, even at the risk of my own life; standing before a gray wall with soldiers aiming their rifles—"Deny Jesus Christ and you can live." I refused, and the rifles fired, and I slumped, and there was weeping in the afternoon and flags at half-mast. It hasn't happened yet. I wanted to write God a check—my life—and now fifty years later I think the largest check I have written to God is 87 cents.

What is it to give your life? It's committee meetings, running to the hospital, talking with someone about their family, a funeral or a wedding now and then, studying for Sunday school class, going with a group to this or that. When do I get to give my life? And so it is a problem for people involved in Christian work that they have too low an opinion of the little bitty things, the checks for 39 cents and 87 cents. And they wonder, "When are we really going to get to do something big?" That's as big as it gets. And those of you—and I think this is most, if not all, of you—involved in doing good and right and Christian things for other people: Don't underestimate just a word, or a card, or a note, or a phone call.

On the plane coming back . . . I was there twice in Washington, for the celebration last week of the retirement of the organist at National City Church, and then I went back Thursday evening for a couple of days talking with some young people who are considering going into ministry. They gather every year to talk with one another and to have someone talk to them. On the way back I went to my assigned seat on the plane. It was 32D. The number of rows on this plane was 32. I was in the back row. I was between the engine and the toilet. I was against the wall. There were two seats on that side. There was stuff on the other side. It was a roaring, noisy mess back there. You get the picture? I'm at the end of it. The little kitchen thing is there, and the flight attendants are there doing their things, and we're getting ready to take off. I said, "I suppose you're going to do what you usually do." And she said, "What's that?" I said, "Start serving at the other end, at the front." And she said, "Well yes, we like to serve going toward people so they can see us coming and let their trays down and have in mind what they want to drink." And she said, "Why?" And I said, "I need a cup of coffee." And she leaned over and said, "I think I can give you a cup before I go down the aisle." I said, "Good!" There was a guy beside me but he was already hooked up to his laptop and earphones, and he was in another zone. I thought, "He doesn't know this; we'll do a little private business here." So before they went down the aisle with the cart, she fixes me a cup and asks, "What do you want in it?" "Just a little milk, that's good." So she fixes me a cup of coffee, and this guy in another zone looks up and says, "I'll have the same." So she fixes him a cup. And the guy in front of me says, "I'll have orange juice." When is she going to stop? They went down the aisle serving backward. And when she got to the front and they came back, she said to me, "Look what you did!" I said, "I just wanted a cup of coffee." I asked her, "Were the people up there mad?" She said, "There was this one guy who was mad, but he was mad when he got on." All I said was, "Can I have a cup of coffee?" Now, if it can work on the plane with a cup of coffee, it'll work in your life. Just a kind word: Can I help you with that? I think I can fix that for you. Is it all right if I come Wednesday? I'd like to visit.

I had a phone call from a woman in Atlanta. I don't know her; I wouldn't know her if she came in. She said, "Last Sunday, we were there to ride the train and see the mountains, and we came to worship."

I said, "Good to have you; I want you to come back."

She said, "I stayed for your refreshment time and got to talking with a woman in your church, and it was so helpful to me, but I don't know her name and I want to write her a thank-you note. I wonder if you can help me?"

I said, "Well, would you describe her? Maybe I'll think of her."

She described you to a tee. I said, "Sure I know who that is!" I gave the name, and she said, "That's it!" I gave her the address, and somebody got a nice thank-you note from a lady in Atlanta when all you were doing was talking and having some nice refreshments. Just a little bit. A check for 41 cents. But they add up.

It is exhausting, especially when you get to that point when you think not everybody's participating. There are just a few of us doing the same things; you notice the same names coming up all the time. Where is everybody? When you begin to get that feeling—you know, like Elijah. Elijah, working himself to the ground as the prophet of Israel, looked around and he was by himself. Where is everybody? He looked up to God and said, "Why don't you kill me and end the whole story?" Do you have that feeling sometimes? Of course you do. Jesus did. He fed the five thousand, the disciples out counting the crowd counted five thousand. Did they have a crowd! But the problem with the disciples was that they didn't know the difference between a crowd and a congregation. Five thousand. They came the next morning for another meal, and Jesus said, "I have but one meal to offer you. My body and my blood. Will you walk with me the thorny way?" They drifted off, and out of five thousand he had twelve left. He said, "Are you fellows going to leave too?" And they said no.

But it does get kind of tiresome when you think you have a big bunch and you really don't. The one thing that really wears you out is when you try to work out your convictions and your service to Jesus Christ and you find opposition and tension and battle with your own people; people who should be encouraging and supporting and joining in are opposing. That's awful. Did you know there are some people who live the Christian life embattled? There was a time a few years ago, a generation ago, that different denominations fought and competed with one another. That's over. Every denomination is fighting itself. Every denomination I know is in a big battle. There's some group or another that wants to change everything, and it's really critical.

In Washington, these hundred and thirty brightest and best had been brought from California, New York, Georgia, everywhere, and I was privileged to talk to them about ministry, and after I finished my presentation, a young woman came up to me and said she was a university senior. There were several of them who wanted to know if I would give them some time after, and I said sure. So there were several of them who waited for me up front near the Chancel—this was at Wesley Theological Seminary in Washington—there were seventeen young women, all women; they were all university seniors from all over the country. They didn't belong to the same denomination. The seventeen represented three different denominations. Now, the spokesperson for the group said, "We never met till we came here. We don't all belong to the same church, but we have one thing in common. We believe that we have been called into the ministry. Our churches say we have not. Why? Because we're women. Do you have any advice?"

I talked with them. I said, "I would like to urge you to stay with the church that brought you up and taught you Scriptures and led you to this point in your life. I would like to urge you to stay with that. It might change, it might change." One of them said, "I'm not the pioneering type. I have to have support and encouragement." "Well, maybe some of you can't, but whatever you do, do it with grace and generosity and appreciate the fact that somebody led you to this point and don't ever stomp on that or be ungrateful for that, even if you have to leave and go to some other fellowship." One of the women spoke up and said, "I am a twin. My twin is my brother, and we both feel that we've been called into the ministry, and my church said yes to him and no to me."

I said, "We shouldn't even be having this conversation." But they're going to make it. I can tell they're going to make it. I believe as surely as anything that God is stirring their hearts for something good and right and Christian for them to do. But it is hard. They'll get tired. I think probably a principal reason people get tired doing Christian work is that they're nervous in the presence of God and they won't go complain to God, so they just complain to one another. Why not just go to the boss? Make an appointment, go to God, and say, "Look, this is exactly how I feel about all this." God's pretty strong.

Bible characters did it. Moses made an appointment and went in to talk to God and said, "So this is how you work. Have a big exodus and we're free of Egypt and we're out here in the desert and we don't have any water and we don't have any food, and you say, 'You're on your own.' And all the other gods around here, all the pagan gods are saying, 'Boy, Israel's God doesn't know how to finish the job.' But if that's the way you want to do it . . . I just thought I'd bring it to your attention." And God said, "Moses, you have a point." God can handle that.

Sarah, Abraham's wife, came on her walker to keep her appointment with God. And when she finally got up there to God's desk, she said, "I'm nearly a hundred; I'm all bent over and worn out, wrinkled as a washboard, and now I get this word I'm having a baby. Do you hear me laughing? I'm laughing about this." And Jonah made an appointment. Jonah was sent to preach to Arabs. He was as Jewish as you could get, and he was sent to preach to Arabs. He didn't want to, but he had to go. He did it, but he thought he would just bring the message of doom, and he started the countdown. But God had kindness and mercy; God's love and forgiveness overflowed. God forgave all those Arabs, and Jonah made an appointment. He walked in there and he said, "I didn't want to go in the first place. I knew you'd chicken out and forgive all those Arabs. We don't like Arabs. All this time we've been doing this, and you don't know the difference between Jews and Arabs? Arabs wear a different headdress. If you'll look carefully, they are different. I don't like you being kind to people I hate." And God listened. If you feel yourself sagging, not enough help, not enough respect for what you're doing for Christ, just make yourself an appointment. It'll be all right.

But I don't know anything like it, the service of Christ, as exhausting as it is. You probably read about it, the group of people whose leader said one Sunday evening, "I want us all to go on a trip." And they said, "Hey, yeah, let's wait and go this winter and go to Aspen and go skiing." "No, I had in mind a work trip." "Work?!" They said it as if he had said typhoid fever. Work? "Over in Eastern Kentucky, in Corbin County, people are very, very poor. Why don't we go up there for eight or ten days and do some work? Repair roofs, sagging porches, broken steps, put screens on windows that never had any screens." These kids were spoiled; none of them worked; their parents gave them everything. Finally, the upshot was that nine went with two adults, who knew what they were doing. They spent ten days up there. They slept in their bedrolls in churches. They ate in the kitchens of folks who gave them collard greens and field peas; they saw some worthless men lying around cursing their wives and drinking beer. They heard children crying in houses where there were twice as many children as there ought to be. They got a baptism into reality. They fixed the porch and fixed the roof and fixed the screens and fixed the steps. They came back home. All the bathing they'd done had been in a dishpan or in a creek; they used outhouses for toilets, these spoiled kids. They got back home and were lying around the parking lot waiting for their parents to pick them up, and one of the kids said, "This is the best tired I've ever been." You know what that is? "The best tired I've ever been."

21

Tell No One Before Easter

Mark 9:2–9

This text is well placed in the Christian year. Our last Gospel reading before Lent. The season of Epiphany, beginning January 6, comes to a close. It is the season in which the church declares publicly to the world who Jesus of Nazareth really is. And this reading is one of the three anchor texts for that proclamation. The whisper of Bethlehem has now become the shout in Jerusalem. The coming of the magi, that is to say the nations worship Christ. The baptism of Jesus, "This is my son, my beloved in whom I delight," said the voice from heaven. And now the transfiguration, "This is my son, my chosen, listen to him."

This text is well placed in the Gospel story as well, as all the Epiphany texts are. Just when the infant Jesus was coming under the threat of a wicked tyrant, the world came to worship him with gifts. In the second text, just as Jesus is joining the others who come to the Jordan to be baptized of John, seemingly no different from all of those confessing their sins and being baptized for forgiveness, still wet from his baptism, the voice from heaven says, "This is who he really is."

And now following Jesus' first statement to his disciples about his approaching death, the voice from heaven says, "But this is who he really is." The curtain lifted, the dazzling splendor of the transfiguration. But for all the timeliness of this text, it comes too soon for Peter, James and John. They're not ready. They're afraid, they're full of thoughtless chatter, they make senseless statements, they're awkward. There are some commentators who criticize them a bit for not being prepared for this. After all they had the antecedents in their own Hebrew Scriptures, Exodus 14, Exodus 24 and Exodus 34. The six days of waiting, Moses going up into the mountain, the cloud, the voice, the shining face, the revelation, the making of a tent, why weren't they ready?

They had continuity with their own Scriptures. They should have been ready, say others by their own experiences. Look what they've already experienced with Jesus: exorcisms, healing, walking on water, feeding multitudes, even the raising of a 12-year-old girl from the dead. Why aren't they ready?

Well, they're not, they're terrified, absolutely terrified. I'm sure if they had known what awaited them on the mountain, they would have done what Israel did. "Moses, we'll wait here, you go on up and when you come back, tell us what you heard and what you saw. We'll be interested."

Luke helps us a bit by softening the whole account. You remember Luke says to them, "Let's go up on the mountain *to pray*. And while Jesus was praying he was transfigured." They were protected from the conversation among the three, Jesus, Elijah and Moses, by a deep sleep. The three of them were talking about Jesus' approaching death in Jerusalem and they were asleep. In other words, Luke tells it not so much like an Easter story as a Gethsemane story.

But Jesus knows they're not ready and he says to them, "Don't worry about it. In fact don't say anything about this until after Easter." After all, someone running around telling a lot of dazzling miracle stories who has never been to the cross can grossly misrepresent what Jesus is all about.

I'm glad that Jesus understands that because it comes too soon for me too. You see, I'm up there on the mountain because I'm the reader of the text. Some people never stop to think about what the Bible does to the reader. The reader is immediately present and if you don't mind, if you won't tell anybody I said it, I will confess to you sometimes I resent the Bible just rushing me in when all I intended to read was a few verses of Bible. And you're there; you don't get a summary statement: "And the disciples had an unusual experience with the dazzling Jesus when they were on the mountain." No, no, no, no, you're up there. You hear them talk. The Bible does it all the time.

Did you know, well, of course you do. As a reader of the Bible, you're on Mt. Moriah when Abraham is offering Isaac. You don't just get a summary statement: "Abraham was willing to offer his son, but God made a substitute sheep at the last minute." No, no, no, you are up there. The gathering of the sticks, the tying of the child, you even hear the father and son talk, "Daddy, we don't have an animal for a sacrifice." You're up there; you see the glint of the morning sun on the blade of the knife.

It happens all the time. You're at the party of Herod Antipas. His stepdaughter dances and he makes a vow in wine, foolish vow, "whatever you want." She runs to her mother, "the head of John the Baptist." You're at the party.

You're present when Paul meets with the elders at Ephesus; such a tender moment. He pulls into Miletus, the elders from Ephesus come, he meets with them, tells them, "It's up to you now, I'm going. You'll never see me again."

They fall on his neck and they kiss him. We hear it, we see it, we're there. What right do we have to be there? We're just readers, for goodness' sake.

The reader of the Bible is in Gethsemane. Nobody else is there but Jesus. Oh, the three are there, say some of the writers, but they're asleep. But we're there, we hear it. "If it be possible . . ." We're there just because we're readers.

We're at the cross. Everybody else has abandoned him and fled. There are some women at a distance from Galilee, but you and I, just because we're readers, we're there. We hear him talk to the other two being crucified. We hear him scream. We even hear him say, at least I thought I heard him say to his beloved disciple, "Take my mother home." Whew!

It's a frightening thing to read the Bible. I sometimes just want to say, "Let me out of here." But I've said that all my life. I said it when I was in the parish, my first parish. I'd been there less than two weeks, the phone rang, one of the grand old men of the church, a hemorrhaging ulcer. I rushed to the hospital, wife is there, daughter and son are there, grandchildren there, and I'm there. When I hear the flap of the condor wing, I'm there. When they slipped the silent sheet, I'm there. Twenty-six years old, what right do I have to be there? I'd preached nine sermons. Just because I went to seminary, I'm to be in that circle when every eye upon his death turned toward me. "Let me out of here."

I've had that experience in this room, in this very room. Just thought I'd go to chapel. Whew! If I had known, I would be overwhelmed. I would have gotten up an hour earlier to try to get ready for what happened. It happens. You know what I mean?

I know I must be kind of weird, it happens to me at movies sometimes. I went to see *Shadowlands*. C. S. Lewis and his beloved Joy, only three years and she dies. Her son up in that attic room, and that man in his early 60s, sitting there together, sobbing. And I'm in the attic with them? Why, because I paid the price of a ticket? It happens all the time.

Others have this experience too. I remember what Thomas de Quincey said of William Wordsworth. He said Wordsworth had such a love affair with nature that sometimes he would go out and on a beach when he would see the evening sun sizzle into the sea or sometimes the thundering cataract, he would be so overwhelmed, he would distract himself by counting rocks or counting trees or estimating distances. What was he doing? Protecting himself; it was too much.

When Toscanini, at least Marcia Davenport says, when Toscanini had finished sixty rehearsals of Bellini's *Norma*, at the dress rehearsal he put down the baton and said, "The concert is canceled." Why? He said, "The music is too great, it's beyond human powers, I can't do it." Do you know what he's talking about?

I recall once in Kansas at a men's retreat somewhere. It was on a little lake; they had pushed all the water of Kansas together and made a little lake. And the instructor leading the retreat, said, "We want you before breakfast in the morning to go out in teams of two for morning prayers." There was there a little man from Wales. He had ridden a bus 200 miles because he heard someone named Craddock was going to speak and he said, "I have in Wales so many neighbors named Craddock, I thought, ah, someone I know." He said, "I don't know you." I said, "No, no, I'm sorry." He said, "Let's go together."

We went out and we sat on a rock by the lake. I had the New Testament and I said, "Do you want to read?" He said, "I never learned to read or write. You have to read." "Do you have a preference?" "No."

I opened to Philippians. I started at verse 3. "I thank my God for all my remembrance of you, making mention of you in my prayers" (au. trans.). And so I read and I was just getting started when he said, "Whoa, whoa, stop, stop, stop." I said, "What's the matter?"

"How much have you read?" I said, "Well, I've just read five verses." "Five verses?" I said, "Yes." He said, "I've just been a Christian about a year. When I started out, I could barely handle one verse. Five verses?" I said, "Yeah." He walked away and said, "Wow, five verses." Some things are too much.

I think I'm with Emily Dickinson. We want the truth but we want it on a slant. I want to look but I want a piece of smoked glass through which to look. Clement of Alexandria promised me a piece of smoked glass. He said, "It's in the nature of Scripture that it's written in brilliant obscurity so that it is not available to every casual passerby. It's concealed." And I've always believed Clement, but it's still too much.

John Calvin promised that it wouldn't be too much. He said, you know his theory of God's accommodation to our frailty and God's revelation comes to us according to our capacity to receive it, and so Calvin said God's revelation is, you know, veiled in flesh and human words and bread and wine so we could handle it. But it's still too much. Maybe, maybe if I had more time. With more time, maybe get ready.

I recall years ago starting college. I was in a little mountain college on the banks of the French Broad River on the rolling hills of eastern Tennessee. Almost monastic-like school in those days, just a few hundred of us, all headed one direction, toward the ministry. We were 18 years old when we started, high school the previous year.

First semester, freshman year, and a fellow named Bill Loft sat back there on the back and asked Professor Lambert a question. A profound question apparently. I didn't quite get the question but it was an extraordinary question apparently. Professor Lambert paused and I thought, "Ha, ha, he doesn't even know the answer." And then his eyes welled up with tears and I thought,

"There's something else here." And then he said, "Mr. Loft, I think it would be better for all of us if I delayed my answer." I didn't think anything about it. When we were seniors in the last semester of our senior year in an advanced class, we were trying to read the Greek, and Professor Lambert stopped and said, "Mr. Loft, about your question."

Whew, that just takes time. If I just had more time, I didn't ask for this, I asked no dream, no prophet's ecstasy, no sudden rending of the veil of clay. I have learned through all these years to piece together a little bit of faith to live by; I just make it out of snippets of things, the question of a child, a burst of laughter, a walk to the mailbox, struggling with the text, a little prayer in the morning, conversation with a friend, an evening meal, coming by the chapel when someone is rehearsing at the organ, listening to the choraliers practice down the hall as I try to think. I just kind of pieced it together really. A whisper here, an aroma there, an intimation there, enough to live by.

But what do you do with this? You can't just come down the mountain and say, "Guess what we saw today." Can't do that, though I must acknowledge, I must acknowledge that of all the sermons that I have preached, I think by far the majority of them, I preached too soon. Too soon.

And Jesus said, "Don't worry about it. I'll lead you into Lent, into Holy Week, to Good Friday and Easter morning. And I think then you will find your tongue and be able to tell of what you've seen and heard."

22

If Only We Didn't Know

Mark 11:1–11

And Jesus said to two of his followers, "Go into the village in front of you. You'll see a donkey tied there. Release it and bring it here and if anyone asks you what you're doing, say the Lord needs it, we'll send it back." And so they did, and so it was, and so they came with the donkey. They put their coats on the donkey, Jesus sat on it, and somebody remembered a prophecy buried 500 years deep in the sacred books of Israel, written by Zechariah. "Rejoice greatly, O daughter of Zion! Shout aloud, O daughter of Jerusalem! Lo, your king comes to you; triumphant and victorious is he, humble and riding on an ass, on a colt the foal of an ass" (Zech. 9:9 RSV).

That's the beginning of a most extraordinary day in the life of Jesus. It was in the spring of the year, about this time. The time for the Jewish Passover, the central festival of all of the Jewish people, a festival fueled by memory, one burning, searing memory, the memory of slavery and the deliverance and freedom, liberation from slavery in Egypt. They remembered it in what they ate and what they did, what they sang, what they said. In every get-together they remembered it. And now it was very, very important to remember because they were almost enslaved again, under the chariot wheels of Rome; Tiberius Caesar and all the cruelties of that empire, crushing them down. And they're hoping again and sometimes the hope turns into revolt and bloodshed. You can take it only so long, and then wild freedom breaks out.

Rome knew that, of course, and so every year at Passover time they increased about three times the size of the military presence in Jerusalem. The military governor himself, Pontius Pilate, came to town in case some real radical decisions needed to be made concerning the citizens. He was going to preserve the peace of Rome, which was preserved, as you know, in the only way they knew: by killing. They were ready. They were ready for the pilgrims; nervous I'm sure.

I recall years ago, 1963, attending a banquet to honor a large professional society in the city of Dallas. The mayor and some of the important city officials were there as our host at the banquet. I sat across from the chief of police. "Well, is everything quiet in Dallas?" I said.

He said, "I hope so. I hope it stays that way, but I'm nervous."

I said, "What are you nervous about?"

He said, "Well, President and Mrs. Kennedy are coming next week. I think I'm ready. We brought in extra troops and security officers, but you never know; there are a lot of crazies out there."

Pontius Pilate was ready, but nervous.

All four Gospels tell this remarkable story of the pilgrims coming to the city at Passover time. It was a beautiful day, a beautiful time, but electric with all kinds of expectations. All four Gospels, Matthew, Mark, Luke and John tell the story of singing and dancing and putting branches on the road and hailing Jesus. But the one that is most unusual is the one that was read a moment ago by Lynn, and that is Mark's account. I don't know why it is different from the others, but it is. For instance, if you compare it with Matthew, it seems so subdued, almost muffled, too restrained. There are not enough balloons in the air. Something is not right.

For example, Matthew says, "Behold your King." Mark doesn't call him King. "Behold the Son of David." Mark doesn't call him Son of David. Matthew says, "The streets were filled with children." Mark has no children. Matthew says, "The whole city was astir." Not in Mark. Matthew says that Jesus talked to the crowds along the way and to his critics in the city. Not in Mark. From the time he sat on the donkey until the next day, until the next day, nothing but silence from Jesus.

Matthew says, "He went straight into the city, through the city to the temple." Mark says, "The parade stopped at the city gates and Jesus went alone into the city and to the temple." Matthew says, "He cleansed the temple." Mark says, "He went in and looked around and saw everything, but it was late and he went out to Bethany." Something eerie about it, something too restrained and subdued to be a festival and a parade and a hosanna occasion.

Now I don't know why. I don't want you to be sitting there thinking, "He's about to tell us why." I don't know why. Mark may have had one of those personalities that just couldn't celebrate completely. You know people like that, they just don't have any playfulness, they just can't turn it loose, there's no sense of spontaneity. I mean they're good people, they make good committee members, but they just, you know, they just don't do that. They come to the parties but they wear gray. You can ask one of them to play Santa Claus in the Christmas parade but they only give it one "Ho" instead of "Ho, Ho, Ho." They're just that kind of people. I don't know, maybe that's it, maybe we should stop there, I don't know.

It could be, it could be that Mark thinks that all this celebrating is a bit inappropriate. There are many folks who do. It's just not appropriate. You can have a party tomorrow night and within 10 miles of your house there will be cars thick on the parking lot of a funeral home with people signing the guest register and trying to calm the nerves and dry the tears of the grieving. Close to your house; are you still going to have the party?

Mary sang lullabies to her baby, her first born, Jesus. She sang to him but you want to say to her, "Mary, hush. Don't you hear Rachel crying?" I heard a voice, the voice of Rachel weeping for her children and she would not be consoled because they were gone. Maybe, maybe Mark thought it was not appropriate.

It could have been that he thought it was just premature, a little too early. Like some people plant their gardens in the spring. We have a couple of warm days, end of February, early March. This is it, they go plowing and digging and dropping the seed, and later they go out and rake away the snow and ice to see if anything came up. You know most things are premature. Every party, every celebration is premature. Don't you think you ought to wait and see?

I said this to the father of the prodigal son. When he came home and the father ran down the road and grabbed him and kissed him and they killed the calf and invited musicians and brought in the neighbors and there was singing and dancing, I said to the father, "How do you know he'll stay at home? He may change shirts, have a good night's sleep, eat the banquet, pack a lunch and hit the road. Don't you think maybe thirty days probation?"

Maybe Mark feels it's a little premature. I don't know. I do know there is something in me that sympathizes with Mark in his muffled and restrained presentation of this material because I confess to you sometimes reading the Bible makes me feel extremely awkward, like I'm not in tune with what's happening.

There are two things the Bible does that sometimes make me very uncomfortable. The Bible invites me, the reader, into places where I don't feel I belong. Example: Jesus went into the home of Jairus whose 12-year-old daughter, sick, is now dead, lying in her bedroom, a corpse. The mourners have already gathered. Jesus comes in, says, "Get everybody out of here." And everybody's put out except the mom and the dad, the little girl, Jesus, Peter, James, John, and you, the reader. You go inside, you hear Jesus say, "*Talitha cumi!*" ("Little girl, get up!"). You see him take her hand, you hear him tell the parents, "Give her something to eat." I don't feel I have a right to be in there. Do you? Some people just read that and, "What lesson is in that for me today?" Well, wait, wait, wait.

Gethsemane: Jesus takes the group, now only eleven, "Watch and pray with me; my soul is so heavy I can't stand it." They all drop off to sleep; the only one awake is Jesus and you, the reader. You're in Gethsemane, you hear him praying, you see the sweat like drops of blood. You hear him say, "Please, God, everything is possible with you. Let this cup pass from me." Hour after hour after hour; I have no right to be in Gethsemane.

And at the cross: Soldiers are mocking, disciples have abandoned him, there is the disciple he loved, and there is Mary, his mother, and there I am, the reader. And I actually hear him say to his disciple, "Take my mother home." I have no right to be there. The Bible makes me nervous sometimes, letting me in on things that I'm not ready for, have no right to.

And the Bible tells me things I don't want to know. Jesus prayed all night. And at the end of praying all night, the next morning, came one of his many disciples named Judas Iscariot. And you know what the writer says? "The one who was to betray him." And after that, every time his name comes up it says, "who betrayed him, who betrayed him." Now I know the Bible is looking back on it but the first time I meet Judas, it says, "He betrayed Jesus." That just messes it all up for me. Judas was one of the Twelve. He was an apostle. He cast out demons. He healed the sick, he preached the gospel. He was with Jesus passing out bread at the feeding of the 5,000. He was in the boat when they all bowed down and worshiped Jesus. He was with Thomas when Thomas said, "Why don't we go to Jerusalem and die with him?" And Judas said, "I'm with you." I want to meet Judas without the writer saying he was going to betray Jesus. That just ruins it.

Like this story. Mark has told me three times, bless his heart, he has told me three times that this parade is going to the cross. This parade is not going to end in City Park with a big rally and a band and trumpets and funny hats. This parade is not going to end with Jesus lifted on the shoulders of everybody, "Behold your King." He's going to be lifted up on a cross. Mark has told me that three times and I tell you, it affects the parade, because I know where it's going.

I want to just go out in the street in Jerusalem and say to that crowd, "Hold it, hold it, hold it. Do you people have any idea where this is going? It's not a parade; it's a funeral procession. What are you doing? You ought to know. You should know. Do you remember when he was still in Galilee among his relatives and friends? They tried to kill him in Nazareth, an assassination plot in Capernaum. Now, if in Galilee, among his own familiar friends, they tried to kill him, what do you think is going to happen here, in Jerusalem, the center of every plot going on in the minds of people around every sticky café table in town? What do you think is going to happen?"

I want to say to them, "Stop the parade. Do you have any idea?" It could be, could be they just don't. It's called blissful ignorance, a state in which I live most of the time. Just don't know; didn't know; sorry I didn't know.

I saw two little girls playing with a balloon, a red balloon that had been inflated with helium; it was floating up. It would go to the ceiling and then they'd try to get the string and the smaller of the two girls would get up in a chair to get the string. They'd pull it down and take turns turning it loose. They were having a wonderful time. What struck me, however, was that this was happening in the lobby of a hospital. In over 200 rooms there was pain and misery and anxiety and grief, and two little girls in the lobby playing with a balloon. Do you think I should say to the little girls, "What's the matter with you girls?" No.

But this crowd, are they in denial? They know, but won't really accept it? The only thing I can figure as a reason for doing what they are doing, shouting and dancing and singing on the way to the crucifixion, singing and shouting and dancing on the way to the Place of the Skull, I think is that it was their extraordinary faith. I know it was true with some of the women. They were in the parade, Mary and Mary Magdalene, Joanna and Susanna, and others. They were there when he was crucified. They were there when he was buried. And on Sunday morning they were out there early to prepare the body because he was buried in such a hurry. And I stopped them on the way out there to the cemetery and I said, "How can you keep doing this? He's dead, for goodness' sake." And one of them, I forget which one it was, said, "We're persuaded that neither life nor death, things present, things to come, height, depth, angel, demon, anything else in all creation, nothing, nothing, nothing can separate us from the love of God in Jesus Christ our Lord."

That's the only way I can explain Palm Sunday to you. So extraordinary.

23

And the Witnesses Said Nothing

Mark 16:1–8

And they went out and fled from the tomb; for trembling and astonishment had come upon them; and they said nothing to any one, for they were afraid. (Mark 16:8 RSV)

What a strange way to end a Gospel! Such an ending turns Easter into an abortion. The one event that makes sense of the cross, God's act vindicating the life and work of Jesus of Nazareth and the net effect is a frightened silence. Such an ending to the story is a contradiction of that natural human response to the news that God gives life to the dead; a leap for joy, not a running away in fear.

Such an ending stands over against the historic practice of the church, to shout more loudly at Easter than at any other time. "Christ the Lord Is Risen Today, Alleluia." And yet Mark says of the women at the tomb, knotted by fear and tongue-tied by ecstasy, running and trembling, they said nothing to anyone. What a strange way to end a Gospel.

And especially it is strange to us who find the silence of these women in such sharp contrast to the everywhere and at all times witnessing in our time. A slow turn of the radio dial picks up witnesses from thirty stations. TV extravaganzas in prime time witness to the risen Christ. Cars passing each other on the freeway blink turning signals over bumper stickers that witness. Leaflets left on the windshield while you're in the market. Tracts tucked into your hand in the airport. A beatific face in the aisle of the grocery or a smiling stranger in the car waiting beside you at the red light, all of them inquire, "Are you saved?" Full-page ads in the morning paper, flashing lights on the marquee fearlessly proclaim Christ is risen. No one can say, "I have not seen, I have not heard."

But of those women at the tomb, Mark says they were strangely, totally silent, a most unexpected conclusion indeed. Perhaps the context will help us.

> And when the sabbath was past, Mary Magdalene, and Mary the mother of James, and Salome, bought spices, so that they might go and anoint him. And very early on the first day of the week they went to the tomb when the sun had risen. And they were saying to one another, "Who will roll away the stone for us from the door of the tomb?" And looking up, they saw that the stone was rolled back; for it was very large. And entering the tomb, they saw a young man sitting on the right side, dressed in a white robe; and they were amazed. And he said to them, "Do not be amazed; you seek Jesus of Nazareth, who was crucified. He has risen, he is not here; see the place where they laid him. But go, tell his disciples and Peter that he is going before you to Galilee; there you will see him, as he told you." And they went out and fled from the tomb; for trembling and astonishment had come upon them; and they said nothing to any one, for they were afraid. (Mark 16:1–8 RSV)

Rather than resolving our questions the context seems to raise new ones. Here are the women who were at the cross. While he was dying they were helpless but at least they were there. When he was buried there was nothing they could do but they were there. And now at the tomb nothing remains to be done but to preserve the body against time and the elements, and so they are there. Where are the stalwart Twelve? They were there once, mixing in those swelling crowds in Galilee. They were there once helping, hoping and full of high ambition, but quite early, Mark says, a shadow fell across their ministry. Their understanding of what a Messiah was to do and be was left dazed and puzzled by the words and actions of Jesus. For example, Jesus withdrew early one morning to pray alone. Simon Peter and others found him and interrupted his prayers. "We have a big crowd in town."

"Let's go elsewhere," he said.

Or again, after the miraculous feeding of 5,000 and 4,000, Mark describes Jesus with the Twelve crossing the Sea of Galilee. The Twelve are discontent, grumbling, blaming one another. Jesus asked them what was the matter. They answered, "We forgot to bring bread."

Eventually, says Mark, Jesus began to speak of his coming passion. Three times he brought up the subject. The first was near Caesarea Philippi. "I am going to Jerusalem and suffer many things and be killed." And Simon Peter rebuked him. The second time was on the road. "I am going to Jerusalem and suffer many things and be killed." And they were not paying attention because they were arguing about who was the greatest. "I am going to Jerusalem and be killed," he said a third time.

James and John raised their hands; "We have a question."

"Yes, what is it?"

"Can we sit in the chief places when you come into the kingdom?"

Inevitably the failure of understanding became a failure in ability to serve. He went up on a mountain with Peter, James, and John and was transfigured before them. The nine others were below waiting when a distraught father came up with his son. "Can you help me? My son has seizures. Sometimes he falls into the fire and sometimes into the water and his mother and I don't know what to do. Can you help us?" And they tried and tried and they could not.

Jesus came down from the mountain. "What's the matter?"

"I asked these your disciples to help and they could not." And Jesus healed the boy.

"Why couldn't we help him?" they asked.

And Jesus said, "This kind can come out only by prayer."

It is then no surprise that these men, without understanding and without power, are, in the critical moment of trial and execution, without loyalty. And so Mark says they all abandoned him and fled. In Mark's Gospel we see them no more. But here are the women. At least we can dress the body, they thought. Then comes the message, "He is not here. He is risen. Now go tell his disciples." And they ran from the tomb, scared, and did not tell anyone anything.

It's no wonder that the scribes, who were copying and passing along the New Testament documents to the church, were bothered by this ending. And so they added other endings, more comfortable verses that assure the reader Christ is alive and among his followers. Some added a short ending; others added a longer ending, extending the chapter for twelve more verses. But when you read those editions, you know what they are, attempts to heal what looks like a broken document.

It is no wonder that Matthew, when he tells the story of the women at the empty tomb, continues the story to tell of Christ appearing to them and of their excitement. It seemed only right to complete the story of Christ appearing to his disciples on a mountain in Galilee and of his giving them the Great Commission. That, the church has said, is a more appropriate ending for a Gospel. It is no wonder that scholars have been puzzled for centuries in seeking to explain this strange ending. Perhaps the scroll was worn and broken at the end and the last verses of Mark have been lost. Maybe so. At least, as it is seems no way to end a Gospel.

But suppose we look at it not as the end of a Gospel, but as the beginning of a story. Mark has made his point about the career of Jesus. Its center and governing event was the cross. All words and actions of Jesus led to it and with it, he ended the narrative. So important was it to tell the story this way that Mark did not take the reader's eye off the cross with appearances of the risen Christ.

But the announcement of the resurrection must be made, not only because the resurrection was God's vindication of the Crucified One, but also because the resurrection began the next chapter of the story. And so the women hear the word and must now carry the word. And the first response? Ecstasy. He is alive. Pilate has not won. Herod has not won. Hate is not the last word. Death is not the last word. He is alive. Then came the fear. He's alive? If he's alive, now what? Are we going to have more trouble? Will there be more killing? Will we have another assignment? Are we to go back home? Where are we to go? Will we be killed? If this is God's way in the world, what next will be asked of us?

And then came the silence. After all, who is going to tell this? To whom are they going to tell it? Who wishes to introduce into the face of laughter or hostility or arrest the news of Christ's resurrection? And all those questions. How do you know? When? Where? Did you see him? Why you women and not the Twelve? And the crowds of the curious: who will control them? If there's a mob, there will be an official investigation and perhaps more crucifixions. Which one will be the first to pronounce these words? Would I? Would you? Who, once struck by the immensity of the powerful presence of God who calls into being things that are not and who gives life to the dead, is going to become chatty and glib? Who is going to be the first town crier? I understand their silence, don't you?

Søren Kierkegaard once said, "Some things are true when whispered but become false when shouted." It is also true that some things become cheap when shouted. When one hears a glib and easy witness, one wonders, where is that awesome distance before God? How can anyone talk freely in God's presence? When one repeatedly experiences the inability to speak when deeply and profoundly moved, then surely Christian witnesses must draw their breath in pain to tell this story. And those closest to God seem to be the ones most sensitive to the strong inclination to keep silence before him.

In his very personal book *The Way to Rainy Mountain*, Scott Momaday, a Kiowa Indian, tells of life on the reservation and of his love for his grandmother. She was a comfort to him and a joy. Her apron was his fortress, her kitchen his storehouse of jam and bread. Between them there was no distance, only intimacy.

One day young Scott ran into her cottage, late into the afternoon, for a quick embrace and a snack. She was not in the kitchen. He went into the one other room of her cabin and there she stood at the foot of the bed. Her kerosene lamp made strange shadows as she lowered and raised her arms in prayer for her people; the Kiowa language on her lips cast mystery into the room. It was almost frightening as she paused over the syllables of sorrow in her intercession for her sad and tragic people. The boy stood motionless and then slowly backed out of the room into the comfortable kitchen. His only thought was, "I have no right to be here. I have no right to be here."

In the intimate distance of that moment our text comes clear. "When the sabbath was past, Mary Magdalene, and Mary the mother of James, and Salome, bought spices, so that they might go and anoint him. . . . And they went out and fled from the tomb; for trembling and astonishment had come upon them; and they said nothing to any one, for they were afraid."

When these women do speak, when they find their tongues, when they are able to witness, I will listen.

24

And They Said Nothing to Anyone

Mark 16:8

The earliest account, which was just read, of Easter morning—Mark 16—begins without any real surprises. Three women, whose names we know—Salome, Mary, called the Magdalene, and Mary the mother of James—went to the cemetery after the funeral. This is not unusual. This has been a practice in my family after the loss of a member of the family; some of us go to the cemetery again later. There may be a card still left in flowers and we need to send a thank-you note; there may be some flowers, still fresh enough that we may need to take to a church or a nursing home. And it's a quiet time because the crowd is gone. It's not unusual to go to the cemetery after the funeral. These three women went because it was up to them to care for the body. Nobody did that officially. The climate was such, the practices such, and in this case with such a hasty burial, that they had work left to do, to put spices on the corpse. No surprise. But then wave after wave of surprises begin. The grave is open. They're shocked and immediately disturbed. Then a young man in dazzling white is standing there, and they say, "Jesus?" "No, he's not here; he has risen just as he said. But he left a message for you; he wants you to go and tell his disciples and Peter that 'I will go before them into Galilee. I will meet them there. They will see me.'" It's too much for the women. Instead of going with the commission that Christ has given them, to go and tell the disciples, they run the other way. They are traumatized, they're amazed, they're shocked, they're afraid, and they are completely silent. The language of the New Testament, the Greek language, allows, as most languages do, that you can break the rules of grammar sometimes in order to emphasize a point. And literally what is said of the women is this: "They did not say nothing to nobody." In other words, totally silent.

Now, since the second century the church has not liked the ending of Mark. This is no way to run a resurrection! Having women quiet, not saying anything, and scared and running. And so starting in the second century scribes began to add to the Gospel of Mark. And if you look in your Bible, most of you will find an alternate ending, a short ending, a mixed ending, taking pieces of the other Gospels and adding them to Mark so that it will have an appearance of Christ, triumphant resurrection morning, belief of the disciples, and a lot of hallelujah. My old teacher in seminary said that the reason Mark ends the way it does is that the end of it apparently got frayed or damaged or destroyed, and we don't know exactly how it ended. I'm comfortable with the way it ended. The women were totally silent. I can understand that. You have to give them some time to doubt this. The men had time to doubt it. All the Gospels say that some of the Twelve disciples doubted it. Matthew says, "They worshiped him; but some doubted." Luke says, "While in their joy they were disbelieving." Feel the mixture there of believing and not believing? And John says Simon Peter said, "Well, I'm going fishing." And Thomas, of the Twelve, said, "Well, I won't believe it till I touch him." Why not let the women have time to question the truth of it? Or it could be that they just don't need any more news. I don't care how good it is; you just reach a saturation point of not needing any more news. And they are in a position to need nothing else. Jesus is dead and buried. They've cleaned out his closet; they've given away what few things he had. They have washed and returned the dishes to those who brought food. They've written the thank-you notes. The dog has been returned from the vet. The guests are gone. Four loads of laundry have been done. And now comes the routine, the blessed, joyous routine, of life as it was. You can complain all you want about routine; there is nothing so composing, so giving of composure, as routine. Let's get back to our routine. They don't need any news, however good it is. They can't hold it. But the text says they were afraid. It doesn't say of whom, maybe the authorities. Very likely the authorities. In order to keep law and order, they killed Jesus. He's a rabble-rouser, got a lot of people stirred up, created a lot of dissension, huddles of people planning and plotting on street corners. We have to get rid of him in the name of law and order! And so they did.

Now let's suppose we go out and say Jesus is alive again. You know what they're going to do? They're going to start with us. And they can squash us like bugs. Because how many do we have? Luke says, after all Jesus' ministry, he had 120 believers. Less than the membership of this one congregation. If Josephus was right and there were more than two million pilgrims in Jerusalem for the Passover, what would this little group of three women do in that kind of throng? They would be run over. What are you going to do?

Roman historians say that at the end of the first century the empire had a population of about seventy million. And they estimate that there were maybe as many as forty thousand Christians. Think of it. In a town of seven thousand people, four Christians. This means that in Gilmer and Fannin counties together after a hundred years there would be what? Seventeen? Most of us don't know what minority is. Think about it. Are they now going to get out the word that this Jesus you killed is alive again? Maybe that's what it is when he says they were scared. It could have been that they were simply unable to talk. Fear does that to you. Those of you who have been in your first play or led your first program or read Scripture in public know what the fear is. Fear of mispronouncing, fear of choking up, fear of losing your voice, fear of falling down, fear of everything. It's hard to talk when you are deeply affected. We can chat about the weather and everything under the sun, but let someone bring up a sacred subject, and most of us get as quiet as these women, and we don't say nothing to nobody. The most common thing said to me in this church, which is run by volunteers, people who are good people—they cut down trees, mow the grass, wash the windows, serve, fix the table, decorate, bring flowers—but the one thing I hear most is this: "Don't ask me to say anything." I'll do anything, but don't ask me to say anything. I'll climb up and change the light bulb, but don't ask me to say anything. Why is it that we can just chatter like magpies, but mention Jesus Christ and it's "Don't ask me to say anything"? I hear an expression a lot these days—it's not enough to talk the talk, you've got to walk the walk. Well, that's nice. The trouble with it is, it's backwards. It's not enough to walk the walk. You've got to talk the talk. Because the most difficult and most effective and most profound thing you'll ever do for Jesus Christ is to say something. And when I ask for talkers, no one comes. If I say, "Let's redo the building," everybody comes. This is no criticism of anyone, but an honest recognition that the fundamental human sacrament is to say something important. And that's hard to do.

Now Nettie and I and some other friends were talking recently with a man whose wife is very ill; she has been for many years. And one in the group asked him, as we were leaving, "Is there anything we can do?" And he said, "Pray for her." Now when he said that, it was not only an indication of how sick she is, but it was a milestone in that man's life. I have known him for fifteen years and I had never heard him say anything so deep as that. It came from way down here. He can talk so freely of golf and the Braves and the Hawks and the weather and politics and the stock market. But I had never heard him say, "Pray for her."

These women couldn't talk. It might have been that they were afraid of the response. You take any good Christian witnesses and run them around a few times through the beauty parlors and the barber shops, through Wal-Mart and into the restaurants and the post office and one of those cafés where men sit all day drinking their coffee, and say "Jesus Christ is risen," and see what happens. Did you hear what those women said? They said he was risen!

You're kidding? No! That sounds like a bunch of women who don't have enough to do. My goodness. Well, how do you explain it? They went to the wrong tomb, they were confused, it was early in the morning, they say it was about dark. They just got confused and went to the wrong tomb.

How do you explain it? Well, they moved the body; he was buried in someone else's tomb. They didn't have time, it was nearly sundown, they had to get him off the cross and get him buried. They just buried him nearby. They were going to move him later to a permanent place. What's the deal?

How do you explain it? They stole the body. Some of his followers stole his body and then started spreading this story about how he's raised from the dead, he's raised from the dead. It's the oldest trick in the world. Now you see it, now you don't.

How do you explain it? Well, I never believed he was dead in the first place. Really? Now, you just think about it. He was on the cross from, what, nine in the morning to a little after three? Listen, I've seen crucifixions, I've seen fellows hanging up there for three and four days, just think about it—they take him down from up there around three o'clock, and he hasn't been up there even a day? Half a day? Now you just think about it. That's premature burial. He came around. That's the way I look at it.

I just hate for our Christian witness to just get all messed up, to go through the rumor mills, and it comes back, and you don't know anything about it.

Now I want to say to you people, as plain as I can on this Easter day that "Jesus Christ is risen from the dead" is a Christian witness. A church witness. It is something believers say. It's not a public statement. The risen never made an appearance in public. The only ones who saw him were his followers. No public appearances. If I had been running it, I would have had him go around to stores, go back into Pilate's hall and say, "Hey Pontius, you want to give it another shot?" That's the way I would have run it. And for people who doubted, agnostics and atheists and those sorts, I'd have had Jesus appear and just scare them to death. But that just shows you how small I am. If you read the New Testament, nobody saw him except his followers. If the world is going to believe it, they're going to believe it because you believe it and you testify to it, that's it. Luke said it just as plain as day. He said, "The life of Jesus you all know, it's a matter of public record. The death of Jesus is also a matter of public record. The resurrection of Jesus? Of that we're witnesses." Do you see? We cannot expect the public, the culture, society in general to sustain the real meaning of Easter. It is a Christian word. A Christian commitment. A Christian belief. One of the darkest, darkest times in the history of the world came when a man stood up in front of his country, his government, and said, "We can't expect the churches and the Christian families to carry the whole weight of ridding the world of atheism and communism. We have to put the power of government behind it." And so Adolf Hitler persuaded the people to put the power of government behind the battle to rid the world of atheism and communism. And he said, "God is with us."

We can neither be seduced nor intimidated by institutions or culture at large. It is a Christian message. Jesus Christ is raised. If the message of Easter is lost, and dwindles down and peters out, it becomes nothing more than colored eggs and rabbits, breaks from school, trips to the beach, spring holiday. If it becomes only that, it's not the schools' fault. Because it is the church's message. And everybody's yelling about how the schools ought to do this and the government ought to pass a law about that—phooey on that! It is the church's message. It is for the church to say.

Now what are we going to say? We can't be like those who didn't say nothing to nobody. This is what I say: Our God is a God who gives life to the dead. It's been that way since creation. He brought into being what didn't exist and out of chaos formed the world. That's the way God is. God gives life to the dead. Or Abraham and Sarah, so old they couldn't have kids, they were over a hundred. And yet they believed God gives life to the dead, and even though both were so old they were dead as far as procreation was concerned, they had a child and named him *laughter*, Isaac. Jesus was dead. He was dead. You ask his friends, he's dead; you ask his mother, he's dead; and yet we believe that God gives life to the dead. You and I, dead in our trespasses and sins, God has made alive. Do you believe that? Can you think of a way of saying that? Can we say that to somebody? It's not enough to walk the walk; we have to talk the talk. We cannot be a church that runs from the empty tomb, silent. Amen.

25

Nothing Is Impossible with God

Luke 1:26–38

"For nothing will be impossible with God." That's the text, and it is a preacher's delight, because you don't have to go into who said what to whom and bring up Samuel or Saul or Moses or Paul or anybody. It's just one of those statements that's true without context. Nothing is impossible with God. You can put it in a bottle and toss it in the sea and have it wash up on a distant shore, and it's true. You can put it on a banner and have an airplane carry it across the sky, and it's true. You can write it on a slip of paper and put it under your pillow; it's true.

Nothing is impossible with God. It's like a proverb. It doesn't need who said it to whom or what or where; it's true. An ounce of prevention is worth a pound of cure. It's better to be safe than sorry. A bird in the hand is worth two in the bush. If your heart is bitter, sugar on your lips won't help. Some things are just true. This is just true. And you are therefore relieved of my having to go into a lot of Bible history in order to establish this. It's true. Now, I know it sounds as if it's from a fairy tale. What is the name of that book of children's stories? *Anything Is Possible?* Elves come in the night to fix things that are broken, and a beautiful princess touches things with her wand and all hurts are healed, and dirt turns to gold. All wishes come true, and animals talk to children, and nothing is impossible with God. It sounds like a fairy tale, but it isn't. It's from Holy Scripture. And it has been the anchor, the rock, the sustenance for people in extremely difficult circumstances. I heard this text once spoken through the bars of a jail to a prisoner who sat in there with his head in his hands crying, wondering what would happen to his wife and child. Nothing is impossible with God. You can write it with Crayola in every orphanage; you can embroider it on a pillow in every nursing home. It is the truth. Nothing is impossible with God.

143

I remember the first time I heard it, it was in Rhea County in the mountains of East Tennessee. A logger working in the hills pulling and snaking out the logs had been killed in an accident, leaving a widow and three small girls. He was already dead when I came to know her. She dressed those girls; they always looked clean; their hair was shiny; and they looked happy running down the road from their little cabin to catch the bus. They wore their little cotton dresses, always clean and pressed. Ruby got a check every month for $147. I said, "Ruby, you can't do it." And she said, "I'm going to be here when those kids go to school, and I'm going to be here when they get home, and I'll just pick up extra money where I can." She did washing and ironing. I said to her one day, "Now, Ruby, you can't do this on $147 a month: why don't you just come clean with me, I'm the minister. You're bootlegging." And she laughed and she said, "Nothing is impossible with God."

It was in Oklahoma, a place called Carrier, Oklahoma, that I heard this. I was a guest in a home. I was a guest in the pulpit, and they had invited me to lunch. I saw on the upright piano a picture of a young man wearing a uniform. "Your son?" "Yes." This was following the Korean War. I said, "He was in the war?" She said, "Yes." I said, "He's home now?" She said, "No." I said, "Was he killed?" She said, "No. He is missing in action." I said, "How many years?" She said, "It's been seven years, but we still have hope." And her husband, sitting at the end of the table, said, "We do not. We have no reason to hope anymore." And he threw his napkin down and walked out into the backyard. I said, "Should I go out there?" She said, "Oh, no. He hasn't given up. You see, nothing is impossible with God."

I don't know if you people know it, I don't know if I've told you, but I said that to myself a lot as we were starting this church. I hadn't planned on all this. As a minister of the Disciples of Christ I've always believed, of course, that people of all backgrounds, economic, social, educational, denominational, can come together in one faith in God as revealed in the forgiving love of Jesus Christ. Whatever things we may believe, I've always believed that. And then you people came along and put that to the test.

Some of you are wastefully wealthy; some of you watch your pennies. Nothing is impossible with God. Some are so shy you stand around counting your shoelaces. Others come bursting into a room and get the name of everybody they've never met before. Some sit outside waiting for someone they know so they can come in together, they are so shy. Others are happy in the presence of strangers. We can't make a church out of that, can we? Nothing is impossible with God.

And how are we going to get any young people interested? Young people like to be where there are a lot of folks; they like to be where there are 150 kids knocking and talking. How can you have a church where there are just a few? They don't like to come where there are just a few. They have a kind of herd instinct, and we don't have a herd.

When we were in west Tennessee for Miss Auttie's funeral, the great-grandchildren were there sitting around on the furniture wishing they were somewhere else. I said to one of them, "Boy, it got cold last night." He said, "Yeah." I said, "I don't know how cold it got, but Miss Auttie has a thermometer out on the porch." And he went out to read the thermometer, and some of the others went, and then six of them went out there to read the thermometer. I said to myself, "We don't even have six." But nothing is impossible with God.

We have people who don't read the Bible, and we have people here who are Bible teachers. Nothing is impossible with God. We have some people who show up every time we have a Bible study or worship. They show up because they want to build their reserve and make deposits on their faith so that when the crisis comes, they can write a check and be sustained. We have others that don't really worry about that. I'll handle whatever comes . . . They don't know that they can't.

When I was a kid, there was a little house on the empty farm next to ours. A family moved in, didn't stay long. It was wintertime, there was a little stove, a woodburning stove, and the man would go outside to the back of the house and pull boards off to burn in the stove. And as it got colder, he pulled off more boards. And it got colder. He pulled off more boards. And it got colder. And he pulled off more boards, and it really got cold, and so he and his wife left, and they cursed the stove and they cursed the house. And there was an ax and a chopping block and a tree and another tree and a forest available, and he burned up his own house to warm his own house. And I thought about how many people there are who think they have their own resources, their own strength, their own power to handle it when the phone rings, the letter comes, and the crisis is too big. I thought, *I don't know*. And the text came back. Nothing is impossible with God. That's where we started. And here we are. But you know me well enough to know that whatever the text is, I cannot pull it out of the context; it is a part of Holy Scripture, and we need to know who said it to whom. Nothing is impossible with God—it is twice in the Bible, I guess you know. It appears once in the Old Testament and once in the New Testament. The circumstances are very similar, but different. In the Old Testament it's in Genesis 18. An old couple named Abraham and Sarah have no children, absolutely none, no kids, and they're old. And a messenger of God comes to their tent one day and says, "You're going to have children. You'll conceive and have a son, and from him will come a nation, and that nation will bless the world." And Sarah laughed and said, "You've got to be kidding!" And she had the son, and she named him laughter, *Isaac*, because it seemed so funny to her.

And from Isaac came the nation we call Israel, and Israel, in spite of being enslaved, persecuted, murdered, ostracized, made fun of, unwelcome, has given the world the basis for a moral and ethical society. You should love the Lord your God with all your mind and heart and soul and strength, and your neighbor as yourself. That's the foundation. You shall not kill; you shall not bear false witness against a neighbor; you shall not covet what your neighbor has. You shall not murder; you shall honor your marriage vows. Have no other God before me, have no idols, and remember the Sabbath day and keep it holy. You need your rest. God rested. And in those commandments we have the basis for the whole Western world's life together. And it started when a messenger said to an old couple, "You're going to have a baby. And the world will be blessed." That's in Genesis 18.

In Luke 1 it is almost the same, but different. To Sarah and to Abraham the messenger said, "Nothing is impossible to God." To Mary, a teenage girl in a little town in northern Israel, unmarried—she had been promised by her family to a carpenter who lived there in Nazareth by the name of Joseph, but they were not yet married—the messenger said, "You're going to have a child." "But I don't have a husband!" "You're going to have a child, and he will bless the world." And she did. And in spite of the fact that he was mistreated, abandoned, made fun of, mocked, beaten, whipped, and executed, wherever he goes, people's hearts are lifted. They become kind and generous. People who remember Jesus will repair their neighbor's house when their own roof leaks. They'll empty their pockets for other people's children. "Is there any way I can help?" They'll love even their enemies. They will turn the other cheek. They'll go the second mile. And all because a messenger said, "You're going to have a child and you'll name him Jesus." And Mary said, "I don't get it." And the angel said, "Nothing—nothing—is impossible with God."

Now folks, I hope we've all learned our lesson by now. It's been two thousand years. If God can give a child to an old couple in a tent in Saudi Arabia and change the world; if God can give a baby to a teenage girl in northern Israel and change the world, why should you ever, why should I ever, give up hope, doubt, wonder, despair, shrug my shoulders? I think, I think, *I think* I have learned my lesson: Nothing is impossible with God.

Write that over the door at your house. Write that on your mind. Write that across your heart. It will come in handy before we meet again. Nothing, nothing is impossible with God.

Amen.

26

And Jesus Also

Luke 3:15–22

Well, finally I'm here. Robin invited me years ago but I wanted to wait to see if he was sincere about it. He told me recently that he'd been here for twenty-three years. I heard of this church before that. Clyde Wheeler, interim minister here for awhile, spoke of you often in words of praise. Now Robin, twenty-three years. It's hard for me to imagine. I hope you'll be patient with him. He's a slow starter, but once he gets started, he slows down.

This is a beautiful sanctuary. I love the worship. I was thinking last night some American businessmen a generation ago purchased the London Bridge and moved it to Arizona. I don't know why, but when I heard about it, I thought, what will happen next? Probably some people will buy the May-flower and move it to Oklahoma, and call it a church. And they have, and they did, and you are. I'm very pleased to be here.

"Now when all the people were baptized and when Jesus also had been baptized . . ." Luke says that Jesus was about thirty at the time, the time when he shook the shavings from his carpenter's apron, folded it on the bench, went into the house to say goodbye to his family, and made his way down to the valley of the Jordan River. We don't really know why this particular day, this particular time. What was the prompting? Maybe something said in the Rabbi's sermon in the synagogue and Jesus knew this was the time. Maybe listening to the reading of the Scripture, he heard his own name. That's what we all do when we listen to Scripture. We listen for our own name, and he heard it. Maybe that was it; I don't know. Maybe some of the other men of the community of Nazareth passed by the shop and said, "Jesus, we're on our way to the Jordan." They'd heard about John and they went away singing "Shall We Gather at the River," and Jesus closed the shop and joined them. I don't know. Maybe in his own quiet meditating time. I don't know how God spoke so much to him. Maybe his early mornings, sitting on the back steps before the family wakes, holding a cup of coffee as though it were a small stove in the cool air. Maybe. Or in the evening walking down the back roads of his mind, beside the rivers of his own memory, looking up and seeing a star and hearing the rustle of a wing, and knowing this is it.

Historians of Jesus have taken to giving his mother credit for the prompting that sent him down to the river. And it might have been; she was a remarkable woman. Luke said she pondered things in her heart. She was not a pushy mother. She let him grow. She didn't shove him into the showcases of the world at age 12. She didn't enter him into all the miracle contests with boys and girls of Galilee. She let him grow, and besides that, she was busy. I don't know how much time she could give to him anyway because after Jesus was born, Mary and Joseph had a lot of children. They had many daughters, says Luke. They had four boys, James, Joseph, Simon and Jude. She was pregnant most of the time Jesus was growing up. I hadn't thought about that before.

But whatever the prompting, why guess? He went. "Now when all the people were baptized and when Jesus also had been baptized . . ." What a strange thing to say. "When all the people were baptized and when Jesus also had been baptized . . ." That's not the way to say it. Luke was acquainted with Mark; he should have said it simply as Mark did, as though there were only two people in the world at that time, John and Jesus, and John baptized Jesus with heaven's approval. That would be the way to do it. Something dramatic. You don't say "and when all the people were baptized and Jesus also." "And Jesus also"?

Matthew would never say a thing like that. In fact, Matthew, when he has John looking down the way, and here comes Jesus, he said, "Whoa, whoa, whoa, I'm not going to baptize you, you should baptize me. It should be the other way around." Jesus says, "Leave it alone, just do what's right, what God wants, go ahead." What a remarkable way to say it.

There was an early church father, name of Epiphanius. This will be on the test so jot this down. Epiphanius said he had heard that when Jesus was baptized, there was a bright light from heaven that shone upon the surface of the water. We know that Jerome, the church historian and translator, said he had heard that when Jesus was baptized, fire spread across the surface of the Jordan. That's the way to tell about Jesus' baptism. This is no ordinary person. At least Luke could say, "John told Jesus, oh no, not with the rest of them. When I get through with the crowd, then we'll have a special private service for you; you are different." But Luke didn't. "And when all the people were baptized and Jesus also was baptized." You know why I don't like that? It sounds like a line, a line of people being baptized and there's John at the edge of the water, saying, "Next," and it's Jesus.

I don't like lines. In lines, everybody just sort of seems the same. We're not the same. I don't like lines in cafeterias, or getting driver's licenses, or paying bills, or registering to vote, or any of that. I just don't like lines. Look at all these people. Where'd they come from? Who are these people? If you want lines, I know how to make lines. One line for clergy, one for laity. One line for those who make over $100,000 a year, another line for those who make less. One line for those who live in gated communities, another line for those who live in trailer parks. I know how to make lines. There's a line for those who own and there's a line for those who rent. I know how to make lines.

Luke doesn't know how to make lines. Luke gives the impression that it's all just one line. "Now when all the people were baptized and when Jesus also had been baptized." That just puts him in line. Do you want him in line? Beyond that, Luke goes on to say who was in the line. What an assortment. The poor were there, says Luke. Of course, they were; the poor always show up. Those who go through life with nothing but a handful of ashes, when anybody comes along preaching the riches of God's good grace, they're going to show up, whether it's in a cathedral or at the Mayflower or under a tent in a Kansas wheat field, sitting on boxes, while an old upright piano double clutches some old song, they'll be there. Why not? Some have theirs now and we'll have ours later, let's go to the meeting.

Luke says the rich were there. Does that . . . no, it doesn't surprise you. The rich were there. Why? Maybe sitting on their patios by the pool, they suddenly discovered that the roof leaked and the rent was due. There's something other than this. Perhaps they're tired of running around with a fistful of $100 bills looking for the market where life is sold. I have no idea why they came, but they came. The Gospel writers even tell of a specific case of a rich person we call the rich, young ruler. We put it all together rich young ruler. Why did he come and fall before Jesus? "Rabbi, what should I do?" What caused him to do that, this man of power and wealth? I don't know. He could have just come from the doctor's office. "Doc, it starts here in the chest and shoots out into my arms and I have to sit up in my La-Z-Boy to get my breath and to get any sleep. What do you think it is, Doc? Do you think it's serious?" Maybe that's why he came. Maybe going down the street, some children of the street, begging, grabbed at his sleeve and said, "Sir, could we have a penny, could we have a penny, please mister, could we have a penny?" "Get away from me, kids, you're getting my clothes dirty." And he walks in at home just in time to hear his wife say, as she scrapes plates of food into the sink, "I don't know what we're going to do to get those kids of ours to eat." And he is just sick of it; it's no way to live. I don't know why, but they came.

The clergy came. That's a clinker, isn't it? The clergy came for the baptism. Along the way, they forgot something, their baptism. I know why the clergy came because I would have been in the group. You can be in the ministry so long that you begin to get used to things like sanctuaries and tables and candles and children singing. You get used to it. Remember now your Creator in the days of your youth, before the evil days come when you say, "I've lost all my appetite for life." And the years draw nigh; the grasshopper drags itself along, the clouds return after the rain, and people say, "Whatever happened to Reverend So-And-So?" And the answer's clear: he just got used to it, couldn't see it anymore, couldn't hear it anymore. The condition is called ennui.

C. S. Lewis had it, that loss of appetite. He said, "It's like a general dampness in the body. I wish it would rain. I'd rather have a rain than this general dampness that sogs my mind." Victor Hugo had it. He said, "I get up every morning and tip the urns of my life to see if there is yet one more drop for me." It happens. The clergy show up.

Most surprising to me, and I don't know why, really, is that Luke said soldiers were in line. Soldiers were in line to be baptized. They represented the power of Rome. They had blood on the tip of the sword and bragged about it. When they raised the sword, it was the power of Rome. When they put on the helmet, the breastplate, the sword, everything, the power of Rome was present. Standing like a giant colossus across the earth, one foot on land, one foot on sea: "We are the power." And yet when they take off those pieces of armor for baptism, they are like every other mother's son, trembling in fear of death. There they are.

I wonder where Jesus was in the line. Was he among the clergy? "How're you doing, brothers and sisters." I don't know. Maybe with the poor; maybe. He could have been among the rich. He went to the homes of the rich. Can you see Jesus standing among the soldiers? "Next, next." I don't like that word, *next*. This is Jesus we're talking about; "when all the people were baptized and when Jesus also . . ."

I was in a line once, a terrible line. DeKalb Medical Center, Decatur, Georgia; I had become paralyzed with Guillain-Barré. I'd never heard of it until I had it, and I was totally paralyzed, suddenly. I taught on Thursday, paralyzed on Friday. Doctors stared at me and said, "We don't know what it is, but we'll try." Nobody knows really what it is. I know I was paralyzed.

Weeks and weeks and weeks of therapy, and finally the leader of the therapy program . . . you know, they're all vicious, those therapists, they'll kill you, she stood up and said, "We have four people we're going to give a chance to stand alone tomorrow. We think they've moved to that point. They will attempt to stand alone." Four, and I was one of the four. I couldn't sleep that night. What if I fall?

The next day everybody in therapy, quite a number of people, gathered around. The instructions were clear. We'll bring those two bars that you hold onto to stand, we'll bring them together, you'll wheel your chair in between them, we'll pull the chair away, you'll pull yourself up on the bars, and then we'll pull the bars away. If you stand to the count of 10, we'll applaud, and you'll get ice cream.

Charlie was first. Old Charlie had a stroke. He drooled, he could hardly speak, his mouth was drawn. He seemed a fine person. He told me he went to school two years; he went through the second grade. He was a dairyman. He was a fine fellow except he drooled, I didn't like to eat with him, he drooled. You know Charlie is the one who was in that plane; maybe you read about it. They put a Holstein cow in an airplane, an old DC-3, and circled over Atlanta while Charlie milked that cow. He's the only person who's milked a cow over Atlanta. He told me that story 897 times.

Charlie was first. He went out there. We were all hoping and praying. They pulled the bars away, Charlie stands, one, two, three, he went down. This hard-nosed therapist said calmly, "Maybe next time, Charlie." They caught him; they didn't let him fall.

Earl was next. Earl worked on these big trucks, 18-wheelers. Big, brawny, tough guy, full of profanity and strength. The jack slipped, he was crushed, and he's in there with the rest of us, and he's mad as he can be. He's next. I saw the clenching of his jaw and I said to myself, "He'll make it just on willpower." They pulled the bars away, they counted to ten, they could have counted to twenty, he was a tough customer, and we all applauded, and he got ice cream.

Elizabeth was next. Elizabeth was a single woman, a retired schoolteacher. She had a single-car accident. "I was not drinking." "I didn't say you were drinking." "Well, you looked like you were about to say I was drinking." "No, no."

She was a nice lady in a way but she didn't like her therapist. I said, "What's the matter?" "She treats me like a child. Why do people treat old people like children, we're not children." I said, "Aw, she doesn't do that. She's a nice person." "Yes, she does. You get on the cot next to me tomorrow in exercise and listen."

So I got on the next cot; she had a crushed pelvis, and the therapist was moving the leg out to one side. Then I heard Elizabeth say, "Oh, oh, that hurts." And the therapist said, "The reason it hurts is that you're feeling a lot of pain in the area of your discomfort." I said, "You're right, Elizabeth."

They pulled the bars away, she stands . . . eight, nine, ten, she made it. We all applauded, she got ice cream.

I was the fourth and last. I waited, I waited, I waited, I wanted to be introduced. Next we have Dr. Fred B. Craddock, Rev. Dr. Fred B. Craddock, the Bandy Distinguished Professor of New Testament and Preaching at Candler School of Theology, Emory University, so on and on and on . . . You know what she said? She said, "Next!" I moved up there; I was determined, trembling, but determined. They pulled the bars away . . . seven, eight, nine, ten. I made it. I stood alone and I was only sixty-four years old. I got ice cream.

I don't like for anybody to call me and say, "Next!" I have a name; I'm different from others. Lines are demonic. I tried to get that clear in my head when I was invited to Riverside Church in New York some years ago. Bill Coffin was pastor and he said, "Can you come up and fill the pulpit? I have to be away, so on and so on." I said "Yes." It was in the summer. I was free. I went to New York. He said, "You can stay in my apartment, it's near the church. I'll tell the super that you're coming."

And so he told the super to let me in and I went into his apartment. He was a bachelor at the time, and you could tell it. It was a terrible apartment. There were sheets of paper on the floor with arrows pointing different directions. An arrow pointed this way that said kitchen, another that way said bedroom, another one this way. I was pleased with that because otherwise I would never have known one room from the other. Bill was a great preacher but he didn't keep the house.

I went into the kitchen the next morning to get something from the refrigerator for breakfast. A note on the refrigerator said, "There's nothing in here, Fred. Don't look inside." Of course, I looked inside; there was nothing in there. He said go to the church and there's breakfast there. I thought, great, I'll eat with the staff, find out where I'm to sit, stand, who does this and that. Complete orientation. Good.

I grabbed my robe, walked to the church. When I got there, there was a line, down the side of the building and around the corner, eventually over 250 men from the street. I got in line. "Next!" I went to the little window and I got a scoop of egg, a sausage patty, a biscuit, a cup of coffee. "Next!" I found a place at table across from a man who had seen better days. He still had links on his cuffs, worn and dirty though they were. We ate. Finally I said to him, "Where are you from?" He said, "Well, here and Albany." I said, "What did you do in Albany?" "Stockbroker. I was doing well, too, but the bottle got me; lost my house, my job, my family, my marriage, everything, and here I am. My daughter said I could live with her as long as I stayed sober but she didn't want to raise her kids around a drunken old man. I was sober for four or five weeks and then, I couldn't do it. So I'm back."

He said, "Where are you from?" I said, "Georgia." He said, "What do you do?" I said, "I'm a preacher." He laughed and said, "It gets all of us, doesn't it?" When he said that to me, I wanted to get up and take a knife to hit on the glass to get everybody's attention, stand up on the table and say, "Listen, you losers. In a few minutes, I'll be in one of the great pulpits of America and you'll be back on the street. I'm not like you." But I didn't, because it would not have been true.

There is a sense in which it does not matter whether you're standing on the center podium at the Olympics, gold medal around your neck, crying through the National Anthem, or wheeled in an iron chair into the back of the sanctuary, there is a sense in which, no difference. You can be at the peak of your earning power or you can put your head in the post office window and ask, "Are the checks going to be late again this month?" There's a sense, it's the same. You can bow your neck to receive the doctor hood from the university, or you can enroll at night in a class on how to read. In a sense, it's all the same. I'm here to announce that the invitation into the kingdom of God is quite simple. A voice says, "Next!"

27

On Being Gracious

Luke 6:27–36

Darrah Rorrer is not here to read the text. I remember when she became a member of the church. I had her repeat her name, Darrah Rorrer, and I said, "It sounds like someone starting a lawnmower." No wonder she's not here. I'll read my own text from Luke, chapter 6, starting at verse 27. This is a section of the teaching of Jesus which, according to Luke, was delivered on a level place.

> But I say to you that listen, Love your enemies, do good to those who hate you, bless those who curse you, pray for those who abuse you. If anyone strikes you on the cheek, offer the other also; and from anyone who takes away your coat do not withhold even your shirt. Give to everyone who begs from you; and if anyone takes away your goods, do not ask for them again. Do to others as you would have them do to you.
>
> If you love those who love you, what credit is that to you? For even sinners love those who love them. If you do good to those who do good to you, what credit is that to you? For even sinners do the same. If you lend to those from whom you hope to receive, what credit is that to you? Even sinners lend to sinners, to receive as much again. But love your enemies, do good, and lend, expecting nothing in return. Your reward will be great, and you will be children of the Most High; for God is kind to the ungrateful and the wicked. Be merciful, just as your Father is merciful.

The Word of God.

Ten years ago today there was no Richard Lumpkin as choir master, no big choir up here taking up all the space. It's hard to imagine. Ten years ago today there was no Teri Slemons leading in worship, even though she became the worship leader and for three years was worship leader every Sunday. Ten years ago there was no Birdie at the piano singing and playing. When I preach Birdie sings; it's in the Bible; it's supposed to be that way.

Ten years ago these windows, beautiful windows that wrap around you while you worship and will be in our new building, ten years ago they were still hanging on the sagging walls of an abandoned and rotting chapel at a cottage hospital in Manchester, England. It's hard to imagine.

Ten years ago there was no Cherry Log Christian Church; that's hard to imagine. Oh, there was some murmuring, a little stirring around. Joe and Doris Burke said one day, "There ought to be a Disciples Church up here." Nettie said, "I think so too." Jack Hall said, "I think so too." Carolyn McGinness said, "Well I think it's a nice idea but Dan and I travel a lot. But I think it's a good idea."

But nothing happened. Joe and Doris Burke again said (I'm skipping the thousand times they said it in between), Joe and Doris Burke said, "Well at least we could have a service, a worship service." Nettie said, "I think we could." Jack Hall said, "I think we could." Carolyn McGinniss said, "I'll try to be there."

And so September 1, 1996, in the Pavilion owned by Jim and Joe Sisson and their families, and by their good graces we used it for some time, we had a service of Word and Table. It was after the pattern of the Disciples, as this is. There were three or four dozen of us there. The spirit was upbeat, we took an offering, and we received, according to my notes on the day, $207.03. The group decided to give it to the Good Samaritan Fund because we weren't a church and had no treasury or anything. It was a good day. We had refreshments; we've always had refreshments. I think that day we had possum pâté and sassafras tea.

I have notes on the day and there were several announcements made. One of them was, according to the urging of the group, we will meet again the sixth of October. Another one was, if we continue meeting we want to make sure that everybody is welcome. We will turn away only the people that Jesus turns away. In my notes it was also announced that there would be no distinction between male and female in positions of leadership. We had a nice day. That was the first day of September 1996.

The gestation period for Cherry Log Christian Church was seven months, during which we had seventeen worship services between September and Easter. Easter 1997, about 10 minutes before 12:00 p.m., the church was born. I think fourteen or fifteen names on the charter. Everybody seemed to have a good time except one man who waited with me with heavy brow and deeper voice. He continued to come regularly but he had an objection about the day. I asked him what it was and he said, "The Scripture you read."

I said, "What was wrong with it?"

He said, "Bad choice."

I said, "Well, those were words of Jesus."

And he said, "Well, there are a lot of words in the Bible that are out of keeping with the spirit of our time. It's just out of touch. What people expect of the church now-a-days is not a lot of talk about cross-bearing and loving enemies, they want to come to church to feel better, be a part of a group that will help them be successful. In a case or two maybe some therapy but otherwise, we get together to mutually enjoy each other, so knock off the 'ought' and 'must' and 'should.'"

I said, "Why?"

And he said, "It sets the bar too high. If you keep doing it, you'll never have a church." He said, "Aw, there'll always be these little cinderblock churches where people meet once a week to make each other miserable and if you're not careful, you'll be one of those. Don't be out of touch with the spirit of the time."

He kept coming; was a sincere and good person. When time came to put the name on the line as a member, he never did. Though he continued to come, he never did. He objected to those words. I read them to you this morning. I read to you this morning the same Scripture that was used ten years ago. "If you love those who love you, what credit is that to you? Even sinners do that."

Jesus, according to Luke, had prayed on the mountain that night, prayed all night. And the next morning, from among the disciples who now followed him, he selected twelve, called them apostles, to be with him and go out in his name and minister. After he selected them, Luke says he went down to a level place. I remind you this is Luke. You know Matthew has this teaching "on a mountain" because he elevates Jesus as the new Moses, bringing the law of God to the earth.

But Luke has Jesus come down on a level place, one of the people. Around him gather three circles, the Twelve immediately around him, the apostles, and then the larger group of disciples from whom they were selected. And then the third ring around him, those who are interested in what he is saying but not quite ready to make any kind of commitment or confession. And to them all he said, "If you love people who love you, big deal. (My translation.) What credit is that to you? Sinners do that. If you do good to those who do good to you, what credit is that to you? Sinners do that. If you lend to people who lend to you, what credit is that to you? Sinners do that."

You are to love and to do good and to lend to people who will have absolutely no thanks to you, no gift in return, no positive response, no love to you, no kindness to you. Why? Because that's the way God does, that's the way God is. If you want to be my follower you do not let your life become dictated by the people around you. The people who reject you determine your life? No. The people who accept you determine your life? No. Enemies define your life? No. Friends define your life? No. The people who hate you, the people who love you do not create your character. Your character is created by the character of God.

Now, what is the character of God? God is kind to the ungrateful and to the selfish. That's what he said. And the critic there in worship that day, September 1, 1996, bless his heart, said, "Now don't start off setting the bar too high. You'll never have a church. Stay in touch with the times, don't get out there in never never land where nobody lives."

God is kind to everybody. You're to be children of God. The people who've attended here through the years know that once in a while I throw out a Greek word to remind them that I know more than they do. The New Testament was written in Greek and in the expression three times repeated, what credit is that to you, the word translated "credit" is the word which everywhere else is translated "grace." What grace is that? If you love those who love you, where's the grace? If you do good to those who do good to you, where's the grace? If you lend to those who lend to you, where's the grace? There's no grace.

This is the principle: We are to be gracious as God is gracious. The final work of grace in anyone's life is to make a person gracious, but don't set the bar too high. Stay in touch with reality. Don't go floating off. It is a beautiful expression, isn't it? God is kind to the ungrateful and to the wicked.

When I'm studying Scripture, I don't know how it is with you, but when I study Scripture, I also take my five senses and try to relate to the text. What does it taste like, what does it smell like, what does it feel like, what does it sound like? This Scripture, "God is kind to the ungrateful and the wicked," when I put it to my ear, what does it sound like?

I recalled boyhood experiences. Our nearest neighbors down in West Tennessee were an African-American family, John and Jeanetta Graves and their sons, Lee Grant and J.W. They had a well in the backyard with a windlass that you used to crank up the bucket and get the water, just like we did. But theirs was a shallow well and sometimes John Graves would come up and call out, "Mr. Fred" and Daddy would go out there and John would have a couple of buckets. "I came to get some water, our well is dry." And my father would always pick up a stone, rub the dirt off of it as best he could and drop it in our well. That's the way he could tell how much water we had. If it was just kind of a shallow, cheap, tinnish splish, my father would say to John, "Well, we're going to have to divide this. Looks like we'll have something to drink, maybe wash our hands, but no bath tonight, John." But when he dropped a stone in there and it went, "kerplunk," my father would say, "Take all you want; take enough to have a bath, John." And John would say, "Now let's not get carried away."

When I read this Scripture I hear "kerplunk"; deep and profound, but I remember what the man said, "Don't set the bar too high." It is a beautiful expression. Stephen Webb calls it the language of sacred excess, beautiful to read, lovely to contemplate, marvelous in our ideals, but, but, but, it's not where anybody lives. You cannot be gracious in the world because relationships are complex and painful and awkward and some need so much attention. And some relationships are so high maintenance you simply can't be gracious.

I remember shortly before our service on that Sunday in 1996, I was down at the post office in Blue Ridge and some prisoners were working on the sidewalk. You know they use prisoners for that work. You could tell by their stripes that they were prisoners. There was a guard with two guns. They were finishing up their work on the sidewalk and when I came out I noticed how nice it was and I said, "Thank you, fellows; it looks real nice. You did a good job." And the guard said, "You don't thank them; they're prisoners." It's hard to be gracious in a world like ours.

During the Vietnam War I was asked to have a preaching workshop for chaplains up at Fort Belvoir in Virginia. In the evening I ate with the commissioned officers, lieutenants and captains. I think there was a lieutenant colonel there. Had a nice meal. Our table was waited upon by a young man in army green. I looked at him several times. I nodded my gratitude to him but he never said anything. I looked at his shirt pocket to see his name. I was going to call him by name but it didn't have his name. So I just said to him, "Well, I would thank you, whatever your name is; I don't see a name." He never said a word. The officer next to me said, "He doesn't have a name. We have several conscientious objectors that work here, that wait tables, clean the toilets and anything else we don't want to do, they do. But they have no names. They're conscientious objectors." It is difficult in a world like ours to be gracious.

Allegheny, Pennsylvania; Robert McCall had aplastic anemia. "Have to have a bone marrow transplant or you're going to die, Robert." He was thirty-nine years old. Found a cousin named David, perfect match, perfect match. Hallelujah! Time came for the transplant and David said, "I'm not going to do it. I'm not going to have the pain. I'm not going to run the risk, I'm not going to do it."

Robert was so angry and so disappointed; he took the case to Common Pleas Court, Judge Flaherty presiding. Made the case before the judge and the judge said, "Robert, we have all kinds of laws in this state about taking life and hurting life, but we don't have a single law that compels anybody to give life, not a one. I can't, this Court can't, make David give you life. And this Court cannot make you forgive David for not doing it. There are some matters beyond the Court, they're matters of the heart." Where's the grace here, where's the grace?

The fellow at the service said, "Don't set the bar too high."

I said, "Well, I'm not setting the bar."

He said, "Yeah, but you picked that Scripture. There are other Scriptures."

I said, "That's true."

He said, "Get real or you'll never have a church."

What I said that day is what I say today. It makes no sense and ultimately I think is of no value for us to think of the grace of God as simply something to wallow around in and feel good, like in a warm bath. To talk about being saved by the grace of God and grace covers all our sins and all that. It's true, it's true, but that's not all that's true. It is also said that if you only love people who love you, give to people who give to you, do good to people who do good to you, where is the grace? Where is the grace? You're to be as God is, gracious.

It came home to me not long ago here in church; I come here now and then. And the Sunday I was here, it was the early part of summer, and a former student was here in worship. I hadn't seen him since the early '80s. He was my student at Emory, in the seminary, made a minister, good prospect; there he was worshiping with us. I went over to him, "You'll have to help me with the name, I remember the face."

He gave me the name. He said, "I know it was a big class."

I said, "Yeah."

He said, "I just came up to tell you that I have left the ministry and I have left the church."

"You came to tell me that?"

He said, "You were gracious to me and I wanted you to hear it from me and not from someone else." And he left. When I went out to my vehicle he was standing in the parking lot.

He came over and said, "Do you remember the time in class when you were stressing focus on the biblical text in the sermon, then say one thing, one thing, one thing, don't go chasing rabbits. Just say one thing. And you said to us, 'Tomorrow when you come to class, bring one Scripture verse. If you had your choice to preach the rest of your life on one verse, what would that one verse be?' You remember that, Prof.?"

I said, "Yes, yes, I remember."

He said, "I don't expect you to remember what mine was."

I said, "Well you're right, I don't."

He said, "Psalm 23, verse 1. The Lord is my shepherd, I shall not want." He said, "Prof., I remember yours." Because they'd heckled me and said, "Come now, come on now, what's yours, Prof., what's yours?" You know students have no respect.

So I said, "What was mine?"

"Yours was Luke 6:35. 'God is kind to the ungrateful and the wicked.'"

I said, "Is your verse still true?"

He said, "Oh, it's still true. I turned loose of God but God has not turned loose of me. The Lord is my shepherd."

I said, "Great!"

He said, "And your verse, is it still true?"

I said, "Yes, yes, still true, still true."

28

But If the Answer Is No

Luke 10:1–11

It would be rather easy to get the impression that Jesus did not want many disciples. Our text last Sunday spoke of persons who would have been his disciples. One said, "I'll follow you wherever you go." And Jesus said, "Foxes have holes, and birds of the air have nests; but the Son of Man has nowhere to lay his head" (Matt. 8:20). That's not exactly inviting. "Lord, I'll follow you wherever you go, but let me first bury my father." "Let the dead bury the dead, you come and follow me." That doesn't draw a crowd. "I'll follow you wherever you go, but let me first say goodbye to my family." "If you put your hand to the plow and look back, you're not fit for the kingdom of God."

It would be easy to get the impression that Jesus did not want many disciples. Of course, historians of religion know that this was the pattern of teachers and wise leaders in ancient times. They screened fairly carefully would-be followers. A guru, a wise man lives up in the mountains in a cabin, isolated. A would-be disciple goes up and knocks on the door. The wise man comes to the door. "What do you want?" "I want to be your disciple." He slams the door in his face. The person goes the second day. "I want to be your disciple." And the wise man spits on him and closes the door. The third day, "I want to be your disciple." And the wise man hits him with a stick and closes the door. Finally the wise man listens. "I want to be your disciple." "Now I see you're sincere; come in."

So it was not Jesus alone; rabbis sometimes did this, carefully screening disciples. When we were at Chautauqua, the president of the Chautauqua Institute was telling me of the young American who wanted to be a Buddhist monk. He went to Tibet, went to the Abbot, "I want to become a monk."

"Really?"

"Yes."

"Well, it means seven years of silence, after which you get two words."

"Yes."

After seven years of total silence, the Abbot called him in and said, "You now can say two words."

He said, "Cold breakfast."

"Are you going to stay?"

"Yes."

"Well, it means seven years and then two words." Seven years of total silence and then two words. The Abbot called him in, "You can now say two words."

He said, "Hard bed."

"Are you going to stay?"

"Yes."

Seven more years, after which he called him in and said, "You now have two words."

He said, "I quit."

And the Abbot said, "Well, it's just as well. You've done nothing but complain ever since you've been here."

It would be easy to get the impression that Jesus didn't just want any and everybody. And yet in our text today he has quite a large group, from which he selects teams, thirty-five teams, to go out before him and preach. He is popular in a way. There are a lot of people who say "yes" to him in spite of the demands. I'm not really surprised, personally. I find that people prefer a challenge, prefer something that's demanding, prefer something that's important, something that demands discipline and sacrifice, rather than just mealy mouthed, watered down, anybody can do it, there's nothing to it, you don't really have to do anything, you don't even have to be there kind of an invitation. People want more. Young people want more than just a ski trip to Aspen when they come to the church. People expect that the God of heaven will expect something of them, sometimes at great cost.

When we were at Chautauqua, I took the liberty of preaching on a text from James in which it was quite clear that one of the virtues of the Christian life in that circle of Christianity was constraint. Curbing appetite, not satisfying appetite, but curbing appetite. Self-control was considered a virtue in those days and I talked about curbing the appetite. In the course of the sermon I said, "Just because you can afford it, doesn't mean you can afford it. Having the money is not a green light to getting it. As long as anybody sleeps in a cardboard box, as long as any child is hungry in the world, you cannot afford it." For what kind of life is it anyway to come to the end of it and somebody says, "What did you do?" "Well, I shopped. Had nice trips."

After the service that day, I didn't know whether I would be stoned or not because these people are, you know, able and sufficient. This elderly woman

(I say elderly, she's older than I am if you can imagine that), said she wanted to talk to me. I said, "Yes."

She said, "I'm in the process of finishing our home, our retirement home." And I said, "Yes?"

"My husband and I have been planning this home for some time and it's about finished."

"Where is it?"

"It's right at the edge of Pittsburgh in the suburbs."

"Nice home, I take it?"

"Yes, $1.4 million."

And she described it. Six bathrooms is the only thing I remember but you know what goes with that. I said, "How many people are going to live in this?"

"Well, it was to be for my husband and me, but he died last year."

"You're going to live in that by yourself? $1.4 million?"

She said, "Well, my husband made a lot of money."

I said to her, "You cannot afford that house. I'm not talking economically, I'm talking about being a Christian." A trophy house at the end of life? Surely not. And she wanted me to say something about it. Just as some of you are ill at ease with the way you spend your money.

So Jesus made it clear. "When you go now, when you tell people about the kingdom of God, I want you not to take a lot of extra stuff. Just go with what you have. Depend on the hospitality of those who welcome you. And when you go, don't move around from house to house looking for the best place. 'Boy, that bed's hard. I'm going to try to find another place tomorrow night.' No, you stay where you are because I don't want anybody to get the impression that you're making economic differences in the name of God. Whether it is a straw mattress or something that causes you to float in midair, you accept it, and whatever they set before you, you eat it. Don't look down at the table and say, 'Oh goodness, okra again.'"

What does he mean by eating what is set before you? He means that what is set before you sometimes will be Jewish food, sometimes Gentile food. "Don't reject one or the other because I do not want anyone to think we make any racial or ethnic distinctions before God; not economic, not racial, national, ethnic, not at all. I want you to make it clear that everybody, whether they eat out of the Community Food Pantry in Ellijay, or entertain thirty guests at table with gourmet food, before God is the same. Is that clear?"

"Yes, that's clear."

"And then I want you to say to them, 'Now, the kingdom of God is here.' That's the good news; God's love and grace is here in the person of Jesus Christ. Now, you will go into some places and they will reject you. You won't be welcome, no hospitality, no food, no anything."

"Well, what are we to do?"

"You are to leave, following the ancient pattern of shaking the dust off your feet, and leaving. In other words, just say, I leave you to God. You are not to fuss at the people."

"But what if they say 'no' to the message?"

"It's not up to you to get anybody to say 'yes' or to get anybody to say 'no.' How they respond is not your business. Leave that to God. You just give the good news."

"But if they reject it . . ."

"If they reject it, the message is the same. To those who accept it you say, 'The kingdom of God is here.' To those who reject it, you say, 'The kingdom of God is here.' The message is the same because I want you to understand that your message, your life, your behavior, your relationships are not determined by other people. Whether they say 'yes' or 'no,' that's not the point. You are to be children of God. Don't you remember the teaching? If you speak to those who speak to you, what's that? Pagans do that. If you're nice to those who are nice to you, what's that? If you invite those who invite you, what's that? If you're generous to those who are generous to you, what's that? You're to be as God is, who gives the rain and the sun, on the good and the bad, the just and the unjust alike. Why? Because God is love and love does not react to anybody and say, 'So, if you're going to be like that'; God is God and God acts out of God's own character, which is love. Now that is the way you are to be. If someone says 'no' that's not the point. Your job is to say, 'Good news, God loves you.'"

I think that is probably, for me at least, the most difficult of the teachings of Jesus. "Do not react to anybody's behavior but act out of your own character as a child of God. For God is kind, even to the ungrateful and selfish." How can God do that? The same way you can; the same way I can.

I spent a lot of time this week flipping back and forth in the Old Testament and the New Testament. Late at night and early in the morning I was using my concordance and my references trying to find a passage that would support us and would justify an occasion in which I would be in the right if I were unkind to somebody, a family member, neighbor, business partner, clerk, client. I was looking for a verse in which I could have scriptural support for reacting to unkindness with unkindness. I could not find a verse; I could not find a single verse. You see, the final work of grace, the top of the stack work of grace in anyone's life is not just going to heaven. "I want to go to heaven." Of course you do. The final work of grace is to make a person gracious, to be gracious as God is. Even to those who say, "No."

29

Familiar Questions, Strange Answers

Luke 13:1–9

Some of you will notice that I have departed from the planned text and sub-ject. Although you see a residue of the former order of worship in the bulletin and on the cover of the bulletin, it seemed wise to change. It means, there-fore, that I will be walking in the sermon outside the area of my knowledge and expertise, but the members here are accustomed to that. In fact, if I only talked about matters in which I was an expert, I would be silent every week.

But I have the good example of Jesus in this regard. He was on his way to Jerusalem and he was teaching the people. Yet he met an audience that was not paying attention because they were preoccupied with two tragedies. They were in shock; they were angry, they were grieving. They felt helpless; they wanted revenge for the actions of Pilate, the governor of Judea, the Roman appointee, ten years the master of their lives in that little land. Pilate had, pro-voked or unprovoked, we do not know, taken the occasion when there were some worshipers in the temple, some pilgrims from Galilee, while they were at their prayers and offering the sacrifice, to send his soldiers to kill them in the act of worship. While kneeling in prayer, they were slaughtered. By that one act, he not only ended a number of lives; he changed forever many more.

The Tower of Siloam had fallen. We don't know a lot about this tower; we do know towers were built primarily of stone and were part of fortification and security. They were built into the walls around fortified cities. Strategic military places had towers, as did other areas needing protection. It might have been, I'm only guessing, that the pool of Siloam, a spring with a reser-voir, was so strategically valuable for the residents or for any attacking army that a tower was built at Siloam to guard, to protect.

Whether someone tinkered with the tower and loosened some stones or whether it fell through faulty construction or old age, we don't know, but one

day the tower fell. How many people were hurt? We do not know. When they
removed the rubble, they found eighteen bodies. The people before Jesus had
questions. Following any tragedy that seems absolutely indiscriminate in its
nature and unbelievable in its size, people have questions, just as we do. The
obvious one, already addressed by Teri, "What can we do?" Pray, give, give
blood, encourage support, help the families, volunteer for common labor in
removal of rubble, anything that can be done to help. That's what we can do.

We have questions about appropriateness. What is the appropriate thing
to do? "Shall we go ahead with the festival?"

"Well . . ."

"Are we going ahead with the birthday party?"

"Well . . ."

"Can we go out and play?"

"No, no, no."

"Can we go to the movies?"

"Well, I don't think that would be appropriate."

"Can we go swimming?"

"Well . . ."

"Well, what about the wedding Charles and Ethel are going to have next
week? Are they going to have it?"

"Well, the family will have to decide."

This seems to be a small matter but it is not a small matter because most of
the time we give attention to what is appropriate and inappropriate. No one
wants to seem unfeeling, unsympathetic. That is not an unimportant question.

And there is a question of justice. In our case, we know there are people
whose task it is to exercise expertise in the locating of criminals and bringing justice in the case of crime, horrendous crime included. Americans trust
that those who have that task will carry it out with patience and precision,
not indiscriminately. Surely we have grown past the point, matured past the
point, when we flail and use our power across the world without discrimina-
tion. Surely we have passed that. It makes you ache to hear already of the graf-
fiti on the doors of garages because the people there are from the Near East.
It makes you sick to hear that in Australia a school bus of Muslim children
was attacked. Why? "Well, we're supporting America." It makes you sick to
see the flames of a Lebanese church burning. Why? It's a Christian group.
"But they are Lebanese and we are supporting our country." Please, haven't
we learned?

In World War I, when we went to war against the Germans, people who
lived in this country who were of German descent and had lived in this country as a family for generations and generations, suddenly, because their name
was Schnauzer or Klein or Rauschenbusch, eggs on the porch, screens cut,

crosses burned in the yard. "What did we do?" "Your name is Rauschen-busch." We've grown past that; that was World War I.

In World War II, we hadn't quite learned. We put in compounds Japanese Americans, many of whom, many of whom, had sons who were serving in the American military fighting the Japanese. Surely we have matured past "blast them all," haven't we?

The people in Jesus' audience had another question and so do we. Why these? Why these victims? What did they do? They didn't even know what was going on. They had nothing to do with it. They are somebody's wife, mother, son, daughter, brother, sister, trying to do their work and suddenly gone. Why these? And they looked at Jesus, the Son of God, and they said, "Why these? Why were these Galileans who, in the hour of worship while they were helpless, their backs turned, slaughtered by a cruel, cruel man who stopped the temple worship, stopped all traffic, closed all the shops and sat grinning at the world?" That's exactly what he wanted. Why these particular ones? "Well, Jesus is the Son of God and he has answers; we'll ask Jesus."

"Jesus, why these?" And he didn't give an answer. You would expect him to talk a little bit about the will of God. A lot of people I've talked to already talk about the will of God. I find so many people saying it so easily but Jesus very seldom. He struggled with it in hours of prayer, and yet others say with certainty, "The will of God." He did not say any of that. In fact, he gave an answer that was not an answer. You know, sometimes the words of Jesus are the most unwelcome words you can get. You just want to close the Bible and get on with your business. There's nothing there that's going to really help us to do the job. "So what do you say, Jesus?"

And Jesus said, "Unless you repent, you will all perish." "What? We're the victims here. What did we do? We didn't do anything. We're not guilty. What do you mean 'repent'? Repent of what?"

I don't know. I'll be personal; you can take it for what it's worth. Some-times I need to repent of feelings of moral superiority. Crises and tragedies tend to make two groups out of the whole universe. The good ones and the bad ones and we're the good ones. There is no question about the moral excellence of American people in crises. What has been given in money and blood and work is just unbelievable. But then I notice that the governor of New York has to call out more National Guard because people are going into damaged buildings and stealing computers and telephones and money. Who are these thieves? They're Americans; just as American as you and I. I must repent of any feeling of moral superiority.

I noticed that they're warning us now about fake charities. Somebody is setting up fake charities, using this terrible tragedy as an occasion to make a lot of money. Who's doing this? Americans, brothers and sisters of those who labor twenty-four hours without rest to help somebody they don't even know. I noticed the mayor in New York said, "We're watching you, those of you guilty of price gouging, charging two prices now for a rental car, charging two prices for gasoline." Who are the people making money off this? My fellow Americans. I have to watch feelings of moral superiority.

A man said to me as Nettie and I were coming back Tuesday evening from Kentucky. We had stopped at a rest stop and a man said to me, "You know, this terrorist stuff really sucks."

I said, "What's the matter?"

He said, "I was supposed to start my vacation this weekend." He looked American to me.

Brothers and sisters, think, be humble, all America united except some of us who are making a buck off this. "Repent," Jesus said. What a strange thing to say. I know in my case I am spending a lot of time raising the question, "Why do people in other countries of the world hate us so? Why do they hate us?" It's not enough to say, "Oh, they envy our way of life. They envy our luxuries; they envy our possessions. They envy our houses and cars, so, so, so." But why hate us so? Is there, is there some unevenness in the way we treat other people in the world? Blessing these with great favor, sending guns and planes and billions in help and over there, not even acknowledging they exist. This one gets the latest jet; that one gets to throw rocks. I don't know. I'm spending a lot of time asking myself by what standard does this country treat people with favored or unfavored status. It may have nothing to do with anything but I just wonder why? I know this much, I know this much, that the most dangerous people in the world are the hopeless people. What is there to lose?

Something I've repented of and I'm kind of embarrassed about this, I'm repenting of the extent to which I have allowed the movie screen and the television screen to tell me what world I live in. We all know it is a fact that what you see tends to be the world you live in. You know the story of the Chinese emperor who saw some men leading an ox down the street, going to the temple where the ox would be slaughtered in the ceremony. The emperor was so moved seeing that ox taken down the street to be killed, he said to his aides, "Go out there and release the ox. Give them a sheep." Later, someone asked the emperor, "Do you like an ox better than you like a sheep?" He said, "Well, no, not necessarily. It's just that I saw the ox." What you see affects you so much.

Two cases against a railroad, same railroad; two families brought suit against the railroad over an intersection that was not well marked and was very dangerous. In the one family, a son, teenaged son was killed at that place by the train. From another family, a son, one leg cut off by the train. Both went to court. The family whose son was killed, asking for several million dollars, got nothing. The family whose son had a leg removed got several million dollars. That does not seem fair. Killed, and nothing? Lost a leg, millions. Well, this is the way it works. The family that had a son who lost the leg wheeled him into the courtroom every day in front of the jury. The other family's son was out of sight in the graveyard.

What we see so creates our world that I forget sometimes that even the news is put on by people who are doing that to make money. News now is show business and yet I fail to remember that is what it is and so I allow myself to think that's the way the world is. And yet, what do they not show me? This crisis has reminded me that they have not shown me pictures of two million Congolese, dead, starved, diseased, beaten, shot. Two million! Where are the pictures?

Three million, over three million, Cambodians killed. Long afterwards, when the bulldozers were piling up these human skulls, "What is that?" Americans asked. "They're the skulls of the killed." "How gross." Three million! No cameras there, no cameras there. That didn't become a part of my consciousness, my groaning, my aching, my praying because they were showing me other things. The American people, I am sorry to say, the American people, have had more camera time on the belly button of Britney Spears than on the dying poor of the world. Is that right or is that wrong? I don't blame them; they're in business to make money. I blame myself. To be so deluded that I let these cameras create my world. A Christian has another camera, a camera of the mind and heart.

There was a man who planted a fig tree. It was time for harvest; it had grown enough to bear fruit. And so he went out with his gardener, but there was no fruit. And the man who owned it said, "Look, I've been looking for fruit for three years. There's no fruit; cut it down." And the gardener said, "Please, sir. Will you let me dig around it? Will you let me fertilize it? And then, after a year, if there's no fruit, we'll cut it down." And the owner said, "OK." In other words, the grace, the patience, the love, the waiting of God is still with us. We still have the grace of God with us and God said, "I'll wait on them. They're at Cherry Log. I'll wait on them—at least another year."

I am amazed at the grace and the patience of God.

30

Party Time

Luke 15:1–3, 11–32

I suppose you've noticed that some people will celebrate anything. It is remarkable actually. She calls and says, "You know that diet I've been on for two years?" "Yes." "Well, the scales say that I've lost five pounds. I thought we'd have a few friends in; I've made a chocolate fudge cake. I bought a gallon of strawberry ice cream; we want to celebrate this."

He calls and says, "You know our plumbing has been backed up for four days. Well, the Roto-Rooter man finally came; he has it unclogged, everything is flushing. Thought we'd have a few folk in and celebrate."

They call. "We've rented the community room at Cherry Log. We have a live band; we're going to have a great time. Like for you to come." "I'll be glad to be there. What are we celebrating?" "It's Tuesday." Good enough for me.

Some people will celebrate anything, but I must say to you there are some times when I cannot go to the party. It's not because I looked over the guest list and somebody will be there that I don't like. If you have that attitude, you'll never go to a party because there's always somebody there you don't like. It's not your list; you're the guest.

It's not because I think the party is premature as some people do. Never celebrate anything because, they say, "It's too early to have that party." A baby is born. "Well, it's too early; you never know how he'll turn out." A wedding? "Well, you never know if they'll stay married." Made good grades? "Well, you better hold off; you haven't graduated yet." There are some people who think all celebrations are premature. I'm not one of those. I simply can't go to some parties because the occasion for celebration I just cannot handle. Such parties seem to me inappropriate.

When I taught at Emory I had a colleague and good friend who was diagnosed after a long delay, his wife fussing at him forever and ever about going to a doctor. He finally went. The large tumor in his leg was malignant. The chemo started and we visited him in the hospital. He was rather upbeat; he was going to get well. The doctor said, "One way we can stave it off is to remove the leg." They took his leg off just above the knee and I received a little invitation. In his hospital room at Emory we were going to celebrate the burial of that leg. A few friends gathered; the leg was buried. The school did not know it. Don't you tell them, but it was buried just outside Cannon Chapel below my window. Not supposed to do that. "Fred, I'd like for you to come, we're going to have a few friends in." I couldn't go. I just could not go. I was with him, supported him, encouraged him, prayed for him, but a denial party produces a kind of giddiness in people that is not celebratory. I just couldn't go.

A young minister I know, a second career minister and a woman, married, several children, decided she needed some space. Her husband was a good man, a Christian man, supportive and encouraging, loving to her and the children. He was well spoken of, but she said, "I need more space if I'm really going to be a minister," so she said, "I've got to jettison my husband." I received an invitation to the divorce. Good student, in three of my classes, fine person, but I couldn't go to celebrate the divorce. I'm not alone, I don't think I am alone, in being unable to celebrate some occasions.

The Scriptures tell us repeatedly that there are some things that God cannot celebrate. God cannot celebrate the death of the wicked, even though I know ministers in churches that seem to enjoy that, looking over the banister of heaven and seeing the wicked writhing in the pit and saying, "You got what was coming to you, ha, ha, ha." God cannot do that. There are some times you just don't think you can make it to the party. One such time comes to mind with this text.

It's going to be a good party; kill the fatted calf. The fatted calf; not those little hors d'oeuvres. I mean, we're talking about serious food here. Wiener Schnitzel, cordon bleu, veal cutlets, plenty of food; not those little triangles, you know, the cucumber sandwiches. Is that what they are? Or the little slice of an olive that sits on a Ritz. No, it's going to be a good party. Live band; that always fires it up. I don't care what kind of party it is, if you have live music, not some DJ playing records, I mean a real band, tuning up their instruments, and here we go. After several sets they may even take requests. If they're old enough, I might have the nerve to yell out "Smoke Gets in Your Eyes." You're not that old, but it's a good one. "Some Enchanted Evening." And if they look like a mountain band, I can go with that. We'll have a sing along: "You Are My Sunshine," or my favorite, "It's Been So Bad Since You've Been Gone, It's Just Like When You Was Here."

It's going to be a good party. Live band; there's going to dancing. You don't have to know how to dance any more. It used to be when you went to a dance, you had to know how to dance. Everything now is regarded as dancing, and if you're getting a little decrepit, wait 'til the shank of the evening and everybody will do the "San Antonio Stroll." It's going to be a nice party and all the invitation said was, "Welcoming home our son." Hey, that's always occasion for celebration, welcome home the son. I don't know where he's been; where's he been? College? Welcome home, son. Spend the summer here, we'll fatten you up. That's good. Where's he been? I don't know. Peace Corps? I'm always moved by young people volunteering to give two years of their lives in the peak of their youth, two years, in some remote place of the world, to live with and work with and serve people. That's marvelous. Is that it? Welcome home, son. What is it? I don't know. Maybe he's sick, maybe several months in the Mayo Clinic up there in Rochester, Minnesota. You know they have McDonald's houses nearby for the families to stay. Stayed there four months; he had some strange disease but, you know, the bone marrow transplant worked. He's coming home. Welcome home, son. Whew! This is really going to be a party.

Where's he been? You idiot, you don't know where he's been? He's been eating with the hogs, living with the hogs, acting like a hog. Took every penny of his inheritance and blew it on wine, women and song. Paid out hundreds of dollars to women who sell their favors, lost his clothes, lost his job, can't find a job except slopping some pigs. And now, once in a while, you can see him over there eating with the pigs. He has abandoned his religion; he has trampled on everything his parents taught him. He has been in the far country. Phew! Then why is he coming home? Because he's hungry.

You get down and out, I don't care how much pride you have, sooner or later you're going to come home. When you hit the wall, you're going to come home. When you hit bottom, you're going to come home. It's not like it used to be; sit at the dinner table and discuss whether you're going to see the opera, or go to see a Shakespearean play, it's a matter of, is there anything to eat? He needs a bed and a bath and a meal. That's why he's home. We all come back when it gets hard enough. In fact, some people not only come back, but they get religion. You can ask every prison warden in the country. "Oh yeah, they can strut around and say, 'I didn't do it; I didn't do it,' but when they hear that gate clang behind them, they want the chaplain and they want a Bible and they find Jesus." Oh yeah, oh, yeah, they come back when it really, really gets rough. That's why he's home.

Then why are they having a party, for goodness' sake? That seems absolutely inappropriate that you would have a party. Let him come home? Yeah, I think all parents ought to let them come home. I don't care what they've done, let them come home. But come in the back door, eat in the kitchen, lay low for awhile, get work clothes on and get back out there in the field and earn your place again. Earn the respect of your neighbors. Earn the respect of your brother. Earn the respect of your family. But a party? I think that party is a little premature and very inappropriate.

You know the woman that celebrated losing five pounds? I saw her in the grocery; she's gained it back and at least twenty more. It doesn't last long. You remember the party we had for that fellow who celebrated six months of sobriety? "Haven't touched a drop in six months; let's have a party." I saw it in the paper, arrested for public drunkenness. They go back around. You remember the party we had for the fellow who got out of jail? Out of jail, never again, celebrate, wonderful party. He's in jail again. What's the percentage of those in jail that go back to jail? Now he has come home, but he gets a few good meals, gets a change of clothes and you know what, you know what? A party? That seems absolutely nonserious. What he has done is serious. I think he needs to be taught a lesson. If you want my advice, the story you heard read this morning by Bill, my response to the family is, teach that young man a lesson. And you can't teach a lesson when you have tables filled with food. "Come in, make yourself several sandwiches, I want to teach you a lesson." That's a contradiction. Music and dancing, Mom and Dad out on the floor doing the Charleston saying, "Son, we're going to teach you a lesson." Where's the lesson in that? There's no lesson in that.

I think he needs to be taught a lesson. And when you pile the table up with food, bring in a live band and have a big dance floor and everybody dancing, what lesson is taught? The only thing, and I'm honest with you here, the only thing I can imagine that he is being taught is this: "We love you, we forgive you, we're glad you're home." That's all I can think of. Is that enough for a party?

31

Looking Around During the Prayer

Luke 18:9–14

To those of us who have been around the barn a few times, it is clear that some of the stories that Jesus told need to be repaired or as we say in the south, they need fixin'. Not long ago we had one of these stories. Luke seems to have gathered the most offensive of them; it was the story of the Prodigal Son. I decided to preach it as it was. I had been invited by a church in north Georgia to preach on that text on that Sunday, and I did. But I gave it just as it was. There was a man who had two sons. The older son stayed home and worked and did the father's bidding. The younger son went away into a far country, lived among Gentiles apparently, fed the hogs, came into terrible times and decided to return home. As he approached the house, the father met him, embraced him, kissed him. And the son said, "Father, I have sinned against heaven and in your sight; I am not worth calling your son. Make me a slave." But they brought the robe and the rings. They hired the fiddlers, they killed the calf, they had a party upon his return.

I thought it was appropriate that I say to the people that God frustrates the proud and gives grace and forgiveness to the humble sinner. After the service my wife and I were taken to lunch by an attorney in that church and his wife. And at the lunch he said, "I really don't know whether to say I didn't like your sermon or I didn't like the text." He says, "It is easier to say I didn't like your sermon because my wife doesn't like for me to speak against the Bible."

I said, "Well, you can here. What's your problem?" And he said, "It's receiving that boy back home and having a party for him." And I said, "Well what would you have transpire?" He said, "He should have been arrested. He broke the law, he ruined the family, lived with Gentiles, ate with the pigs, totally against the law. He should have been arrested." I said, "And given a mandatory sentence?" He said, "At least six years."

174

He was serious. I tried to make light of his comments and he would have none of it. So I decided that story needs to be fixed, it was running into problems. So when I was invited to a church to teach an adult Sunday school class some distance from here, it was Sunday morning about 9:20 when I was called, "Can you teach our class?" I said, "It's Sunday already." They said, "Well, yes, but our teacher's just called and is ill. Can you come and do it?" I said, "Well I have to have time to prepare." "Oh you can do it, it's the New Testament, it's a parable. We're studying parables." "Well, which parable?" "The Prodigal Son."

I said, "OK" and I decided to fix it on the way. It had not gone over well before. And so I said, "There was a man who had two sons, the older son stayed home, did his father's bidding, worked hard on the farm. The younger son took his money, wasted it in a far country, came into hard times, decided he should come home, confess his wrong. Well, when he drew near the house, he heard music and dancing and he called one of the servants and said, 'What is this party going on?'"

"And the servant said, 'Well, you know your older brother stayed here and worked, your father appreciates him, and he's giving him a party.'"

I couldn't even get myself straightened up in front of this class before some woman yelled from the back, "That's the way it should have been." So now I knew how to deal with this Bible business.

Then Luke a few chapters later does it again. Two men at the temple to pray, the one a Pharisee, and I hope that word is not too flavored in your mind. He was a man committed to the law, oral and written law. One should obey the Word of God, night and day, twenty-four hours a day, waking and sleeping. He gave a tenth of all he had for the poor and the needy, prayed and fasted regularly, and kept himself clean. Not like adulterers and thieves and rogues. Not even like this tax collector. Give him credit. He could have run for office without any fear of someone pulling things out of the closet and getting him disqualified immediately. He was OK. He was proud of being OK.

The other, a tax collector, was a reprehensible character. He had decided to collect taxes for the Roman government from his own people. He was a political traitor. He was, in terms of citizenship, a nonentity. He couldn't serve on a jury. He couldn't do anything a normal citizen did because he was out. He couldn't even look around, he couldn't look up, he couldn't look down, he couldn't look within. He just beat his breast and said, "Please, God." And he went home justified.

Now I knew with an audience like this, that wouldn't go over so I have fixed it. When you get old, you like for people to like you. The way to make this acceptable is to consider the Pharisee is really the rogue, narrow minded and brittle, judgmental, bigoted, harsh, cruel in his treatment of others, condescending in his attitude, pinch-nosed. But the publican. I meet these all the time.

This is Joe, the bartender, a nice guy, an outsider. We love outsiders, someone who can say, "God, I thank you that I'm not like these Pharisees and all these other people who do their religious duty. I'm free of all that." He sits behind the bar, takes counsel with the people, helps those who are in distress. And is generally the healer, counselor, and pastor of the real people. Now it's all right for him to go home justified because we've given a reason within himself to be justified. He's a nice guy.

The other one with a reason not to be justified, he's a religious bigot. This is a little exercise you have to go through to make these stories acceptable. To find a reason in the person for being acceptable because there is in many of us, I can't speak for you, but there is in many of us, a fundamental idea that people should just get what they deserve. And stories like the father with two sons, the two who went up to the temple to pray and other such stories, are offensive because they deal with that rare and strange experience known as forgiveness, in which most people do not believe. Why is forgiveness so hard?

Rodney King, pulled from a truck, beaten almost to death, finally recovers, faces his attackers, goes over, shakes their hands, "I forgive you." And the reporter says, "Uh, we understand that Mr. King suffered some permanent brain damage." Why is it so hard to believe that he forgave them? You don't just forgive somebody, for goodness' sake.

I've been thinking a good deal lately about George Wallace, who died recently. I remember him first, that square-jawed man, who stood across the path to equal opportunity. "Segregation yesterday, segregation tomorrow, segregation forever." It was not just a southern disease. In the presidential primary, he took the city of Boston. He brought out a certain quality in people. They found a voice in George Wallace. George Wallace changed. I believe he really changed. The people who had supported him felt betrayed. Those who had opposed him were still suspicious, but I looked at the line of mourners as they went by his casket, all ethnic groups, all races, all kinds of people went by to pay their respects. I think he changed. Given what he did for education, given what he did for politics, I think he really changed, but before he died, he said, "I still don't understand why the American people have not forgiven me." Well, George, it's hard.

I was this week at Vanderbilt, my old graduate school. We were dilly-dallying around there having some ceremonies and talking and we fell into reminiscences of the school when I was there and a classmate of mine, Jim Lawson, a young man, a black man, now a very significant minister of the United Methodist Church in southern California. He was engaged in a sit-in in downtown Nashville, he was arrested and he was, by the chancellor of Vanderbilt University, B. Harvey Branscomb, expelled from school. Last fall, Jim Lawson was back to receive an honor, a distinctive honor. Harvey Branscomb, at that time almost 103, asked to go to the ceremony. He went to the ceremony in a wheelchair, and he asked to be taken up to Mr. Lawson, and he put out his hand and said, "Reverend Lawson, do you forgive me?" And Jim said, "I've already forgiven you" and took his hand.

One of my old teachers, bless his heart, was there on that occasion and he was heard to mutter too loudly, "It's not that simple. It's just a show." Why couldn't he accept that? Because forgiveness is very hard. It's hard to believe that it really, really takes place. Why? Part of it is just getting a lot of bad advice. People who are in a situation that calls for forgiveness get a lot of advice from friends and neighbors and relatives. "Don't you ever forgive him. But what you're to do is pretend that you do but keep bringing it up every once in a while and you will have power over that creep. For as long as you're married, you'll have it."

Others said, "Hey look, who are you? You're not perfect; nobody's perfect. Who are you to judge? Cut him a little slack for goodness' sake. My land, we're all human." Bad advice everywhere. That's probably the reason, I don't know, probably it's the fear of what other people will think.

When Helen found out Jim was having an affair, she went home to her mother. She was there for about six weeks and she had been in communication with Jim; she had decided to return and was packing her suitcase. Her mother came into the room. "What are you doing?"

"I'm packing a suitcase."

"Well I see you're packing a suitcase. Where are you going?"

"I'm going home."

"You are at home."

"I'm not at home. I'm going to my home."

"You're going back to your home? Jim will be there."

"I know it. I forgive him. I love him and I forgive him."

"What?"

"I love him and I forgive him."

"You mean, you're . . . ?"

"Yes, Mother. I'm going back. I love him and I forgive him."

"I never thought a daughter of mine would condone a thing like . . ."

"Mother, I didn't say I condoned it. I said I forgive him."

"Well, it looks the same to me. Now what are other people going to say?"

"OK, what are other people going to say?"

"One thing they're going to say for sure is that you're soft on sin, pretty soft on sin. The way you prove you're not soft on sin is never forgive anybody anything. Show your moral courage. Show your moral stature. Never in my lifetime. Then everybody will know you stand for what is right."

"Even though I personally cannot think of anything more immoral than not forgiving?"

What makes it so difficult? One day Jesus was teaching his disciples and right in the middle of the lesson, they raised their hands and said, "Whoa, whoa, whoa." That's the Greek, it's hard to get it over into English. And they said, "Increase our faith, teacher, increase our faith. What you're asking is more than we can do." What was he talking about? Going the second mile, turning the other cheek, giving your coat, feeding your . . . no, you know what he was talking about? Even if someone sins against you, repents and turns and asks for forgiveness, seven times a day, you will do it. And they said, "Increase our faith, we just can't do it."

It's extremely difficult. Why is it difficult? I think part of it is that many people feel that you have only one of two alternatives. To just cut everybody some slack and say well, you know it's not all that bad, is it?

My oldest brother when he was in the school of journalism at the University of Missouri got married one weekend, his sophomore year. It wasn't too many weekends later that they were going to be divorced. I don't know, must have had a lot of bad weather in Missouri. But he got married; it didn't work, had death written all over it. He called me and said, "Do you know any minister in Columbia, Missouri?"

I said, "Yes, I know some."

"Could you give me the name of someone with whom I could talk?"

He was absolutely devastated. And he went to a minister I suggested. He made an appointment, went in and talked to the minister, the minister said, "What's your problem, Bill?"

And he said, "Well, I think we're going to be divorced."

"That's your problem? You're on a campus, for goodness' sake. We have marriages and divorces all the time. Welcome to the club."

I don't know how many years it was before my brother returned to the church because he said, "I expected to be taken seriously."

But see many people think the only alternative they have is to be nonserious. Oh, everybody has problems. You're a liar and a cheat, somebody cheats on the spouse and all like that . . . but nobody's perfect, hey, that's the way the world is. On the other hand you have other people who choose the alternative, which they feel to be rigid, immovable, stand firm, crucify them, never let them off the hook.

And the fact of the matter is forgiveness is another alternative. Forgiveness looks like, looks like, you didn't take it seriously but feels extremely the pain of it. In order for there to be forgiveness there has to be the pain of the one who stands for what is morally right. There has to be the release of the one who says let him go.

As Reinhold Niebuhr put it, "Forgiveness negates and yet fulfills all righteousness." The only person who really can forgive is the one who has been hurt by what happened. The rest of us don't. Sitting around proving how liberal we are, how conservative we are doesn't amount to a hill of beans because it is not our case. Drink gallons of coffee, sit in all the shops, go into all the cafés, make huddles at night. "What do you think? I don't know, what do you think, what do you think? Well, the way I look at it is . . ." Do you know why we're so free with those opinions? Because we don't hurt.

But the one who feels violated, "something in me just wants to die," is the only one who can say, "I forgive you." This is why God is qualified to say, "I forgive you." This is why you have been or will be qualified to say, "I forgive you." I am willing to turn loose of my pain, this pain that has really become my identification, this pain which I have vowed to carry with me because this is who I am now, the hurt one, the victim. I am going to turn it loose.

I saw a couple recently whom I've known for years. But about eight or nine years ago, he violated the marriage vow. I was there when he said as clear as crystal, "Keep thee only unto her as long as you both shall live." And I heard him. He said, "Yes." He didn't, he didn't. It was so terribly destructive to her, to him, to the children, to the friends, to the parents. Whew! I saw them recently. They were walking along, talking, having a good time with another couple, just as happy as dead pigs in the sunshine. Or so it looked, so it looked. But were they really, were they really? Do you believe? I'm asking you a question now. Do you believe that she could really forgive him?

32

Wanting but Not Wanting the Blessing

John 9:1–25

It's good to see you again. It's a beautiful day here in Jonesboro. Is this typical or are you just showing off? Very, very nice.

I'd like to share with you this story from the Gospel of John. It is an unusual story and works a reversal upon all who read it and think about it. And I think the unusual and demanding and surprising nature of it takes us all off guard.

I noticed recently a Chamber of Commerce advertisement from a little town in northeast Wyoming, a little town that was very comfortable and settled in, wasn't growing, wasn't losing and was doing fine suddenly found itself sitting on top of rich deposits of coal, oil and gas. It's a boomtown. Population has quadrupled, people are coming night and day; they live in tents, house trailers. They're living upstairs, downstairs, in basements, whatever they can get. It's a boomtown.

The Chamber of Commerce, not wanting the town to be overwhelmed, trying to bring some order and sense and stability in the community, has put an advertisement in newspapers and written a lot of letters, personal letters in that area of the world, making a strange request. What they're advertising for? Some good churches. They would like for some good churches to come to that town. I don't think they mean it in any derogatory way about the churches they have; they just want some more good churches.

Do you have any idea of what they want? They said good churches. I don't know what they want. My guess would be that the Chamber of Commerce there is like the Chamber of Commerce would be in many places. They like to put up a sign at the edge of the town that says, "Good schools and good churches."

That's a worthy objective and a sensible desire, good schools and good churches. Everybody wants it. Even people who don't go to church want

180

good schools and good churches. If you ever, because of your work, have to move to another town and the big truck comes, gets the furniture, the mover will likely say, "We'll have your furniture there promptly in three months." And you are in your station wagon, you've got the kids and a few lampshades and the Saint Bernard and you're driving along ahead. You reach the brow of the hill just before coming to your new home, first thing you do is search the skyline for spires and steeples. Good churches. And if you didn't see a spire or steeple you wouldn't live there. You must have good churches. I wouldn't live where there weren't good churches, even if I didn't go to church.

People tell me this, including those who never attend, "Gotta have good churches. Gotta have an institution that preserves our values and takes care of things. You like to go out on Sunday morning, 10:30 or 11:00 o'clock in the morning in your bathrobe to pick up the morning paper and hear the church bells ringing. Like to know that somebody somewhere is doing the right thing. Want the kids to know the stories of Jesus. Like to know that somebody's singing the hymns. I like to spread my morning paper and get my good hot cup of coffee out on the patio and know that somewhere there's some people saying, 'I believe in God the Father Almighty, Maker of Heaven and Earth, and in Jesus Christ his only Son, our Lord, conceived of the Holy Ghost, born of the Virgin Mary, suffered under Pontius Pilate, crucified, dead and buried.' Somebody needs to be saying that and I just wouldn't want to live in a town that didn't have good churches, to preserve the values that we all hold dear and not let disruptive forces disturb."

There are, however, some people who believe that a good church is a church that witnesses to the very clear possibility and some actual cases of life being radically changed, a community changed, a family changed, people actually changing their habits, their speech, the way they spend their money, the values actually changing radically. Now not all church members expect this. I find church members as surprised as anyone else when there's really any radical change in anybody.

That's the story in the text that was read by Charles a moment ago, the ninth chapter of John. It's the story of the healing of a man who was born blind. And it's the story of a religious community that had absolutely no expectations. God isn't going to do anything different. We have a nice community but nothing unusual is going to happen. There is a man sitting by the way. He's blind; perhaps was begging. The disciples see the man and they don't expect anything to happen, for him to be healed, for anything to be different. What they want to do is discuss it. "Who sinned, this man or his parents, that he was born blind?" It was a very common opinion in that day and among some people today that if anything goes wrong in your life, you did something wrong.

I know a pastor who, when he calls in the hospital, says to the person in the bed, "What sin did you commit that this happened to you?" I was in the hospital room one day with a friend who had just discovered she had breast cancer. This man, her pastor, walked in and said, "Well, what sin have you committed?" I thought the husband was going to hit the preacher.

Some people believe it, some don't. But what the disciples wanted to do was not help the man, not look to Jesus for changing the man's condition, but discuss it. Everywhere you go there are people like that. They'll change the kingdom of God into a discussion group. "Who's going to make the coffee next week?" And the church becomes a great book club.

We don't really expect anybody to change but isn't it interesting? It really is interesting, isn't it? Who sinned? This man or his parents that he was born blind. What's your view on that? "Well, my view is, what book can we read? Let's get a good book and take turns chapter by chapter." Here they are. Nothing's going to happen. The man himself did not expect anything to happen. He's sitting by the side of the road and I want you to remember he doesn't say, "Jesus have mercy on me, Jesus heal me." He doesn't know it's Jesus, he doesn't believe in Jesus. That's important for you to remember, that God not only answers prayer but God answers some people who didn't even pray. Sometimes God will do something for you you didn't ask for. You wanted it but you didn't want it.

And the man is there suddenly discovering himself under instructions and his eyes are opened. He didn't ask for the blessing but now he can see and he starts home. Next scene, the neighbors looking out the window. "Is that our blind neighbor? Well, it looks like him."

Others said, "No, no, that's not the one. Notice how he walks. He doesn't have his dog or his cane."

"Well, it sure looks like him. Does he have a brother?"

"No, I believe that's the same one."

"But he didn't stumble at the curb."

"But it can't be the same one, the other one's been blind since he was born."

"But it looks like . . . no, it's not the same one."

It never entered their minds that he could be healed, never once. What is so surprising about the story is all of these are religious people who are shocked when somebody is different. "Well, that can't be the same one."

"Well, it looks like him, must be his brother."

"No, no, he looks a little taller."

"No, he looks a little shorter."

"I think it's the same one."

"I don't think it's the same one. Watch him at the curb."

Did you ever have anybody report to work where you work and the word is out early Monday morning? "Did you know that she made a confession of faith Sunday? She's become a Christian."

"Oh you're kidding; she's become a Christian? Oh no. That won't stick. She must have been upset."

And they start watching and listening, watching and listening. And the first little stumble, "Ha ha ha, see, I knew. You can't fool me; I've known her for years."

The family; they go to the family and they say, "Is this your son?"

"Yes."

"Born blind?"

"Yes."

"Can he now see?"

"Look, we're not in on this; he's grown, let him answer for himself. We're not in on this." And the family gives the man absolutely no support. Now this is most extraordinary. You would expect, you would expect a family to be the first to support anybody who had just been blessed by Jesus Christ. But no, no, no, no. I learned a long time ago that sometimes if you are genuinely Christian, I'm sorry to say this, it distances you from people of your own family.

I have a student, a graduate of Yale University, just entered seminary. Her family came down from Connecticut, very important people and very wealthy people, to rescue her from seminary. And during the break they went to the Caribbean on a cruise. When they came back, the reason for the cruise is clear; they thought they'd get out of her mind this notion she had that she wanted somehow someway to minister to people. They talked to me about deprogramming.

I said, "Now wait, wait, wait."

"But we had such plans for her. We had such plans. Can't you talk to her?"

I said, "I do talk to her. She's one of my students."

"But I mean, can't you really talk to her?"

I'm talking to this young woman who has said before God and the world, "I want to give my life to help people in need." I'm talking to her mother and her father who had such great plans.

There was a certain church in which the young people as Christmas approached wanted somebody in the church to play Santa Claus. They went to this one man who was a leader in the church, a banker, very very close with his money, but very faithful in the church. They went to him and said, "Will you be Santa Claus at our Christmas party?"

And he said, "I guess so." In a moment of weakness he said that. They didn't ask him because he was generous or had the qualities of Santa Claus.

They asked him because of his shape. He'd make a good Santa Claus so they said, "Will you be Santa Claus?"

And he said, "Sure, I'll be Santa Claus." As the time approached he got nervous; he growled at supper every night. To his wife he said, "I can't do this; I can't be Santa Claus." "Sure you can, dear; just put on that silly suit and pretend. It's no big deal."

The night arrived for the church Christmas party. He was so nervous he could hardly get in the suit. "God, help me to be a good Santa Claus," his wife heard him mumble. "Dear, you are taking the fun out of it. Relax."

He went to the church and by the end of the party he had given to the poor all that he had.

"But how could you? Nobody expected you to *be* Santa Claus, for God's sake!"

33

More Than Anything in the World

John 14:1–9

"Lord, show us the Father, and we will be satisfied." We do not know, of course, whether Philip whispered these words, hoping no one else would hear, or shouted them above the noise of many conversations. We do not know if he spoke in a tear-filled voice or blurted out his request. We do not even know if he realized the importance of what he asked. What we do know is that he spoke for all of us: to know God is a fundamental human longing, so deeply imbedded, in fact, as to rise very seldom to our lips. Why?

Perhaps it is pride. One has to swallow pride of self-sufficiency in order to form the words of this request. A man paces back and forth outside a church door before entering. This is strange territory. Inside a friendly face wearing an usher badge hands the visitor a worship bulletin and with a smile says, "Welcome; we know you are here in search of God." "Well, no, I just had an hour to kill and thought I would drop in."

Perhaps the difficulty in expressing a desire to know God lies in the fear of exposing one's emotion. After all, the desire is not solely cerebral; it is visceral as well. A patient lies in a hospital bed awaiting surgery early the next morning. Through a partially open door he sees his pastor coming down the hallway toward his door. "Pastor, what are you doing here? You should be visiting other patients who are really sick. Of course, I have a little surgery tomorrow to remove my kidneys and liver, but no big deal. A piece of cake. But some folks in here are nervous and could use a good visit by a reverend." What's with the frivolous chatter? What's going on? The patient doesn't want the minister to come over to his bed, take his hand, and pray. What he really wants is for the minister to come over to his bed, take his hand, and pray. But he doesn't want to cry.

Or perhaps the request "Show us God" sticks in the throat because of a suspicion that the request will go unanswered. Maybe the preacher in Ecclesiastes is right: "God has set eternity in our hearts, but we can't know the beginning or ending of anything" (Eccl. 3:11, au. trans.). After all, just because you're hungry doesn't prove there is bread. I recall hearing Professor James Crenshaw of Duke describe this grim view of life as being similar to a huge Easter egg hunt. In the morning all go out with baskets and full of anticipation. During the day, now and then, someone yells, "I found one!" but in the evening most go home with empty baskets. Maybe that eloquent agnostic of another generation, Robert Ingersoll, had it right: "Life is a narrow vale between the cold, barren peaks of two eternities. We know not whence we come or whither we go."

But suppose a kind fellow traveler wished to give some answer to my request, to what or to whom would I be pointed? After all, the author of our text has already acknowledged, "No one has ever seen God." The answer most readily available is creation. "The heavens are telling the glory of God; and the firmament proclaims his handiwork" (Ps. 19:1). Even Paul, in his own way, holds that all humanity, including those beyond access to Scripture, is without excuse. "For what can be known about God is plain to them, because God has shown it to them. Ever since the creation of the world his eternal power and divine nature, invisible though they are, have been understood and seen through the things he has made" (Rom. 1:19–20). Luke agrees: "(God) has not left himself without a witness in doing good—giving you rains from heaven and fruitful seasons, and filling you with food and your hearts with joy" (Acts 14:17). Even John, who raises the question of knowing God, at least implies the Godward pointing of creation (1:1–5).

And our own experience of nature offers a strong Amen. It is so in the spring when the world is a poem of light and color, when "butterflies flutter up from every little buttercup." It is so in the summer, when trees and vines hang heavy with fruit, provisions for all God's creatures. It is so in the fall, when a chill nips the air and autumn weather turns the leaves to flame. And it is so in winter, when the long fingers of barren trees welcome a blanket of snow. There is hardly a square inch of earth so barren and desolate but what one can see in the lower right-hand corner the initials of the artist—G.O.D. Take a walk "down the back roads and along the river of your memory" and among your thoughts—God. Sit alone on the back steps with your fingers cupped around your early morning coffee and see how long it takes for God to enter your thoughts.

Then why is this not enough? Why is Philip still standing there, waiting for an answer? He has eyes and ears and heart; he has the same access to creation as we do. So why is he still asking, "Lord, show us the Father, and we will be satisfied"? Probably because it is not satisfying simply to have witnesses in creation that there is a God. There is nothing saving, nothing redeeming, in believing there is a God. Our desire is to know God, to know what God is like, what is God's relationship to us. Show us that; no cloud, no bird, no leaf, no sunset can tell me.

Philip's question was not only poignant, it was urgent. His only hope for an answer had just announced to his followers that he was going away. "Do not let your hearts be troubled. . . . In my Father's house there are many dwelling places. . . . I go to prepare a place for you . . . so that where I am, there you may be also." His followers are confused. They are children playing on the floor only to look up and see Mom and Dad putting on their coats. The children have three questions, always three questions: Where are you going? Can we go? Then who will stay with us? Jesus responds, "I am going to my Father and your Father. You cannot come now; you can come later. But I will not leave you orphans. I will send another friend, another helper who will never leave, but who will stay with you forever."

Hearts heavy with the news of the approaching death of their leader and friend cannot grasp these words. It is too much. Questions tumble upon questions, until finally Philip speaks, not only for himself, not only for the Twelve, but for all of us. We are all full of questions about life, death, and what we do next. But our minds and hearts will find satisfaction if we can know God. Show us God.

Show us God? Is that your question, Philip? Where have you been? All this time together and you don't know? Were you there when the lame man at the pool stood and walked? Were you there when the blind man saw his family for the first time? Were you there when the centurion's son left his sick bed? Were you there when the hungry crowd was fed? Were you there when Lazarus was restored to his grieving sisters? Yes, I was there and I believe in miracles, but I want something more; I want to experience God. And so Jesus took a towel, tied it around his waist, and in a basin of water washed their feet. Oh no, not this; show us God. And so Jesus took up a cross and as he walked up to Golgotha, he turned to Philip, to the Twelve, and to all of us, and said, "Whoever has seen me has seen God." Jesus healing, feeding, caring, serving, dying: this is the portrait of God.

But is that the end of it? The class in theology is over, students dismissed? By no means! Jesus has shown us God in order to show us ourselves as believers. To be a believer in the God revealed in Jesus is to heal, feed, care, serve, die. Whether or not Philip understood it, we do: knowing God carries the assignment to live out the character of God.

"And we will be satisfied." Are we? I must confess I did not realize that in knowing I would be known, in finding I would be found.

When I was a child I played hide-and-seek with my brothers and sister. You remember the game, don't you? One of the group is It, which means hiding one's eyes, counting to one hundred, then announcing, "Coming, ready or not." Now It goes in search of the others, now well hidden. The first one found is now It. When my sister was It, she cheated. "One, two, three, four, five, ninety-seven, ninety-eight, ninety-nine, one hundred; coming, ready or not." But I didn't care that she cheated because I was well hidden—under the porch and under the steps of the porch. Behind trees, in the barn, in the corncrib, round and round she searched. She passed by me again and again. I was confident; she will never find me here. But after awhile it hit me—she will never find me here! So I stuck out a toe, she saw it, you're It, you're It! I crawled out muttering, "Aw, phooey, you found me."

What did I want; to be hidden? Well, yes, but what did I really want? To be found, just as every person in this room.

And then we will be satisfied.

34

Being a Friend of Jesus

John 15:9–17

It strikes me as strange that I have never heard a sermon on this text. Stranger still, I myself have not until now prepared a sermon on this text. Who knows why? Here is a passage with depth, with sufficient density to tease the mind of the preacher, with an extraordinary offer to the listener, hiding in plain sight. Maybe it is avoided because its promise is too magnificent and, therefore, too demanding. Some texts are like that. Even Martin Luther found the story of Abraham offering Isaac simply too much for a sermon. Or it could be that John 15:9–17 makes an offer to which the heart feels it must say, "No." Listen: "I do not call you servants any longer, because the servant does not know what the master is doing; but I have called you friends, because I have made known to you everything that I have heard from my Father" (John 15:15). From servant to friend—do you welcome, will you accept, the promotion?

I must acknowledge that my trembling before John 15:15 has an antecedent in a sermon heard almost twenty years ago on a kindred theme: Abraham was called a friend of God (Jas. 2:23). A combination of misfortunes put me in the fortunate position to hear the sermon. A cancelled flight; a last-minute reservation in a motel near the airport; a search for a church within walking distance, since the next morning was Sunday; a housekeeper at the motel pointing in the direction of one six blocks away; my arrival at a cinder block building in which a few tired souls had already begun singing gospel songs. The preacher, a large man, made painfully awkward by a number of maladies, including poor eyesight, moved to the pulpit and read in crippled speech his sermon text: James 2:23.

His opening words were, "Abraham was a friend of God. I'm sure glad I am not a friend of God." His sermon was an explanation of why he was pleased not to be a friend of God.

I cannot recall being so engaged in a sermon. His delivery was without ani-
mation; his physical condition denied him that. His speech was a bit halting, but
each word was clear and pronounced with respect. All of us in the small congregation were helping him preach by our total silence and attention to what he
said. He recalled the story of Abraham, pilgrim and wanderer, who, after years
of homelessness, died and was buried in a land not his own. "Abraham was a
friend of God," he said; "I'm glad I'm not." He then spoke of others who had
been called friends of God, faithful in spite of dungeon, fire, and sword. He
concluded with a story of Teresa of Avila, remembered by the church as a friend
of God. He recalled her begging in public to raise funds for an orphanage. After
a series of setbacks—flood, storm, and fire repeatedly destroying the orphanage—Teresa in her evening prayers said to God, "So this is how you treat your
friends; no wonder you have so few." The sermon closed with counsel: If you
find yourself being drawn into the inner circle of the friends of God, blessed are
you. But pray for the strength to bear the burden of it.

Because of that extraordinary sermon in that little church (I do not remember its name, nor that of the preacher), I am somewhat prepared to hear Jesus'
words, "I do not call you servants any longer . . . but I have called you friends."

No longer servants but friends: it sounds like a promotion. One could
make a case for such a reading. Had not Jesus, in that very room, on that very
night, dramatically impressed upon the disciples the posture and action of a
servant by washing their feet? Had he not said plainly that they were to wash
one another's feet? Had he not reminded them of a fact not to be overlooked
in the life of a disciple: "servants are not greater than their master"? (13:16).
"Servant" is the operative word to speak of our relation to Christ and to the
community of faith. Nothing strikes us as so unbecoming a follower of Christ
as arrogance, as the pursuit of position and power, as the desire to be served
rather than to serve. Such living is a stark contradiction of the teaching and
the example of Jesus. Of course, we sing with feeling "What a Friend We
Have in Jesus," but who among us would say, "What a friend Jesus has in
me"? None of us would or should claim that position.

No, suddenly and shockingly, Jesus bestows the title that no one among
us could claim: *friend*. It feels like a title; but, in fact, the word describes a
relationship. It implies love and mutuality. Even if it is not a title, it still feels
like a title. If you have been all your life a servant of Jesus; if you have chosen that role; if being a servant of Jesus, faithful in word and deed, has been
the total definition of who you are, then to be called by Jesus his friend is an
overwhelming gift. "Jesus has called me his friend"; who can pronounce the
words? It is too much.

Of course, "friend" is heard as a promotion. No longer servant but friend—
receive it for what it obviously is, a promotion from one station to another.

Think of it: out of the cabin into the big house; off the back porch to the patio; off the bench up to the dining hall; out of the field onto the lawn; off the floor and into the big bed. No more, "Tote that barge, lift that bale"; instead, "Come, friend, let us walk together." Can there be in all God's kingdom a delight greater than this? No, absolutely not; it is impossible.

Jesus continues: "I do not call you servants any longer, because the servant does not know what the master is doing." That's the truth; the whole of my life was to do what I was told. Plough, plant, weed, harvest; that is what I did when told to do it. I did not know what went on in the big house; I did not know what went on in the master's head. Deals, trades, profit and loss: these were his responsibilities, not mine. His lamp burned late, not mine. When my day's work was done, it was done. After that, it was bread and bed for me. Don't ask me any questions about my master's business; I don't know. I mind my own business.

Jesus continues: "But I have called you friends, because I have made known to you everything that I have heard from my Father." In other words, a friend of Jesus shares in the knowledge of God's operation in the world, what God is doing and how God is doing it. God is creating a community of love that is to embrace everyone. A friend has this love and extends it toward others, but it carries a price. The world that does not know God will hate the friend of Jesus as it hated Jesus for practicing this love. Jesus paid the full price for so loving, laying down his life for those he loves. We have no reason to assume a friend of Jesus would be exempt from the same. Through knowing what Jesus heard from God, the friend of Jesus shares in the responsibility of that knowledge. "What a friend we have in Jesus" is a pleasant and encouraging thought, but "what a friend Jesus has in me" is beginning to feel burdensome. I am beginning to wonder if the move from servant to friend is really a promotion.

It is true the servant does not know what the master is doing, but that has its bright side. The servant doesn't take his work home with him. For him the day ends when he puts aside the shovel and the hoe. But sometimes the master is up all night, pacing and worrying. If the servant becomes the friend of the master, then the master's burdens become the servant's own. It seems friends of Jesus are never completely free of the duty to bear the fruit and to pay the price of love.

"Because I have made known to you everything that I have heard from my Father." But really, who wants to know? Most of us carry within us large areas of deliberate ignorance. From childhood we carry the warm and inspiring image of General George Washington with his troops in the biting snow at Valley Forge. Who wants the picture spoiled by the information that Washington was quartered in a large and comfortable farmhouse nearby? From English literature class we embrace William Wordsworth as the tender and sensitive poet. Why enroll in a graduate course on Wordsworth and be disillusioned by his practice of using a knife already smeared with butter and preserves to cut apart the pages of books newly arrived at the home of his host? Who wants to hear a poor child say, "Mommy, I'm hungry," and to read a marquee announcing "All You Can Eat, $7.95" all on the same evening? Comfort demands avoiding those rallies where passionate and informed speakers assail our ears with the news: 13 million children in America go to bed hungry every night; over 9 million have no health insurance; every 30 minutes a child is shot to death in the United States. There is a lot of information that I prefer not to know.

Is this what it means to be a friend of Jesus, to be told the uncomfortable truth that carries unavoidable duty, the duty to love, to love as God loves, to lay down one's life if need be? The life of the servant is looking better all the time. I recall the first time I saw the inside of a pulpit. The church of my upbringing had a beautiful pulpit with a succession of most attractive tapestries. I admired them every Sunday from my seat near the back pew. The pulpit was awesome. Then I was called to be a minister. On a Christmas break from school, I was asked to preach. It was a trembling experience. Among my memories of that day is the unforgettable image of the contents of the pulpit. Piled inside on two shelves were old bulletins, a scum-covered glass of water, a baseball cap, a faded stole, a coverless hymnal, an old Bible, a few sheets of music, pages of handwritten notes, a broken alarm clock, and a burned–to–the–base candle. Needless to say, the view from the pew was much more pleasant. I did not at the time feel I had been given a promotion. In fact, there are plenty of days when being a servant has stronger appeal than being a friend. The old cabin out back looks more attractive than the big house.

I will never forget the first time I was invited as a friend to spend the night in the big house, God's house. I was, of course, excited as a new friend of Jesus and a first-time visitor to the House of Many Rooms. Angels showed me around and answered my endless questions. The food was heavenly and at bedtime I was shown to a room of my own. With a, "Goodnight, sleep well," I was left alone. The excitement of the day finally resolved into weariness and weariness into rest. My bed was a cloud. To the soft sound of music coming from everywhere, I drifted into sleep.

Sometime during the night my sleep was interrupted by sounds from the next room. I did not know who was in that room, but somebody was having a bad night. The noise was not snoring, nor did it seem to be sleep-talking. I listened more carefully; maybe it was groaning or moaning accompanied by tossing and turning. I thought once to knock on the door, but was afraid to do so. I dared not call out lest I add to that person's discomfort and perhaps wake others. So I tolerated it till morning, catching only snatches of sleep.

At daybreak I heard the person next door move about the room and then step out into the hall. I did the same, wanting to see who it was, and, if appropriate, express regret that the night was so restless.

It was God. I was shocked; God restless and unable to sleep, the God who blesses with peace beyond understanding, the God who hushes even a whimpering child? I was speechless.

God said, "I'm sorry if I disturbed your sleep. I know my groaning was a disturbance, but I couldn't get my mind off all my hurting children down there."

What did that "I-don't-remember-his-name" preacher in that "whatever-it-was" church say to the congregation? "If you find yourself being drawn into the inner circle of the friends of God, blessed are you. But pray for the strength to bear the burden of it."

35

What Do We Do after Easter?

John 21:1–17

The Scripture text for today is called an epilogue to the Gospel of John but don't let that fool you. This portion is as much a part of the story as any of it. It captures the mood and the dilemma of the church and of all the followers of Christ in the days immediately after the Resurrection. Is that all there is to Easter? Just what do you do after Easter anyway? And Simon Peter said, "I'm going fishing."

What do you do after Easter? Check the attendance records for Easter Sunday and the Sunday following and together they will form both the confession and the denial of the Christian faith. There was a time when churches planned very special events for Easter in order to build the crowds. Now churches expect the crowds to be there on Easter but they plan all kinds of special events for the Sunday after in order not to be hurt and embarrassed by the noticeable collapse in attendance and activity. And so on the Sunday after Easter, one church will bring in a professional athlete to speak or a beauty queen or a movie star. Another church may have a midget come to speak while another may get a magician to do some tricks, or perhaps some fellow to yo-yo while reciting Scripture. Of course, many churches go the cheaper route and just fuss all day Easter, shaming the people into coming back the next Sunday.

How are we to understand this phenomenon? Shall we simply attribute it to the shallow and fickle church? Treat it as a documentary on human sins, and trudge on our way as best we can? I think some reason for it lies in the rhythm of human life. Life, as we all know, moves in a kind of rhythm between expansion, new adventure, excitement on one hand, and rest, contentment, and reflection on the other. It is not realistic to expect high enthusiasm all the time. Unless, of course, you're afraid if you do pause and reflect, you will discover there was nothing to the enthusiasm. This may explain why some

194

people try to stay noisily enthusiastic all the time in order to make their empty house sound occupied.

One is reminded of the childhood game of skipping rocks on the water. If the rock had the momentum it might skip all the way across the pond to the other side. But if it ever slowed down it would sink. I'm thinking just now of a number of churches that keep the ministers busy manufacturing momentum and enthusiasm. The plain fact is life is not one long ecstasy or a repeat of ecstatic moments such as that very first Easter. On that day, for the very first time, lips formed the message; "Jesus Christ is Risen Today, Hallelujah"! Anxious women running, an appearance to Simon Peter and to James and to the Twelve and to above five hundred brethren at once. And then what? Is that all there is to Easter?

It was a beautiful wedding. I don't recall how many attendants. I think a dozen. She was beautiful; he was handsome. Everyone was nervous, mothers were crying. Rice was showered; they sped away in a car painted with all kinds of friendly urgings. But after the honeymoon he was back to work in the oilfield and to the little mobile home he brought his bride. The mobile home was out in the middle of nowhere with a few others like it. He was gone most of the time; she sat alone. It was muddy outside but there were some planks placed along so that she could make her way to the community laundry not too many yards away. Other bored wives moved about sluggishly in this muddy field. She sat among strangers and she cried over the album of those beautiful wedding pictures. Is that all there is to a wedding?

John, of all the Gospels, was most aware of the problems created by Easter. You see Easter is the resurrection of Christ to be sure. No one denies that. But John understood, more than any other writer, that Easter is also the departure of Christ. The Gospel of John consists of twenty-one chapters. The public ministry of Jesus ends at Chapter 12. And what is the rest? The rest is farewell, a farewell meal, farewell discourses, a farewell prayer, and then the farewell. The pathos in this portion of material is deep and real. "Let not your hearts be troubled. You believe in God. Believe also in me. In my father's house are many rooms" (John 14:1–2, au. trans.).

What is he talking about? The disciples are like children sitting on the floor playing with their toys when suddenly they look up to discover that Mom and Dad are putting on coats and hats. The questions are always three and they're always the same. "Where are you going? Can we go? Well, who will stay with us?"

"Where am I going? I'm going to my Father and your Father."

"Can we go?"

"Where I am going you cannot go now. You can go later."

"Then who will stay with us?"

"I will ask the Father and he will send the Spirit and he will be with you always."

What do you do after Easter? Simon Peter and six others went fishing. Easter was over. The whole life with Jesus of Nazareth seemed to be over. It was beautiful while it lasted. There was that spot called Camelot, but it was over. It was wonderful to be sure, but you can't squeeze a lifetime out of one moment. "I'm going fishing." And while they fished Christ appeared. And after breakfast he looked at Simon and said, "Simon, do you love me?"

"Well, frankly, that question is embarrassing; it makes me uncomfortable. It isn't that I'm unaccustomed to questions. I like questions. I liked the three years we spent together with questions and answers. I like to discuss and entertain ideas. There's something about uncertainty that keeps my mind open. And I like the sophistication of considering various viewpoints on every issue. I like to be tolerant and open. That's why your question is embarrassing. 'Do you love me?' Maybe if you would rephrase the question. Ask me: 'Are we good friends?' I can answer that. We're good friends, yes, but I don't like questions to be too certain, too absolute, too clear-cut, too either-or. Those bother me. They remind me of all those people who have certain answers to everything.

"Like the evangelists I used to hear as a boy. They would lead you right up to the presence of God and then call you up to the front of the church if you would say *Yes* to God. I hated the awkwardness of those moments, having to say yes or no. Sounds like Paul with his one dramatic unambiguous *yes* near Damascus. I recall Augustine in a park in Milan. Yes or no. Or John Wesley. He said it was on Wednesday, May 24, about a quarter 'til nine. Your question is too much like that old revivalist approach. 'Do you love me? Yes or no?' I really think I'm a little intimidated by this question. Why don't we bring the chairs around in a circle and let the other six disciples join in and let's have a group discussion. John is here, what about him? What's he going to say? Why do you just pick on me all the time? I feel too much pressure here really to be enjoying this experience. In fact, I don't think you've asked me the right question. What difference does it make whether or not I love you? That's not the important thing. Faith has its own objective reality and we shouldn't go around talking about how we feel. We should just present the message as it is in and of itself. Ask me another question that is more appropriate to the three years of learning that I've had with you. None of those old questions that make a person feel guilty. Ask me about Christology or ecclesiology. I like essay questions."

"But, Peter, it is the right question. What is to prevent your being arrogant when you're successful if you have not really answered this question? What is to prevent your being depressed at failure if you have not clearly faced up to this question? In the final analysis it is the quality of the relationship you have with me that will make all the difference in your life."

"Would you repeat the question?" "Yes. Do you love me?" "Yes, Lord, you know that I love you." "Then tend my lambs and feed my sheep." In that assignment Easter is translated into life and resurrection morning is made meaningful every morning. I don't mean to get sentimental. It's a tough assignment. To tend my lambs is to face the fact that some are going to stay lambs for forty years and never become sheep. Feed my sheep; not simple at all. Some of them refuse to eat. Now what am I going to do?

The Apostle Paul wrote to the church in moments of exasperation reminding them that he was their father, he was their nurse. It was a tough and difficult assignment but in that assignment, the long-term meaning of Easter is revealed.

"What I was doing," says Jesus, "I want you to keep doing. As the Father sent me so I send you."

All across the country there are churches trying to recapture Easter, trying to keep it going or to get it back. And there are many sincere church people feeling they have lost something, feeling guilty that they do not remain excited by Easter. May I suggest that the feeling of enthusiasm and exhilaration at Easter needs to be turned into common energy? Tend the lambs and feed the sheep.

Have you ever been to one of those meetings where you got excited about the problems of ecology and then nothing specific was proposed? And you went home only to grow cold. Have you been to one of those meetings where you became disturbed, heavily disturbed, about world hunger but nothing was proposed? And it was not long until you were back surfeiting off the fat of the land without any heaviness at all.

Have you ever been to one of those meetings where you became incensed and angry over the mistreatment of children in this country but nothing specific was proposed? And now it has been some time since you've given any thought to it. What's the answer? Go back to those meetings and see if you can get back the ecstasy, get back the guilt, get back the pain?

Suppose you have a ten thousand dollar bill. My goodness. Wow! A ten thousand dollar bill. Look at that. A ten thousand dollar bill. But after several days of admiring it, being in awe of it, showing it to your friends, what do you do with it? You don't go for coffee and say, "Here, I'll just take care of it out of this ten thousand dollar bill." You don't say, "Let me pay for the hot dogs out of this ten thousand dollar bill." That ten thousand dollar bill will have meaning only after you have changed it into a sack full of concrete acts of grace.

What do you do after Easter? "Tend my lambs and feed my sheep."

36

You Shall Receive Power

Acts 1:1–8

In the first book, O Theophilus, I have dealt with all that Jesus began to do and teach, until the day when he was taken up, after he had given commandment through the Holy Spirit to the apostles whom he had chosen. To them he presented himself alive after his passion by many proofs, appearing to them during forty days, and speaking of the kingdom of God. And while staying with them he charged them not to depart from Jerusalem, but to wait for the promise of the Father, which, he said, "you heard from me, for John baptized with water, but before many days you shall be baptized with the Holy Spirit."

So when they had come together, they asked him, "Lord, will you at this time restore the kingdom to Israel?" He said to them, "It is not for you to know times or seasons which the Father has fixed by his own authority. But you shall receive power when the Holy Spirit has come upon you; and you shall be my witnesses in Jerusalem and in all Judea and Samaria and to the end of the earth." (RSV)

"And you shall receive power." That promise hardly stirs the blood any more. Not because we don't believe that the promise will be kept; it's just that most folk are not interested in power any more, not even political power. Oh, there was a time, a generation ago, even ten years ago, when there was ambition for political power but disenchantment has set in, disenchantment by false hopes of what power can do, disenchantment due to corrupt uses of power. And then came the apathy and the inertia. Now the promise of power brings nothing but a yawn.

There's not even an interest in personal power. There have been times in our history when a premium was put upon power to change, power to be different from what we are and the way we are. There was preaching which stirred a divine discontent within us and the "ought" of religion awoke in us the conscience. In my mind I serve God but in my members there is another force at work and I do not do what I ought. I can will what is right but I cannot do it. O wretched man that I am. Who will deliver me? This is what many people were saying, not just the Apostle Paul. How can my life become qualitatively better? How can I overcome those forces, those habits, those manners, those ways of life that hinder my being what I know I ought to be?

"And you shall receive power." The promise was claimed by many but the promise is not interesting any more. You see the desirable word now is not power. The word is acceptance. We ought not to say "ought." Don't lay any guilt on me. The whole point is to accept yourself and to accept each other exactly as we are. Any program or any desire to change, to be different, or to help anyone else change, is viewed as an admission that you have not accepted yourself. Nor have you accepted God's acceptance of you. As you are, my friends, just as you are.

And so everywhere the churches have been serving up small dishes of soft grace. Who needs power? Power implies that you want to be able to be different and that's not the point. What you want is to embrace what is, as it is. Drop from the vocabulary of the faith words such as ought and should. Lie back and be mellow. But for those first disciples to whom this promise was given, it was a proper word. They were a little group totally immobilized with a sense of powerlessness. They had been wrong, so totally wrong, about Jesus and the nature of his purpose and his ministry. They had two swords under their robes when they went up to Jerusalem with him. They were ready. They went up to Jerusalem humming "The Battle Hymn of the Republic." "Soon," they said, "the drum will speak to the trumpet and the trumpet will speak to the cannon and the cannon will speak to the sky." Then Jesus was arrested. Affections cooled, hopes died, disenchantment took over. There was the crucifixion. It was over.

But now God has raised Jesus from the dead. God has vindicated Jesus Christ. Something new is astir again and so they come again asking, "Now, Lord, will you restore the kingdom to Israel? Now can we bring out the seventy-six trombones? Now can we raise the flag? Now can we march against Rome?" And again they're disappointed. "No, no, that's not your business, but you will receive power."

"Do you mean to say the Spirit of God is going to come upon us like it did upon our ancestors? As the Spirit came upon Samson and he was powerful over his enemies? As it came upon Gideon and he became the champion of the people? As the Spirit came upon Saul so that he amazed all his contemporaries with his leadership? Do you mean to say the Spirit of God will come upon us and we shall deliver our people?"

"No."

"Then perhaps you mean we're going to receive personal power for moral and ethical achievement. That we're going to be better people. That there's going to be personality development and self-assertion."

"No. You shall receive power to witness. That is to say you shall receive power to share the message of the Christian faith."

Now that is disappointing. Who needs power to witness? If you want to tell it, tell it. You don't need any power from heaven, any Holy Spirit to do that, do you? Well, it isn't that simple. There is a kind of enabling, a kind of encouragement, a kind of power that is necessary. It is necessary if you are really to overcome a sense of self-disqualification. That's what hinders so many of us. We disqualify ourselves with those statements that sound, on the face of it, quite Christian. Who am I that I should be talking to other people about the faith when God knows I have so many problems of my own? I certainly am not perfect. I have enough difficulty with my own life. Who am I to speak to others? And so we spend our time getting ourselves straight first with the illusion that once we get everything straightened out about ourselves, then we will be qualified to speak to others. And so here we sit before a green light with the traffic backed up all the way to Toronto tinkering with our own souls to get them adjusted just right so that we'll be qualified to witness.

Now suppose, just suppose that the first Christians had been of this mind. Suppose they had said, "When we clean up all of our problems, then we'll be able to speak to others." How long would it have taken? In the membership of that first church was Judas. Don't you imagine the church was tongue-tied about that? "Who are we to go out and talk to others? They might bring up Judas."

"Who are you to be talking to us with a Judas in your group?"

And Simon Peter, who cursed and swore that he never knew Jesus, three times denying him. Can a church headed up by Simon Peter really witness? Or, for that matter, look at all the Twelve. Mark says that they all forsook Jesus and fled in the hour of crisis. Are they now going to witness? Then there's the leading missionary among them, Paul, his hands dipped to the elbows in the blood of the church. It was he who tried to stab that church in its cradle and kill all the Christians. And he is a witness? Do you mean to say that a church that was made up of grumbling widows, claiming they didn't get their share of the blankets and the food, a church that had several of its leaders in jail most of the time, a church that had members like Ananias and Sapphira who lied about their offering, do you mean to say that church is going to witness?

Yes, because witnessing is not talking about one's self. You don't take the stand in the courtroom to explain to the judge and jury how you happen to feel about the accused or how you happen to feel about the whole case. You sit there to tell what you know, what you have witnessed. Personally I think we're all beginning to get a little weary of this kind of witnessing in our time, that has become subjective, so captive to itself, spending its Sundays and some of its weekdays taking trips through its own psyche while the world is essentially unaddressed on the grave issues that face the human race.

"You shall receive power to witness." Of course we need it. We need power if we are going to overcome our hesitation to speak at all. Most Christians are not glib, and thank goodness for that. We pause before the task of finding the appropriate word to say about God or about the Christian faith. We hide from that assignment; we hide in statements such as, "Well, it's the life you live that really counts. It doesn't really matter if you say anything." We hide behind a preferred busyness. "I'd rather paint the sanctuary again really than to go out and say anything to anybody." Of course we'd rather not speak because that is the most difficult assignment of all. Beware of anyone who talks easily and freely and painlessly about intimate and important things. Of course it's difficult; that's why the promise: You shall receive power. You will be enabled; you will be emboldened to speak.

"You shall receive power to witness." Of course we need power to witness because witnessing means one has to overcome prejudice against a large number of people to whom we do not speak at all, much less about the Christian faith. Those to whom Jesus addressed the promise of power to witness were Jews of Palestine, primarily from Galilee. And the assignment he gave them was to witness in Jerusalem. Now that's a toughie. Jerusalem was where he was arrested, where he was killed. But perhaps they're thinking, "We're courageous; we'll be a little scared but we can witness in Jerusalem."

"And you shall be my witnesses in Judea."

"Well that's a little bigger territory but we can handle that. In fact we have a number of friends in Judea. We know those people, speak the same language. Yes, we can do it."

"And you shall be my witnesses in Samaria."

"What?"

"In Samaria."

"But Samaria is where those people live who are, you know, half-breeds. They speak a different dialect, have different political views, different religion and only part of a Bible. Are you sure you mean Samaria?"

"And to the ends of the earth."

"You mean among the Gentiles?"

"Yes."

"We're to witness to Gentiles?"

"Yes."

Now are you beginning to sense the need for power? At each step of the way the barriers were there. The barriers were real and they did not come down easily. At first the members of the church were Jews, comfortable with each other. Then some began to admit into the church those who were called Greek Jews. They spoke Greek; they were more liberal, having accommodated themselves to the ways of Gentiles. Tensions and quarrels developed. Next you read that one missionary baptized and brought into the church some Samaritans. What is happening to our church? And then an Ethiopian eunuch. Can you imagine bringing an Ethiopian eunuch into the membership of the church? Ethiopian is bad enough, but a eunuch? And then Gentiles, here they come. Italians, Turks, Greeks, Romans, all of them. What is happening to our church?

At every step of the way, the prejudices were strong, the tensions were deep, the arguments were heated. The first conference the church held was to discuss the whole issue. Are we going to continue to bring into the church all these different kinds of people and regard them as equals? Seemingly immovable stood the ancient walls of language, custom, dress, food, social and economic structures.

"But you shall receive power." And when the book of Acts ends, the church has moved all the way from Jerusalem to Rome. All the barriers that were there are still there. Rich and poor, black and white, male and female, young and old, labor and management, hawk and dove, the barriers are still there. But so is the promise. The promise is still there too. "You shall receive power." That promise lies there, often unclaimed, but still available for those who would receive it. Are you interested?

37

Witnessing to the Resurrection

Acts 2:14a, 22–32

I want to thank those who are participating in the worship; they are as busy as the rest of us. Robert had no choice; he's in my class. I've asked three graduate students to participate. We sometimes forget about the graduate students. They, too, have souls. At least they did when they came. I don't know what happened. And Meg, thank you very much. When Meg was in my P301 she couldn't do a thing. In fact, after I heard her sermon, I said, "Have you thought maybe of music?" Thank you very much.

It's Easter; we're in the fifty days of joy, but even Easter is not a time of unambiguous joy. I recall a young fresh preacher coming to our little church years ago and on Easter Sunday he had printed those mock newspapers, "Jerusalem News." It had stories about the resurrection as though they were public news. He was jumping up and down and full of "Alleluias" and "Christ is risen."

On the way home my mother said, "It's apparent our new minister hasn't experienced Easter yet." I said, "Well, he seemed excited enough." And she said, "Yes, but he hasn't understood that if the dead are raised, then they leave us." Jesus' disciples finally understood that, and so you weep even at an empty tomb.

I know this is the spring of the year. Some of you will be graduating and leaving. I'm not supposed to make this any kind of a closing event, but I am not unaware of the fact that some of you will be leaving and that is a fulfillment of Easter, but in the heart it is also an interruption of Easter.

The text, which Bryan read, is known to all of you. Acts 2 is the narrative of the birth of the church. The disciples were all together in one place; the city is Jerusalem. There was the sound of the rushing of a mighty wind that filled the room and tongues like fire sat upon their heads. They began to speak in tongues and most extraordinary, everyone heard what they said in his or her own language, a miracle of the ear as well as of the tongue.

There were people there from every nation under heaven, Luke says. Parthians and Medes, and Elamites and Capadocians and Libyans and Romans . . . from every place. They saw what was going on and they said, "These people are filled with new wine," and Peter stood with the eleven and said, "They're not drunk as you suppose. It's only 9:00 o'clock in the morning. This is the fulfillment of the prophet Joel. 'I will pour out my Spirit on all flesh.'"

And having explained the extraordinary occasion, he preached Jesus Christ. They were deeply stirred and many of them were brought to faith. Three thousand, says Luke, were baptized. That's the text.

Frequently in classroom and in chapel and in lecture and in sermon, the students complained about not having anything to think about during the lecture or the sermon and feel themselves not very well employed during the time. I anticipated that problem because it's an old problem. Even in the first century in synagogues the question came up. "What are we to do if we have an old senile Rabbi and we don't get anything?" And the instruction was this. If you have an old senile Rabbi who stands up there and gives you nothing but the toothless reminiscences of his youth, take your books and study during the sermon. After all an hour of study is in the sight of the Holy One as an hour of prayer.

So I anticipated this problem and I've made some assignments for you to think about while I'm talking. I've jotted these down; all of these are based on the text that was read by Bryan earlier, or at least from the narrative of Acts 2. Those of you whose last name begins A through F, I want you to think about this: The inclusiveness of the church on the day of its beginning. Now that's your thought. They were there from every nation under heaven and the prophecy of Joel was "I will pour out my Spirit on all flesh." You get that? "Sons and daughters will preach." Hear that? "Maid servants and men servants will prophesy. Young and old, young will see visions, old will dream dreams, and whoever calls on the name of the Lord shall be saved." Anybody left out? Nobody. Very inclusive. So think about that.

You might want to think of some other things that come to your mind. For instance, the question that was asked the Rabbis. "Why is it that our Law, the Law of Moses, was given to us before we got to the land? It was given to us at Sinai in Arabia." The answer: "So that we would always remember it is not for us alone but for the world." You remember that?

Or, you may think of that parable, that marvelous parable, of God assigning a committee of angels to take care of the parting of the water at the Red Sea so Israelites could cross. And so the angels stood at the banister looking over and when the Israelites got to the Red Sea, they parted the waters and then when the Egyptians came, they released the water. Chariots and horses and soldiers and all tumbling, drowning in the sea and the angels were congratulating themselves on this assignment and were jumping up and down and applauding and singing. The Almighty came by and said, "Why are you so happy?" They said, "Look, look, look, we got 'em, we got 'em, we got 'em." And the Almighty said, "You're dismissed from my service." "Why? We got 'em." "But the Egyptians are also my children." A through F: Inclusiveness.

G through M, think about what was preached. You may not recall it exactly from the text but what was preached? When Peter stood with the eleven, it doesn't mean they were all talking at once. It means this is the apostolic preaching. This is normative. This is what C. H. Dodd researched, apostolic preaching. This is what they said. Notice, Jesus' way of life you all know, attested by the power of God. Jesus' death you all know, in fact, you're implicated in it. God raised Him from the dead and God lifted Him to the right hand of the throne where he sits and pours out the Holy Spirit upon the church. That's what they preached. Think about the need for just that being preached.

Recall times when you've been to church and the preacher just put his or her finger on a pulse and called it theology. This is the message. That's G through M.

N through S, what I'd like for you to think about while I'm talking is how God is the subject of the story. Notice God is the subject of the story. Jesus' life and ministry, "God confirmed by mighty works." Jesus' death by the foreknowledge and will of God, Jesus' resurrection, God raised him from the dead. Jesus' elevation, God exalted him to the throne. They preached the mighty acts of God. God is the neglected subject of preaching today.

You can go to church sometimes, think about this N through S, you can go to church sometimes and hear so much Jesus talk and so much Holy Spirit talk, you forget that the proclamation is the mighty act of God. That's the subject. And if you want to sit there and be disturbed by how this is so neglected, it's all right, it's all right to be disturbed by it. But don't create a disturbance.

T through Z, I would like for you to reflect on the closing of the sermon which, according to Luke, here Peter and the others were interrupted. "God has made him Lord and Christ, this Jesus whom you've crucified." And the people said, "But what are we to do?" Now that was preaching, wasn't it? Preaching that stirred the question "What are we to do?" How many sermons I've heard in which it was assumed somebody asked the question and so we had sermons on what we are to do. Eight steps of salvation, four steps of salvation, whatever steps of salvation, droning through all of that when nobody has asked. Preaching of the Gospel stirs the question, you see? And if you want to sit there and quietly weep over the deadness of the pulpits that do not raise that question, it's all right.

Now those are your assignments and if you carry them out I will feel much more free to speak briefly about a theme in the story that is somewhat muted, but is by no means minor. I recall for you the language. This Jesus of Nazareth, his way of life you all know. That is to say, it is a matter of public record. The facts about it are accessible to historians, to the researchers, to the journalists, to the reporters. It's out there, public domain.

This death of Jesus you all know. It was very public. Even passersby saw what was happening. It is publicly visible. No secret, nothing private. No faith required; it's just there. At the hands of lawless men, killed. That God raised Him from the dead, now watch it, that God raised Him from the dead, of that *we* are witnesses. You see the shift? His life you all know; His death you all know. His resurrection, of that *we* are witnesses.

Now for Luke, the preaching of the gospel is to witness to the resurrection of Jesus Christ. For instance, in the choosing of a successor for Judas, they chose Matthias to do what? To be a witness to the resurrection. And with great power, they gave their witness to the resurrection. Paul, when he was on trial, said, "I'm here because of the resurrection." In the text that Bryan read, one verse on life, one verse on death, nine verses on resurrection. But what I want to point out to you is, what does that mean? We're all going to live in the hereafter? Well, Paul developed that, but we're talking about Luke. What did it mean to witness to the resurrection? It meant that Jesus Christ has been elevated to the right hand of God and is Lord of the church. That's what Luke says. Luke says that the resurrection means that Jesus Christ is at the right hand of God pouring out the Holy Spirit for power and for guidance upon the church.

The resurrection of Jesus Christ means that the world has come to a critical corner and it is now turned. Peter said it in Jerusalem and Paul said it in Athens, Greece. Peter in Jerusalem said, "You have killed the Lord of Glory but I know you did it in ignorance, but now repent. This is a new day."

And Paul stood on Mars Hill in Athens, Greece, and said, "The times of ignorance God overlooked but now He commands all of us to repent by the announcement of the resurrection."

The world has come to a new place. That's what the resurrection means. What does the resurrection mean? It means that the life of Jesus of Nazareth has been vindicated by God and therefore this is the life and this is the way the church is to live. What He did, we do. What He said, we say. That's why, as you know, the Gospel of Luke and the book of Acts tell the story twice. Jesus' story and the church's story, it's told the same way. What He did, they did. He fed, He loved, He cared, He preached. They fed, they loved, they cared, they preached.

He ate with all kinds of people and brought them together. And the church did. Oh, it was tough. The book of Acts says it was tough. They had councils about it and everything. How are you going to have at the same table people who have different languages, dress differently, eat differently, have different histories, their names are different. They just have everything different. People who have sworn, "I wouldn't be caught dead together with those folk." How are you going to get them around the table? The church said, "We have to, because He did."

Now that's what witnessing to the resurrection means. And preaching means witnessing to the resurrection. But the point I want to make is this. That you and I are called on to speak when we don't have public approval or knowledge. There's no indication that the public believes this, cares for this, knows this. His way of life you all know, His death you all know, but to His resurrection, we are witnesses. It means to give a minority report in the room. It means to stand up and say something that doesn't have general consensus. It means sometimes to be the only one who says it. That's frightening.

It's no wonder the churches run to historians and scientists to get a little evidence. How preachers brag, "You know, Dr. So-and-So who's a known scientist, has come to believe so-and-so. And such and such a historian, teaches at Princeton, has come to believe." And we think, hey, we're getting some help here. We're getting some help here. We're not getting any help; there is no help. We are witnesses to the resurrection.

It means, therefore, to stand up and speak with courage. Of course the temptation is strong to get some proof. If we just had some proof. I hate to just stand up and say that and have somebody snicker. That Christ is raised from the dead, I need some proof. I wish a lot of times God would support me a little more in things I say so that I have a little miracle and people say "Wow!"

It started a little bit in Matthew, in Matthew's account of the resurrection, having the soldiers there, the guards and the rumor "it really happened." He's already trying to prove it. I know the feeling. And in those post New Testament documents, Christian documents, the writers would have the risen Christ appear in public. On the street, you know, going into K-Mart and everywhere, just scaring people. "Isn't that Jesus? That's Jesus." Because the church wanted so much for everyone to believe it and we just wanted to prove it.

Faith doesn't come at the end of proof. Faith is in response to the witness but that takes courage, real courage. To speak it in the face of cynicism, speak it in the face of indifference, speak it in the face of laughter, speak it in the face of greed, trying to get the attention of people who are on their way to some other sensational thing to quicken a flickering life. And you're trying to catch them on the run. Speak it in the face of people who have gone through the world for sixty or seventy years with nothing but a handful of ashes and they have no reason to believe this marvelous thing you're saying. And you keep saying it. Of course we're scared.

Easy thing for me to just say it when I'm with Christians. Get together with folk who already agree with me. I can sound the Easter trumpet there. Let all other sounds cease and I can blast the trumpet because I know everybody in the room already agrees. But when I look around and nobody has ever heard this before, the easiest thing in the world for me is to retreat into a radical subjectivism and just tell you how I feel about it. And you ask me how I know He lives and I say He lives in my heart and I know that you can't get at me because who can examine another person's heart? In fact I could even become a little arrogant with that kind of witnessing. No, no, no. And it doesn't mean bravado, a few scattered screams over the fence now and then over some issue that may even be dead by now.

It means courage. Of course we're scared. There's some Farmer Oak in every one of us. You remember Thomas Hardy's character Farmer Oak? Ah, that pitiful man. He stood at the window and saw a young woman go every morning and every evening to milk the cows. And he just watched her go with the pails empty and full. He watched her every day and he fell in love with her behind the glass, in the house, looking out the window. He fell in love with her but she never knew. Because he was afraid, he was afraid to say anything. There's some of that in all of us. Of course we're afraid. To get up and speak is frightening.

I recall when I started to school. We went to a little rural school that had the third, fourth, and fifth grades in the same room with one teacher. You may not understand all of this but each class would go up to the front and recite and the others would sit in the back and read while we were reciting. Then the next class would go up. There was a recitation bench and you had to go up to the recitation bench and then you went through those oral drills, spelling, math, sentences, grammar. Had to stand up in front of all those kids and give the capitals of the states. The teacher would just call out "Idaho" and you'd stand up and give the capital. If you didn't know it, it was embarrassing. And if you did, it was frightening. All your friends at the back snickering, hoping you'd miss something. "All right, stand." And she gives you the word "hypotenuse." And you think hypot, hypote, hypotenuse. Oh it's awful. It's a frightening thing to stand there right in front of everybody. Make sentences, add numbers; how painful!

It's no wonder we're afraid because in a few minutes you're going to be asked, you're going to be asked to stand in this room in front of these people and say your faith. We call it the Apostles' Creed. It's the apostolic preaching. It is frightening, but that's what we're asked to do. To make the center of life, to act out of, move out of, live out of, the belief that God gives life to the dead. God gives life to the dead. God calls into being that which did not exist.

Abraham and Sarah were dead. Could they have children? No. She was dead; he was dead. But they believed that God gives life to the dead. Jesus of

Nazareth was dead. You ask the soldiers, he was dead. You ask His friends, He was dead. Ask the women from Galilee, He was dead. Ask His mother, He was dead. But God gives life to the dead. And you and I, dead in our trespasses and sins, God has made alive. To say that, to get up every morning with that as the governing consideration of my life, this is not to be narrow-minded and say "Close off all the options." Of course we're open. Do we believe God is doing and saying other things in the world? Of course. We don't want to be narrow, rigid, literal, repeating what others said and did.

I went to church with a friend of mine. It was a small rural church. It was different from where I usually go. They had the Communion service. I was welcome; I participated. After the Communion, we sang a hymn. We went outside. I said, "Are we going to have a sermon?" He said, "Yeah, yeah." After we went outside, we all came back in and had the sermon. I said, "What was that about?" "The Bible says that after the Lord's Supper, they sang a hymn and went out." I said, "You've got to be kidding!" "That's what the Bible says."

To be a witness doesn't mean that you just shut everything down and close everything off. We are aware of all the roads to God and from God. What I'm saying is we don't spend a lifetime pondering all those roads and calling it being "open." The fact of the matter is you've got to take one. You've got to take a road. It's not a matter of serving afternoon tea to every position on every issue because you are open. If you do, without ever taking one, without ever drinking a cup, without ever breaking the bread, you will probably go to your grave having been very interesting company but having witnessed to nothing. Nothing.

38

Sit at My Right Hand Until . . .

Acts 2:22–36

All of you have probably noticed that one of the strange practices of Christians is to declare as true many things that are not true. In fact some even celebrate events that have never occurred. For instance, Christians say, "We have been raised with Christ and made to sit with him in heavenly places." Christians have announced that statement as the truth and have enjoyed it, but is it true? When did it happen? Or for instance, Christians say, "We have died to sin. Sin no longer has power over us." That's a wonderful statement, but is it true? Will all of those for whom that is the truth, please stand.

Or for instance, Christians say, "Christ has broken down the wall of hostility and made us one in him." Broken down the wall of hostility. We are one people in Christ. Is that true? Is it really true? In every town through which you pass, large or small, I daresay at least half of the churches in that town began as split-offs. We are one in Christ Jesus? Or for instance, listen to the Christian announcement in our text.

> This Jesus God raised up, and of that we all are witnesses. Being therefore exalted at the right hand of God, and having received from the Father the promise of the Holy Spirit, he has poured out this which you see and hear. For David did not ascend into the heavens; but he himself says, "The Lord said to my Lord, Sit at my right hand, till I make thy enemies a stool for thy feet." Let all the house of Israel therefore know assuredly that God has made him both Lord and Christ, this Jesus whom you crucified. (Acts 2:32–36 RSV)

The writer of Acts is here presenting the sermon of Simon Peter in Jerusalem on the day of Pentecost. At the center of this sermon is the word that this Jesus whose life and death they all knew, God has raised from the dead. Of that truth, he says, we are witnesses. But in order to confirm it in the minds of the listeners beyond what a mere word of witness might do, Peter draws upon the Old Testament and in particular that portion of the Old Testament most often used in the New Testament, Psalm 110.

"The LORD says to my lord, "Sit at my right hand, till I make your enemies your footstool" (RSV).

I'm tempted to pause here to remind ourselves that in the early church the primary meaning of the resurrection was not the assurance of personal life after death. In no way would I minimize what that came to mean and does mean to all of us, thanks especially to Paul's development of the theme of the resurrection of God's people. But the fact is, the central interpretation of the resurrection was the exaltation of Christ to God's right hand as Lord of the church. It is true, of course, that Luke, in the book of Acts, separates the resurrection and the ascension of Christ by forty days. We're all aware of Luke's style of translating the theology of the church into history. But even though he separates these two themes by the space of forty days, in reality he joins other writers in the New Testament in concentrating upon the resurrection of Christ as his exaltation to the right hand of God.

Resurrection without ascension simply means resuscitation of the dead. Listen to the way others say the same thing. You will recall in the Gospel of John that as Jesus approaches the cross, he says in prayer to God, "Father, now restore to me the glory I had with you before the foundation of the world." That is to say, the resurrection was the restoration of Christ to God's right hand. Or, as Paul puts it, "He humbled himself and became obedient unto death, even death on a cross. Therefore God has highly exalted him and bestowed on him the name which is above every name, that at the name of Jesus every knee should bow, in heaven and on earth and under the earth, and every tongue confess that Jesus Christ is Lord, to the glory of God the Father" (Phil. 2:8–11 RSV). Notice how the statement of resurrection appears as really a statement of the exaltation of Christ as Lord.

Or, again, from the Epistle to the Hebrews. "When he had made purification for sins, he sat down at the right hand of the Majesty on high, having become as much superior to angels as the name he has obtained is more excellent than theirs" (Heb. 1:3–4 RSV). In other words, when he had been crucified, then he sat down at the right hand of God. The image of the exaltation of Christ as Lord is shaped and nourished in the New Testament by Psalm 110, which is an enthronement psalm. When the king of Israel was crowned, this psalm was used, declaring that the throne of the king was actually at the right hand of God and to him God said, "Sit here beside me until I make your enemies a stool for your feet."

Think of this coronation psalm in connection with the crowning of Israel's first king, Saul. Saul, the son of Kish, was sent by his father to find some straying asses. While he was looking for the asses, he met the prophet of God on the road. At the prophet's direction, the servant attending Saul was sent away and Saul himself was commanded to kneel. The oil of anointing was poured by the prophet Samuel over Saul's head and the prophet declared, "God has chosen you as king over Israel." This big country boy from the hill tribe of Benjamin all of a sudden is king of Israel and God says, "Sit at my right hand." Now I ask you, is he a king really? How would the word be received at home if he came back from the field and said to his parents and brothers, "I am a king"? How would his friends downtown receive it? How would that word sound on the street? "Saul is a king." A king? He has no crown; he has no capital; he has no army; he has no ambassadors; he has no government; he has no flag; he has no seal. But God has crowned him king? And God said, "Sit at my right hand." Is he then a king? Why sure, he's a king, because God said that he's a king. But really, he's not a king. Is he?

Recall the coronation of Israel's second king, David. The scene is Bethlehem of Judea, the house of Jesse. The prophet has been told that the next king of Israel will be of the house of Jesse. Jesse has many sons and when the prophet arrives at the house, he has Jesse bring his sons around so that the right one may be selected. It's interesting that all of the boys were at home. I don't know why. Maybe they were sitting around combing their hair waiting to be king. To the prophet each one looked good enough to be king but God spoke in his heart and said, "No, no, no, no." So Samuel said to Jesse, "Are these all your sons?"

Jesse said, "I have one other, the young boy out keeping the sheep, David."

"Then you'd best send for him."

And as you know, it was David. Kneeling before his family and the prophet, David was anointed king of Israel. Now is this boy a king? Tell his brothers that and see if they bow down or laugh. Suppose David refuses from this time on to do any chores around the place because, he says, "After all, I am a king." Surely his mother would accept that as reason enough for not cleaning his room or emptying the garbage. God said, "Sit at my right hand until I make your enemies a stool for your feet." Is David a king? Why, of course he's a king. God has anointed him king. But now really, is he a king? Well, no, not really a king. Is he?

Recall the coronation of Jesus. This Jesus whom you crucified God has raised from the dead and he is seated at the right hand of God and God has said, "Sit here until I make your enemies a stool for your feet." Now is Jesus really crowned as Lord? Is he really a king before whom every knee should bend, in heaven, on earth, and under the earth? Well of course he is. Because God has christened him, anointed him, made him the Lord and Christ. And God said, "Sit at my right hand." But really, is he Lord? Well, in a way he is, but in a way, he isn't.

Ask Simon Peter. He's the one who preached the sermon. He's the one who said this. Ask him. And Simon Peter says, "Of course he is. He is the Lord of the church and he is Lord of all. And this word is not only to you but to your children and to your children's children and to all the nations of the world, regardless of race or place or language. He is the Lord." Simon Peter's conviction is absolutely unwavering. But in the same book that records this sermon and this conviction, only a few chapters later, this same man is called upon to preach to some Gentiles, an Italian soldier and his family and friends. But Simon Peter says, "No, I have never gone into the home of a Gentile. I have never eaten with Gentiles." It is only after repeated visions and prod-dings that the man who claimed that Jesus is Lord of all people finally con-sents to break the race and custom barrier. Is Jesus Christ Lord, Simon Peter? Of course. Well, yes, however . . .

Ask the Apostle John. John said it in a most beautiful and dramatic way. In the Apocalypse, the Revelation, John paints on a huge canvas, the lordship of Christ over all opposing forces, including death. Caught up in this grand vision, John says that the last enemy, death, is defeated. There is no more death. Death is dead. Jesus Christ is Lord even of death. Is that true? Is that really true?

A friend and colleague of mine died last year. About five years ago she was at home in her apartment grading papers. She heard a knock at the door. She went to the door and there in the doorway stood Old Death with his yellow face. She slammed the door, bolted it, and went to the doctor. He said, "It is malignant." There was surgery, medication, and she was back at work. She really looked good. Her weight was right, she was cheerful and hopeful.

About two years ago she was at home alone one evening. She heard a knock at the door, went to answer it, and there stood Old Death with his yellow face. She slammed the door, bolted it, and ran to the doctor. There was more surgery and chemotherapy. Her hair came out; she got a wig. She returned to work and we joked with her. "You should have been wearing a wig all along. It looks good." And her spirits were bright.

Last year she was at home alone one evening. She heard a knock at the door and went to answer. There stood Old Death with his yellow face. She slammed the door but the lock was broken. She was afraid; she could not keep him out. She called friends and family and we gathered from far and near. We took turns, twenty-four hours a day, leaning against that door. We could keep him out. We did it so well; we grew cheerful in the chore. We even joined with her in laughing and talking and remembering good times.

Once in a while one of us would go to the window and look out, just to see if he was still there. And he was, with his yellow face. But one day she said from her bed, "Back away from the door." Surprised, we did as she said. The door opened and there Death stood with his yellow face. But I felt sorry for him really; in his hands were not his usual poison darts of pain and fear. One hand now held peace and the other hand rest. It was evident as I looked at him that this once feared enemy was an angel of God. Christ is the Lord of death? Yes. But the friend is dead; she's no longer here to enjoy and to be enjoyed and to share life. That's true, but you should have heard us sing at her funeral.

Jesus Christ is Lord. How can we say it really? Christians say a lot of things as though they were true when they aren't true. Are they? The only reason I have been able to come up with to explain why Christians keep saying things are true is that they really are. Jesus Christ is at the right hand of God, Lord of life and death. Do you believe that? Before you answer, let me remind you that it is not wisdom only to be wise and on the inward vision, close the eyes. It is wisdom also to believe the heart.

39

Table Talk

Acts 2:43–47

And fear came upon every soul; and many wonders and signs were done through the apostles. And all who believed were together and had all things in common; and they sold their possessions and goods and distributed them to all, as any had need. And day by day, attending the temple together and breaking bread in their homes, they partook of food with glad and generous hearts, praising God and having favor with all the people. And the Lord added to their number day by day those who were being saved. (RSV)

In those lively sentences, Luke sketches a vivid portrait of the early church in the vigor of its youth in Jerusalem. Since Luke writes, in part, to provide a model for the church in his own day, we should not be surprised to find him touching upon those qualities central and normative for the church anytime and anywhere. The author has just described the Holy Spirit's launching, through the apostles, that new fellowship, which we call the church. It was not altogether new, says Luke, because it was the fulfillment of the promises of God to and for his people from the beginning.

The place is Jerusalem, for the word of the Lord is to go forth to all peoples from Jerusalem. The time is Pentecost, a festival celebrating not just the early harvest but the giving of God's revelation at Sinai. The assembly consists of Jews from every nation, for through them are all nations to be blessed. In that setting, says Luke, God poured out his spirit on all flesh. The apostles preached, witnessing to the resurrection of the crucified one. Thousands repented and turned to God and something old, yet new, something new, yet old, was begun.

It is the habit of Luke, following an account of activity or conflict in that church, to pause and, in reflection, describe the quality of life within that

Christian community. These descriptions are brief, clear, and always positive. Such is the nature of our text. In five succinct lines, that vibrant church is characterized. Vigorous leadership: signs and wonders were done by the apostles. Evangelism: and the Lord added day by day those who were being saved. Fellowship: All who believed were together and had all things in common. Stewardship: and they sold their possessions and goods and distributed them to all, as any had need. Worship: attending the temple together and praising God. But why, among those tall phrases describing the ideal church in its model behavior, are we told they partook of food with glad and generous hearts, breaking bread in their homes? Is the writer interrupting himself to say that, in the midst of ecclesiastical business those Christians did take time to eat? If so, could we not have assumed that? One hardly pauses in documenting the lives of God's people to say that they cared for creature needs. Perhaps we should just wrap that sentence in parentheses, mutter a few comments about those strange Near Easterners and move on. Hardly.

If I were to ask you to sketch a picture that would be properly entitled *The Church*, what would you draw? A beautiful little building with a spire, a sanctuary with pews of worshipers, a small group in a circle studying the Bible, an altar and a pulpit? When Luke portrays the church, whatever else is included, he always places in the center a dining table. More than any other Gospel writer, Luke describes Jesus at table. Read through this Gospel and you probably will be as surprised as I was to discover how many of the great lessons Jesus gave were given while he was at the table.

In the home of Martha and Mary, he spoke of pots and pans and the kingdom. Sitting at the table of Simon, the Pharisee, he taught of love and forgiveness. When he was a dinner guest at a certain home, he warned the other guests about seeking the places at the head table. While he was at a banquet, he said that when you're giving a big banquet, make your guest list of those who are financially unable to return the courtesy. He was at dinner when he said that the kingdom of God is like a man who gave a great banquet. Those invited made excuses and so the room was filled with people of the street. The most beautiful parable that Jesus ever told was a parable of a dinner party for a prodigal who had returned. It was at a meal with his friends that Jesus spoke of his death.

After his resurrection, Luke says that Jesus' appearance to his followers began when two of his disciples were walking home from Jerusalem, discouraged and downcast. As they trudged toward Emmaus, a stranger joined them and he asked them what they were talking about. They began to share with him their disappointment at the death of Jesus in whom they had hoped. The stranger listened and then began to explain the Scriptures, filling their minds concerning those things that would happen to the Messiah. The day faded into evening and so the two asked the stranger to stay for dinner. When they were at the table they asked him to say grace. And he took the bread and broke it and said the blessing. And the Lord was made known to them in the breaking of bread.

In the second volume of his work entitled *Acts of Apostles,* Luke pictures the risen Christ with his followers. And he says that while they were staying together—the expression "staying together" is literally "sharing the salt." In other words, while eating together, he gave them the Great Commission to witness in all the world. But this witnessing in all the world was possible only if the great barrier between Jew and Gentile was broken. And how was it broken? Of the many stories he tells, recall only two.

Luke says Simon Peter was on a housetop in Joppa, hungry and waiting for his lunch. As he napped, he had a vision of a sheet come down from heaven and on the sheet were all kinds of creatures that it was not kosher to eat. "Rise, Peter, kill and eat." Three times he saw the vision and each time Peter refused. The voice from heaven became unmistakable. "What I call clean, do not call unclean." When that beautiful story ends, Simon Peter has entered the house of a Gentile, an Italian army officer in Caesarea, and has eaten with the man, his family, and his servants.

The second story concerns Paul. It also occurred about noon near Damascus and he, too, through a vision, was called to preach to Gentiles. Broken and penitent because of his efforts to destroy the church, for days Paul refused food or drink. Then the pastor of the Christian community in Damascus came to him, called him brother, embraced him with understanding, and baptized him. The congregation surrounded Paul and accepted him fully as demonstrated by their eating together.

Why is it so vital to Luke to picture the church sitting around a table? Because for him sharing the food is basic to the definition of a church. There is nothing more spiritual anyone can do for another than to share the food. In a certain village there was a rabbi whose absence on the eve of the Day of Atonement was explained by the congregation in this way. "Our rabbi has ascended to heaven to make intercession with his people." A visitor in that synagogue heard that explanation and made light of it saying, "No one ascends to heaven; that's foolish." The next year the same explanation occurred and from this one came the same refusal to believe. "That's foolish; no one ascends to heaven." The third year this unbeliever determined to find the truth so he hid under the bed in the rabbi's cottage, waited and watched. Early one morning the rabbi got up and gathered what food he had into a sack and started out through the woods. He traveled some distance through the forest, pausing at one time to chop down a tree, cut it into fuel, tie it in a bundle, and put it on his back. He continued his way through the forest until he came to a clearing where a very humble cottage housed a widow and her children. The rabbi gave the food and fuel to this poor family. The next Sabbath the congregation explained the absence of the rabbi by saying, "The rabbi has ascended to heaven." But the former doubter arose and announced; "He has gone even higher." You cannot go higher than sharing the food. Wherever some eat and some do not eat, you do not have church.

But it was not just in the bread that Christ was present, it was in the breaking of bread, in the sharing of the bread. The very nature of the church is contradicted when some have to eat alone. So painful was the thought of having to eat alone that it came to the mind of the Apostle Paul only in one moment of extreme anger and disappointment. He had learned that the church in Corinth had grown so permissive that one of the leaders was living with his father's wife. And even worse, the congregation was not raising any objection. Paul was incensed. He demanded that this man who had set such a poor example and brought such disrepute on the church be punished severely. Paul searched his imagination for the worst possible penalty and he finally concluded that that man was not to eat with the church. He must eat alone. It is hard to conceive of a harsher punishment than that. It apparently worked because the church in extreme cases of violation of its morals or its teaching continued the practice and called it excommunication.

The secular world followed and reserved for its hardened criminals that terrible sentence, solitary confinement, and it remains the awful fact that the church in many places even today, without imagination and thought, allows that practice to continue by its neglect of the increasing number of the aging and widowed. Of course there's no punishment intended but the pain is no less severe. If you don't think so, just ask those who sit alone somewhere amid stainless steel trays, forced to eat alone when their only crime is that they have gotten old. But in that church Luke describes, eating together was the test and the proof of their common life. Was there full love and acceptance each for the other? Of course, they ate together, didn't they? Evangelizing and baptizing people with whom one would not be willing to eat was not allowed.

You recall that very tense moment in the church at Antioch, which Paul describes in his Letter to the Galatians. He and Simon Peter were attending the fellowship dinner there in that church made up of Jewish Christians and Gentile Christians. The remarkable fact is that they were eating together, Simon Peter included. But there came in certain brethren from the church in Jerusalem. They whispered in the ear of Simon Peter and he along with several others formed a separate table. Paul stood, walked over to Simon Peter and said, "You are condemned before God for this hypocrisy." One can hardly imagine a more tense moment than this, the two great apostles standing eyeball to eyeball and the table fellowship interrupted. It is a crisis of major importance. What was at stake? Everything was at stake.

When you form a separate table you have destroyed the church. It is not a church where some refuse to eat with others. How profound is this simple portrait of the church drawn by Luke. The church is a group eating together with glad and generous hearts. It is theologically central, not just quietly beautiful, that he began his story of the resurrection with that account of two men asking a tired stranger to stay for supper. They didn't know who he was; they only knew that the hour was late, the trip was long, and they were hungry. Wherever the church exists, now as then, God's people will break bread at home and partake of food with glad and generous hearts and now, no less than then, the Lord will be made known in the breaking of bread.

40

May I Also Be Included?

Acts 8:26–39

I do regret if my tight schedule has created any anxiety for Jim and the worship planners for today but this late rush is no big deal. In the spring I plan to do a parachute drop into the courtyard.

Now to the text for today. It involves one of those church meetings that we, most of us I think, hate to attend. Not in spite of the fact that it was a church meeting but because it was a church meeting. Church meetings can be the most incendiary of all. We knew it was going to be rough; it was a called meeting. We knew it was going to be rough because the notice said everyone should select delegates for the meeting. We knew it was going to be rough when we got to the room and found a note under the door: "Will the Antioch delegation meet thirty minutes before the plenary." And then arriving in the great hall it looked like a forest of microphones. It's going to be confrontive. I don't do well in that kind of setting. I'd rather go shopping and then come back and say, "How did it go? I wish I'd been there."

It was a single-issue meeting, Luke says; a single-issue meeting. The issue was clear: Are we going to continue to admit into full standing and fellowship in the church foreigners, persons who have never belonged to the people of Israel, persons who do not know the Old Testament, the story of creation, have never believed in God, do not have the moral and ethical standards of Israel, do not know the tradition of the exodus, who yesterday worshiped before idols? Shall we simply, upon their confession of faith, admit them into the fellowship? Is that enough? That was the question. (See Acts 15:1–29.)

The people were divided. Luke in his own modest way says, "There had been much debate." He says, "No small dissension arose among them." It was not simply that the Christians, and they were Christians all, it was not simply that the Christians disagreed with each other, but individual Christians disagreed with themselves. Their own hearts were torn and sometimes when we lash out at someone else because of their position, the reason for the intensity is that I'm at war with myself. And when I'm at war with myself, my tendency is to make casualties even out of people I love.

I know that was true with Simon Peter. "How shall I vote?" It was he who stood up in Jerusalem that first day, the day of Pentecost, and preached. It looked so good; a big crowd. Luke says that they were from every nation under heaven, Parthians, Medes, and Elamites, and dwellers of Mesopotamia. From everywhere they came. Peter was carried away in his oratory and when he had finished that sermon he said, "This promise is not only to you but to your children and your children's children and to all that are far off Gentiles, as many as God shall call." Great day.

And then he had a vision to go to the house of a Gentile and preach and he said, "No." It's one thing to preach, it's another thing to do. It's one thing to have your voice heard in a crowd that is not approving, it's another thing to be in a crowd that agrees with you. Have you ever had a minority position and you were sort of pleased that you were in the minority? Then you went to a gathering and everyone agreed with you and it scared you. That happens, you know. I think my view is going to pass. It's scary. Maybe that's the way it was for them.

I know he must have been divided in his own heart. Paul said Peter was at the fellowship dinner at Antioch. He started eating with Gentiles but some others came in and he, with Barnabas and some other Jewish Christians, formed a separate table. A painful thing for that church and for Paul and I'm sure for Simon Peter himself. Because you see, it is one thing to say, "I know we should include these people." It is another thing to believe in your heart "we should include these people." That's the longest trip you'll ever make in your life, between the head "I know" and the heart "I know."

And in between there was no small dissension and much debate. So they argued. They went to the microphones. "Microphone Three." "Yes, we're here from Antioch. And we have good Bible study groups, Super Six Bible class every Tuesday night. We've been studying Ezra. We all believe the Bible and Ezra says, 'Get rid of the foreigners. Even if you're married to one, divorce her. Get rid of the foreigners.' That's all I want to say. Thank you."

"Microphone Two, we'll hear from you, Microphone Two." "Well, we also have a nice church and a nice Bible study group and we're from Berea. We've named our class the Berean Class and we've been studying. In our women's group we've been studying Ruth. Such a wonderful woman, she was the ancestress of David and the ancestress of our Lord, as you know, and she was a Moabite. And if our Lord had Moabite blood in his veins, isn't this OK for us to do this? Thank you, Mr. Chairman."

"Microphone Five." "Well, I don't know but one of the really great prophets of Israel was Amos and Amos said, 'You alone,' talking to the Jews, 'you alone.' Do I need to define 'alone'? He doesn't say etceteras, it says alone. 'I have chosen from among all the nations you alone.' Thank you."

"Microphone Nine." "Yes. I don't have anything to say but I remember when I was just a child I memorized a Bible verse about, I don't know, I can't say it now, but uh, uh, 'The mountain of the Lord's house will be the highest of all the mountains in all the nations, all the nations.' I think it says all the nations shall flow into it. Thank you."

Oh, me. I'd rather be shopping. Whose fault is it? I mean here the church is doing fine, started off with thousands and thousands, multiplied and spread out from Jerusalem and is just doing great. We've got little congregations in all the towns and then this. It's just going to split us wide open and then what's going to happen? Just when everything was going so well.

"You know whose fault I think it is? I think it's Stephen's. When he made that speech against the temple in Jerusalem that's what started it. Now he was appointed to wait tables but he thought he had to preach; everybody wants to preach. And that's what started it."

"No, I don't think so, I think it was Philip. He went up there and baptized some of those Samaritans. He baptized some of those Samaritans and when you let those Samaritans in, the camel's nose is in the tent."

"Well, no, I really think it's Simon Peter. He doesn't want us to know about it but I happen to know because I have a sister who lives in Caesarea. He ate with some Italians. Yes, the word is out, the word is out. We're supposed to think of him as one of our leaders, an Apostle."

"Isn't it really, though, the fault of Paul? Running around here claiming this vision, claiming to be an Apostle to the Gentiles. He just takes in everybody, just lets them all in. 'You all come.' And look at his churches. Holding their bulletins upside down, don't know an introit from a benediction. He just lets in everybody and that's when it all turned sour as far as I'm concerned."

"No, I really don't think so. I think it was Barnabas. Bless his heart, he's such a fine person, but you know how we'd all agreed in Jerusalem, if Paul ever shows up here, he can fellowship with us, he can take the Lord's Supper with us, but he is not to preach. Oh, he can have the benediction or something; he is not to preach. But Barnabas took him around and worked him in and pretty soon there he is preaching. Now Barnabas should not have done that. He knows better."

Whose fault is it? Luke says that the fault is God's. That God sent the Holy Spirit to push and shove the church. Push and shove the church beyond ethnic borders, national borders, social borders, economic borders. That repentance and forgiveness be preached to all nations and the Holy Spirit pushed and pushed and pushed and pushed. But every once in awhile, Luke turns the camera around. Instead of giving us this painful pushing scene of the Holy Spirit moving the church beyond its own prejudice, once in awhile, Luke turns the camera around and lets it focus upon one of the outsiders whose future is at stake, one of these people whose fate is being debated in the church. Shall we let them in or shall we not let them in? Luke turns the camera upon one of these people. What does it mean to the person standing outside waiting upon the word of the church? "How did it go? Will I be admitted or not?"

And the strangest of all the stories that Luke tells is that of the Ethiopian eunuch in his chariot riding from Jerusalem to Gaza, the one to whom Philip spoke. He's an Ethiopian. I don't know if Luke wants us to take that literally or not. There was an Ethiopia, somewhere near Khartoum or Aswan today, but the word Ethiopia, since the days of Homer, had been sort of a nickname or a symbol for the end of the world. "Oh, they tell me he's from Ethiopia." Ethiopia just meant the jumping-off place. Ethiopia meant the same as in my culture we said Timbuktu. We didn't know if there was one or not, but we'd say, "I don't care if she goes to Timbuktu." That just meant as far as you can go and then a little more. Just the end of it. Timbuktu.

Well in the literature of that day, that's the way Ethiopia was used. I mean how far out and away and distant can you be? "He's an Ethiopian." And he's a eunuch. A eunuch is a man who either by accident or by surgery was rendered sexless. Usually such persons found gainful employment, and sometimes powerful and wealthy employment, in palaces, especially in the service of queens. For being sexless, they were not derailed by their own private interests, harmless around the harem, never having to be late because they were driving the carpool that morning. No wife, no children, no anything to distract. Devoted, single-minded, loyal, they were very useful in such occasions. Plutarch says it was very common. I think it was Josephus who said, "One nasty thing about Herod is that he had three eunuchs in his palace." Even though, even though the Jewish Scripture was very clear. Deuteronomy 23:1: "The eunuch shall not be permitted in the assembly of the people of God" (paraphr.). Any questions? "The eunuch shall not be permitted in the assembly of the people of God." Then what in the world does it mean when it says he had been up to Jerusalem to worship?

What kind of man is this who would walk around the outside, stand at the edge, look over the fence, ask people what's going on. "How was the service? How was the sermon? What did the priest do? Were there many people there?" Peeking through knotholes, getting stuff secondhand, looking over fences, walking the edge of the crowd. Worship?

I ask you seriously. Why will any human being continue to knock at a locked door and stand there with bloody knuckles and refuse to go home?

Why? The door is locked. Shall I read it again? You are not welcome. It's clear. Why doesn't he just make it easy on himself? Is he one of these people who entertains the notion that if you rise to a certain level of power, a certain level of wealth, then the rules don't apply to you anymore? He is a wealthy man. He has his own Bible, it says in the text; he must have been wealthy. He's in a chariot. He is in the service of Candace, the Queen of the Ethiopians. He's the treasurer of the country. "Maybe the rule doesn't apply to me."

I don't know. I certainly wish he'd make it easy on himself. He's simply increasing the pain. Lingering at the edge of the people of God with that verse staring at him day and night. Why does he do it? Even if somebody, even if a careless usher, even if somebody who didn't know what it was all about admitted him, he wouldn't fit in. The moment he got inside it would be obvious to everybody. "You don't fit in; you just don't fit in. I mean even if we let you in, you don't fit in."

I'm borrowing the phrase "don't fit in" from my first student church. It was up in East Tennessee. I worked there in the summers as a seminarian and it was about twenty miles from Oak Ridge. Oak Ridge had gotten into place. The atomic energy thing was booming and folk were coming and construct- ing that little town into a city. Folk were coming from everywhere. Hard-hat types, in tents and trailers and little temporary huts and all kind of lean-tos. They covered those beautiful hills with temporary quarters, wash hanging out on the fences and little kids crying through the muddy places where all these things were parked.

My little church, an aristocratic little church, white frame building, beauti- ful little church was near by. It was a nice church, wonderful people. I called the board together and said, "We need to reach out to those folk who are here. They just come in from everywhere and they're fairly close. Here's our mission." The chairman of the board said, "Oh I don't think so." I said, "Why?" He said, "They won't fit in. After all, they're just here temporarily, living in those trailers and all." "Well, they may be here temporarily but they need the gospel, they need a church, now why . . . ?" "No, I don't think so."

The board meeting lasted a long time. Called the next meeting for the next Sunday night. The upshot of it all was a resolution. The resolution was offered by one of the relatives of the chairman of the board and the resolution basically was this: "Members will be admitted to this church from families who own property in the county." It was unanimous except for my vote and I was reminded I couldn't vote. "They won't fit in; they won't fit in."

Since we've been back at Candler I wanted to take Nettie, my wife, up to see the scene of my early failures. Had a hard time finding the church because of Interstate 40 through there and all that now but I finally found the road, the county road, and back nestled in the pines, still there, shining white, just beautiful. Just like it was except now cars and trucks were parked everywhere, just everywhere, cars and trucks. And a big sign out front: "Barbecue. All you can eat, chicken, ribs, pork."

I said, "Well, we might as well go in for lunch." Went inside, they still had those beautiful oil lamps hanging on the wall, beautiful oil lamps, still had that old pump organ, one of the kids always had to stand there and pump it while it was being played in the service. Beautiful; now it's decoration.

The pews which had been cut from a single poplar tree were around the walls and people waiting to get seated at a table; there were a lot of those aluminum-legged plastic tables. And the place was full of all kinds of people. Listen, they're Parthians, Medes, and Elamites, dwellers of Mesopotamia. And I said to Nettie, "It certainly is good this is not a church now. These folk would not be welcome. They wouldn't fit in."

Why does this Ethiopian eunuch keep doing it? You know what he's doing? You do it yourself; I do it myself. He's flipping the pages of the Bible to find his own name. Everyone in the world wants that. I want to find my name. I want to find a verse that says, "for me" and I'll write it in the margin. That's who I am. Just a little promise, just a phrase, just something; he's looking for his name. We all do that.

I have a friend whose son, a university student, was killed in a wreck and my friend kept saying it was God's will. I couldn't stand it. You don't argue at a funeral but weeks later when we were talking, I said, "Charles, you can't say that anymore, that it was God's will that he be killed in a car wreck. Don't say that." He looked at me with level gaze and said, "Leave me alone. I will say that." He said, "What's the alternative that you've got to offer? You'll probably say it was an accident. Now which do I prefer, to believe that God knew my son, that God had something in store for my son, that God had a purpose for my son? Or your theology that says, 'It was an accident.' I'll take mine; leave me alone." Even in death people want to say, "Ah, there's my name. God knows me."

And so he's reading in Isaiah and he finds it; he thinks he finds it. It's almost too good to be true. There it says it, Isaiah.

> No longer let the foreigners say surely the Lord will separate me from his people. No longer let the eunuch say I am but a dry tree for thus says the Lord God. The days are coming when the eunuch, who hears my voice and obeys my law and keeps my covenant, I will give him a place in my house and I will give him a name and it shall be to him as generation and generation and generation of children. Better than sons and daughters it shall be to the eunuch. (Isa. 56:3–5, paraphr.).

Ah, he reads in Isaiah. "As a lamb that's led to the slaughter, as a sheep before a shearer is dumb, he didn't open his mouth. Who will declare his generation?

Who is going to declare his generation? He was cut off out of the land of living. He had no children; he had no generation. He had no one to remember him. He had no one to carry on his name. He was just cut off, killed without any children. Who's going to declare justice for him?" (paraphr.).

And Philip said, "Do you understand what you're reading?" He said, "No, I don't have anybody to help me, but I found some good stuff here. Now is the prophet talking about himself or is the prophet talking about someone else?" Philip said, "Let me tell you who that is. That's Jesus."

"You mean he was cut off without any children? He didn't have any other generations and grandchildren and people to keep his name?"

"No, he was cut off from the land of the living."

"Do you mean to say that maybe this other verse up here, maybe, I know, I know, I'm just an Ethiopian and I don't know how you feel about Ethiopians, but it says here, no longer, no longer let the foreigners say surely the Lord will say, 'get out.' I know I'm a eunuch and I know what it says in Deuteronomy but it says in Isaiah, 'No longer let the eunuch say I'm just a dry tree. Listen I will bless you and you will be remembered and it will be better than children, grandchildren, great-grandchildren forever.'"

"Uh, Philip, do you suppose it's possible, I know I'm just an Ethiopian. I know I'm a eunuch, but do you think it is possible, could I be a member of the church?" And Philip said, "I can think of a hundred people who are going to be upset but, yes. I don't know how this is going to go over back home, but yes. In fact, I feel a little awkward myself because I've never been in this situation and I'm not handling it well, but yes. In fact, I'm surprised at hearing myself say this, but yes. Because the fact of the matter is, who am I to say no when it is clear that God has already said yes."

Do we have to put it to a vote in this group? Or may we accept it by acclamation?

41

Surrounded

Acts 26:12–18

I don't know if you were listening very carefully to the reading of the text, but I was and frankly I felt some distance between that text and myself. It was not the fairly common distance of unfamiliarity. I am familiar with the story the text narrates. Three times in the book of Acts and once in a letter, the Letter to the Galatians, the story of Paul's conversion and call to the ministry has been given. Saul, or better known as Paul, was a persecutor of Christians. The accounts agree he was on his way to Damascus, Syria, in the pursuit of his ugly business when his life was turned around. He was in the company of several others and about noon, as they approached the city, he saw a light and out of the light a person. He heard a sound and from the sound, a voice. As a result of that experience he was turned from dealing death to the Christians to a life of missionary work on behalf of the gospel. That work took him to Syria, Turkey, Greece, and finally Italy.

I know the story and you know the story. We experience no distance of unfamiliarity here. The distance I feel is rather that of being unable to identify with the story. Here is a man on the wrong track and he is halted by vision and by voice. In front of him is the person of Jesus of Nazareth and behind him, according to this text, moves some unnamed pressure, which is prompting him and goading him toward what is right. "It is hard for you to kick against the goads." In other words, he is surrounded, unmistakably, by the influences of God.

Now the distance I feel is simply this. God has, in my experience, been much more timid, applying very little pressure at all. In fact, at times I hardly know God is there. Now don't get me wrong. I believe that God communicates but my experience of his communication is that of whispers, not shouts. And sometimes the whisper is a very low whisper. In fact, sometimes I'm not even sure of God's word or of God's will. I believe God acts but when you're the only one around who saw what God did, you begin to wonder if God really did it. For example, sometime after recovering from an illness, say, "God restored my health," and say it among your friends and relatives. Do you suppose you will get strange glances? Why? You do believe that God restored your health. But it was not obvious, was it? Or after some major turn in your road, say, "God answered my prayers." Say that in the midst of friends and relatives and see what response there is. Probably they are thinking, "You always were lucky or what a coincidence that that should happen," but they cannot identify with God answering prayers.

There are some people who feel that their lives have been so victimized that the problem they have with God is God's fairness. Such has not been my case. My problem with God is God's timidity, God's quietness. Even on the most religious occasions, God stands back in the shadows. Ask the people around you, "Do you think God is here today?" Some of them will say, "Of course." Others will say, "I hope so." Others will say, "Well, I never thought about it." Others will say, "I'm not into that kind of stuff."

The story in the text for today impresses this matter on my mind. How can I think about it? Is it true that God once encountered people with vision and voice unmistakably loud and clear but now God has changed strategy? Or maybe God still does that for those who have faith and I simply do not have the faith. Or is it that the writer who reports these things in the Bible has misrepresented the case? Certainly it is helpful to take time to realize that there are huge differences in the language writers use to relate a faith story.

In the book of Acts, for instance, it is quite obvious that the writer narrates history as God's story. His accounts are given as though God obviously were the principal character in everything that happened and he projects it all on wide-screen and in Technicolor. For instance, he tells the story of the death of Herod Agrippa. Now Herod Agrippa died of gout and the general effects of severe intemperance. However, the writer of the book of Acts says, "God sent worms and they ate him." In the book of Acts, there is the story of Christian missionaries being released from a prison due to a big earthquake. The writer says, "God sent an earthquake." There are visions everywhere; there are angels everywhere. That's the way the writer tells the story.

Now in contrast, the Apostle Paul in his letters very seldom speaks of anything unusual. He is very soft on visions and miracles. In fact, the story we have just read about his own conversion and call to be an apostle, he himself tells very very quietly. In the Letter to the Galatians he says, "When God was pleased to reveal his Son in me." That's quite different from saying there was a voice and a light and the figure of Jesus. He tells it much more reservedly without the loud voice, without the bright colors. This is not to say that Paul was less Christian. This is not to say that Paul had less faith. Part of the difference lies in the way you tell something. It is also helpful to read the text very carefully.

We will discover that even in passages like this one before us, passages that seem to be full of visions and voices, things are not as obvious as they seem. For instance, Paul went to Damascus in the company of several others but the experience on the way to Damascus was his alone. Those who were with him did not see Jesus of Nazareth. Those who were with him did not hear a message from Jesus of Nazareth. Only Paul heard it. How are we to understand this? One way to understand it is, even in marvelous, extraordinary passages like this, the writer still makes it clear that only the ears and eyes of faith get the message.

Recall the scene in the Gospel of John when Jesus lifted his voice to God and said, "Father, glorify your name." John said the voice of God said, "I have glorified it and I will glorify it again." Some standing around thought it thundered. Others said that an angel spoke to him. What really happened? According to the writer, much depended on the kind of ear you brought to the occasion. This perspective is generally true of the Bible. Those marvelous stories of the miracles of Jesus, which may seem so persuasive to a Christian reader, remember they are told in such a way that some people standing nearby could come immediately after an exorcism or a healing and say to Jesus, "Show us a sign that you are really one with this authority." It is easy to say, "How blind can anyone be? Where were they? Didn't they just see what happened?" Obviously they did not. Sometimes we tend to criticize unreasonably the people that did not see and hear when actually what they missed was really not all that obvious.

I am convinced that God has always whispered and that God has been heard only by those who lean forward. Of course, what faith has heard, faith has then shouted. But with all that shouting, we have to remember that to the hearer, it is always a whisper. Isn't it the case that God has always stood in the shadows? When faith sees God, faith describes God in bold colors but we should understand that there is always plenty of room for reasonable people to say, "I do not think God was there." In other words, God does not overwhelm us. God leaves everyone room to say *no* so that when they do say *yes*, it will be a freely decided and responsible *yes*.

Having said that, I must go on to affirm that faith does see, does hear and we are still in these postbiblical times, surrounded by God's presence. If you don't believe it, just go out and read the face of nature. God has never been left without witness. This is not true only when the snow falls fresh upon the earth. This is not true only when you're looking at a lake glistening in the sun or see ripe peaches heavy on the tree or a newborn white-faced calf standing for the first time on wobbly legs. This is not true only when you see yellow pumpkins asleep among the sentinel shocks of grain or view the evening sun sizzling into the sea or flying clouds on a frosty night or green meadows turning somersaults of joy. Read the face of nature in barren places, too, and you will discover that there is more life even in the crack of a sidewalk than you ever noticed before. There is more life stirring in the desert than the speeding tourist ever sees. Not one square inch of the universe is so deprived or neglected that what, upon looking closely, you can see God's initials in the lower right-hand corner.

Or read your own heart; take a stroll down the back roads and along the rivers of your mind. Are you looking for anyone? Our fathers in the faith said we were made for God. We are seeking after God, searching in hope. The poet of ancient Greece, without the inspiration of Jewish or Christian Scripture, was still able to sing "In Him We Live and Move and Have Our Being." No blinding vision, no heavenly voice, to be sure, but it is real nevertheless. God still surrounds us even though whispering and standing in the shadow.

Or look around you; look at the persons beside you or across the table from you. Do you see anything unusual about them? Of course you do. For when God had created everything else, pine cones, squirrels and everything, God said, "That is good." But it was only when God made those people beside you and across from you that God said, "This is my own image, my own likeness." Had you noticed that before? You can see it, too, when you're looking in the mirror. That is, if you look carefully.

Sure, we're still surrounded; you just have to look and listen. You say that's not enough. Well, permit me one last word. No one has ever really seen God but there was a man who dwelt among us, a man who was so transparent, so free of selfish grasping for himself that many looked upon Jesus of Nazareth and said they saw God. Is that not enough? If it is final proof you seek, we have none. We can only speak of what we have seen and heard.

42

Remembering Tomorrow

Romans 9:1–5

I am speaking the truth in Christ, I am not lying; my conscience bears
me witness in the Holy Spirit, that I have great sorrow and unceasing
anguish in my heart. For I could wish that I myself were accursed and
cut off from Christ for the sake of my brethren, my kinsmen by race.
They are Israelites, and to them belong the sonship, the glory, the
covenants, the giving of the law, the worship, and the promises; to
them belong the patriarchs, and of their race, according to the flesh,
is the Christ. God who is over all be blessed forever. Amen. (RSV)

To be a Christian is, to a certain extent, an exercise of memory. I say that, I
realize, as a person who is himself growing older. I say that over against a culture that has sometimes been obsessed with now and at times with tomorrow.
I say that in reaction to having been made ashamed of remembering a few
years ago. Our culture made fun of remembering, laughed at remembering
patriotically or religiously or educationally or culturally or domestically. No
one does that any more, we were told. And some of us, trying to keep pace
with the young, quit remembering.

We have, however, come to realize we made a mistake. There is hardly any
posture for a human being that can replace the posture of reflection and recollection. It is essential to the health of a community and of a person. This is not
to mention the fact that remembering is also a source of tremendous pleasure.
You don't really take a trip until you remember the trip. Recall that last trip
you took. You had your camera, snapped all those good pictures, sent the film
away and finally got the slides back. Then you invited in some unsuspecting
friends to see a few thousand of your pictures. While they dozed off to sleep,
on into the night you revisited and remembered. Now that you were free of
suitcases, sickness, and the fear of losing your tickets and passport and all that,

now that you were back home you could look at the pictures and almost, for the first time, take the trip.

Many of our experiences become ours only in reflection. Do you recall your wedding ceremony? Probably you don't remember very much except a sense of relief when you discovered that you had gotten through the whole thing without falling on your face. You mumbled what you were supposed to say, made it down the aisle and out the door and it was over. You tried to listen but you couldn't at the time. But afterwards, looking through the album, you reflect upon it, and the meaning of marriage continually grows out of the profundity of those two words *I will*.

To be a Christian is, to a certain extent, an exercise of memory. I say that in spite of the traps and dangers there are in memory. It can be a trap you know, a place to hide. Some people hide in their memories and refuse to face the realities of today or tomorrow, longing for the way it used to be even though it never was. Sometimes it is dangerous to trust the memory because the memory gets to be rather selective. We forget the splinters on the old oaken bucket as we brag about the pure cool water from the well where we drank as children. The fact of the matter is the water was not safe but we don't remember that. Our young people get tired of hearing us talk about how it used to be. They know what we know but won't admit: our memory is a little bit inaccurate.

Our sons and daughters drag in and say, "Whew, did I have a hard day!" Our response is, "You don't know what work is. When I was your age . . ." Youth says, "Boy, was it hot today." And we say, "Hot? You've never seen it hot. When I was your age . . ." One of our youngsters moans, "Am I broke! I really could use some money." And we interrupt, "Broke? Why, you don't know what it is to be poor. You young people don't know the value of a dollar. When I was your age . . ."

To hear us tell it, when we were their age we went to school every day, twelve months a year, made straight As, went to church every Sunday and listened to every word. Of course there are traps and dangers in the memory and some are even more serious. There are those who use their memories for demonic purposes. They absolutely refuse to forget certain things. For them memory is a cave for nursing hatreds and grudges. It is as though they go out into their own little backyards every day and lift a rock to make sure the snake is still there. "I will never forget what she said. I will never forget what he did." But in spite of all that, memory is vital to life. Prisoners of war have survived and kept their sanity by memory, recalling the names of schoolteachers, the names of classmates, street numbers, a thousand insignificant things. They kept themselves alive by reaching into the chest of memory, holding onto yesterday, hoping somehow to guarantee a tomorrow.

If you haven't grasped how vital to life memory is, walk into the hospital room and see her. She's a grandmother, she's had a stroke, she can't remember. Her daughter comes in from California and is treated as a stranger. The daughter is hurt. She brings in the two beautiful grandchildren. "Mother, these are your two grandchildren. This is Ben and this is Kathy." Grandmother stares at them, puzzled. "Ben and Kathy? I don't believe I've met Ben and Kathy." Beautiful years now locked forever in the brain are gone.

In the early church there were some Christians, rather heretical in many ways, who had a significant term to describe what it was to be lost. The word they used was *amnesia*. To be lost in the world is to have forgotten who you are. To be a Christian is, to a certain extent, an exercise of memory. How far back can you remember? When you were five? Maybe four? Some people can remember when they were three years old. I met a young woman in Texas who told me that she could remember when she was ten months old. Otherwise she seemed normal enough. How far back can you remember?

There are some people that believe there is such a thing as a racial memory, that somehow in the mind of every person there remains a recollection of the evolution of the race, that is, all the stages of evolution leading up to full humanity. Under certain conditions, they say, those previous stages will emerge, such as the animal-like tightening of the upper lip and the raising of the hair on the body in anger or deep distress. In other words, the body remembers. Then there are some who believe they can remember when they were here before, holding to some doctrine of the recycling or reincarnation of the soul. These claim a memory of having lived before, another time, another place.

And there are many who believe there is in all of us what could be called a memory of Eden, a memory of how it was to be close to God and to be in perfect harmony with one another. Back through all the discord and strife and sin and violence and frustration that marred our lives, there remains a residue, or as Professor Bultmann used to say, "There is in all of us a faint recollection of Eden."

Perhaps so, but what I wish to assert, without question, is that whoever cannot remember any farther back than his or her own birth, is an orphan. Now I don't mean that in any mystical sense, as though you should have remembered a previous life. I simply mean it in one sense: our memories should tie us to life that precedes our own birth and extends beyond our own death. It is to recognize that our identities, the meaning of our lives, our futures, and our purposes entail being enrolled in the story that is larger than our own personal story. It is part of the conceit of our time that some folks seem totally disinterested in that which preceded their own birth or succeeds their own death. Between the narrow parentheses of my birth and my death, all that is important occurs. Whoever lives in such a way is an orphan.

This kind of amnesia, this lack of memory can plague a whole community. The early Christian movement engaged in a major debate. Shall we keep our ties with Israel? Shall we keep the Old Testament as a part of our Bible? There were some young radicals who said, "No. We can find our identity only by saying no to yesterday." But thank God, common sense prevailed and the church recognized that it had its purpose, its place, and its meaning in the larger story of what God is doing in the world. Jesus said, "I did not come to destroy the law and the prophets, I came to fulfill them." The Apostle Paul in our text for today speaks gratefully of his own life in relationship to his people, the Jews. "They are," he says, "the roots of all that we are. To them belong the covenant, the worship, the promise, the patriarchs. In fact, from them came the Christ. We cannot forget."

But we do. There are many Christian people who have no memory at all. How much we could learn from the Jewish people who instill in their young a memory of who they are. It is not uncommon among them for a young person, in the beginning of the teen years, to recite: "When we were in Egypt, God heard our cry and brought us out with a strong arm and a mighty hand." Who is saying that? A thirteen-year-old boy who has never been out of the city. But in a deeper sense he is right; we were in Egypt. The history of his people is his own history.

I recall being in Israel and being shown about the country by a man who was very zealous for his nation. One day as we traveled in his little car from Tel Aviv to Jerusalem, he asked if he could take me another way. When I agreed, he took me along a back road, pulled off to the side and began to describe a previous battle between the Jews and their enemies. He explained that the road at the base of the hill was the expected route the Jews were to take into battle and the enemy had stationed themselves in the trees above the road. "But," he said, "we heard of the planned ambush, came around the backside of the hill, over the top, and we were able to destroy them." When I asked my host to what war he referred, he said, "The Maccabean War." The Maccabean War? That was in 165 BCE. I said to him, "Do you realize you told that story as if you were a member of that army? *We* were coming along the road and *they* were coming down the hill and *we* came around behind them and *we*. . . . Do you realize you told it as if you were there?" He said, "I guess I was."

I don't hear Christians say, "*We* were in Antioch. *We* were in Jerusalem. *We* were in the catacombs. *We* were in Rome. *We* were at Plymouth Rock." Oh no, we have our own private experiences and we like this and we dislike that. Isolated and cut off, orphaned, without memory. I recall hearing Scott Momaday, a Kiowa Indian, tell of his life as a boy. He told of being taken early one morning by his father to the cottage of an old squaw. There his father left him. All day long the old squaw told him the story of the Kiowa.

The beginnings of the tribe at the headwaters of the Yellowstone River, the movement of the Kiowa south into Nebraska and Kansas, the wars with other tribes, the buffalo hunts, the coming of the white man, the terrible winters, moving on south until finally being conquered by the white man and being moved to a reservation in southern Oklahoma. She told the story and she recited the songs. At sunset his father came for him. "Son, it is time to go." Mr. Momaday said, "I left her house a Kiowa." It is the sad fact that most of our young people leave our church buildings on Sunday after Sunday without a sense of "I left that house a Christian."

To be a Christian is, in part, an exercise in memory and whoever cannot remember any farther back than his or her own life is an orphan. "If I forget thee, Bethlehem, if I forget thee, Nazareth, if I forget thee, Jerusalem, Athens, Rome, if I forget thee, may my right hand forget her cunning and may my tongue cleave to the roof of my mouth. For if I forget, I will, without a doubt, become a victim of the future" (Ps. 137:5–6, paraphr.).

Our Father, it seems so light a thing that we forget. Yet it is so heavy a thing that we be forgotten. We who wish to be remembered, especially by thee, help us not to forget, especially thee. In Christ's name, Amen.

43

Why the Cross?

1 Corinthians 1:18–31

As you know, to be a Christian is to believe in God. Not just any God, not just any belief, as though all faiths were the same, not "well, as long as you believe, what difference does it make?" or a lot of other tripe like that you hear, but belief in the God we have come to understand in Jesus of Nazareth. Jesus is the one who came to reveal God. When you think of it that way, the gospel becomes a rather beautiful and comforting story, because this man Jesus was so caring and gentle, going around teaching and preaching and healing. He was a blessing to everybody he met, regardless of who they were. So we can say to ourselves, "This is the way God is; not cruel and judging and harsh and mean, but caring and lifting and loving." It is a beautiful thing to believe in God.

Sooner or later, though, somebody is going to say to you, "Then what happened to Jesus?" Then you have to tell the truth: he was sentenced to die and was executed. He was about thirty-five years old when he died. He was executed by the Roman government in order to maintain the peace of Rome. Jesus seemed to be a threat, a disturber of the peace, a gatherer of peasant people with some false notions, and it was expedient that he die. And that was that.

The means of Jesus' execution was not a lethal injection or an electric chair. Rather, he was hanged on a stick, a cross, where he was left to die. It took some people who were executed by this means several hours to die; it took others days to die. Mercifully, Jesus died within a matter of hours.

When you answer the question about what happened to Jesus—this beautiful, gentle, kind, and caring man—and you tell the truth, some people walk away. They are not interested in a man who died like that, and they are not interested in any group that centers itself around such an event. "Why can't we just leave that part out?" they say. "Why can't we just tell the stories about Jesus healing and touching and teaching and preaching?" Indeed, why not, as some people have done, take some of the best teachings of Jesus, the best teachings of Gandhi, the best teachings of Muhammad, and the best teachings of Gautama the Buddha, put them together, and call it a way of life? Why not say, "Now *this* is the way to live! Have a good family, have good relationships, be wealthy and successful and wise." But there is no cross in there—no cross in there.

We hear about people, especially in the entertainment industry, who have left their churches to join Scientology. They testify to receiving what they did not get in their traditional churches, namely, a sense of caress and comfort and health and coping and healing. There are no crosses. As theologian Reinhold Niebuhr said some years ago when he was teaching at Union Theological Seminary in New York, "This is a view that insists on a God without wrath bringing men and women without sin into a kingdom without judgment through a Christ without a cross."

Paul said, "I cannot do that. I cannot give up on the truth that I have resolved to know nothing among you except Jesus Christ and him crucified." Paul paid a dear price for that conviction. When he went to Corinth, addressed in today's text, he said, "I arrived among you shaking, scared, and feeling very weak." He had just come from Athens, the cultural center of the world—beautiful Athens, Greece, a monument to the nobility of the human mind and spirit. In Athens, sculpture, art, music, poetry, philosophy, all were unsurpassed. Paul stood on a hill there and preached about Jesus, and his listeners treated him in the worst way any preacher could ever be treated: they laughed. What would this vain babbler say? Paul said, "I have to tell of the cross. I *have* to preach the cross, even though the culture regards the message of the cross as foolish, as something that makes absolutely no sense."

Where was Jesus when he was killed? He was in Jerusalem. Did he live there? No, he was from Nazareth, about eighty miles north. Then why did he not get out of town? He did all his good work and he taught and he healed and he went to Jerusalem. His followers ran like crazy, but he stayed there in Jerusalem. How foolish can you get? Did he not know the danger? Had he not received the threats? Did he not know what was going to happen to him? Why didn't he leave? Talk about senseless killing, the kind of thing people say about drive-by shootings: absolutely senseless. The one who pulled the trigger did not even know the person who was killed. It makes no sense!

Jesus' death makes no sense either. In fact, it is still a bit offensive to the cultural despisers of religion. As Philip Rieff once observed at the University of Chicago, "Any church or any preacher who keeps preaching on the cross is not going to grow. The preacher will not be a success and the church will not grow, because in our culture what we are interested in is success, not sacrifice." If you talk about sacrifice at your church, then you are going to sit there with your little huddle of people like a covey of quail while the other churches will be blooming all around and promising that if you give God a nickel, then God will give you back a dime. Those churches say that the way to health and wealth and happiness is to come to Jesus.

That is what the architect was told when he started designing one of those huge churches in California. "We do not want any crosses on the church, either outside or inside. None. We don't want anybody to think failure and weakness. Why would we want a symbol of a man slumped dead on a cross after his few friends have gotten out of Dodge? All that were left were a few women crying. You talk about weakness. What does that do?"

The Ku Klux Klan knows what to do with this cross, this weak, dying stuff. They put on their white hoods, ride into a neighborhood, put one of those crosses in a yard and set fire to it. You can hear the screaming of children nine blocks away. The Klan knows how to take that weak cross and turn it into terrifying and vicious power.

In 1967, a pastor in San Francisco got up before his congregation and said, "The cross has been the symbol of sacrifice and the acceptance of pain and suffering, and we are tired of it. We are not going to be a part of this anymore." And he got up there and tore down the cross from the church. No more suffering. No more weakness.

Paul said, "I *have* to preach the cross." Why? Let me introduce the answer by saying, "I don't know." What I say from here on is what I think. I think that the cross is a reminder—and I am sorry we have to have it—of the cruelty and violence and sin in the world that affects people who had nothing to do with it. Even in high places, proper places, white-collar places, there is a lot of ugly, cruel, evil power that crushes and hurts. You know that this is so.

A few years ago, a very fine writer and novelist by the name of Jack Abbott was in federal prison in Atlanta. He wrote an article and sent it in to a New York literary journal. It was published and acknowledged as one of the most beautiful things written in our generation. I can almost remember a line from it: "Over the wall, the smell of magnolia, and peach, and soft, late evenings almost change a man." Some of the powerful people in New York, literary figures and political figures with influence, said, "Anybody who can write like that should not be in prison." They exercised their power and got his sentence reduced. Before long, Jack Abbott was in New York, "over the wall, the smell of magnolia, and peach, and soft, late evenings." He dined at a nice restaurant in New York a few weeks after he got out. After he finished a long evening of eating and drinking, he came out with his friends and said to the parking valet, "Bring my car." The valet said, "Just a moment. There are some in front of you." Abbott said, "Bring my car!" and the valet said, "You'll have to wait your turn. We'll bring it in a few minutes." Abbott then pulled out a long knife and killed the attendant. "Over the wall, the smell of magnolia and peach." And he killed again.

We need to be reminded that just because people have been to school and just because they have a nice income and live in the better part of town, and just because they are children of some of the best families, they can still be responsible for some of the ugly cruelty in the world.

At the National Cathedral in Washington, there are flags flying inside that beautiful place from all the states in the union, and the flags represent significant people from those states. In recent times, there have been three flags from Georgia. One was for Martin Luther King Jr.; one was for Woodrow Wilson, who began his law career in Georgia and married a woman from Rome, Georgia; and one was for Robert Alston. Many people asked, "Who was Robert Alston?" He was from Atlanta, and he owned the land that is now East Lake Golf and Country Club. He was a member of the Georgia Legislature, and he was absolutely incensed at the ugliness and corruption of that body.

One item in particular offended Robert Alston. It was the custom in those days for wealthy and influential people to use state prisoners to work on their mansions, or to build their commercial buildings, or to farm their plantations. All you had to do was to provide lunch. You did not have to house these workers or pay them. You were not obligated to provide insurance—just lunch. Did you know that a lot of the fine commercial buildings and a lot of the nice old homes in Atlanta were built on the backs of prisoners who were hauled out of prison and worked all day for the wage of a lunch? Robert Alston said, "This is worse than slavery." He spoke to his fellow legislators, but no one else seemed to be interested. They were making money and their wives were sipping drinks at the country club because of the system.

So Robert Alston announced, "Tomorrow I will introduce a bill into the legislature to make this practice against the law. It is absolutely inhumane." The next morning he came in with his bill. A fellow legislator from one of the nice families—if I mentioned the name you would know it—came over to Alston and said, "Mr. Alston, are you going to introduce your bill today?" Alston replied, "Yes, I am." The man reached inside his coat, pulled out a derringer, and shot Robert Alston dead.

I do not know for sure, but I think Paul had to preach the cross to say that this is not only the way the world is, this is also the way the Christian life is. The Christian life says you get involved in other people's lives, sometimes at a risk to name, reputation, fortune, money, and job. You get involved because it is your business to do so. They do you wrong on radio, on television, or any other pulpit when they say, "If you just believe in God, everything is peaceful, serene, and beautiful, and the dying winds move your ship sailing toward the sunset in beatitude."

If you believe in God, that is sometimes when your trouble starts. One day Jesus said to his disciples, "Get into the boat and go to the other side." They did what he said, and they hit a storm. It was not because they disobeyed that they hit a storm; it was because they *obeyed* that they hit a storm. Believing in God means putting yourself in situations that may cause you to say, "Why did I do *that*? I thought God blesses you when you do right." Because of their faith, some people have stopped the mouths of lions, have won wars, have raised the dead, have had every kind of triumph in the world. But other people, because of their faith in God, have suffered. They have been chased, and pushed, and hurt, and talked against, and imprisoned because of their faith. Faith is not a success story; faith is a story that says, "I take this up as my way of life."

But I think the primary reason Paul had to preach the cross is because the cross tells us how God is. God identifies with human suffering; God comes to us and suffers with us, and that sympathy is extraordinarily powerful.

Some years ago, Greek author Nikos Kazantzakis wrote *The Last Temptation of Christ.* The book was made into a controversial movie that was protested and boycotted all over the country. In his novel, Kazantzakis basically said that when Jesus got into Jerusalem and the noose was tightening around his neck and there was no way out and death was in front of him, he thought, "Why don't I just go back to Nazareth, marry, have a family, take up carpentry again, and get out of this? Nobody seems to care anyway." If Jesus had done that, if he had slipped out of town, gone back to Nazareth, married, had children, lived like everybody else, would we be able to sing "What a Friend We Have in Jesus"? No, no, not at all. If he had skipped out before the pain started . . . But he did not do that. He went to the cross.

Sometimes a child falls down and skins a knee or an elbow, then runs crying to his mother. The mother picks up the child and says—in what is the oldest myth in the world—"Let me kiss it and make it well," as if mother has magic saliva or something. She picks up the child, kisses the skinned place, holds the child in her lap, and all is well. Did her kiss make it well? No, no. It was that ten minutes in her lap. Just sit in the lap of love and see the mother crying. "Mother, why are you crying? I'm the one who hurt my elbow." "Because you're hurt," the mother says, "I hurt." That does more for a child than all the bandages and all the medicine in the world, just sitting on the lap. What is the cross? Can I say it this way? It is to sit for a few minutes on the lap of God, who hurts because you hurt.

Paul said, "I have to preach that." So do I.

44

Praying through Clenched Teeth

Galatians 1:11–24

For I would have you know, brethren, that the gospel which was preached by me is not man's gospel. For I did not receive it from man, nor was I taught it, but it came through a revelation of Jesus Christ. For you have heard of my former life in Judaism, how I persecuted the church of God violently and tried to destroy it; and I advanced in Judaism beyond many of my own age among my people, so extremely zealous was I for the traditions of my fathers. But when he who set me apart before I was born, and had called me through his grace, was pleased to reveal his Son to me, in order that I might preach him among the Gentiles, I did not confer with flesh and blood, nor did I go up to Jerusalem to those who were apostles before me, but I went away into Arabia; and again I returned to Damascus.

Then after three years I went up to Jerusalem to visit Cephas and remained with him fifteen days. But I saw none of the other apostles except James the Lord's brother. (In what I am writing to you, before God, I do not lie!) Then I went into the regions of Syria and Cilicia. And I was still not known by sight to the churches of Christ in Judea; they only heard it said, "He who once persecuted us is now preaching the faith he once tried to destroy." And they glorified God because of me. (RSV)

I'm going to say a word and the moment I say the word, I want you to see a face. To recall a face and a name, someone who comes to your mind when I say the word. Are you ready? The word is bitter. Bitter. Do you see a face? I see a face. I see the face of a farmer in western Oklahoma, riding a mortgaged tractor, burning gasoline purchased on the credit, moving across rented land, rearranging the dust. Bitter.

Do you see a face? I see the face of a woman forty-seven years old. She sits out on a hillside, drawn and confused, under a green canopy furnished by the mortuary. She is banked on all sides by flowers sprinkled with cards. "You have our condolences." Bitter.

Do you see a face? I see the face of a man who runs a small grocery store. His father ran the store in that neighborhood for twenty years and he is now in his twelfth year. The grocery doesn't make much profit but it keeps the family together. It's a business. There are no customers in the store now and the grocer stands in the doorway with his apron rolled up around his waist, looking across the street where workmen are completing a supermarket. Bitter.

I see the face of a young couple. They seem to be about nineteen. They're standing in the airport terminal, holding hands so tight their knuckles are white. She's pregnant; he's dressed in military green. They're not talking, just standing and looking at each other. The loudspeaker comes on; "Flight 392 now loading at Gate 22, Yellow Concourse. All aboard for San Francisco." He slowly moves toward the gate; she stands there alone. Bitter.

Do you see a face? A young minister in a small town in a cracker box of a house they call a parsonage. He lives there with his wife and small child. It's Saturday morning. There is a knock at the door; he answers and there standing before him on the porch is the chairman of his church board, who is also the president of the local bank, and also the owner of most of the land roundabout. The man has in his hands a small television. It's an old television, small screen, black and white. It's badly scarred and one of the knobs is off. He says, "My wife and I got one of those new 44-inch color sets but they didn't want to take this one on a trade, so I just said to myself, 'We will just give it to the minister. That's probably the reason our ministers don't stay any longer than they do. We don't do enough nice things for them.'" The young minister looks up, tries to smile and say thanks, but I want you to see his face. Bitter.

Will you look at one other face? His name is Saul, Saul of Tarsus. We call him Paul. He was young and intelligent, committed to the traditions of his fathers, strong and zealous for his nation and for his religion, outstripping, he says, all of his classmates in his zeal for his people. While he pursues his own convictions, there develops within the bosom of Judaism a new group called Nazarenes, followers of Jesus. They seem, at first, to pose no threat. After all, Judaism had long been broadly liberal and had tolerated within her house of faith a number of groups such as Pharisees, Sadducees, Essenes, and Zealots. So why not Nazarenes? As long as they continue in the temple and in the synagogue, there is no problem.

But before long, among these new Christians a different sound is heard. Some of the young radicals are beginning to say that Christianity is not just for the Jews but for anyone who believes in Jesus Christ. Such was the preaching of Stephen and Philip and others. It doesn't really matter if your background is Jewish as long as you trust in God and believe in Jesus Christ. This startling word strikes the ear of young Saul. "What do they mean it doesn't matter? It does matter. It is the most important matter. No young preacher can stand up and say that thousands and thousands of years of mistreatment and exile and burden of trying to be true to God, of struggling to be his people and keep the candle of faith burning in a dark and pagan world, means nothing. What do they mean it doesn't matter to have your gabardine spat upon and to be made fun of because you're different. Of course, it matters."

Imagine yourself the only child of your parents, but when you're seventeen years old they adopt a seventeen-year-old brother for you. When you're both eighteen the father says at breakfast one morning, "I have just had the lawyer draw up the papers. I am leaving the family business to our two sons." How do you feel? This other fellow just got here. He's not really a true son. Where was he when I was mowing the lawn, cleaning the room, trying to pass the ninth grade, and being refused the family car on Friday nights? And now that I'm eighteen I suddenly have this brother out of nowhere and he's to share equally? How would you feel? Would you be saying, "Isn't my father generous?" Not likely.

Then imagine how young Saul feels. Generations and generations and generations of being the people of God and now someone in the name of Jesus of Nazareth gets this strange opinion that it doesn't matter anymore, that Jews and Gentiles are alike. You must sense how he feels. All the family and national traditions, all that you've ever known and believed, now erased completely from the board? Every moment in school, every belief held dear, every job toward which your life is pointed, now meaningless? Everything that grandfather and father and now you believed, gone?

Of course, he resolves to stop it. The dark cloud of his brooding bitterness forms a tornado funnel over that small church and he strikes it, seeking to end it. In the name of his fathers, in the name of his country, in the name of God, yes. Now why does he do this? Why is he so bitter at this announcement of the universal embrace of all people in the name of God?

Do you know what I believe? I believe he is bitter and disturbed because he is at war with himself over this very matter, and anyone at war with himself will make casualties even out of friends and loved ones. He is himself uncertain and it's the uncertain person who becomes a persecutor. Suddenly, like a wounded animal, he lies in the sand near Damascus, waiting for the uplifted stroke of a God whom he thinks he serves. But Paul knows his is a God who loves all creation. He knows; sure he knows. Saul has read his Bible; he's read that marvelous book of Ruth, in which the ancestress of David is shamelessly presented as a Moabite woman. Sure God loves other people. He has read the book of Jonah and the expressed love of God for people that Jonah himself does not love.

Paul has read the book of Isaiah and the marvelous vision of the house of God into which all nations flow. It is in his Bible. Then what's his problem? His problem is the same problem you and I have sometimes. It's one thing to know something, it's another to know it. He knows it and he does not know it and the battle that is fought between knowing and really knowing is fierce. It is sometimes called the struggle from head to heart. I know that the longest trip we ever make is the trip from head to heart, from knowing to knowing. And until that trip is complete we're in great pain. We might even lash out at others.

Do you know anyone bitter like this? Bitter that what they're fighting is what they know is right? Trapped in that impossible battle of trying to stop the inevitable triumph of the truth? Do you know anyone lashing out in criticism and hatred and violence against a person or against a group that represents the humane and caring and Christian way? If you do, how do you respond? Hopefully you do not react to bitterness with bitterness. We certainly have learned that such is a futile and fruitless endeavor, just as I hope we have learned that we do not fight prejudice with prejudice.

A few years ago many of us found ourselves more prejudiced against prejudiced people than the prejudiced people were prejudiced. Then how do we respond?

Let me tell you a story. A family is out for a drive on a Sunday afternoon. It is a pleasant afternoon and they relax at a leisurely pace down the highway. Suddenly the two children begin to beat their father in the back. "Daddy, Daddy, stop the car, stop the car. There's a kitten back there on the side of the road."

The father says, "So there's a kitten on the side of the road. We're having a drive."

"But, Daddy, you must stop and pick it up."

"I don't have to stop and pick it up."

"But, Daddy, if you don't, it will die."

"Well then it will have to die. We don't have room for another animal; we have a zoo already at the house. No more animals."

"But, Daddy, are you going to just let it die?"

"Be quiet, kids; we're having a pleasant drive."

"We never thought our daddy would be so mean and cruel as to let a kitten die."

Finally the mother turns to her husband and says, "Dear, you'll have to stop."

He turns the car around, returns to the spot and pulls off to the side of the road. "You kids stay in the car, I'll see about it." He goes out to pick up the little kitten; the poor creature is just skin and bones, sore-eyed and full of fleas. But when he reaches down to pick it up, with its last bit of energy, the kitten bristles, baring tooth and claw.

He picks up the kitten by the loose skin at the neck, brings it over to the car and says, "Don't touch it, it's probably got leprosy." Back home they go. When they get to the house, the children give the kitten several baths, about a gallon of warm milk and intercede, "Can we let it stay in the house just tonight? Tomorrow we'll fix a place in the garage."

The father says, "Sure, take my bedroom; the whole house is already a zoo." They fix a comfortable bed fit for a pharaoh. Several weeks pass. Then one day the father walks in, feels something rub against his leg, looks down, and there's that cat. He reaches down towards the cat, carefully checking to see that no one is watching. When the cat sees his hand, it does not bare its claws and hiss. Instead it arches its back to receive a caress. Is that the same cat? Is that the same cat? No, it's not the same as that frightened, hurt, hissing kitten on the side of the road. Of course not, and you know as well as I what makes the difference.

Not too long ago God reached out a hand to bless my family and me. I looked at God's hand. It was covered with scratches. Such is the hand of love extended to those who are bitter.

45

Throwing Away the Good Stuff

Philippians 3:4–14

I once took advantage of my wife's absence to make a couple of trips to the landfill. In the past my life had been rather simple. I had a formula: take care of what you have and when it is broken, used up, or of no value, then throw it away. Then I got married, and the formula changed: take care of what you have until it is broken or useless to you or anyone else, and then store it in the garage.

So I went to the landfill. In my opinion, what I threw away was useless. There were boxes, the bottoms of which had rotted out, and they seemed to be candidates for the landfill. There were creek waders that had a lot of holes in them. I tossed them. There was some bad birdseed. (At least, I assumed it was bad. I had planted some of it three times, and no birds ever came up. So I tossed it.) I made two trips.

This is a common drama in everybody's house. It is as ordinary as having a family. Things get used up. That is why we have garbage dumps. Things get broken, are no longer of any value, and they have to be disposed of. But once in a while, just once in a while, there is a case of somebody throwing away that which is very valuable. Something very good and very right gets tossed.

I am not talking about careless families, families that are full of waste and indifference toward the things they have because they have more than they can use and so just scatter it everywhere. I'm not talking about that. I'm talking about those rare occasions when something good and valuable is thrown away. You can think of such times. They do not occur very often. Suppose, though, a man in a very expensive Brooks Brothers suit sees a child drowning. He goes into the water. He can't swim with all that on, and he removes this valuable suit in the water in order to rescue the child. The suit is still good, but compared to the life of the child? He throws the suit away.

246

Imagine pioneers moving west, trying to get to California and Oregon. They come to the Rocky Mountains and the snow is beginning to fall and those Conestoga wagons are heavy, squeaking wheels straining, horses pulling; they can go no further. They go up as high as they can, but they cannot go up any higher, and the leader says, "We're going to have to unburden some of the wagons." The children are crying; the parents are crying. But over into the rocks and into the ravine go furniture, chests of precious things, a piano. The group cannot go on if they hold onto these things. Even in the Bible I have read of ships at sea tossed by storms or hanging onto a sandbar that had to unburden themselves of cargo—precious cargo, good cargo, fine clothes, jewelry, furniture, all kinds of good things tossed away. It's a matter of life and death. In view of the crisis, even that which is good has to go.

It is very likely that no such occasion will arise in your life. This is more the stuff of novels and movies. Interesting and moving, but so what? Well, even though it is rare, even though it may never happen to you, I still feel I ought to share with you a case of someone who tossed away what was extremely valuable.

His name was Paul, and he said when he wrote to his friends in Philippi in northern Greece, "If I were to enter a bragging contest, I would win. Not for what I have, I'm not a wealthy man, but for *who* I am. My identity, my genealogy, my family tree, my connections, my standing in the community—I can win any bragging contest. I want you to know that I am a Jew. I am proud of that. I am a member of the house of Israel. We have been mistreated severely. We have had our gabardines spat upon in every country of the world. We have been literally destroyed in community after community. But I remind you that we have clung to faith in God. We have kept the light on when darkness was everywhere. We have given the world the basis for all moral and ethical standards, the Ten Commandments, and we have contributed the writings that have shaped three of the great religions in the world: Judaism, Christianity, and Islam. I'm proud that I am an Israelite. I was born a Jew."

I know in some places it is very popular to join a synagogue if you fall out with your church. Around universities and colleges, it is a rather popular thing for those who decide they do not believe what they used to believe or who take the view that their church back home was moss covered or too restrictive. It is popular to say, "I think I'll just junk it all and join the synagogue." In places where I have taught and where I have studied, it was quite popular for Gentiles to join synagogues. Paul said, "Not me. That was not how I got there. I was *born* a Jew. I did not come to this late because a lot of my bright intellectual friends thought it was the thing to do. I was circumcised on the eighth day of my life. My family, Benjamin, the smallest tribe, did not amount to much in a lot of people's eyes, but God has always used the smallest and the weakest and the least known in order to accomplish what God wants to do. And so it was with my tribe. Did you know that my tribe, Benjamin, contributed to Israel its first king, King Saul? I am named for him, you know—Saul of Tarsus—and I am proud of that.

"My denomination? Pharisee. I know there are other Jews who have different views, but I am proud to be a Pharisee. Being a Pharisee simply means that we believe in the Bible; we follow the Bible. When the Temple was destroyed, we built a substitute for the Temple called the synagogue, and we are zealous about the synagogue. We establish synagogues everywhere we go. But the one thing that we hold at the center is how important it is to know the Scripture, to listen to the Scripture, to obey the Scripture. I am proud of that. As for myself, I have kept true to the Scripture. You can ask my teachers. I outstripped all my classmates in zeal for the Scripture. You can ask my family; you can ask my friends. I live by the Book. I am proud of that. In fact, I am so conscientious about this that I have a passion against anybody who weakens the Scripture, distorts it, trades it for something else. I cannot stand it. I am proud of that zeal. If I went into a bragging contest, I would beat out everybody. My standing, my character, my family, my genealogy—it's all unsurpassed!"

And yet Paul said, "I count all this as garbage. I've tossed it. I took it to the dump." Why?

We do not have a story here of a man who regrets his past, a man who is all torn up inside and burdened with guilt, a man who is depressed at night and cannot sleep, saying, "Oh, what am I going to do?" No, no. This is not about guilt. All of his zeal and achievements, all that I have recited to you, is good. Also, we do not have here a case like you hear about so often of a new Christian being asked to give up terrible old habits. "If you're going to be a Christian now," they say, "you've got to give up all those bad habits and clean up your language and quit beating on your kids and be nice to your wife and all the ugly things you've ever done. You've got to lay them down and come to Jesus." While that may be true in some situations, we are talking here about a man who said that if one reviewed his past before he came to Christ, one would find only good stuff. "Nevertheless," said Paul, "I took it to the dump."

Why? Was the church an occasion for some sort of upward mobility? Did Paul say, "Well, it looks like everybody who is anybody is joining the church, I might as well switch my membership from the synagogue"? No, no, no! Then why did he do it? He did not have to do it. Every church that ever existed would have been glad to have him. He is the kind of folk we need in the church—good, clean, upright, honest, productive, love the Bible, do what is right, follow the Ten Commandments kind of folks. Is there a church anywhere that would say no to Paul? He does not have to do all this tossing of his past. Just add Jesus and join the church—that would have sufficed. In fact, Paul could have done what some other people do: join the church and then just pick and choose the parts you like. Come now and then, give a little now and then, do a little now and then, maybe serve on a committee now and then. And now and then you die and now and then you hope to go to heaven. Maybe. There are many people who do that. Paul could have done that. Who would have objected? Yet he threw it all away.

Why would Paul throw away what he has just called good? This man believed that Jesus Christ was with God but that he did not count being with God and being equal to God something to covet or to grasp. Instead, Jesus Christ emptied himself, became a human being, and was obedient to the hour of death, even death on a cross. That is what Christ is like—not upward mobility but downward mobility. He came from the presence of God, from all that was so good. He came from the ivory palaces, from the throne, from the glory, from the angels, from the praise. He possessed all that is so good, but he tossed it and became a human being like you and me, obedient even to death. Paul says, "How can I, how can anyone, claim to be a follower of that man and still seek upward mobility? How can I still keep my own agenda, keep my own pride, keep my own investments, and just add in church as it may or may not fit in? How can I tack on my Christianity around the edges but keep my life intact when this new faith is in the name of Jesus, who gave it all up, took it to the heavenly dump, and came down here and became a servant?"

Do you know what Paul thought? Paul thought that if you are going to be a Christian, then you should be like Jesus. So then, what do you do with your pride? What do you do with your own agenda? What do you do with your own selfishness? What do you do with your own independence? What do you do with your own calendar to which you may or may not add a little church? You take it to the dump in order that you might be like him.

This unusual man Paul had the idea that the ideal Christian life would be to be like Jesus: to love, to care, to give, to serve, to suffer, and to sacrifice like he did. "I am not there yet," he said, "I do not mean for you to get the idea," he protested, "that I have arrived, that I have attained my goal. Oh no. But I'll tell you this: being like Jesus is the one thing on my mind. I'm running toward this. I'm running toward this, temples pounding, heart pumping, bones breaking, muscles aching, face sweating, running. If I could just be like Jesus."

I know Paul is unusual. You may never in your lifetime meet anybody who takes Jesus that seriously. But I felt obligated to bring it up to you today, because once in a while somebody does, and I had the feeling it might be you.

46

A Note of Thanks

Philippians 4:10–20

As many of you know, many scholars believe that this little piece of material originally was a separate note of thanks, sent to the church at Philippi, when Epaphroditus arrived where Paul was in prison, bringing a gift from the church. There is much to be said for that position. The letter of Philippians does seem to be a collection of fragments of interchanges between Paul and that church, put together so that now it seems to be one letter. And yet, an argument can be made for it as one whole letter.

Whether you take this little piece in chapter 4, which has its own beginning and ending, and is thoroughly complete within itself, and seems chronologically to have been sent first before anything else, or whether you take it to have been a separate letter, or to be in the proper context where it is, doesn't matter. It is a note of thanks. Just as certainly as it is a note of thanks, it is a strange note of thanks.

In the first place, it's too long. Notes of thanks just aren't this long. You can tell when you open the envelope it's a thank-you note, because it opens top to bottom instead of side to side. "Steve and I thank you for the fondue pot. Of all the gifts we received at our wedding, it is my favorite, because that happens to be the only thing I can fix. But I do plan to cook other things. Love, Carolyn." Now that's enough. And it doesn't matter that she says in all the notes, "Your gift was the favorite one." We want to feel good. This is the thank-you note. The thing cost fourteen dollars!

Look at Paul's note: it's so long. It's a page and a half. And it starts out the wrong way. "I rejoice in the Lord that now, finally, you have renewed your concern for me." Now that's not the way to start. The killer in there is the word "finally." "You finally thought of me again." That's not the beginning of a good thank-you note.

Paul realizes, once he puts it down that way, "Oops—that's kind of barbed." So he softens it. And then in the next sentence says, "Well, you did have concern for me. But you had no opportunity." It's a beautiful image from the spring of the year. "You were not bearing fruit because it was not the season." And then he says, "Not that I complain of want . . ." (Now this is the thank-you note!) "Not that I complain of want. I don't sit here in my cell, rattling a tin cup across the bars, saying, 'Has the mail come today?' No, no, no, no. I know how to get mail; I know how to get no mail. I know how to receive packages. I know how to sit here with no package. I know how to have a lot. I know how to have nothing. I know how to have plenty. I know how to be totally without. Because I have learned in whatever condition to be content. I am adequate in every situation through Christ who gives me strength."

"Not that I seek the gift . . ." (He can't quit, can he!?!) "Not that I seek the gift. I seek the credit that goes to your account because of the gift, because you really didn't give it to me. You gave it to God, a gift, an offering accessible and acceptable to God. And my God will supply every need of yours in Christ Jesus." That's the thank-you note. How would you feel if you received that?

"You Philippians know you were the only church that entered into giving and receiving with me." This is an extraordinary relationship. For you know from the letters of Paul that he did not let churches give to him easily, slipping a few bills in his pocket as he came and went. No. He would spend his energy and risk his life raising money for the poor saints, famine stricken. But to give something to Paul? "I work with my own hands. I pay my way. You know, night and day I took care of myself. I needed the freedom to preach free of charge."

But the church at Philippi was honored above all other churches in this one regard: he allowed them to give him a gift. "Even when I went to Thessalonica you alone helped me. Time and again, you helped me then. Not that I seek the gift. Not that I am in want. Not that I really needed it. It was good for you to give it." That's the way he talked. How are we to understand it? This strange note of thanks in the latter part of Philippians has puzzled and fascinated students of this letter for centuries and centuries. It is unusual.

Part of its unusual nature can be attributed to the fact that he's talking about money. And Paul knows, as you know, that you cannot discuss that subject in simple sentences, just cause and effect, flattened out. It is a complex matter. The Bible argues with itself. Some of the writers in the Bible say prosperity is a sign of God's favor. "The person who delights in the law of the Lord is like a tree planted by the water, and everything he does will prosper" (Ps. 1:3, paraphr.). "Show me a prosperous man, I'll show you a righteous man, because I have never seen a righteous man hungry, nor his children begging for bread" (Ps. 37:25, paraphr.).

As one of the great benefactors in the history of America once said, "Show me a poor man, and I will show you a sinner." But other parts of the Bible said, "No, the opposite is true." "Blessed are the poor. Blessed are the poor." What did Mary sing? "He has filled the hungry with good things. He has sent the rich empty away." Luke says, "A rich man and a poor man died. The rich man went to hell, the poor man went to heaven." You don't know anything else about them, except one ate and one didn't eat. And that was it.

The Bible argues with itself. It's a very complex issue, just as it is with us. You can say "Thirty pieces of silver," and the ugliest scene of which we know anything comes to mind. Dark and gruesome, an ugly and foul story: "Thirty pieces of silver." What's the worst thing you could say about this man? "He did it for the money." What's the worst thing you can say about her? "Do you know what? She married him for the money." And yet, there's hardly anything in the church that we do that's more beautiful than giving our money as an offering to God. The tortured nature of the gift of thanks is due, in part, to the complexity of the subject.

Part of it is a kind of awkwardness of the apostle. He stands before this gift from the church, and he's standing on one foot, and he's standing on the other foot. And you can tell he's awkward. "I thank you for the gift. You remembered me again. I know you thought of me. You just didn't have a chance. I didn't really have any wants. I don't really want for anything. I don't seek the gift, but I thank you. You're the only church . . ." You see? You feel the awkwardness.

No wonder it's awkward. Paul is at that moment, that rare juncture in human life, that is the most fragile, and yet the strongest, the most beautiful with the possibility of being the ugliest of any transaction we can ever know: the giving and the receiving of a gift. That's a tender moment. It is a beautiful moment.

The New Testament thinks of that as such a beautiful moment that, at times, it will use exactly the same word for giving it and for receiving it. The word is *charis*. We translate it usually "grace." It can be translated "gift." It can be translated "thanks." You don't know whether it's being given (thanks), being received (grace), or being given (gift). Eucharist—that's it! Charisma—that's it! Charismatic—that's it! The whole thing is one word, that marvelous transaction, which in its most beautiful form is an exchange in which the same quality and temperament characterize the person who receives and the person who gives, and no difference, really, is made. No wonder the apostle is awkward here. He is at the juncture of the most beautiful and the most rare moment we know.

But there is another factor here. Paul says, "I have learned to be content." And he uses a stoic word. "With reference to things in this world, I learned to be apathetic. To have no feeling. To make the heart a desert and call it peace." "I don't have any feelings in this matter." There are some people who arrive at that. Some after very painful experiences, of totally losing all appetite for anything. Not that it's a virtue, but they just lose all appetite for anything.

I've wondered if, perhaps, that might have been the case of the rich ruler the Gospels tell about, falling at the feet of Jesus: "Good Teacher, what must I do?" I wonder if he had reached that point. Maybe going home from work in the afternoon with his beautiful robes, children on the street grabbing at his sleeve, "Penny, mister, mister, penny? We're hungry, mister. You give us . . . ?" "Get away, kids, you'll get my clothes dirty." And he gets home just in time to hear his wife say, as she scrapes plates of food into the disposal, "I don't know what I'm going to do to get those kids of ours to eat." And he's just sick of it. The magnificence of life's promise, lost in the poverty of its achievement. "And the very thing I thought I wanted I have, and I don't want it at all."

Like Macbeth wading through blood, even of relatives, to get the throne of Scotland. And when he gets it, what do you see? An old man sitting on the side of his cot, twirling a crown in his fingers.

The awkwardness in this thank-you note—what is it? If I didn't know better, I'd say, "Here's somebody who's had a bad experience with gifts, and doesn't want to get too involved." "Thanks for the gift, but, but I really didn't need the gift." You have that feeling. Some of you know what that's like, because some of the ugliest things that ever happen involve gifts. Gifts can be very painful, treacherous, and demonic. Gifts can!

When I was briefly in the parish, a painful thing occurred in the membership. He was an officer in the church, and did well at it, but he was gone most of the time. His work took him away. His wife spent most of her time ironing, washing and ironing, washing and ironing, white shirts for him. Packing the suitcase. Emptying the dirty clothes. Washing them, putting them back in the suitcase. He was on the road most of the time. She began to discover in the clothing the evidence that he was having an affair. She was convinced of it. One day when she could explode, while he was home for lunch, she dumped the whole thing on him. She told me later he just sat there and stirred his food. Didn't eat anything. Didn't say anything. And left. He came in at three o'clock in the afternoon, called her name. She said, "I'm in here." She was doing some needlework. He walked in and said, "This is for you," and tossed something into her lap. She picked up two keys. He said, "Look out there!" And outside she saw a new yellow Plymouth convertible. She stopped to see me on the way to the lawyer. And she said, "I think I would have been able to forgive his infidelity. But I could not forgive him the gift. What did he think I was?" Gifts can be very painful.

When I was in third grade, the government had a hot-lunch program if you could prove that you deserved one. It was a free-lunch program, so I got my credentials together, and established myself before the government, and they said, "You get a hot lunch." And this is the way it worked. Our teacher (bless her heart, she intended nothing wrong by it) said, "Now boys and girls, the bell rings at five till twelve. Those of you getting free lunches, stand beside your desks. March to the cafeteria. The second bell will be at ten after twelve. Those of you buying your lunches, stand beside your desks. March to the cafeteria." Five till twelve, the bell rings and I sit there. Because there's something worse than being hungry, and that's walking in front of your friends as a freeloader. If you're ever going to do something nice for somebody, please lay it gently on their pride . . . because that may be all they have.

You almost get the impression that Paul has been burned by gifts. I don't think he has, but he surely is ginger in his comments. What is it? I don't think he's tiptoeing at all. In my judgment, his expressions about the money, or whatever the gift was that they sent to him, are the expressions of a man who is *free*. He is absolutely free in relation to things. To money. His freedom is not the freedom of a spiritualist, who translates everything into spiritual terms, and then laying "his finger beside his nose, up the chimney he rose." Like a gnostic of some sort. I don't know when we're going to get it straight in the church that it is not enough to rail against physical indulgence. There is also spiritual indulgence. And to wallow in spiritualism is just as debilitating—perhaps more so—than in physical things. He doesn't do that.

He doesn't handle the problem of money as a crusader. The difficulty with being a crusader (and Paul, I don't think, could ever have been a crusader) is that a crusader lets the opposition or the problem or the issue determine the agenda. And Paul brought his agenda with him, his relationship to God in Jesus Christ. You see, the crusader always asks only one question, as the crusader goes out into the world, ferreting out the problem: "Who is it? Who is it? Who is it?" But the Christian asks a question the crusader never asks. The Christian doesn't always ask, "Who is it?" The Christian asks, "Is it I?"

Paul isn't solving his problem as a moralist, though he was interested in moral issues. He doesn't solve it as a moralist, who reduces the world to a set of bad habits, and then enjoys not doing them. Paul handles it another way. He expresses his freedom. He is free from having to have money. He is free from the illusion of all that it will do for him. He's learned that's not true. He doesn't have to be wealthy. How did he learn? He says, "I've been initiated into the secret." I don't really know how he learned it. He says, "I know how to have a lot, how to have nothing. I don't have to have a great deal."

Some of the really pitiful things you run into in the world are scenes where people have not learned that yet, where people haven't gotten the secret yet. You see them in stores: "I'd like to buy some time." "We don't have any time, but we can sell you a clock." "Can I buy a friend here?" "No, no, don't have any friends. We can sell you a companion for the night." "I'd like to buy a drop of rain." "No, can't sell you any rain, but we can have some water piped to your house." "Can I buy some salvation here?" "Oh, no. Got some nice Bibles. Sell you a Bible?"

See a man in a hospital corridor with a fistful of twenty-dollar bills, going up and down, stopping every orderly and every nurse: "My wife's in 306, in there under the oxygen tent. I can't lose her now. We've been married thirty-three years. There's a little something extra if you'll check in on her once in a while. Run in . . ." "Look, we'll take care of your wife. Put your money away." "Well, just . . ." He doesn't understand, does he? He doesn't understand that the fundamental fabric of human relationships is totally unrelated to money. How sad it is to think that giving will do it, or not giving will destroy it! The mother who puts a ribbon in her little girl's hair doesn't put it in there to make her pretty. She puts it in there because she is pretty. And when you give a gift to somebody, it's not "in order to." It's "because of."

Paul has learned that. And you know, he has learned to be absolutely free from the need to be poor. "I know how to have a lot. I know how to have nothing. I can take it either way." He doesn't have to be either way. He doesn't have to be wealthy, but remember, he doesn't have to be poor.

I used to think just being poor was a virtue. We used to have evangelists come to our town. And I liked to hear them preach those sermons against wealth. They knew everybody in the house was as poor as Job's turkey and mad about it. And they have these sermons against the rich. The assumption was, if you have money, bad news for you! And if you don't have money, you're going straight in through the pearly gates. They preached those marvelous sermons, and in those apostrophes, those flights of oratory against the wealthy: "Oh, with your big house on the hill, racks of shoes in every closet, room and bath for everybody, enough for all the neighbors! But the day will come when all of that will turn to a box of rags and the roof will leak and the rent is due. Then where will you be?" And then he paints this scene of one little room up over a store, one string of light cord with a fifteen-watt bulb, and lying across a mattress without a sheet, and on the floor, old cigarette butts floating in stale beer. And we said, "Sic him, preacher! Yeah!" Lord, help the rich! They got theirs now, we get ours later.

You know, the trouble with that mindset is that a person who has no money can be as materialistic as someone who has money. There are two kinds of people who worry about money: those who have it, those who don't have it. And there's many a child reared at a wealthy table, and many a child reared at a poor table, and they hear the same conversation, nothing but money, money, money. "Because we have it," or "if we had it." Money, money, money. You can inflate in the opinion of those children what money will do and what it will not do.

"I don't have to have a lot," Paul says. "I don't have to be poor, and I don't have to be rich. Because I have learned the secret that has absolutely set me free from the destructive power of this grasping, grasping thing." He learned in that mystery what Flaubert was later to say in that marvelous line, "A demand for money being, of all the winds that blow upon love, the coldest and most destructive." "I can have it; I cannot have it, because I have learned something else." Paul uses an unusual expression in talking about that relationship with Christ. "I have been initiated into the secret (or the 'mystery')." Do you have any idea what that is? The secret? "I've been initiated into the mystery."

It happened in our family that our daughter graduated from college in the same year our son graduated from high school. In a smooth move, I decided on gifts for both at the same time. It would be the same gift. I wanted to give them a poem. But I didn't want to hand them this poem, you know, photocopied or something. So I went to the university, and in the art department, there was a calligrapher who wrote it on that brown paper that makes everything look like it's real old.

It was a Yiddish poem called *"Der Ikker"*; in English, "The Main Thing." I wanted to give them a beautiful copy of this poem. She made this in a beautiful scroll for me, ten dollars apiece. And I went by the dime store and got the frames. It cost me about twelve or thirteen dollars a kid. But when it's your own kids, you blow it all, you know. Wrapped those up, put them on the bed. After their ceremonies, and we took all the pictures we wanted to take, they opened gifts, and they saved Daddy's gift to last, because it looks small, but they know there's really something in there . . .

So they get to my packages and they open these poems. I can see the disappointment. I said, "Go ahead and read it." I said, "John, read the poem." He read the poem. I said, "You get it?" He said, "I don't get it." I said, "Laura, you finished college. Explain the poem to your young brother." And she read it and she said, "I don't get it." I said, "Well, just think about it. It will come to you." And so, they took those gifts.

Last time I was in Laura's house in Oklahoma, it was on the wall in the den. I said, "Do you read that?" And she said, "Every once in a while I read it." I said, "Do you get it?" She said, "I don't get it." And I recently saw it hanging in the kitchen at John's. I said, "John, do you read that?" And he said, "Yeah. What does that mean?" Ah, they'll get it. It's the secret. It's the secret.

The poem says:

> If your outlook on things has changed—
> this is not the main thing.
> If you feel like laughing at old dreams—
> this is not the main thing.
> If you recall errors of which you are now ashamed—
> this is not the main thing.
> Even if you know what you're doing now
> you'll regret some other time—
> this is not the main thing.
> But beware, light-heartedly, to conclude from this
> that there is no such thing as the main thing.
> This is the main thing.
>
> Hirsch Oscherovitch

And they said, "What is the main thing?" I've never told them. I'm going to tell you. I hope you won't tell them. I want them to figure it out.

But as far as I'm concerned, in all seriousness, to be initiated into the secret of the fundamental relationship with God that sets you free is gratitude. I have never known a person grateful who was at the same time small, or mean, or bitter, or greedy, or selfish, or took any pleasure in anybody else's pain. Never.

I was thinking that if I were on a search committee, looking for a minister for the church, and we were talking about, and with, a certain person, I really think before I would even ask (and you know how important this is to me!), before I would even ask, "Can this person preach?" I think I would ask, "Is there any evidence that this person is grateful?"

"I have been initiated into the secret. I thank God that you have revived your concern for me. I'm not in want. I'm content, because in every situation in life, I'm adequate because of Jesus Christ." You can call it "grace." You can call it "gift." You can call it "gratitude." But that, my friends, is the heart of the matter.

47

Handling Preferential Treatment

James 2:1–7

Good morning. What are you doing here? This is Monday morning, you know! You need to get a life. Or maybe I should say, what sin have you committed that you have come to confession? I'm still enjoying yesterday; it was a remarkable day. I didn't get through enjoying it and was a little hesitant to start another but when I thought of the alternative, I thought we'd better go ahead. I was really surprised about yesterday. Nettie and I have never been here on the first day of the season, but I didn't expect everything to run so smoothly and so beautifully. The first day of things has a kind of awkward grace to it and I figured we'd all have to sort of pitch in and help. You know after the winter the battery's dead, the tires are low, the oil is low, so everybody get behind and push. Let's clean up the brush and trim the lawn. But it was as though it was mid-season and I don't know when everybody got ready for that, but it was a remarkable day. We are grateful for it and grateful for today. Today, I'm speaking not simply *about* but *to* the gifted and strong, and that is you, in case you forgot.

You heard the text that was read a moment ago from James 2. The writer of the text is absolutely appalled at the preferential treatment being given to certain people who come into the assembly, into the sanctuary. One comes in wearing gold rings and a fine white toga and everyone jumps around and says, "Here, sit here. Get up, get out of your seat, let Mr. and Mrs. sit here." And then someone comes in in rags, one who is poor. "What are you doing, who let you in here? Sit over there, sit over there in the corner." The writer cannot believe that such distinctions are being made, is absolutely flabbergasted that this kind of preferential treatment would be given in the House of God.

The people know, the readers of the letter know, the people addressed by this letter know; it is against God's law. You remember it as well as they do.

"You shall show no preferential treatment, you shall make no distinctions between the rich and the poor." It's clearly stated in Leviticus 19. It is in the teaching of Jesus. You don't say to one a favored word because that person favored you. You're not generous to one because that one is generous to you. You're not kind to someone because they're kind to you. You do not take your behavior from the nature of the other person, you take your behavior from the character of God who sends sun and rain on the just and the unjust, and that's what you're to do. Make no distinction.

Even the complex Apostle Paul got the point after a few years and wrote to the Romans and said, "With God there is no partiality." How can these people do this? Why are they doing this? Make a distinction on so flimsy a difference as economic status. As though identity was tied to a twenty-dollar bill, for goodness' sake. How stupid can people get?

I had occasion some years ago to observe within the frame of one week two beautiful sixteen-year-old girls who seemed to be worlds apart. One was in a beautiful blue dress coming down a spiral staircase to a waiting and applauding and admiring group of family and friends. Sixteen years old, pretty as a speckled pup. Everybody was delighted.

Within the same week I saw another sixteen-year-old girl. Pretty, standing on the porch of a mountain cabin in eastern Kentucky. She had, as they put it, a young'n on her hip. The father of the child long gone and she's standing there alone, about a half-dozen scrawny chickens pecking in the yard, nothing in the cabin, nothing for her, one diapered child. She looks out upon a gray world without any hope.

What's the difference in those two pretty sixteen-year-old girls? In my prayers that evening, I said to God, "Did you notice the difference? Why is it in this world, down the spiral staircase, standing with a baby, sixteen years old? Now, why the difference?" And when I paused in my prayer, God said, "I didn't notice any difference." God's getting a little old, have you noticed that? Losing eyesight and a little senile. Anybody can see the difference except God.

I don't know why these people in the church addressed by the book of James are making such distinctions. It's against their law, it's against the tradition, it's against the community, it's against the very nature of church. It might be that it was just kind of a heady business to know somebody who had gold rings and a white toga, noble person, politician. I don't know; that's kind of heady business.

Some years ago when I was briefly a consultant to someone running for the presidency of the United States, I was on a couple of occasions in Washington and I was shaking hands with people who before had simply been names in the paper. This could get to you if you're not careful. I was ready to call Nettie and say, "Sell the house, I've found a place here." But after a few days

I knew better than that. Maybe the people addressed just feel important by association. Maybe, maybe they're expecting some patronage; maybe they're expecting some political favor for the church. After all, it is a tough business to sing doxologies and follow the liturgy in the shadow of Caesar who stands with one foot on land and one foot on sea, astride the world. Caesar is Lord and here is this little hovel of Christians trying to say, but not too loudly, "Jesus is Lord, but would you sit here please. Here, take this . . . you, get up, let the man sit down." I almost understand it.

It could be that they just get some identity by that association. There are people, and this will surprise you I know, who have no sense of self-worth, who just attach themselves to someone who does, and think by that process, that association, they become somebody. "See that picture over there on the piano. I was at Graceland, had my picture taken with Elvis." "Hey, that's worth a lot, you know. The autograph seekers stand four hours in the rain in a long line to get the autograph of Hank Williams Jr." Why? It gives one some worth, doesn't it? I don't know, I don't know.

What is most amazing in this text is this. Why are you catering and giving preferential treatment to those people who are the very ones who abuse you and suppress you and deny you and mistreat you? They double the rent, they cut the wages, they won't give you a fair price for your produce. They oppress you and abuse you in every way and here you are kowtowing and bowing, "Oh please, have my seat. It's great to have you. Did you notice who's here this morning?"

Why, maybe you can answer, why is it that the abused still cater to the abuser? Why does the woman, who spent those years with a violent alcoholic husband, once divorced, marry another alcoholic? Why does the battered woman finally get free only to return to the batterer? The writer says, "I don't understand it. The very ones who put you down, you elevate."

Well, I'm just as flabbergasted as he is so I don't want to talk about it any more. I don't want to talk about those who give preferential treatment, I want to speak to the gifted and strong who receive preferential treatment. It starts out innocent enough. Wasn't it Somerset Maugham who said, "The most deeply ingrained, the most deeply rooted instinct in civilized humanity is the desire for the approval of other people"? It's natural and it starts out without any diseased condition at all. We all have it.

My student in preaching class, after one semester, is invited to preach in the home church. We know what Sunday it was; it was the Sunday after Christmas when nobody's there, or the Sunday after Easter. Came into the pulpit all full of himself. "Prof., they gave me a standing ovation." "A standing ovation?" "A standing ovation." "And you preached that sermon?" "Yeah, yeah."

And here's my poor student hanging onto the shrubs and the furniture to keep from ascending. First sermon. But it's innocent enough; it's innocent enough. I know the feeling. When I finished graduate school and had finished the Ph.D. and full of "Dr. Craddock," I went into the barbershop. The man who shined the shoes and swept up the loose hair, opened the door for me, "Come in, Doctor." Sounded good. I was getting my hair cut when the town drunk stumbled in and he said, "Come in, Doctor." This is not working too well.

It starts off almost natural with all of us, just a little preferential treatment, but then it becomes meat and bread. Then it becomes the very air we breathe. We begin to expect it. Disappointed, hurt when it doesn't come. The minister standing at the door: "Good sermon, Reverend. That was your best, the best one you've preached. I've never heard a better sermon." Now what am I going to do? If that was the best, what am I going to do next Sunday? The Reverend is not only competing with predecessors; he is competing with himself, a deadly thing, a deadly thing.

But already it's beginning to work. I have to have that, I need that. Then begins the decline. What can I do to get it? I tell you, give people what they want. Find out what they want and then say that. Find out what they like, give them that, even if it's just bread and circus, meet their expectation. That'll do it. Or one thing that always works is publicly confessing your weaknesses or your failures; they'll think you're honest. It comes across as honesty. Become one of the people so they'll say, "Even though he has the gold ring and the fine toga, we saw him in blue jeans the other day working in the yard. Oh that's good, I'll vote for him."

There was a southern senator, I won't name him, he's long dead, who was a master. Time for reelection, he would put on old clothes. He had in the garage an old, old Plymouth that he drove during election years. And he would drive it around in the country; he'd stop at a farmhouse. "You know I'm your senator, been working for you and would like for you to vote for me again. And by the way, I'm sorry to say this but while I'm here, I need to go to the restroom."

"Oh yes, just come in here, just come in the house. I haven't cleaned it up but you're welcome to use our restroom."

"Oh no, no, no, no, I'll just go out here behind a tree somewhere." Reporters followed him once and said he went to the toilet thirty-seven times one morning. Got the vote. You can manipulate, even if you are the gifted and strong.

Then comes the final stage, the forgetfulness. To forget, to forget, that neither popularity nor unpopularity are the measure of the merit of your life, the character of your life. Has absolutely nothing to do with it. And all people gifted and strong know that, but it is forgotten.

When I started out in teaching and preaching in the '60s, it was the thing to be unpopular. Ministers wanted to be unpopular because that was a sign they were prophetic. It was embarrassing if the church was growing. There must be something wrong. So the minister turns cynical and negative and then says, "There were over 300 in worship when I went there. I've been there two years; 78 last Sunday." Ah, a true Prophet has risen among us.

It never occurred that we were just actually obnoxious and weren't prophetic at all. Unpopularity doesn't mean that you are frank and truthful and cutting-edge prophetic. And popularity doesn't mean you're not. Neither has absolutely anything to do with it.

Forgetfulness number two: It is the task, it is the obligation, it is the duty of the gifted and strong not to satisfy a common appetite but to elevate it, to transform the expectations of society. It is wrong, it is wrong for gifted and strong people to contribute to the degeneration and decline of a society. There should be the elevation of the expectation and the hope to change the value system, even at a cost.

I remember a group of fellows saying to their leader, "You shouldn't be doing that. You're our leader, you're not supposed to do that, that's not for someone like you to do." And he acted as though they weren't even talking. He went right ahead with what he was doing. And he took a towel and a basin and girded himself and he washed their feet. You talk about gifted and strong. Wow!

I commend to you Jesus of Nazareth.

48

Weighing the Trifles

James 2:10–13

It's good to see you again, you have returned. It's obvious that you have need of more religion than I can provide so there is a busload of chaplains coming in today to help us out every morning. I'm speaking not only about, but speaking to, the gifted and strong who are the people of Chautauqua. Since I retired in 1993, I've been making a list of all the benefits and advantages of getting older. This has been a boost to my own morale although it has been a great deal of work because I have not been, in the past, a person who made lists. But I've been making a list and in the eight years since retirement, I have one thing on the list so far and that is: it is easier now to say, "I don't know."

In my teaching career, those words were hard to say. As a teacher you are tempted to bluff, to do a little verbal footwork to make the student think you know what you are talking about. It's easier to say now. I should have said it more then. "I don't know." I exercise the privilege this morning to say, "I don't know." I don't know the situation being addressed by the little book of James in the New Testament. It is a book that belongs to the ancient tradition of wisdom, a tradition in which Jesus stood, and the writer of Matthew, and, of course, many writers of the Old Testament.

At the point of the Scripture reading today, there is this unusual thing, which I find great difficulty in absorbing, much less defending. Whoever is responsible for the law is responsible for all of the law and if you break or violate the minutest part, the whole thing comes down around your ears. That's a different translation but you get the point. Whoever breaks the small part of the law is guilty of breaking the whole law. I don't know what situation is being addressed that would press a writer to insist on that. I have the feeling that it's a situation of moral panic, that there is in the community addressed a decline in moral responsibility. Sometimes when a nation or a community or a church feels the loss of moral strength, the weakening of moral fiber, the breakdown of ethical responsibility, a sort of panic sets in. We have to stop this. We have to stop this and one way to do so is to tighten up, tighten the screws, become even more rigid, and become even more legalistic. Anybody who breaks even one of the little laws is guilty of breaking the whole law. Would you ever say that?

Do you know what that smells like to me? It smells like zero tolerance. Doesn't it? Zero tolerance. I hate zero tolerance. I think the principle is absolutely irresponsible. It puts into one category the kindergarten girl who has a little bitty play knife made of rubber in her lunch bucket and the thug who has a switchblade in the alley and comes to school with it. And somebody stands up and says, "A knife is a knife is a knife." But she's a little girl, five years old, and her little knife is made out of rubber and plastic. It's an inch and a quarter long. He is a thug with a record and has this switchblade. Does it say in the rule, "except for little bitty knives"? Does it make a distinction? No! A knife is a knife is a knife and your five-year-old granddaughter is expelled. But . . . no, no, no, no, zero tolerance. Zero tolerance is the panic point you reach when you are unwilling to assume the responsibility of making moral and ethical distinctions between the lesser and the greater. That's just a personal opinion. I have a feeling it corresponds with ultimate truth.

When I read this in James, I think of that. Now I know what James is doing. James probably belongs to a very long tradition of what is called "The defense of the solidarity of the law." Many Jewish rabbis did it; a lot of the Greek moralists did it. And that is to say, you don't break the law; you don't violate the law, you violate the lawgiver. And if the laws that are for the community of faith are given by one lawgiver, God, to break one of them is to violate God, to sin against God. It is called "the solidarity of the law."

Now I find it more comfortable, much more work, but more comfortable, to make distinctions as are made in our courts. First- and second-degree manslaughter, voluntary, involuntary manslaughter, malice murder, felony murder, capital murder, justifiable homicide, these are reasonable distinctions. Even the church has dipped into distinctions and talks about venial sin and mortal sin and deadly sin. Distinctions surely can be made. And yet, I keep listening to the text and there comes to my mind what may be, I don't know, what may be in the mind of the writer; that is, when you begin to calibrate greater, not so great, medium, light, trivial, you start playing a game that can be dangerous. Dangerous in this way, that you presume to know the difference between what is major and minor, what is greater and lesser. I don't think we always know. Some of the great tragedies in human relationships begin with this word: "I was slighted." That's just a sliver of a word. I was "slighted."

Alienation can follow as great as the ocean. "Slighted." What's little, what's big? Shakespeare said, "Trifles light as air are to the jealous confirmations, strong as proofs of holy Writ." Trifles, trifles, light as air. Who knows what is big and what is little? Petrarch said, "If you want to take the measure of the greatness of a person, don't count the ships that have been launched and the battles won and the books written, but catch the person in that moment of insignificance attending to a matter, trifling apparently, and you will have the real revelation of the character of that person."

Thomas de Quincey was of the literary circle with Coleridge, Wordsworth, and others, a strange man, an opium eater, but brilliant mind. He wrote an essay entitled "On Murder." I'm sure many of you are familiar with it; it's absolutely brilliant. He says, "Many a person who upon committing a murder begins a downward slide and soon may come to robbing and then Sabbath breaking, may even sink to incivility and finally, arrive at procrastination. You never know once you begin this downward slide where you will end. Many a person can date his ruin from some murder or other that he thought little of at the time." Do you see what this strange genius is saying?

Turn it upside down and think about it. What really is major? What really is minor? I don't know, not at all. I do know this. In the exercise of my religion, I set great premium on little things because in all the years of my relationship to God, I've never had a big report to deliver to the brothers and sisters. Nothing big; only intimations, hints. I firmly believe, for instance, that God wanted me and wants me to be in the ministry of the gospel. I am, in the language of the church, called to be a minister, but I was not called in a voice loud enough for the whole family to hear. I have spent my life trying to say, "But it's true." It was so slight, that whispering of God. Why not broadscreen Technicolor so everybody could say, "Wow"? I haven't had that.

I brought one of my favorite poems this morning. It is from a woman who attended one of my classes for non-seminary trained ministers in rural Appalachia serving small churches. I was in the mountains of eastern Kentucky in a poverty-stricken community having a class and this woman, I would guess middle-aged, came to the classes because, she said, "I like the stories about Jesus." As an expression of gratitude, she gave me this poem.

> There is the hint of quiet rain coming soon,
> Not much, enough to soothe the greening needs
> Of outstretched leafy arms and hidden moss,
> Shy and quietly waiting for the damp.
> There is the hint of quiet moments coming soon,
> Not much, enough to soothe the thirsting needs
> Of outstretched, anxious hearts and hidden selves,
> Private and silently waiting for the peace.
> Louise Davis (unpublished poem)

The hint, not much, enough. Please don't put my best moments, her best moments on the lower end of the scale, saying, "But a trifle."

This, then, is my point. When we begin this calibration of distinctions, great, not so great, down to very, very minor, there is the temptation to trivialize the major portions of most people's lives. Those who are gifted and strong; you, gifted and strong, sit at long tables of decision, take up matters of great pith and moment, and affect the lives of many. Somebody has to do it, of course. But what a temptation when you're dealing with matters of major importance to miss the little things. "It was only one family." "It was only one church." "It was only one little community." "It was only one person." And when you enlarge the screen of your awareness of the hugeness of a matter, it can be a way of copping out from attending to one little thing.

I recall some years ago when we were living in Oklahoma, I went to Oklahoma City to take part in a discussion of what could be done among the Christian communities and Jewish communities of that area to relieve a tragic situation that existed in a small tribe of Native Americans on a reservation in southwest Oklahoma. This was the branch of the Arapaho tribe that moved south, not the northern Arapaho. Many of them were living near the Kiowa. We settled around a table, had our cups of water, had our coffee breaks, our refreshments and all that as we discussed the problem, a serious problem. Somebody said, "But isn't that the problem we have with all Native Americans? Isn't that a problem, really, that they all deal with?" Well, yes, I suppose so.

Then somebody said, "And think of the growing Hispanic population." We gave an hour or so to that and then the other minorities, Asian and Black. The screen grew larger and larger and larger and at five o'clock in the afternoon, this committee of the gifted and strong were sitting there in a pool of pity for the world. And that poor little subtribe in southwest Oklahoma received no help from us. We had to look at the big picture.

"What do you mean, child? Coming to me with a splinter in your finger? A splinter in your finger? Did you know that there are children all over the world having their arms and legs blown off by landmines? And you come with a splinter?" Let's get the larger picture here.

"Now what is it exactly that you and your husband do?"

"Well, we have a foster home for children. We have a rather large house. We've had as many as eleven but now we're down to eight. But we take especially those who have learning disabilities."

"Listen, let me tell you something. Do you have any idea how many children in this country are homeless, how many children in the world with learning disabilities and you have eight? A drop in the bucket." Let's get the big picture.

The danger for the gifted and strong is to sit at long tables and consider the big picture but never improve the playground for the children in the neighborhood where they live. Do you understand? The fact that millions, millions in the world are starving is not a reason for me to spend my time pondering that, but never volunteering one hour at the soup kitchen of my church. "But a trifle."

In the third decade of the first century of the Common Era, things were falling apart in the Roman Empire. Caesar Augustus had brought it together, having defeated Antony and Lepidus and Cleopatra. He had one great empire and he was probably the greatest Caesar of them all. Now his nephew Tiberius is ruling, but enemies are rising, armed forces at the east, the need to increase military personnel, which meant greater taxes on everybody in the empire. Seventy million people threatened. It's falling apart, dissension in Rome, hunger everywhere, fringe groups, and small countries within the empire having civil strife and revolutions. It's terrible.

And God looks it over to get the big picture and the next sound you hear is a baby in a little obscure town; a Jewish baby named Jesus, mewling and puking in his mother's arms. This is what God is doing? Did not God see the big picture? What can that baby do? Good question. What can that baby do? And Jesus said, years later, "I want all of you to understand that even a cup of cold water given to a child does not go unnoticed by the God who smiles upon it."

Not a trifle; not a trifle. Amen.

49

Curbing One's Appetite

James 4:1–3

The young people who are scholars of the International Order of King's Daughters and Sons who have been reading the text for us have done such a good job, I feel a little bad that the texts I've chosen have a grim quality to them. Maybe if I'm ever back, I'll choose something delightful from the book of Psalms for them to read.

It is a bit grim, as those of you who have been here and have been listening to James talk to us know, that "A" if not "The" primary function of religion for James is restraint, the exercise of restraint. He is battling in the church what he calls hedonism, that is, pleasure seeking, desire, unrestrained seeking after things and after pleasures. This is very much on his mind, especially in the reading today. It is obvious he puts a great premium on restraint in the function of religion.

In my home church, whether or not they were into James, they certainly got that message. My recollection of the primary function of religion in my home church was restraint. I mean we didn't have any laughter. We didn't have any applause. It was fairly dead. I think the only hymn our church knew was "'Tis Midnight and on Olive's Brow" and the only Scripture I recall was "Well done, good and faithful servant. Enter into the misery of your Lord." Preachers with a cadaver face would get up and spend long minutes talking about how we had to restrain ourselves about all kinds of things.

It was a heavy business and it affected me. I recall once going with a friend to his church, a different denomination. It was a Sunday they were having the Communion, the Lord's Supper. The one presiding at the table said, "We come now to the time for celebrating the Lord's Supper." He used the word "celebrating." When I got home I told my mother they had the Communion but they celebrated it. And she said, "Well, now you understand why that church has never grown." Celebrating? My goodness.

Then I went away to school and as I told you in the little testimony on Sunday evening, it was a very strict and conservative school. It was a work college; you had to work your way through. Large Holstein herd had to be milked at 3:30 in the morning and 3:30 in the afternoon and the school program was built around that. Chapel was required every night but it had to be over at 8:00 because you had to go to bed at 8:00 in order to be up early the next morning. Well, there was somebody preaching at us one evening. It went well past the eight o'clock hour but in the course of the evening, it was the spring of the year, there were no screens, but somebody had opened the windows and a big bat came into the sanctuary. We thought it would dismiss the service, but the preacher said, "You will notice, boys," we were all boys, "you will notice, boys, that it is not the dove of the Lord; it is a bat from Satan to distract us from the Word." He just went on and on and on while this bat swooped down over us and flew under the preacher's nose.

It was obviously well past 8:20, 8:30; he was still going, but the bat was beginning to win. Finally we were taking off sweaters and swinging them when the bat came by. Somebody at the back had a broom and . . . well, you can't hit those bats. Someone in the back yelled, "If you'll turn off the lights, make it dark in here, then the bat will go outside." So the lights were turned off, maybe a minute, two minutes. When they were turned back on, there were only six students left. My sad report is that I was one of the six.

I had not learned that to be a Christian is to be light on your feet and humor is not a contradiction but an expression of the freedom of the grace of God and gratitude for every day. It doesn't conflict with the high purpose of our lives before God, not at all. Seriousness of purpose does not require heaviness of manner, but I hadn't learned that. I was in the restraint business at the time.

Now James is not alone in recognizing that restraint is, in a sense, a Christian virtue. Second Peter agrees very much. Remember that marvelous passage, in which the writer says, "As you orchestrate your life, include self-control, restraint." Paul even lists self-control as one of the gifts of the Spirit. The Holy Spirit in your life is evidenced through self-control. But the Apostle Paul recognized also that restraint is not the only quality of one's life if you live before God in good faith. In fact, restraint can be counterproductive. He wrote to the Romans and said in chapter 7 of that book, "I don't understand my own actions. I try to keep the law. The law says you shall not covet, that is, you shall not lust." But that planted a seed in my mind. You shall not lust. You shall not lust. Lust, yeah, lust. And he said, "I wouldn't have known lust except the law said you shall not lust."

Sometimes, he said, even what is good and holy and right can be counter-productive. Many of us would agree with that. Restraint, as the primary definition of religion without some understanding that faith means also release and freedom and joy, can produce a cramped and stuffed person who will have problems and later will have to go either to a therapist or to the bottle or to drugs. Restraint alone is not it. Restraint is never invited to the party.

Now I don't want to give you the impression that I am opposed to restraint. I recognize the benefits of restraint. I used to say to my students all the time that restraint or discipline or self-control is essential if you're to have a productive life. It's essential if you're going to have any kind of freedom. Freedom is a prison flower; it grows only where there is restraint and discipline. If you get up in the morning and there is nothing disciplined and laid out for you, the chances are the day will be wasted. Give some time to study every morning. Get up early enough. After breakfast when you're in your parish, every morning, at least an hour and a half, study, study, study and it will be to your benefit. You'll build a reservoir of abilities that will help you in the crunch and in the emergency. Every morning, every morning. And read in the evening before you go to bed, just pleasure reading, maybe twenty minutes.

In the ministry you're not going to have big stretches of time. "When I get time, I'll do this . . ." Learn to use fifteen minutes, ten minutes, discipline, restraint, discipline. If you'll read twenty minutes in the evening, just for pleasure, something good, at the end of the year a big table will not contain the books you will have read. But if you wait until you have time to read, at the end of a year even a small table will contain all the books you've read plus a couple of elephants. You will not have done anything.

And it will free you from a sense of guilt. You know some people say, "I need some recreation," but all the time they're on the tennis court, they're thinking, "I really should be studying." But when they're studying, they think, "I really should be getting some recreation." And they enjoy neither the studying nor the recreation. Discipline, discipline; it's the key to productivity, to establish the habit. Habits, my friends, are our friends. In fact, strangely enough, even paradoxically so, restraint is the key to a lot of pleasure because restraint is the birthplace of anticipation and there is no greater source of pleasure than anticipation, to look forward to something. If you have everything now, do everything now, then what?

I used to say to my students, "When you call in the nursing homes on the people who are confined, don't just show up on Thursday and say 'How are you doing, Mrs. Brown?' That's no good. Call Monday. 'Mrs. Brown, this is your pastor. I wonder if I might come out to see you, say Thursday afternoon at three? It's Monday. May I come, Mrs. Brown, at three o'clock on Thursday?' She says, 'Well, I'll pencil you in, Reverend.' And then she goes up and down the halls of the nursing home, saying to her friends, 'My pastor made an appointment with me. He's coming on Thursday. When does your pastor come? Does he ever make an appointment? Mine made an appointment; he's coming on Thursday. This is Monday, you know. Made an appointment, Thursday afternoon at three.'" She has the time to brag about it; she has the time to prepare for it. She has the time to anticipate it.

Now I know, I know, I know, sometimes the anticipation of the pastor's visit is better than the visit. But the anticipation is a marvelous thing. That's the key, you know, to a good book. A good book doesn't give you the whole thing at the beginning. It is restraint, restraint, restraint; it keeps you there. Good speakers know this. They don't just start off telling you what they're going to say. Like beginning a joke with a punch line. Restraint, restraint, restraint.

Everybody knows that's how plays and experiences unfold. Even those who write commercials for television know this. There is one I like very much about some kind of headache medicine. This woman comes on the screen and says to you quite clearly, "When you have a headache, you don't want something to relieve the pain. You don't want something to lessen the pain. You don't want something to ease the pain. You want something to stop the pain." That's good. Some of us stupid people would just go out there and say, "You want something to stop the pain? Here." No, no; restraint.

I remember an interview some reporter had with the late Carl Sandburg. "Mr. Sandburg, you're a man of words, you've written poetry and history and biography. You write songs. As a man of words, what to you is the ugliest word in the English language?" Sandburg was in his eighties, shock of white hair down over his brow. Looked at the reporter and said, "The ugliest word? The ugliest word? The ugliest word? The ugliest word, the ugliest word? The ugliest word? The ugliest word is, the ugliest word is, exclusive." I remember that; it was twenty years ago. Someone with lesser ability would say, "Oh let's see, my idea is just my view, of course; everybody's different on this, but my own opinion about it, for what it's worth, would be exclusive, but you know . . ." Restraint.

I want you to understand. I'm going to quit this little side trip in a minute, but I want you to understand that restraint in and of itself is a great source of productivity and pleasure. But the striking thing about James is this: in the passage that was read by Elizabeth this morning, restraint is applied to material things. The writer has three groups of people in his congregation. First, there are those who want but cannot have and so they commit violence to get it. After all, it's only so long you can press your nose against the window looking at the joyful things inside and have somebody say, "You're poor, you can't have it." After awhile, you take a brick, shatter the window, and take it. There are those who want and can't have it and so they're violent.

The second group to whom he advises restraint are not violent people but they covet. They look around and see those who have things and they want those things and they're all in the church together. But the poor are coveting the things of the people who possess them and in that coveting, they create tension and division in the life of the congregation. James says, "Restraint."

And then surprisingly enough, and this is amazing to me, there is a group that is quite spiritual, so they are praying for these things, that God will give things to them. James says, "You're not going to get it, because it's not what you need, it's what you desire. It's hedonistic. It's pleasure-seeking. You ask amiss." God doesn't give you a new car. But here they are praying for it. I think of this text every once in awhile when I listen to people preach the gospel of wealth. Give God a nickel, God will give you back a dime. This Christian religion really pays off.

When in a church in Birmingham years ago, I was invited, following the service, by some couples who said, "We have a prayer group. We'd like for you to come to our prayer group." "Fine, I'll come to the prayer group." They never had a prayer all evening. What they were doing was counting and listing the answers to prayer. We never had prayer. The leader went around the room, there were probably twenty people there sitting in a circle in this nice home. One of the group sat at the dining table with an adding machine, adding up the answers to prayers. I can recall a few of them. There was a mink stole. The woman said that God answered her prayer. There was new luggage. There was a trip to Honolulu. There was a young woman there who had gotten a date with Mike, whoever he was. He was an answer to prayer. And so it went, this list of luxurious things. The leader said to me, "Would you like to add to our list?" I said, "I have nothing to add to your list." "Don't you believe in prayer? Jesus said, 'Whatever you ask in my name, you'll get it.'" I gave them a little exhortation and that was the end of that. The one at the dining table reported, "We have now had 321 answers to prayer" and there was applause around the room, and we left. There had been no prayer.

James said, "Some of you are praying for things that will give you pleasure. You're not going to get that. Those who seek what they cannot have and gain it by violence: Restraint. Those who covet: Restraint. Those who pray for these pleasuring things: Restraint." But what occurred to me is this: what would James say if he were talking to people who could afford to have these things? I speak to the gifted and strong. I speak to the "haves," not the "have nots." It is one thing to say to people who live in a world in which desire and availability are poles apart, "Never in your lifetime." "Then how do I manage that gulf between what I want and what I have?" Restraint.

But what would be his word to people who want and can have? They can afford it. Daddy can afford it, Mama can afford it, we can afford it. "You mean you're building at this age in your life a trophy house worth $1.3 million dollars? Just you and your wife?" "Well, we can afford it." "You mean you're going . . . ?" "Well, we can afford it. We can afford it." What would James say? We know what he says to those who cannot afford it. Restraint. But what does he say to those who can afford it? I don't know and since James is not here, I'm going to tell you. "You cannot afford it." A whole long closet full of clothes. As long as there is anybody without clothing, you cannot afford it. All that food and you can't eat it; where does it go? With hunger everywhere, you can't afford it. One point three million dollar trophy house in your old age? When brothers and sisters are sleeping in cardboard boxes in downtown cities, you cannot afford it. I don't care how much you have. As long as there is a limit to our natural resources, we can't afford it. A limit to the trees and the flowers and the grass, we just cannot afford it. "But I can afford it." Oh, no.

I remember the Apostle Paul said once when he wrote to the Corinthians: "I don't exercise all my rights. I don't exercise all my freedoms. I'm free to do this and have that. I'm free to be this and to be that. I'm free to enjoy this and to enjoy that. But I don't exercise all of them. I exercise restraint because," he said, "I am under divine restraint. There are things I have to do." "I have to"; what an ugly expression. I have to do it. The divine restraint. The divine necessity that spreads its broad wing over our place and says, "You have to do this."

Have you ever been at a social where people are standing around the punchbowl, nibbling those little cucumber sandwiches, wondering when we're going to eat? You're talking to people. "It was a nice day, wasn't it." "Yeah, kind of cool." "Well, it's beginning to warm up. Sun was out, thought we were going to have rain." You know all that heavy conversation just drains your mental powers. And then somebody walks in. "Who's that?" Everybody turned and looked. "Oh, you don't know her?" "No, no." "That's Barbara Harris." "That's Barbara Harris?" "Yeah." "You've read about Barbara Harris, you've heard about Barbara Harris. She's a woman of means and she's gifted and she's strong. You know what she does? She spends her time working with police departments to improve the condition of children who are put in jails. On her own, her own resources." "Is she paid?" "No, no." "Who pays her expenses?" "She does." "Well, you mean she . . ." "Yeah, yeah." You go over and say, "Barbara, is it true you're . . . why are you doing it?" You know what she said? "I have to. Somebody has to do it."

I think, personally, I think the key to achievement, the key to freedom, the key to real profound joy is to feel the burden, the wonderful burden of divine restraint. "I have to do it." Now that's really good news.

50

How Long Does Easter Last?

1 Peter 1:3–9

Have any of you ever been to the reading of a will? I am sure some of you have. The family, the relatives, and any others who expect to be involved in the distribution of the inheritance gather in a judge's chambers or in a law-yer's office, and the will is read. It is a very exciting and anxious time; indeed, for some it is an extraordinary moment.

I thought about this when I read the text from 1 Peter. Sometimes I for-get that this is what we do every Sunday: read the will. That is what we are here for, to read God's will so all the children of God can know what their inheritance is. Sometimes I forget that this is what we are doing. But today's text reminded me that we have, by virtue of the resurrection of Jesus Christ, a permanent Easter benefit, an inheritance that cannot shrink, that cannot be removed, that cannot be altered, that cannot pass away. It is according to 1 Peter, "kept in heaven," which means "guarded in heaven" or, as we would say, "under lock and key in heaven," to be distributed to us. That is why we are here.

So have you been to a reading of a will? Some people don't even show up because they do not want to be embarrassed. They say, "What if everybody is sitting there having their names called out and finding out what they get, then they don't call my name and there I sit? Then what? I think I'll just not show."

According to the Old Testament, in ancient Israel there are some people in the family who may as well not show because their names will not be called. The widow—we call her the "poor widow" because that is exactly what she was in the economic system of that day—did not get anything according to the law. Zilch. She could sit there all day, but her name would not be called. That may seem strange to you (it does to me too) but I am just telling you how it was. Part of her "problem" was that she was a woman, a fact that accounted for a lot of the things that she suffered. Inheritance went through the men-folk, so she did not get any. Moreover, if the deceased had daughters, they need not show either. Their names would not be called. If you are a daughter in Israel, do not come to the reading of the will; you will not hear your name. Now if the deceased had *only* daughters and no sons, then the daughters could make a claim: "We're the closest thing to the son our father never had." But even then sometimes they did not get heard because the money would go to the brothers of the deceased who had sons. There was no need for the daughters to show.

Today we do not have these Old Testament rules and regulations because in our legal system wills and inheritances are up to the decision of the one who is the benefactor. I say that the inheritance is up to the benefactor's decision, which actually means that person's current love, hate, or whim. The will can be changed, you know, and then changed and changed and changed again, and you can sit there as a daughter or a son and not have your name called. Or maybe your name is called: "I leave to my son, Ralph, my dirty socks." Having his name called can be a way of slapping Ralph in front of everybody. Why should Ralph show up? Why should anybody show up when the inheritance is up to feeling and whim?

Many a person who has a great deal of money also has a son or daughter who, as that person gets old, suddenly becomes really, really nice. "Would you like some more soup, Daddy? Can I bring you anything, Daddy?" Up until that time, Daddy did not exist. "Maybe he'll change the will. Maybe I'll get more than the others. Maybe I'll get something big." And then the will is read and the family is torn apart. Brothers and sisters do not speak to each other anymore because one got this while another didn't get anything.

The benefactor can leave it all to the cat. "All that I own I want to be turned into cat food and given to our cat, Sylvia, and to the caretaker of the cat." That can be done. Now this leads to lawsuits. Was he really of sound mind? Was he under undue influence when he changed the will? It can be an ugly thing. I do not know whether it is worth it to show up at the reading of the will.

Some people do not show up because they have no name. How can your name be called when you are nameless? My brothers and I used to mow the lots at Rose Hill Cemetery in Humboldt, Tennessee. It was a way of helping support the family. In the cemetery, across a strong, rather high fence, were maybe sixty or seventy graves. "Do you want us to go over the fence and mow the grass over there?" we would ask. "No," we were told. "That's the potter's field. Those graves don't even have a name." Who were those people? Who cares? They died in jail, they died paupers, they died without family. "Don't go over there. Just let the weeds grow." Why show up when you do not have a name?

We're going to rededicate a cemetery in Fannin County in June. It is a restored cemetery, a beautiful, walled cemetery with twenty-seven graves, each with a stone bearing no name. They were slaves, and there is not a single name. Why show up for the reading of the will if you do not have a name?

One of the most painful things to me about the horror of the Kosovo refugee situation is the recent news that the oppressors are not only driving the refugees out of their homes, but they are also destroying the legal records that show they ever had a home. They are destroying the identity of these people so that they cannot prove they ever existed. You may ask, "When are those people going to go back home?" The answer is: What people? What home? They do not exist. Then why show up for a reading of the will? You do not have *anything*, not even a name.

One time I was conducting a chaplains' retreat at Fort Belvoir, Virginia. They treated me very well. I ate in the officers' mess, and the soldiers who waited on us wore sort of sad green fatigues. However, on their uniforms where normally a soldier would have a nametag, there was nothing. That nametag had been ripped off. I said to the fellow waiting on me, a very nice young man, "I see you don't have on your nametag. What's your name?" He didn't answer me. I said to the officer beside me, "Why didn't he answer? What's his name?"

"He doesn't have one," the officer said.

"What do you mean? Give me a break here. What's his name?"

"He has no name," the officer repeated.

"Who are these people waiting on us?" I asked.

"Conscientious objectors."

This was during the Vietnam War, and these were conscientious objectors. They do not exist; they have no names, so eat your lunch. Can you believe that? No names.

I think the saddest group that does not show up for the reading of the will are those who, in terms of expecting anything, have eliminated themselves. These are the folk who have disqualified themselves because of their low station in life, or because of something horrible they have done, or because nobody accepts their lifestyle. Some people during their lifetime gradually erase themselves and stand looking at their shoelaces and say, "I am nobody. Why should God include me? I'm not anybody."

I remember that marvelous prophecy in Isaiah 56 where the Lord says, "I do not want foreigners to say, 'I do not have a place among the people of God.' I do not want the eunuch to say, 'I am just a dead tree.' The day is coming, the day is coming," says the Lord, "when the stranger, the alien, the foreigner, the transient will have a place in my house. And the man who cannot father children will have better than many children because I will put his name on a marker in my house and everybody will know him forever. That day is coming," says the prophet, "when God's house shall be called a house of prayer for everybody" (paraphr.). What a wonderful thing!

Yet I still run into people who have disqualified themselves, some simply because they think they do not have the right thing to wear. Can you believe it? What is the right thing to wear? But here in 1 Peter, we find a group of people gathered to the rafters for the reading of the will. They are all here, jammed into the room, excited. I don't know why they are there, because a lot of them are women. You have read 1 Peter, and you know that many of the people being addressed are women. You know their names are not going to be called. Some of these people are slaves. You have read 1 Peter, and you know that some of the members of that church were slaves. Do you think they should show up? I think that is the Sunday they need to go fishing. Are they going to have their names called? Why are they there? They are all excited, all excited for the reading of the will. Women, slaves, and what 1 Peter calls exiles, foreigners, and transients. That is the way all of the Christians back then were regarded. They were people without a country, non-people. I tried to think this week about what would constitute a modern analogy to the way Christians were regarded by the culture of that time, and the only word I came up with is *gypsies*. Gypsies are nobody. Where do they live? Where is their place? What is their name? Nowhere. Nobody.

Yet in this little church addressed by 1 Peter, the folks had all gathered for the reading of the will. Strangers, exiles, nobodies, slaves, women, everybody; they have all come and they are all excited because they said, "The will has been kept guarded in heaven, under lock and key, and nobody can change the will. The value will not go down. It is imperishable. The will is unchangeable, and it is not the whim of the one who made out the will to change it and change it and change it." These people are confident that they are going to be taken by the hand outside the building and allowed to walk off the size of their inheritance as the children of God and then taken back inside and run through the unsearchable riches of God's love and grace. Every one of them is expecting it.

The leader gets up and reads the will. He says, "First of all, there is no silver or gold here. You have come to the wrong place if that is what you're interested in. This is a church, and there is no silver or gold. There is, however, boundless mercy, and, when push comes to shove, that is the part of the inheritance that every one of us will want more than anything else: the boundless mercy of God, not what we deserve, but what love gives."

The reader continues with the will: "There is hope, and that is what keeps us alive." Indeed, hope keeps all of us alive, keeps the student alive, keeps the soldier alive. When we were in Oklahoma, I saw that it was hope more than anything else that kept the farmers alive. There they were, driving those mortgaged tractors across that dry, dry land, burning fuel they bought on credit, and seeing not a sprig come up. "Well, maybe next year." Hope. Hope, not because it is spring and everything is beginning to bloom, but hope that is built upon the nature of God who calls into being what does not exist and gives life even to the dead. *That* is the basis of real hope.

"There is security," the reader of the will goes on to say, "security that God is with us and guides us and guards us. Even when we walk the thorny way and endure suffering, there is the security of God's grace." And finally the reader says, "The last gift to all the children of God is joy." Joy. You see it once in a while. I don't mean the silly kind of joy; I don't mean just smiley faces on a little card on your lapel: "God loves you, and I do too." I don't mean that. I mean real joy, the kind that even has tears in its eyes and it is still there.

Next February my wife, Nettie, and I are going on a one-week mission to an island in the Bahamas. I have never been to that part of the world, so I do not know exactly what to expect, but we have been told that the people there are extremely poor, many of them illiterate. The preachers do not have any education, and I am to spend a week helping them with their sermons. Nettie and I are going to go down there and have a good time with those people, preach in their churches, and eat at the table with them.

Thinking about this mission trip reminded me of an experience I had some years ago. I was the visiting preacher at a church, and on Sunday afternoon, a van pulled up in the church parking lot and a number of young people got out. They looked like they were thirteen, fourteen, fifteen years old, maybe as old as eighteen. There were ten or twelve of these young people, all members of that church, and when they got out of the van with their sleeping bags and bedraggled clothes, they were the most awful looking bunch of kids you have ever seen. "What is this?" I asked, and I was told that they had just returned from a work mission. In one week these young people had joined with others and had built a little church for a community. They were exhausted, worn out, and they looked terrible. They were sitting on their bags waiting for their parents to come, and I said to one of the boys, "Are you tired?"

He said, "Whew! Am I tired!" Then he said, "This is the best tired I've ever been." That is what joy is. Do you feel that? "This is the best tired I've ever been." I hope someday the young people in this church will get that tired. I hope we all get that tired. Just the best tired there is. In your Bible, it is called joy.

I want to ask you something. Do you know of any people who live near where you live who do not show up for the reading of the will because they think they are not going to get anything? Do you know any people who for any reason have excluded themselves? If you do, I want you to go to them and say, "Last Sunday we read the will, and your name was called out, but you were not there." And then tell them this: "We are going to read it again next Sunday." So bring them to this place to hear it. There is nothing like hearing your name called out, nothing like hearing the voice call your name and say, "Child of God, this is yours."

That is what we do here. We read the will.

51

When Is the Promise of His Coming?

2 Peter 3:8–13

I am grateful that you extended to me a second opportunity to be here. We live only eleven miles from this building but it took me a year to get here. And I'm grateful to those four who filled in last year when I became ill, Brooks Holifield, Tom Frank, Barbara Brown Taylor, Walter Brueggemann. When I was in the hospital, when anyone is in the hospital, you have very few pleasant thoughts but the nurse once in awhile would come by and see me smiling and say, "It's good to see you smiling; what are you smiling about?" I never would tell her but I was entertaining a wicked thought that when I fell ill, it took four people to replace me. I am grateful to them and to this church and to John Simmons for the pulpit.

This is the Epistle for this second Sunday of Advent. I paraphrase:

> Here is something, dear friends, which you must not forget. In the Lord's sight one day is like a thousand years and a thousand years like one day. It is not that the Lord is slow in keeping his promise as some suppose but that he is patient with you. It's not his will that any should be lost but that all should come to repentance. But the day of the Lord will come like a thief. On that day the heavens will disappear with a great rushing sound. The elements will be dissolved in flames and the earth with all that is in it will be disclosed. Since the whole universe is to be dissolved in this way, think what sort of people you ought to be, what devout and dedicated lives you should live. Look forward to the coming of the day of God and work to hasten it on. That day will set the heavens ablaze until they fall apart and will melt the elements in flames.
>
> Relying on his promise we look forward to new heavens and a new earth in which justice will be at home. In expectation of all this, my friends, do your utmost to be found at peace with him, unblem-

ished and above reproach. Bear in mind that our Lord's patience is an
opportunity for salvation.

This text is a cutting from a very thorny bush. Some people don't even
want to touch it, understandably so. They argue, after all it's a small book
tucked away near the close of the New Testament, under the eve of the great
Revelation, hardly seen at all against the splendor, the terrible splendor of
that book. It's late in writing, perhaps the latest in the New Testament. Not
all of it is original, copied a great deal from the book of Jude, very difficult to
read, fifty-five words in it used nowhere else in the New Testament. And it is
very argumentative, very argumentative. And we don't much like arguments
in church. But when you remove the nettles, when you remove the thorns,
what we have is a debate, an argument.

The issue, the subject, is Advent, the coming of the Lord. It is a subject
about which the writer, the author of this book, feels very keenly. It is a very,
very important subject to the writer. In fact, in the course of the book, he
goes on a rhetorical rampage, using all the devices available. At one point
he goes into a valedictory, a sort of deathbed speech. "Our time is near,
the Lord said I was going to die, now I'm going to die." And he gathers the
church around the foot of the bed. That's very impressive, the last words of
the old writer.

At other times he gets up on his hind legs and just screams bad names at the
opposition, a lot of name calling. What has him so exercised? It's Advent. He
insists he is talking about the apostolic tradition, true, unadulterated, straight
from God, this is the tradition. Like a thief in the night, the Lord is coming. And with his coming there will be a cosmic holocaust, burning flames
and melting down and the truth about every living thing will be disclosed.
And then there is the vision of the new heaven and the new earth and in that
time and place, the justice of God will be at home. That, he says, is the truth.
That's what we preach.

Now, I know, I know, I know, our forbears in the faith, those first generation Christians, believed it was going to come in their lifetime and it didn't
come and it didn't come. And it didn't come in our parents and it hasn't come
in ours and some time has passed, I know that. They believe some standing
here will not taste of death 'til it comes. And time is short; the fashion of the
world is passing away. I know they believe that but what you don't understand, friends, is you've miscalculated.

"A day is like a thousand years, a thousand years is like a day." How can
you count God's time? You're way off base in this. And even if Christ is being
delayed, even if he's being delayed, it's simply another case of the patience of
God, not wanting any to perish but that all repent. He says that's the truth.

Now the other team, the opposition, those who scoff at this, find the Advent a very, very important topic. In fact, they say, you've been preaching that for seventy-five years. We've been standing around waiting for the Lord to come and the Lord to come and some sold their property and we've been going up on every hillside, waiting, and this is it, now's the time. Nothing has happened. Oh, a lot of people believed it when you put Crayola markings on a piece of cardboard and said, "The Lord is coming soon." But now when you put up a sign of concrete, reinforced with steel, most of us don't believe it anymore. Your words have lived way past the conviction.

Now some of us, he says, some of us have already deleted from the Apostles' Creed that stuff about descended into hell. Now we want to take out another element that's just a little old fashioned. "From whence he shall come to judge the quick and the dead." For the truth of the matter is this, there is not a single documented case of God intervening or God acting in the life of any people or any person anywhere at anytime. Has God ever started anything or stopped anything or modified anything or helped anything or hindered anything or healed anything? No. Everything has continued from the beginning of time the same, the same, the same deadly same. Now that's the truth.

Now, preacher, if you want to go on entertaining yourself with those quaint notions about the presence of God and answers to prayer and visions of a new world where justice is at home, if you want to engage in that sort of activity, you go ahead but not in public and not from the pulpit. It's embarrassing to the rest of us. The fact of the matter, the truth of the matter is this. This world, your life, my life, is going nowhere.

Life is not a line with a rise or a slope, ending somewhere, good or ill. Life is a cycle, just a cycle. The rain falls into the rivers and the rivers go into the sea and the sun pulls up the water and the rain goes into the rivers and the rivers go into the sea and the sun draws it up and it rains into the rivers. And that's just the way it is, and that's just the way it is. And you give me one case otherwise.

Now some of us, of course, are not fully persuaded by the writer's arguments about the coming of the Lord. But I'd like to say a couple of things to those who scoff at it then and now. First of all, when you insist that there be a clear public proof, a clear demonstration, unmediated, unadulterated, unambiguous proof of the word and the presence and the power and activity of God, you don't really want that, do you? I don't think so, I don't think so. You couldn't stand it. The people of God have been claiming that all along. They screamed at Moses, "Where is God? We're hungry, we're thirsty. Where is God? You promised this, I don't see, God is not here. We need a God. There's no God here." And finally Moses came to the mountain, said, "This is it. Get ready, for the Lord is near." And there's rumbling in the distance.

And the committee came to Moses and said, "Moses, you go up the mountain and when you come back, tell us what God said." And when Moses came down from that mountain with a blistered face, they cried. They didn't want it; not face-to-face.

When the high priest once a year goes in through the Holy Place, behind the curtain into the Holy of Holies, into the very presence of God to sprinkle the blood on the altar for the year, the Day of Atonement, the people wait outside, breathless. "He'll not come out alive. He'll not come out alive. In the very presence of God, I wonder what is going on in there? I don't think he'll come out alive." And then when the priest comes out, "What did God say? What was in there? What did you hear? What did you see? Give us the blessing." Oh, we can't stand it ourselves.

I used to say, lots of times I've said, when I was a parish minister, I said it a lot. "God, do something, wide screen, Technicolor to shake these people up. Preaching is like a hypodermic in a tombstone. I'm not getting anywhere. Give us a big one some Sunday morning and they'll say, 'Whew, I believe, I believe. That's really it.'"

I go around saying "God has heard our prayers" and they wink at each other and say, "Well, you know he's paid to say that." "Answer one of my prayers in a real loud voice." You know I said to them, "I was called to the ministry" and they grinned and said "Yeah." If God had only called me in a voice loud enough for my family and the whole church to hear. I wanted God to do something that was not mediated and through other channels but just straight and pure, but I didn't, I didn't. Oh, it would have scared me to death.

I heard a minister in Portland, Oregon, say some years ago, he said, "I call on the sick in my parish, I go to the hospital, I call on the sick, I pray with the sick. I went to the hospital; one of my parishioners was in there. Before I could have prayer she said, 'Would you pray for me, Pastor.'" And he said, "I did, I prayed for her. And when I said 'Amen,' she sat up in bed, she put her feet down on the side of the bed, she stood up, she put on her robe, she put her feet in her scuffs and said, 'I'm well, I'm well.'" And she danced around; she grabbed the minister and hugged him around the neck, "Oh thank you, thank you." In the parking lot, he stopped to have a little prayer and said, "Don't ever do that to me again."

When you ask, when you ask for a good, clear, strong documented case of the plain unmediated presence and power and voice and act of God, do you really want it? But more importantly, to these who laughed at the preacher, may I say that the problem is not theological, the problem is not a problem of calculation of the second coming, the problem is one of character. For I want you to notice that those who attacked the preacher of these words are scoffers, they're condescending, they're arrogant, they feel superior. They know better, they put the preacher down. They belittle the preacher. That, my friends, is not a theological matter, it is not a matter of exegesis of Scripture, it is not a matter of interpreting the text; it's a matter of human sin, for there is no place, no place in the human community for one person to feel superior to another. Where would I be placed? Where would I be placed so that I could justifiably feel superior to those around me? Among children? Among the sick? Among the dying? Among the poor? Among the illiterate? Among the unskilled? Among the disabled? In what company, in what company would any one of us have a right to say, "No, no, in this group, I am superior"? On what grounds, on what grounds?

May I say this to you just straight out? If there is in you, if there is in any one of you any pretended claim to feel superior to any other human being, let your prayer be that Christ will snatch that from your soul, throw it into hell and let it burn to a crisp. For if there is anything totally inappropriate and unbecoming among the people of God, it is arrogance, especially in matters of faith.

It is criminal sometimes in academic communities the way some of us talk about God as though we knew what we were talking about. I sometimes find myself and hear others talking as though we had walked all the way around God and taken pictures. No, no.

A few years ago at Princeton some of us preacher types had gathered and were being addressed by an internationally famous physicist, a man of science, of great acclaim. He permitted a question/answer session. Someone asked, "What is it that ministers could learn from scientists?" And without hesitation this man said, "humility." "Oh, that's a surprising answer, I thought all scientists were rather arrogant in all that they know." He said, "No, oh no. You may have met one here and there, but the great scientists are all very humble people because they stand every morning before the mystery of all they do not know. And if anyone should be that humble, it would be the minister who every morning stands before the mystery of the Creator and Sustainer and Redeemer of the world."

Of course all views are not equally the same. Of course they're not. Argue, yes. Disagree, yes. Debate, yes, but never superior. The thing that has haunted me through the years is in the process of my own growth; I thought I had to register with other people the fact that I had grown by telling them in a laughing way about what I once believed. "I once believed this, I once believed that." And I had to belittle the path which I had taken. I had to sort of be superior to all those teachers who taught me things that I don't believe anymore. Of course we grow. But who is the person that would drive by junior high school and say, "phooey." That's the way you got to high school, which gets you into college, which gets you into graduate school.

I recall hearing Scott Momaday tell about an ugly incident in a little southern Oklahoma town. They had Frontier Days in that town; many towns in Oklahoma celebrate Frontier Days. The women put on the old dresses of ages ago and the men let their beards grow and they act like frontier people. It's a good time, lot of bar-b-que, a lot of horses in town and things like that.

He said that some of the young bucks in that little town to celebrate Frontier Days went out to the edge of town where an old buffalo was grazing with the cows. Brought it into town, found an Indian, a Comanche Indian, an old man. Put him up on a horse, gave him bow and arrows, tried to get the old buffalo to run, slapped the haunches of the horse to get it to chase the buffalo and told the Indian, "Shoot, shoot, shoot, we'll pay you." And he would try to shoot and try to shoot, and the exhausted and hot buffalo fell on the pavement. They pulled the old Indian off the horse and gave him a couple of dollars for his trouble. That's great, good fun, Frontier Days, whew.

There was a time, there was a time when that old buffalo could shake his craggy head and woo the others to follow and fifty thousand of them sent the earth trembling from the Rio Grande to Canada. There was a time when that Comanche could jump astride his horse and ride like the morning wind and put fear in the heart of every settler across the continent, but now those days are gone. Is that any reason, is that any reason to make fun? Oh, it's easier, it's easier, it's easier, rather than expressing what I believe, to have you express what you believe and then I can belittle it. I can make fun of it and I can point out the flaws. What do you think about that? That's ridiculous.

You see I'm not vulnerable that way. It is much easier, much easier to be cynical than to be confessional. I just sense it in our culture. Am I wrong in this? In the news reporting and everything you read and now in the churches, some real cynicism, as though people were going to church who did not believe in the power of Christ's presence and the Word of God, but just . . .

I noticed in the paper, I don't know if it's accurate, but the man, Reginald Denny, who was beaten up in California, was present for the taping of a show for Phil Donahue and one of his assailants was there also. Reginald Denny went over to his assailant and took his hand and shook his hand and said, "I forgive you." And Donahue said, "Cut, cut, cut. If this is going to be realistic, you've got to be more bitter." And the reporter said, "I understand that Reginald Denny is suffering from some brain damage."

Is it possible, is it remotely possible that one human being actually forgives another? Oh, I just hate to see this kind of thing creeping, creeping, creeping into the church.

A student came to seminary a few years ago, we fell into conversation. I said, "Where are you from?" He said, "Iowa." "Huh, we don't get too many from Iowa. Where are you from in Iowa?" "Well, between Ottumwa and

Keosauqua." He thought he was throwing me there you see. I said, "Between Ottumwa and Keosauqua, where?"

"Well, I came from a farm; it wasn't really a town. It's just called Taylor Community." I said, "Is that little community church still open there in the Taylor Community?" He said, "You know about that church?" I said, "In the '50s I was invited there because that church had been closed and some people wanted to start it again and thought maybe I could help them. I stayed there about twelve to fifteen days, working in that community." He said, "It's still open."

I said, "When you were there, did you ever know a woman, she's a crippled woman, she walked with a cane, her name was Josephine." He said, "Oh of course, she was my Sunday school teacher for five years; she's the principal reason I'm going into the ministry. Do you know her?" I said, "Yeah, she was eighteen when I met her."

I was traveling around in the community seeing if there was any interest in opening that old church again and I stopped at a dilapidated farmhouse. I started to get out, there was a big sign that said "Beware of the Dog" and I beware of dog. So I sat in the car bewaring. I didn't want to honk the horn, I hate honking horns out in front of houses but I sat there awhile and nobody came so I gave it a slight gentle, sort of Christian, tap. She came out, eighteen years old, right nice-looking young woman, but severely crippled, walking with a stick. We talked, I told her who I was and what my business was. She said she'd heard about it and that she'd like to come. I said, "Well, why don't you come?" She said, "Well, I don't know. I'll have to go in and ask my folks." And I said, "Shall I come in and speak with them?" "No, no, no. They're very hostile toward church."

She came out in a few minutes and she said, "Daddy said if I'll do my chores early, I can come, but he's not going to bring me, I'll have to find my own way." I said, "Sunday I'll come by. After that, someone else will."

Sunday I went by, she was dressed up, she had a different cane, a nice cane. She was quite happy but nervous as a cat, drawn in a knot sitting there. I said, "What's the matter?" She said, "I'm kind of nervous." I said, "Why are you nervous?" "Well, going to church." I said, "Have you ever been to church before?" And she said, "No."

I said, "Well, it's nice and the people are nice and you'll enjoy it. It's a wonderful place." She said, "I think I'll know all the people but everybody will be talking about God and I don't know anything to say about God." That's it. She had it already and she'd never been.

"But in church you talk about God." She's right, we do and sometimes this is what we say. Advent is not a season. Advent is our way of responding to a God who comes to us. We didn't invent this. It is in the nature of God. God is the one who comes to us. Not always according to our calculation, not always in the way we would desire, but God does come in ways that are appropriate to God's justice and to God's grace. Have I said that right? Do you believe that? I believe that.

Shall we pray? Gracious God, sometimes how stale, flat and tasteless seem all the uses of this present world. It seems we gather to rehearse what never happens. We scatter to address the inhumanity in the world only to find ourselves like children with teaspoons standing before an ocean. There needs to be an end to things. There needs to be a beginning to things. And yet we grieve over endings and we're afraid of beginnings. O God, be the Alpha and the Omega of our lives and the life of the world for the sake of Christ. Amen.

52

Does God Have Too Many Children?

1 John 3:1–3

I have looked forward for some time for this occasion to speak to you. I am grateful to Chris. I'm grateful to Richard and the choir. All you have to do is give Richard the two threads of topic and Scripture and he weaves the tapestry of appropriate worship, he and the choir. And, of course, I'm grateful to Birdie who has been a gift to me since the days we were in the Pavilion. It was a small room down there; she played a little loud for it and after about three weeks of repairing broken glass, we decided we needed a bigger room for Birdie. That's why we moved here, but it's not big enough so we're going to move again. Thank you, Birdie.

Today is the Third Sunday of Easter. Easter as you know has eight Sundays. It will end this year on the fourth of June, Pentecost Day. The readings for today, following the common lectionary readings, are three and all three of them are miracle stories. From Luke 24, the appearance of the risen Christ to his disciples, a miracle. Acts chapter 3, the healing of a crippled man at the beautiful gate in Jerusalem, a miracle. And the text that was read by Bill a moment ago, 1 John, chapter 3, a miracle. But of the miracles, I have chosen the biggest for myself. It's my birthday; I can do that if I want to.

First John, chapter 3: "Look at the love that God has lavished upon us that we should be called the children of God" (au. trans.). And that is what we are. The passage makes three clear statements: (1) We are the children of God. (2) It is not yet clear what we shall be. In the hereafter what will we be like? We don't yet know, but there is a hereafter. We don't speak about it enough I think in this church, but that started off as my fault. There is a hereafter and what we will be like, we don't know, but we will be like Him because we will see Him as He is. (3) And the third statement is this: Whoever has this hope, this heavenly anticipation, keeps life clean and just and pure.

There is a sanctifying influence granted by the anticipation of the hereafter. We are children of God. But it has occurred to me over the last few years that God has too many children. That may sound strange to you and I'm not really the one to make that judgment, but it's my birthday. God has too many children.

Now I know that's a relative matter. How many is too many? For Kathleen Maddux of Cincinnati, Ohio, one was too many. She was sixteen years old when she had the baby; didn't know exactly who the father was. Left the charitable ward of the hospital with the baby. Didn't even take the time or the care to give it a name; the band on the little wrist said, "No Name Maddux." She left him with neighbors and cousins, went on her way. "I don't need a baby holding me back. I have my own life to live."

When he got old enough he followed her. She left a trail of bad debts and crime from New Jersey, Ohio, Kentucky, everywhere. He went to jail after jail looking for his mother. In the course of it, she married a man who said, "I'll give the boy a name." The man's name was Bill Manson and he named the boy Charles.

Charles went looking for his mother and she turned him in every time. He was in reform schools. Then he graduated to jails and prisons and of his first thirty-five years on earth, twenty-two of them were spent in jail. Finally he decided, I'll just have a family of my own, so he gathered some sociopaths like himself and formed the Manson Family, still in prison for mass murder. He and his family killed over forty people, especially those who seemed to be happy.

"One was too many," Kathleen said. "I don't need a young'n on my hip. I've got a life to live."

In my family, five was too many. I thought four was just right; I was the fourth. And it worked out real nice, whether we were having popcorn balls or sorghum molasses taffy pulling or whether we were going to have snow cream, whatever it was, my mother would say to the others, "Now leave something for your little brother." I liked that. Then after about four-and-a-half years, they had another boy, my younger brother, who took my place. He was a worthless sort, but I can hear my mother now saying again, "Leave something for your little brother." I tried to give him away. Had some neighbors, a black family who lived next to us on the farm, and I asked J. W. Graves, my buddy, if they'd like to have a little baby at his house. He said, "We don't need a baby at our house, especially if it's white." Five were too many.

How many children are too many? Molly Shepherd who lived on State Road 33 going west of Kingfisher toward Watonga, Oklahoma, an Arapaho Indian, had fifty-seven children. Gave birth to none, gave love to all. She adopted in her eighty-eight years fifty-seven children and they weren't all just cute little babies. She adopted teenagers. Angry, sullen, smart-mouth teenagers; she adopted them. But she had her rules, "You'll help with the chores, you'll stay in school and you'll help take care of the younger ones." Fifty-seven.

She didn't have a very big house. I never was in the house but it looked small. A neighbor of hers down the way toward Fort Sill, Scott Momaday, a Kiowa Indian, who later became a professor of literature, knew about grandmothers being mothers. He said, "My grandmother's house had just two rooms. After school I'd go by her house and go into the kitchen; one room was the kitchen. If I'd had a good day, we ate jam and bread and laughed. If I had a bad day, we ate jam and bread and cried. She absorbed all my pain. Went in one day, I was running a little late. She had already lit the kerosene lamps. 'Grandma!' No answer. 'Grandma!' No answer." He said, "The other room, into which I had never been, was where she slept. The door was ajar and I peeked in and pushed the door open a little bit to see. And I saw my grandmother at the foot of the bed, bowing and having her evening prayers." And he said, "It scared me to death. I have no right to be in this room. I have no right to be in this room." Fifty years later he said, "That was the formative influence of my life. Just two rooms. One where you eat and have fun, cry, laugh, take care of each other, embrace each other. And another one where you're just silent before God."

I thought about that when I thought about our new building. I hope it's not too late to change the building. We just need two rooms. One to love and care for each other and one to be silent before God in a sanctuary. You can do it in one room though. We did at the Pavilion. I remember when Nettie had made the cross and put it out the first time when we were beginning down there. Put it out for the Holy Week services and Nicholas Patterson was sitting on the front row. He was about twelve, I guess. Is Nicholas here? Anybody who sees Nicholas, tell him I miss him. He was on the front row and when Nettie placed the cross, it was right in front of him and he looked up at it. He said, "That gives you a funny feeling." You know what he was doing, don't you? He was getting the point. He was worshiping.

"Fifty-seven," Molly said, in her eighty-eight years. "Not too many." But God, I think, has too many. Now how do you calculate too many? The way I calculate too many is quite simple. If you can't take care of them, you have too many. If you have more than you can take care of, you have too many. And it is obvious to me that God can't take care of them. There are in this country twelve million who are wearing clothes, twelve million children, let it soak in, who are wearing clothes that were bought and worn and tossed aside by somebody else first. If you can't clothe them, you shouldn't have them. And if you can't feed them, you have too many.

I'll never forget that experience over at Clemson University. There was a Bread for the World meeting. I was there. A slender young woman got up, with a quiet voice, holding a tablet, and read the same sentence sixty-five times in sixty-five languages. The last language was English, and she read, "Mama, I'm hungry." If you can't feed 'em, don't have 'em.

I think about our kids now at the close of school. Most families say, "Hurray! School's out." Kids are saying, "Hurray! School's out." But there are a lot of children who are not saying, "Hurray! School's out" because when school is out—well, they had breakfast at school, they had lunch at school, and now school is out.

There's supposed to be provisions for the summer. Those of you who live in Fannin and Gilmer, would you check to see if that is still working? You live there. Would you see about that? And Pickens, and Cobb. If you can't feed 'em, don't have 'em. And if you can't provide a safe place for 'em, don't have 'em.

The Department of Family and Children's Services (DFACS) called the Center. "We understand you have a closet full of stuff or a rental room or something." I said, "Yes, we have a storage place." "We understand you have furniture and all." "Well, we do, we have a little inventory of things. I'll have to check to see what we have." "Well, I have a mother here with three children, and they're all on the floor. If they don't get those children up off the floor within two weeks, we're taking the children." Take them where?" "Foster home." "Where is that? Who's the foster family? How many foster families do you have?"

I didn't know, do you know? Those of you who live in Gilmer, how many foster families? Is that enough? Is that enough? DFACS is always having to go in because of meth and jail and painful stuff like that. Would you check it out? Just take a few minutes, the county where you live. Would you check it out and see if there are plenty of foster homes? I have a feeling there are not and they're doubling up. One foster mother said, "I just can't keep them, but I can't say no." I said, "What's the matter?" "Fourteen."

If you can't provide a place, if you can't protect them . . . Every thirty-five seconds a child in this country is abused. Every thirty-five seconds. Every day, mark it on your calendar, every day eight children are shot to death. That's 2,000, what? 2,920 a year—shot. Children. If you can't protect them, don't have them. And so I said to God in my prayers, we get a little frank sometimes, and I said, "You have too many. It's obvious you can't take care of them." And God said, "You know my plan." "What plan is that?"

The plan is the older ones take care of the younger ones, or to put it another way, those who are able, take care of those who are not able. And it works out. Some of you are from big families and you know it works out. "You'll have to take care of your little brother." How I hated that!

My mother would say, "Your daddy and I are going into town. We'll be gone a little over an hour; you take care of your little brother." And my question was the same as your question; "Do I have to?" And she said, "Yes, you have to."

That was the end of it. I didn't like it, but I had to because that's the way it works. God said to me in answer to my prayer, "The way it works, the ones who are able take care of the ones that are not able. The older ones take care of the younger ones, the well ones take care of the sick ones. That's the way it works. And everyone is cared for."

I said, "That's putting a big load on the Christians. What about the Muslims?" Muhammad said, "If you see an injustice, change it. If you can't change it, speak out against it, if you can't speak out against it, then at least detest it in your heart."

I said, "Well, what about the Jews?" And the Rabbi said, "Do you know why there's so much violence in Israel? Because we love money more than we love children." And I asked Jesus and Jesus said, "You have the children come to me and if anybody hinders, if anybody stands in the way, if anybody is an obstacle, it would be better for that person to have a millstone tied around the neck and be tossed into the sea." The way we treat children is the revelation of the soul of society.

Some years ago, I think it was about five years ago, I was reading the *Journals of Kierkegaard*. He lived in the 1840s, 1850s in Copenhagen, Denmark. He was brilliant, but kind of a weird duck in a lot of ways. When I was preaching regularly here, I would share with the church what I was reading. Once, I told them about an entry in his *Journal*. He'd been out on the town in Copenhagen. He noticed a girl with a beggar's basket, leading three musicians down the street, begging. The musicians were blind. They were trained, classically trained. They were playing Mozart and Beethoven; it was just marvelous music, and around them gathered a little crowd of street people who didn't have any money. And down the street, clattering in their chariots, went those who had money, going to the evening's entertainment. Kierkegaard wrote in his *Journal*: "There are two kinds of people in the world; those who are willing but cannot and those who are able, but will not."

Kierkegaard was wrong. There are three kinds of people: Those who are willing but cannot, those who are able, but will not, and then there's you . . . then there's you.

In Memoriam

Doxology

*Romans 11:33–36: Sermon preached on the Sunday
following the death of my brother, Bill*

In the fall of the year, even after days grow short and the air crisp, I still go out on the patio alone at the close of the day. It usually takes only a few minutes to knit up the raveled sleeve, quietly fold it, and put it away. But those few minutes are necessary; everyone needs a time and a place for such things.

But this particular evening was different. I sat there remembering, trying to understand the painful distance between the day as I planned it and the day as it had been. The growing darkness was seeping into mind and heart, and I was as the night. Looking back on it, I know now that it was this evening on which the Idea came to me. But frankly I was in no mood to entertain it.

It was not really a new Idea, but neither was it old. It was just an Idea. And it returned the next evening. I was relaxed enough to play with it a little while before it went away. The following evening I spent more time playing with the Idea and feeding it. Needless to say, I grew attached to the Idea before long, and then I had the fear that it belonged to one of the neighbors and that I would not be able to keep it. I went to each of the neighbors.

"Is this your Idea?"

"No, it isn't our Idea."

I claimed it for myself and exercised an owner's prerogative by giving it a name. I named it Doxology.

I took Doxology inside to our family supper table. Supper is family time, and conversation is usually reflection upon the day. If all are unusually quiet, I often ask, "What was the worst thing that happened today?"

John answers, "The school bell rang at 8:30."

"Well, what was the best thing that happened?"

"It rang again at 3:30."

Tongues are loosed and all of us—Laura, John, Nettie, and I—share our day. Supper is a good time and pleasant, and the whole family agreed Doxology belonged at our table.

The next day Doxology went with me downtown for some routine errands. But somehow they did not seem so routine. We laughed at a child losing a race with an ice cream cone, his busy tongue unable to stop the flow down to his elbow. We studied the face of a tramp staring in a jewelry store window and wondered if he were remembering better days or hoping for better days. We spoke to the banker, standing with thumbs in vest before a large plate glass window, grinning as one in possession of the keys of the kingdom. We were delighted by women shoppers clutching bundles and their skirts at blustery corners. It was good to have Doxology along.

But I had to make a stop at St. Mary's Hospital to see Betty. Betty was dying with cancer, and the gravity of my visit prompted me to leave Doxology in the car. Doxology insisted on going in and was not at all convinced by my reasons for considering it inappropriate to take Doxology into the room of a dying patient. I locked Doxology in the car.

Betty was awake and glad to see me. I awkwardly skirted the subject of death.

"It's all right," she said. "I know, and I have worked it through. God has blessed me with a wonderful family, good friends, and much happiness. I am grateful. I do not want to die, but I am not bitter." Before I left, it was she who had the prayer.

Back at the car, Doxology asked, "Should I have been there?"

"Yes, I'm sorry I did not understand."

Of course, Doxology went with the family on vacation. This summer we went to the beach down on the Gulf. What a good time! A swim before breakfast, a snooze in the afternoon sun, and a walk on the beach for shells in the evening. Doxology enjoyed watching the young people in dune buggies whiz by and spin sand over on the old man half-buried beside his wife, who turned herself in the sun like a chicken being barbecued. It was fun to walk out into the waves. These waves would start toward us, high, angry, and threatening, but as they drew near, they began to giggle and fall down. By the time they reached us, they had rolled over, we scratched their soft undersides, and they ran laughing back out to sea.

There is no question: Doxology belongs on a vacation.

Too soon it is school time again. I return to seminary classes, explaining all the while to Doxology that really Doxology is unnecessary, superfluous at seminary. After all, do we not spend the day every day talking about God, reading about God, writing about God? We do not need Doxology when we are heavily engaged in theology.

I was leading a group of students in a study of Paul's Letter to the Romans. The class soon discovered, however, that in this weightiest and most influential of all Paul's letters, the argument was often interrupted by Doxology. Early in the letter, in the midst of a discussion of the spiritual state of all those who live out their lives without Bible or knowledge of Christ, Paul insets a burst of praise to the "Creator who is blessed forever. Amen." After a very lengthy treatment of the tragic situation concerning the Jews, from whom came the Christ but who had not believed in Him, Paul breaks off his argument suddenly and begins to sing:

> O the depth of the riches and wisdom and knowledge of God! How unsearchable are his judgments and how inscrutable his ways!
> "For who has known the mind of the Lord?
>   Or who has been his counselor?"
> "Or who has given a gift to him,
>   to receive a gift in return?"
> For from him and through him and to him are all things. To him be the glory forever. Amen.

(Rom. 11:33–36)

Time and time again Paul breaks the line of thought with a doxological reservation, as though suddenly reminding himself of something. Why?

Probably because Paul is aware that the Doxology is most appropriate to his task as a theologian. Theology begins with words not *about* God but *to* God. People discern first what is sacred, and from there move to what is true and right and good. Worship does not interrupt theological study; theology grows out of worship. And we do not attach chapel services to seminary life in order to provide something extra; we worship because of what has already been provided. A mother does not put a ribbon in her daughter's hair to make her pretty, but because she is.

But more especially, the Doxology is appropriate for Paul's own life, who he is. Who is Paul that he should write of the grand themes of creation, the history of salvation, and redemption in Jesus Christ? He is himself a creation of the very grace of which he speaks. He offers himself as Exhibit A in evidence of the effective love of God. Why not break into song now and then?

Nothing, in my opinion, could be more appropriate for any of us, whoever or wherever or however. Whether we spend our time at sticky café tables talking revolution or sit in calm indifference on suburban patios, Doxology is not out of place.

While on sabbatical in Germany a few years ago, I was taken by friends to a small hotel near Salzburg, Austria, where we had dinner and heard a young woman sing. She was Julie Rayne, a Judy Garland-type singer from London. Her songs were English, German, and American, and so many of my old favorites were included that I soon melted and ran down into the cracks of the floor. During her performance, Miss Rayne sang one number of an unfamiliar tune but very familiar words:

> I will lift up my eyes to the hills;
> From whence comes my help?
> My help comes from the Lord who made heaven and earth.

What is going on here? If entertainers move into the field of religion, some of us will soon be out of work. I asked to speak with Miss Rayne and she consented. My question was, Why? Why, in the midst of popular songs, Psalm 121? Did it seem to her awkward and inappropriate? Her answer was that she had made a promise to God to include a song of praise in every performance. "If you knew what kind of person I was, and what I was doing," she said, "and what has happened since I gave my life to God, then you would know that Psalm 121 was the most appropriate song I sang."

Once in a while we have a seminarian who gives it up. Not suddenly but slowly; zeal cools, faith weakens, appetite for Christian enterprises disappears, the springs dry up, the soul is parched, and you can see it in eyes grown dull and flat. What happened? Did evil storm his citadel and take over? No. Did much study drive him into doubt? No. Did attractive alternatives to ministry turn his head? No. Nothing quite so dramatic. He simply made the fatal error of assuming that spending so much time talking *about* God was adequate substitute for talking *with* God. He lost his Doxology, and died.

Is there ever a time or place when it is inappropriate to say, "For from him and through him and to him are all things. To him be glory forever. Amen"?

It was from the class on Romans that I was called to the phone. My oldest brother had just died. Heart attack. When stunned and hurt, get real busy to avoid thought. Call the wife. Get the kids out of school. Arrange for a colleague to take my classes. Cancel a speaking engagement. And, oh yes, stop the milk, the paper, the mail; have someone feed the dog. Who can take my Sunday school class? Service the car. "I think I packed the clothes we need," the wife said as we threw luggage and our bodies into the car.

All night we drove, across two states, eyes pasted open against the windshield. Conversation was spasmodic, consisting of taking turns asking the same questions over and over. No one pretended to have answers. When we drew near the town and the house, I searched my mind for a word, a first word to the widow. He was my brother, but he was her husband. I was still searching when we pulled into the driveway. She came out to meet us, and as I opened the car door, still without that word, she broke the silence:

"I hope you brought Doxology."

Doxology?

No, I had not. I had not even thought of Doxology since the phone call.

But the truth is now clear: If we ever lose our Doxology, we might as well be dead.

"For from him and through him and to him are all things. To him be glory forever. Amen."

God's Child

*A memorial homily on the occasion
of the death of Elizabeth Hale*

Some time ago on a real bright day, not a cloud in the sky, one of those rare days that's fit for nothing but picnics and poetry, God called in the Angel of the Chosen. I don't know if you remember this angel. The Angel of the Chosen has one duty, only one duty and that is, upon God's bidding, to find persons for special assignments. They're usually difficult assignments but have their own delight. The Angel of the Chosen had a good record, was proud of some of the searches and discoveries. The Angel of the Chosen had found Sarah and Abraham, had found Rachel and Jacob, and the largest plaque on the angel's wall was Mary and Joseph.

This angel was a little nervous to go into the presence of God, not because of fear, but because the Angel of the Chosen doesn't get to go in very often, sometimes there are centuries between assignments. The Angel of the Chosen, who had not been in God's presence for 200 years, went in. And God said, "I have an assignment for you. I have a special gift I want to go to the earth. It's an unusual gift, full of pleasure and joy, but it's a very complex gift. It's a little girl. All little girls are complex. This little girl is more so because in her you might say the elements were so mixed that she would need more than the usual amount of love and care. Therefore I want you to find me a couple that has a strong marriage. It has to be together, bound with hoops of steel, because this assignment is going to put a strain on it. They have to have abundant love. After everyone else runs out, they still have to love. They'll have to have miles and miles of patience. They'll have to have faith that is almost as tenacious as a bulldog; faithfulness, always consistent."

The Angel of the Chosen interrupts and says, "This is getting to be a tough assignment."

"Be quiet, I'm not through. I want you to find a couple that's very resilient. I mean they have to be able to change their plans at a moment's notice, postpone this, change that, make a few phone calls, go in another direction. Has to be that way. I want you to find a couple that has the wisdom to resist all the good advice of their close friends. I want a couple that has the will power to attend to this gift and at the same time continue with their own lives. I'm not asking them to give up their own lives. They must continue their own professions, their community work, their church life. They cannot be destroyed, immobilized, or consumed by this assignment. I'm talking about a very special couple."

The Angel of the Chosen said, "I don't . . ."

"Wait, I'm not through. This has to be a couple that can celebrate little things, just little things, just a scrap of a song, just a corner of a smile and be able to live for days on a crust from the bakery of God."

Well, it came to pass that the Angel of the Chosen came back after awhile and said, "I think I've found the couple, but . . ."

"But what?"

"But they're in Georgia."

And God said, "Where is Georgia?"

The Angel of the Chosen said, "You know that new country called the United States? It's there."

"Where in that country?"

"Well, do you remember a couple of hundred years ago when that young country was in crisis and needed a leader? No one was to be found and you sent me to find a couple that would give birth to this leader. And you remember I found this couple, Tom and Nancy Lincoln. And you remember how pleased you were when they named their son Abraham."

"Oh yes, yes, Hodgenville, Kentucky."

"Well, Georgia is south of there."

"Well, I really don't care. You found Abraham and Sarah in the Ur of Chaldees and I'd never heard of that either."

And so the gift came. And so began the thousand delights as they chronicled with camera and notes the life of this growing child. Beautiful and bright, precocious, full of pleasure. Every day something new. Never a week passed, never a week passed but one of the couple said to the other, "We should have brought the camera, we should have brought the camera."

There were the signs; there were the signs, the dark signs, beginning to show up. "What is it, Doc?"

"Depression, I think."

"But she's so young."

"But I think it's depression."

"What is it, Doctor? Manic depression?"

"Bipolar we call it now."

"We don't understand. She's so young, so lively."

"Well, there's medication. She can continue and you can continue."

"But Doctor, she's so full of joy and she loves life. She makes friends so easily. She's sunshine wherever she goes. Can't we just lighten up these dark spots and go ahead? We can't handle this. I don't like her to be sick. Two days, three days, and we're climbing the walls."

And the doctor said, "If it's more than a day but a week, and if it's more than a week but a month, and if it's more than a month but a year, and if it's more than a year but years, it wears you down, it wears you out, especially the one who is ill."

Just as Elizabeth said to her mother a few days ago, "My soul is tired." I think, I think that was probably the signal, the signal that Elizabeth knew she was standing close to the edge. I don't know, but I imagine there were times when she would put out one foot and curl her toes over the edge.

I remember once when Jesus was in a certain village there was a man who came to Jesus with his son. And he said, "We don't know what is wrong with our son, must be possessed of demons. Sometimes he falls in the fire, sometimes he falls in the water. His mother and I are worried sick. We can't leave him alone. One of us has to be there all the time. Jesus, can you do anything?" And he did. And said to his followers, "This is difficult. It comes out only with prayer."

And he went from there. He went to a place called Gadara. In Gadara there was a man that the family didn't recognize anymore. There was something wrong, terribly wrong. The community didn't know what to do. Sometimes they tried to confine him. Confinement sometimes is necessary but is very seldom helpful, but what else can you do? Jesus approached the man and said, "What's your name?" The man said in a voice that was not his own, it was another voice, it was a voice coming from a hollow echo, somewhere else, dark and deep. Nobody who knew the man recognized this voice that said, "My name is Legion for we are many." Jesus did not turn to his disciples and say, "This comes out with prayer."

Sometimes it is more difficult; sometimes it takes stronger procedures. Sometimes God personally has to take over. That's why I wanted to tell you this, so that you would understand what happened early Thursday morning. God said, "Thank you, Charlotte; thank you, Floyd. You've really done a good job, but I'll take over from here."

Once in a Blue Moon

A eulogy for Hugh Golightly

Once in a blue moon there comes along a person
   who opens a new window on the world,
   providing us a fresh breeze
   and a view of what we have overlooked.
Once in a blue moon there comes along a person
   who offers a different commentary on life.
   Life is not getting and spending but sharing,
   Life is not impressing and being impressed but enjoying.
   Life is not being first in line but it is serving those who stand in line.
Once in a blue moon there comes along a person
   who takes our old vocabulary and pronounces
   the words as though they had been newly minted.
   Grace, faith, hope, love, peace, joy are not ancient
   teachings of the church.
   They are stations along the path of the worshiping heart.
Once in a blue moon there comes along a person
   who gives new categories for understanding
   and expressing our faith.
   It is not enough to think only of true and false
   but also of appropriate and inappropriate.
   It is not enough to think only of right and wrong
   but also of beautiful and ugly.
   It is not enough only to walk the walk,
   it is sometimes proper to dance.

> Once in a blue moon there comes along a person
>   who does not save his wisdom and considerable gifts
>   for the learned and cultured few, withholding them
>   from the unlearned and undeserving, but who gives
>   who he is and what he knows to clerks and cleaners,
>   fixers and menders, children and passersby.

You understand don't you why Hugh Golightly is our church organist? Of course, it is the case that he was able to play the organ only three or possibly four times. That doesn't matter, not at all. That is not even important. What is important is that he is the music of this church. That is why Hugh is, rather than was, our church organist.

Next week or the next or the next or the next, if you worship here you will open the worship bulletin and you will see at the top of the bulletin: Hugh Golightly, Organist. And when you read that, you will settle into your chair and be prepared for worship by a pleasant memory of the days when the moon was blue.

Scripture Index

CPSIA information can be obtained
at www.ICGtesting.com
Printed in the USA
LVHW020032281118
598382LV00001BA/158